TERRORISM:

Defensive Strategies for
Individuals, Companies and Governments

D1301360

Edited by Lawrence J. Hogan

Dedicated to the memory of those who have lost their lives through the violence of terrorists.

TERRORISM: Defensive Strategies for Individuals, Companies, and Governments
Edited by Lawrence J. Hogan

ISBN 0-9659174-5-2
Published by: Amlex, Inc.
P.O. Box 3495
Frederick, Maryland 21705-3495
Telephone: 301-694-8821
Fax: 301-694-0412 or
E-mail: amlex@radix.net

Library of Congress Control Number 2001-132013.
Hogan, Lawrence J., Editor. Authors: Peter H. B. Lejeune, Lawrence J. Hogan, Vaughn E. Wagner, David W. Siegrist, George H. Balestrieri, Richard J. Evans, Sean Carr, John Kane, Haven P. Simmons, Michael Sheehan, George J. Tenet, Oliver "Buck" Revell, Robert T. Thetford, Timothy R. S. Campbell, and Eric K. Noji.

TERRORISM: Defensive Strategies for Individuals, Companies, and Governments
1. Terrorism
2. Biochemical Weapons
3. Airport Security
4. Public Works and Terrorism
5. Medical Aspects of Terrorism
6. Media/Public Information and Terrorism
7. Trends in Terrorism
8. Chemical and Bioterrorism
9. History and Anatomy of Terrorism
10. Local Law Enforcement's Preparation for and Response to a Terrorist Act
11. Personal Protection
12. Protecting Dignitaries
13. Cyberterrorism
14. Case Studies: Oklahoma City Bombing, Tokyo Sarin Attack, World Trade Center Bombing
15. Terrorism and Public Policy
16. Terrorism and Technology

First Edition

Printed in the United States of America

Table of Contents

I   About The Authors
Chapter 1   The Worldwide Threat *By George J. Tenet*   1
Chapter 2   Terrorism and Public Policy *By Lawrence J. Hogan*   11
Chapter 3   Chemical and Bioterrorism *By Vaughn E. Wagner*   29
Chapter 4   Medical Aspects of Terrorism *By David W. Siegrist*   55
Chapter 5   Biological Agents as Natural Hazards and Bioterrorism
              as a "New" Natural Disaster Threat *By Eric K. Noji*   73
Chapter 6   SLA-C4I Multifunctional Cross-Border Airport Security
              System *By George H. Balestrieri*   81
Chapter 7   Public Works and Terrorism *By Richard J. Evans*   95
Chapter 8   Terrorism and Technology: Threat and Challenge in the 21st
              Century *By Oliver "Buck" Revell*   101
Chapter 9   Dignitary Protection *By Sean Carr*   109
Chapter 10   Local Law Enforcement *By John Kane*   119
Chapter 11   Media/Public Information
              and Terrorism *By Haven P. Simmons*   187
Chapter 12   Trends in Terrorism *By Michael A. Sheehan*   197
Chapter 13   History and Anatomy of Terrorism *By Peter H. B. Lejeune*   203
Chapter 14   The Challenge of Cyberterrorism *By Robert T. Thetford*   239
Chapter 15   Case Studies *By Timothy R. S. Campbell*   259
Chapter 16   Personal Protection *By Lawrence J. Hogan*   273
Appendix A   Patterns of Global Terrorism, 2000   291
Appendix B   US Government's Commitment to Anti-Terrorism   297
Appendix C   Africa Overview   307
Appendix D   Asia Overview   313
Appendix E   Eurasia Overview   325
Appendix F   Europe Overview   331
Appendix G   Latin America Overview   345
Appendix H   Middle East Overview   349
Appendix I   Overview of State-Sponsored Terrorism   361
Appendix J   Chronology of Significant Incidents, 2000   371
Appendix K   Background Information on Terrorist Groups   399
Appendix L   US Counterterrorism Efforts   441
Appendix M   National Commission on Terrorism Recommendations   443

Postscript: Terrorists Attack America   446

THE AUTHORS

GEORGE H. BALESTRIERI

George H. Balestrieri, a naval officer graduate of the Italian Navy Command School and the Naval College, has 36 years of experience in security matters, 20 years in the strategic planning, marketing and technical assistance, evaluation and implementation of advanced technologies in complex cross-border systems and more than 16 years experience in NATO and National operations.

Commander Balestrieri is a Life Member and 2000-2001 President of the Armed Forces Communications Electronics Association Founders' Chapter. He is a member of the American Society for Industrial Security and of the ASTM F 12 Committee on Security Systems and Equipment.

He pioneered the total airport security concept with the design of the Intelligent Airport Security System (IASS) for "facilitation and security" in airport operations. In 1985 the design included baggage reconciliation with positive passenger identification, leading to today's

SLA-C41, the Multifunctional Sea, Land and Air Cross-Border Management System.

A team player in SMI's international marketing activities, Mr. Balestrieri redesigned the Explosives and Drugs Interdiction and Control System (EDICS) to include IW and C41 for wide-area surveillance and advanced non-invasive inspection technologies and methodologies. The updated EDICS/IW-C41 makes the best use of state-of-the-art systems such as SMI's ABACoS and the method of tagging and detecting drugs, crops, chemical-compounds and currency with perfluorocarbons tracers. (Balestrieri/Kaish US Patent # 549839.)

TIMOTHY R. S. CAMPBELL

Timothy R. S. Campbell, a consultant on emergency services and public safety, has been certified by the Pennsylvania State Fire Academy to instruct incident command, essentials of firefighting, volunteer emergency services management and hazardous materials first responder awareness and operations. He is certified by the US Environmental Protection Agency (EPA) as a hazardous materials technician.

He has been deputy chief, president and ambulance chief of a large volunteer fire company. From 1978 to 1997 Mr. Campbell was the Director of Emergency Services for Chester County, Pennsylvania, an agency serving 73 cities, 123 public safety agencies and 420,000 citizens.

He has held various positions on the local emergency planning committee, the Southeastern Pennsylvania Emergency Health Services Council and the County Emergency Medical Services Committee.

From 1991 to 1997 he also was the Director of the Chester County Public Safety Communications Project, coordinating contracts to relocate the communications center without interruption. He implemented enhanced 911 emergency telephone service, an 800 mhz radio system, computer-aided dispatch, automatic vehicle location, and a mobile data system.

He is a director of the Pennsylvania Firefighters' Legislative Federation, serving on steering committees for EPA's Region III Chemical Emergency Preparedness Conference and the Pennsylvania Fire Services Leadership Retreat.

Mr. Campbell serves as an instructor for Integrated Emergency Management Courses at the Emergency Management Institute, including the "Consequences of Terrorism" course. He was a member of the National Fire Academy's focus group for Fire Service Fiscal Management and the course development team for Emergency Response to Terrorism: Incident Management. He helped to rewrite the IEMC-Hazardous Materials curriculum and the Model Community Update.

He has been involved in the development of IEMC-Response and Mitigation, IEMC-Preparedness and Response, US Department of Transportation/Federal Emergency Management Agency hazardous materials curriculum, and the Nunn-Lugar-Domenici Senior Officials' Policy Workshop on Weapons of Mass destruction. He teaches the latter course through the US Army's Soldier Domestic Preparedness Program. He wrote a chapter on communications in the International Management Association's revision of Fire Services Management.

SEAN CARR, B.A.

Sean Carr has been a member of the City of Philadelphia's Police Department since 1977. He is currently the Lieutenant of the Emergency Response Division and is assigned to the administrative staff of the First Deputy Commissioner.

He was the first Director of the Philadelphia/Camden (New Jersey) High Intensity Drug Trafficking Area (HIDTA) program and was instrumental in establishing this program which combines federal, state and local enforcement efforts in a unified, intelligence-driven offensive against illegal drug distribution.

In this work, Mr. Carr commanded the Philadelphia Police Department's Narcotics Strike Force of 150 highly trained uniformed officers who saturate areas where drug dealing is prevalent, using innovative tactics to disrupt and dismantle street corner drug-dealing operations. The unit was noted for making more arrests and receiving fewer complaints against police officers than any other unit.

Mr. Carr has also commanded narcotics field teams that use covert investigative techniques to discover and bring to prosecution large-volume, drug-trafficking organizations.

As one of the originators of the Philadelphia Police Department's Environmental Response Unit, he was made its first commanding officer. In this work, he developed and presented to the entire Department the first program to train police personnel to the Hazardous Materials First Responders' level while managing the Department's investigative and mitigation efforts regarding environmental crimes.

His earlier police work included urban and mass transit patrol during which time he designed and commanded a pro-active unit that specialized in performing police decoy operations and investigations to arrest repeat offenders of violent crimes.

Lieutenant Carr has been certified by the Commonwealth of Pennsylvania's Municipal Police Officers Education and Training Commission as a Municipal Police Instructor at the recruit and in-service training levels. He has also been an instructor at the Philadelphia Police Academy and the Philadelphia Police Advanced Training Facility. In connection with this instruction, he coordinated and developed all training provided to the 480 members of the Philadelphia Police Department's Narcotics Bureau.

He is an adjunct instructor at the Federal Emergency Management Agency's Emergency Management Institute, teaching various courses, including the "Consequences of Terrorism."

Mr. Carr received a Bachelor's degree in Criminal Justice from Temple University. He is also an alumnus of the School of Police Staff and Command, the Northwestern University Traffic Institute and the Police Executive Development Institute at Pennsylvania State University.

RICHARD EVANS, B.S.

Richard Evans, a registered professional engineer in civil and traffic engineering, is the former Director of the Public Works Department for the City of San Francisco, California. That Department is responsible for the oversight and maintenance of the City's infrastructure which involves providing engineering and architectural services, operating a facility management system, and overseeing asbestos control, hazardous waste and underground tanks. Among the highlights of his five years as Director are the direction of response to the October 1989 earthquake and the reorganization of the Department to address issues of management responsibility, safety, and performance.

Mr. Evans began working in the Director's office in 1980, first as assistant to the Director and then as Deputy Director of operations before being appointed Director. Previously, he had worked in the Department's Bureau of Engineering, holding various levels of responsibility in traffic engineering from 1958 to 1977 and becoming Assistant to the City Engineer in 1977.

He has made presentations to national and foreign governing bodies, including an international symposium in Lisbon on earthquake recovery and reconstruction. He is a member of the American Public Works Association.

Mr. Evans received a B.S. degree in Civil Engineering from Clarkson University in Potsdam, New York, and has attended numerous courses and seminars in management and emergency management. He is an adjunct instructor in the Federal Emergency Management Agency's "Consequences of Terrorism" course.

LAWRENCE J. HOGAN, A.B., M.A., J.D.

Lawrence J. Hogan is an adjunct instructor in the Federal Emergency Management's "Consequences of Terrorism" course. He has been developing and teaching courses for both the Emergency Management Institute and the National Fire Academy since 1982.

His career in public service includes two years as a member of the Maryland Governor's Commission on Law Enforcement and the Administration of Justice and six years as a US Congressman from Maryland. During his service in the US Congress, he played a leading role in the enactment of the District of Columbia Court Reorganization and Criminal Procedures Act (D.C. Crime Bill) and in the revision of the Federal Rules of Evidence.

From 1978 to 1982 he was the elected County Executive of Prince George's County, Maryland. He served with the Federal Bureau of Investigation for ten years and received eleven commendations.

Mr. Hogan retired from the practice of law in 1993. He taught law courses at the University of Maryland for many years.

He is the author of "Legal Aspects of the Fire Service," "The Osage Indian Murders," and was the editor of "Finally Heard, Heroines of the Uncivil War," and "Terrorism: Defensive Strategies for Individuals, Companies, and Governments."

Mr. Hogan received Bachelor of Arts and Juris Doctor degrees from Georgetown University and a Master of Arts degree from the American University. He has pursued further graduate studies at the University of Maryland and San Francisco State University.

JOHN KANE, B.A., M.A.

Lieutenant John Kane is Watch Commander for the Sacramento, California, Police Department. Lt. Kane has worked as a Police Officer in the City of Sacramento for twenty-five years. During his career he has worked almost every assignment you can have as a police officer. He has walked a foot beat, been a Field Training Officer, and worked the plain clothes Crime Suppression Unit. As a Sergeant, he supervised the communications center answering 911 calls, and led a patrol team on graveyard watch. As a Lieutenant in the Detective Division he has commanded the burglary/Sting/Pawnshop Unit and the Sexual Assaults and Child Abuse Unit. He has commanded the Police Academy along with the Personnel and Training Division, and since 1990 has been the Day Division Watch Commander in the Patrol Division.

Because of his expertise in the emergency operations field, he was also placed in charge of Disaster Planning and Emergency Preparedness for the Sacramento Police Department.

Lt. Kane has an extensive military background. He was a 2nd Lieutenant in the US Army at the age of nineteen, and served in an infantry company with the 82nd Airborne Division in Vietnam from 1968 through 1969.

He commanded a Military Police Company for five years in the Army Reserves; and was honorably discharged from the Army with the rank of Captain. He was awarded the Bronze Star, the Army Commendation Medal for Valor. He was wounded twice in combat and holds two Purple Hearts.

Lt. Kane has both Master's and Bachelor's Degrees from Sacramento State University, majoring in Criminal Justice with a minor in Government. He is currently on the faculty of the Federal Emergency Management Agency (FEMA) as an adjunct instructor, teaching at the Emergency Management Institute. He teaches law enforcement response to disaster events such as Earthquakes, Floods, Hazmat events, and Terrorist incidents. He is a graduate of the National Fire Academy as a Hazardous Materials Incident Commander, and the FEMA Incident Command System Train-the-Trainers course, along with many other schools.

In May of 2000 FEMA chose him as part of an expert group to write the lesson plans and teach local law enforcement agencies how to respond to a terrorist act.

Lt. Kane has been serving on the California Governor's Committee of Law Enforcement Specialists in the Standardized Emergency Management System (SEMS) for over four years. While on this committee he helped to write and develop the manual known as: "The California Law Enforcement Guide for Emergency Operations."

Lt. Kane is an acknowledged expert in the field of disaster preparation and response. He has commanded over sixty critical incidents, and was the Incident Commander at the April 1995 Unabomber attack in Sacramento.

After a five-year research project, he founded his own company, D-PREP, LLC, and developed the three-day course entitled SEMS, and Disaster Preparation and Management for Law Enforcement Managers. Since 1996 he has taught components of this course to more than 2,000 law enforcement and civilian personnel. He has written an extensive 130-page manual for this course, along with his manual, "The Local Law Enforcement response to a Suspected Terrorist Attack."

He has also received California POST Certification for another three-day course entitled, "The Tactical Refresher Course for Field Supervisors," which is now being taught throughout California.

His wife Sharon, is a twenty-two-year veteran of the Sacramento Police Department and is currently assigned as a Detective in the Street Gang Unit.

PETER H. B. LEJEUNE

Peter H. B. Lejeune is a co-founder and director of BLE Incorporated, a consulting firm specializing in bringing to clients state-of-the-art knowledge in nuclear safety, defense technology, security, technology transfer, law, and risk management.

He is an expert on threat assessment and the technological and operational aspects of countering domestic terrorism. He has held senior management and consulting positions in both the public and private sectors.

Mr. Lejeune has directed crisis management, contingency planning, business continuity planning, operations reorganization, security and Counterterrorism projects for government and businesses throughout the world as well as holding senior operations management positions.

He spent several years as a consultant to Puerto Rico's superintendent of police, advising on operational systems. Subsequently, he was appointed director of emergency planning and response for New York City. In this capacity he reorganized the Office of Civil Preparedness to respond to changing demands for interagency coordination during city-wide crises, including labor strikes, natural disasters, hostage situations and hostile acts.

He has performed antiterrorism and security threat assessments for Fortune 100 companies, financial institutions, retailers, manufacturers, pharmaceutical companies, warehouse operators, and distributors. In addition to performing these assessments, he has assisted clients in conducting risk and business interruption analyses and documenting and testing plans to cope with the consequences of disasters.

Mr. Lejeune co-founded the New York Contingency Planning Exchange, one of the first organizations created to improve emergency response through the exchange of ideas and enhanced coordination.

Mr. Lejeune, an adjunct fellow for nonproliferation and Counterterrorism matters at the think tank Potomac Institute for Policy Studies, is also a member of several advisory groups and panels advising the US Department of Defense, the US Department of Energy and the private sector defense industry regarding the threat from terrorists' use of weapons of mass destruction. He also has been certified as a trainer by the Commonwealth of Pennsylvania for the Weapons of Mass Destruction Train-the-Trainer Course.

He wrote the proceedings reports of the 1997 Conference on Countering Biological Terrorism, and the 1999 Conference on Defending the Subways Against Biological Terrorism -- Transit Policing.

For several years he has served as an instructor in the Federal Emergency Management Agency's course on the "Consequences of Terrorism."

ERIC K. NOJI, M.D., M.P.H.

Eric K. Noji serves with the Centers for Disease Control and Prevention (CDC) in Atlanta, Georgia, as Chief of the Epidemiology, Surveillance and Emergency Response Branch within the Office of Bioterrorism Preparedness. Prior to this position at CDC he was Chief of the Emergency Health Intelligence Unit in the World Health Organization's (WHO) Department of Emergency and Humanitarian Action in Geneva, Switzerland, responsible for assessing the needs of, and monitoring, the health of emergency and disaster-affected populations around the world.

Dr. Noji also served as the coordinator of WHO's Health Information Network for Advanced Planning (HINAP), a global database and surveillance system focusing on the health and nutritional status of refugees and forcibly displaced populations.

Prior to working at WHO, Dr. Noji was Chief of the International Emergency and Refugee Health Program at the Centers for Disease Control responsible for coordinating the CDC's medical and public health response to international requests for assistance for disasters, and other humanitarian crises (e.g., refugee and displaced population situations). He also served as the Director of the CDC's World Health Organization Collaborating Center for Emergency Preparedness and Response.

Dr. Noji's career at the CDC has included an assignment as Chief of the Emergencies and Populations in Transition Team in the International Health Program Office, where in addition to responding to complex humanitarian emergencies, one of his responsibilities was overseeing USAID-funded programs in the Newly Independent States of the former Soviet Union. From 1990-1995, he was Chief of the Disaster Assessment and Epidemiology Section in the Centers for Disease Control's Division of Environmental Hazards and Health Effects responsible for investigating acute health effects of natural and man-made disasters.

Dr. Noji completed his university studies in biology at Stanford University, and received his medical degree at the University of Rochester in the State of New York. He subsequently completed his residency training in Internal Medicine and Emergency Medicine at the University of Chicago and his public health degree at the Johns Hopkins University School of Hygiene and Public Health (1987).

For the six years prior to coming to the CDC, he was a faculty member of the Johns Hopkins University School of Medicine and an Attending Emergency Physician at the Johns Hopkins Hospital.

He also held a joint faculty appointment in the Department of International Health at the Johns Hopkins School of Hygiene and Public Health. Dr. Noji is an Adjunct full Professor of International Health at the Tulane University School of Public Health and Tropical Medicine. His major area of academic interest concerns the medical and health response to natural, biological and technological disasters, including complex humanitarian emergencies and terrorism.

Current research interests include the development of methods to rapidly assess health care needs in disasters, the development of casualty estimation models for different types of disasters and epidemiologic studies of injuries, illnesses, and medical response to several recent natural and technological disasters, and humanitarian crises. Dr. Noji is the author or co-author of over 130 scientific articles and publications on toxicological emergencies, disaster medicine and disaster Epidemiology, and Public Health Consequences of Disasters (Oxford University Press). The Eric K. Noji Excellence in Teaching Award is awarded annually by the Center of Excellence in Disaster Management and Humanitarian Assistance (a WHO Collaborating Centre) to recognize exceptional teaching and educational achievements in the areas of disaster relief and humanitarian assistance.

In addition to his responsibilities at CDC, he serves as a member of several national and international committees for disaster and emergency medical services. Dr. Noji is a Captain (O-6) in the Commissioned Officer Corps of the US Public Health Service.

OLIVER "BUCK" REVELL, B.A., M.A.

Oliver "Buck" Revell is the founder and president of Revell Group International, global business and security consultants, in Rowlette, Texas. He served five years as an officer and aviator in the US Marine Corps, being discharged in 1964 as a Captain.

During his 30 years with the Federal Bureau of Investigation as a Special Agent and a Senior Executive (1964-1994), Mr. Revell directed or participated in virtually every major FBI case, including the John F. Kennedy assassination, Watergate, the Iran hostage crisis and the Gulf War antiterrorist operations.

From 1980 until 1991 he served at FBI headquarters first as Assistant Director in Charge of Criminal Investigations (including terrorism); then as Associate Deputy Director in charge of the Investigative, Intelligence, Counterterrorism and International programs of the FBI (1985-1991).

He served on the President's Council on Integrity and Efficiency (1980-1991), on the National Foreign Intelligence Board (1987-1991) and the Senior Review Group of the Vice President's Task Force on Terrorism (1985-1986). He was Vice Chairman of the Interagency Group for Counterintelligence (1985-1991) and on the Terrorist Crisis Management Committee of the National Security Council.

In September 1997, Mr. Revell was placed in charge of a joint FBI/CIA/US Military operation (Operation Goldenrod) which led to the first apprehension overseas of an international terrorist. President Ronald Reagan commended him for his leadership of this endeavor.

On May 1, 1992, the US Attorney General ordered Mr. Revell to Los Angeles and placed him in command of joint Federal law enforcement efforts to suppress the riots and civil disorder. He also coordinated the law enforcement activities of the assigned military forces. He received the Attorney General's Special Commendation Award for this work.

He was Special Agent in Charge of the Dallas Division of the FBI at the time of his retirement in 1994 with the rank of Associate Deputy

Director. In 1989 President George Bush awarded Mr. Revell the Presidential Distinguished Senior Executive Award and in 1990 the Meritorious Senior Executive Award.

In 1991 he was awarded the FBI Medal for Meritorious Achievement and the National Intelligence Distinguished Service Medal.
In October 1994 Mr. Revell received the Albert J. Wood Public Affairs Award by the Middle East Forum for his "efforts in the fight against international terrorism."

He is a graduate of East Tennessee State University and holds a Master's degree in Government and Public Administration from Temple University. He is also a graduate of the Senior Executive Program in National and International Security of the Kennedy School at Harvard University.

He is President of the Law Enforcement Television Network (LETN); Chairman of the Greater Dallas Crime Commission; President of the Institute for the Study of Terrorism and Political Violence, Washington, D.C.; Chairman (emeritus) of the Board of Regents, Association of Certified Fraud Examiners (International); a member of the overseas Security Advisory Council (OSAC) of the US State Department; the Executive Assessment Panel of the National Institute of Justice; member of the Steering Committee of the Global Organized Crime Project of the Center for Strategic and International Studies (CSIS), Washington, D.C.; Chairman of the Advisory Board of the Southwestern Law Enforcement Institute; a Trustee of the Southwestern Legal Foundation; Vice President of the Dallas Council on World Affairs; member of the Executive Board of the Circle Ten Council of the Boy Scouts of America; President of the Dallas Rotary Club; Life Member of the International Association of Chiefs of Police (IACP) and founding chairman of the IACP Committee on Terrorism; and a member of the International Association of Professional Security Consultants.

During his distinguished FBI career, he hunted down Mafia hit men, domestic hate group terrorists, and Eastern Bloc spies, and developed investigative strategies, innovated specific surveillance techniques, and championed special FBI units such as Special Events Management and Hostage Rescue.

"Buck" Revell is one of the United States' leading authorities on terrorism and national security issues. He lectures frequently for law enforcement, professional and civic groups on criminal justice and national security issues.

He is the author of "A G-Man's Journal," a book about his FBI career.

MICHAEL A. SHEEHAN, B.A., M.A. (2)

Michael A. Sheehan assumed his duties as Coordinator for Counterterrorism at the Department of State in December 1998. He was confirmed by the full US Senate on August 3, 1999, with the rank of Ambassador at Large. His office has primary responsibility for developing, coordinating, and implementing US Counterterrorism policy.

The office chairs the Interagency Working Group for Counterterrorism -- to develop and coordinate policy -- and the Department of State's task force -- to coordinate responses to international terrorist incidents. It coordinates US Government efforts to improve Counterterrorism cooperation with foreign governments, including the policy and planning of the Department's Antiterrorism Training Assistance Program.

Previously, Sheehan was a Deputy Assistant Secretary in the Bureau of International Organization Affairs where he worked on UN reform and peacekeeping policy in the former Yugoslavia. From 1995 to 1997, he also served in the White House on the staff of the National Security Council. He was Director of International Organizations and Peacekeeping.

From 1993 to 1995, he was Director of Political Military Affairs and Special Counselor to then US Ambassador Madeleine Albright at the US Mission to the United Nations in New York. During this period he also served on peace-keeping operations in Somalia and Haiti as a Special Advisor to the Representative of the UN Secretary General. From 1989 to 1993, Ambassador Sheehan served two tours on the National Security council staff. His responsibilities included counternarcotics, foreign assistance and peace keeping.

He retired as a Lieutenant Colonel in the US Army in June 1997 to join the State Department. His overseas assignments in the military included duty as a Mechanized Infantry Company Commander on the DMZ in South Korea, as a Special Forces "A" Team Leader in Panama (in a Counterterrorism unit), and as a counterinsurgency advisor in El Salvador.

Ambassador Sheehan is a 1977 graduate of the US Military Academy, and has Masters degrees from the Georgetown University School of Foreign Service (1988) and the US Army Command and

General Staff College in Fort Leavenworth, Kansas (1992). He is also a graduate of US Army Airborne, Ranger, and Special Forces courses and Colombian Airborne and Lancero (Commando) courses.

DAVID W. SIEGRIST, B.A., M.S., M. A.

David W. Siegrist is a Research Fellow and the Director of Studies for Countering Biological Terrorism at the Potomac Institute for Policy Studies. He has managed and led all aspects of two studies supported by private foundations and government agencies, and has been a leading contributing author.

The first study was a collected volume, an in-depth study on the multidisciplinary challenge of countering biological terrorism. It included nationally known authors including the former US Ambassador for Counterterrorism, the retired Commandant of the Marine Corps, and many others.

The second study was conducted in coordination with the National Defense University and included sponsorship by the Department of Justice. Mr. Siegrist currently serves as a consultant to the Defense Advanced Research Projects Agency (DARPA) on advanced consequence management.

Mr. Siegrist was a featured speaker and threat panel chair at the First National Symposium on Medical and Health Response to Biological Terrorism.

Other speakers at the conference included former Health and Human Services Secretary Dr. Donna Shalala, Deputy National Security Advisor Richard Clarke, and Nobel Laureate Dr. Joshua Lederberg, among other very distinguished panelists. Mr. Siegrist headed the threat panel, and spoke on "Reality of the Threat: Why is there Concern now?" (A written version of his remarks is in the Centers for Disease Control's journal, *Emerging Infectious Diseases*.

He also directed a project co-sponsored by the National Defense University Center for Counterproliferation Research to identify and prioritize advanced technology needs for biological terrorism consequence management. The Institute identified a number of developmental technologies and conducted a seminar game with users to prioritize needs and to begin developing a national investment strategy. Copies of this report, "HotZone'99," were distributed by the US Department of Health and Human Services to all the cities developing a Metropolitan Medical Response System for mass casualty care. The Association of

Computational Machinery published an article by Mr. Siegrist on information technology needs to counter biological terrorism.

He has lectured before the US Department of State and the Marshall Center of the US European command in Garmisch, Germany, on the prospects for mass casualty terrorism. He has moderated panels with the Michigan State Emergency Management Department on biological emergency response that included representatives from the FBI, FEMA, Centers for Disease Control, and the Army Medical Research Institute of Infectious Diseases.

He has been consulted by Congressional offices seeking information on countering biological terrorism. He is a civilian member of the Interagency Contingency Communications Working Group convened by FEMA and the National Guard.

He also was an invited participant at a seminar hosted by the National Defense University on the psychosocial impact of a biological attack hosted by the National Defense University. He has also participated in an advanced biomedical surveillance workshop sponsored by the Centers for Disease Control and the Defense Threat Reduction Agency. He briefed the Washington, DC Metropolitan Council of Governments on biological terrorism consequence management.

Previously, Mr. Siegrist has served as Executive Secretary of a Senior Panel chartered by the Defense Advanced Research Projects Agency to identify Information Technology needs to Counter Transnational Threats.

Mr. Siegrist has been an advisor to the National Guard and the Air Force Research Laboratory Information Directorate on their plans to counter Weapons of Mass Destruction. He has been published in the *Journal of Defense Research*, and briefed the 1997 Defense Science Board on Transnational Threats.

Mr. Siegrist is a former Principal Staff Member of BDM Federal, a professional services consulting firm. He has been a long-term consultant to the Defense Department, where he has analyzed a broad range of national security technology issues. Among other efforts, he was a lead analyst for the Joint Program Steering Group (JPSG) in Military Operations Other Than War/Law Enforcement (MOOTW/LE), where he had special responsibilities in the Information Technology and Simulation and Training areas.

He conducted a study at the Army War College to prioritize requirements for MOOTW training to inform the development of interactive simulation trainers for military and law enforcement personnel. He also was a leading consultant to MOOTW's Information Technology project, which developed secure wireless and wireline communications to heterogeneous mediated data sources, using natural language queries.

From 1986-present, Mr. Siegrist has been an Adjunct Faculty Member at Georgetown University. Mr. Siegrist is also a former National Strategy Public Policy Fellow of Georgetown University. He has designed and continues to teach four different continuing education courses on Intelligence and National Security. His students have included foreign diplomats, Pentagon officials, Congressional staff, and many others.

He received a Master of Science in Management degree from the National Louis University, a Master of Arts in Government, Magna Cum Laude, from Georgetown University, and a Bachelor of Arts in History, Summa Cum Laude, from Montclair State University. Some of his publications include the following:

- Books -- "HotZone'99: Advanced Technology Needs for Consequence Management of Biological Terrorism." Study Director and Contributing author. Arlington, VA.; Potomac Institute for Policy Studies; 1999.
- "Countering Biological Terrorism: Issues and Status." Dobbs Ferry, NY; Oceana Press; May 1999. Project leader and contributing author.
- Articles -- "Information Technology to Counter Biological Terrorism."
- Newsletter of the Association for Computational Machinery Special Interest Group: *Biology*, August 2001.
- "Reaction Time." *Jane's Defense Weekly*. April 5, 2000, pp. 20-25. (Cover feature).
- "Technology Needs to Counter Biological Terrorism." *National Defense,* September 1999.
- "No False Alarm." *Washington Post,* August 28, 1999.
- "Reality of the Threat: Why is there Concern now?" Paper given at First National Symposium on Medical and Health Response to BioTerrorism, February 18, 1999, Arlington, VA. A written version of these remarks has been published in a special edition of the Centers for Disease Control's journal, *Emerging Infectious Diseases*, July-September 1999, pp. 505-508.

- "Biological Agents: A Threat the Guard Can Handle." *National Guard Magazine,* May 1999.
- "Defending Subways against Biological Terrorism." *Transit Policing,* Fall 1998.
- Presentations -- "Operational Issues In Biological Terrorism Consequence Management: Integrating Hospitals Into The Medical Response, North Carolina Department of Health and Human Services Bioterrorism Symposium and Exercise in Raleigh, NC, November 16, 2000.
- "The US Consequence Management System." Enhanced Consequence Management Planning and Support System Technical Meeting, Albuquerque New Mexico, November 15, 2000.
- "Advanced Technology for Biological Terrorism Consequence Management." Society of Professional Industrial Engineers conference Photonics, East Boston, MA, November 6, 2000.
- "Prospects for Super Terrorism." Presentation to the US State Department Office of the Inspector General, Arlington, VA, January 2000.
- "Biological Terrorism: Reality of the Threat." Presentation to the Indiana State Medical Association; Indianapolis; October 8, 1999.
- "Prospects for Super Terrorism." Presentation to the Senior Executive Course, the Marshall Center, Garmisch, Germany; September 14, 1999.
- "Behavioral Aspects of a Biological Incident." Presentation at the Convention of the Association for Politics and the Life Sciences, Atlanta, September 2, 1999.
- "Advanced Technology to Counter Biological Terrorism." Paper given at Threats of the Technological Age, Holon, Israel, March 17-18, 1998.

HAVEN P. SIMMONS, M.A., Ph.D.

Haven P. Simmons is an assistant professor of communication arts at Salisbury University in Maryland where he teaches public relations and crisis communications. He previously taught criminal justice, urban politics, media and public relations at the University of South Florida. He earned his M.A. in journalism and Ph.D. in mass communications from the University of Iowa.

He was a police reporter for the Sarasota (Florida) *Journal and Herald-Tribune,* and covered numerous law enforcement stories as a reporter for WXLT-TV, the ABC affiliate in Sarasota. He was also a public information officer a total of six years for two law enforcement agencies in Bradenton, Florida.

He presently teaches the media/public information component of emergency response classes at the Federal Emergency Management Agency (FEMA), including the "Consequences of Terrorism" course.

In addition to his doctoral dissertation, he has recently authored articles on public policy and law enforcement media relations in the *Newspaper Research Journal, Communications and the Law,* and the *National Information Officers' News.*

GEORGE J. TENET, B.S.F.S, M.I.A

George John Tenet was sworn in as Director of Central Intelligence on July 11, 1997, following a unanimous vote by both the Senate Select Committees on Intelligence and the full Senate. In this position he heads the Intelligence Community (all foreign intelligence agencies of the United States) and directs the Central Intelligence Agency. Mr. Tenet served as the Deputy Director of Central Intelligence, having been confirmed in that position in July 1995. Following the departure of John Deutch in December 1996, he served as Acting Director of the CIA.

Mr. Tenet previously served as Special Assistant to the President and Senior Director for Intelligence Programs at the National Security Council. While at the NSC, he coordinated Presidential Decision Directives on "Intelligence Priorities," "Security Policy Coordination," "US Counterintelligence Effectiveness," and "US Policy on Remote Sensing Space Capabilities." He also was responsible for coordinating all interagency activities concerning covert action.

Prior to serving at the National Security Council, he served on President Clinton's national security transition team. In this capacity, he coordinated the evaluation of the US Intelligence Community. Mr. Tenet also served as Staff Director of the Senate Select Committee on Intelligence for over four years.

In this capacity he was responsible for coordinating all of the Committee's oversight and legislative activities, including the strengthening of covert action reporting requirements, the creation of a statutory Inspector General at CIA, and the introduction of comprehensive legislation to reorganize US intelligence.

Prior to his appointment as Staff Director, Mr. Tenet directed the Committee's oversight of all arms control negotiations between the Soviet Union and the United States, culminating in the preparation of a report to the US Senate on "The Ability of US Intelligence to Monitor the Intermediate Nuclear Force Treaty." Mr. Tenet came to the Committee in August 1985, after working on the staffs of US Senators.

Mr. Tenet, a native of New York, holds a Bachelor of Science in Foreign Service from the Georgetown University School of Foreign Service and a Masters in International Affairs from the School of International Affairs at Columbia University.

ROBERT T. THETFORD, J.D.

Robert T. Thetford, is a native of Montgomery, Alabama, where he now practices law, specializing in mediation procedures and consulting for police agencies and private industry. He has provided legal advice and instruction to a wide variety of agencies.

In 1998 he co-founded the Institute for Criminal Justice Education, Inc., a nonprofit organization of which he is the managing director.
He is a graduate of The University of Alabama Law School. He serves as an adjunct professor of criminal justice at Faulkner University where he teaches a variety of legal courses, including terrorism and web-based investigations.

He has over 25 years' experience as a prosecutor and Special Agent of the FBI. He also served the FBI as Division Legal Counsel. In addition to investigating political corruption, white collar crime and terrorism cases, he worked as a Certified Police Instructor, Legal Instructor, and Government Mediator. He served as an FBI Relief Supervisor for over ten years.

Awards received during his last assignment in Alabama included selection as Federal Law Enforcement Officer of the Year (Middle District of Alabama) and a Director's Commendation with Presidential Recognition for coordination of the investigation into the murder of a Federal judge.

VAUGHN E. WAGNER, B.S., M.S., Ph.D.

Vaughn E. Wagner is a noted scientist with years of experience in environmental toxicology and medical parasitology. His experience includes "hot zone" assessment of health effects during catastrophic disasters such as train derailments; air and health issues related to a Great

Lakes gasoline tanker explosion; and pesticide drift as a result of a major pesticide warehouse fire. He has also assisted in the mitigation of domestic terrorist/activist group-initiated toxic releases. Currently, Dr Wagner is working on the health effects of bioaerosols in indoor air environments, particularly involving hypersensitivity reactions. He is also a recognized expert consultant to the legal community in toxic tort cases.

Dr. Wagner has a Ph.D. from Michigan State University; an M.S. from Pennsylvania State University and B.S. from Grove City College. He is Board Certified in Medical Entomology specializing in human health effects of parasitic bioagent exposures. Professional appointments include an Adjunct Faculty position at the Federal Emergency Management Agency's (FEMA) training centers at the National Emergency Center Training Center, Emmitsburg, Maryland and the Emergency Assistance Center, Mt. Weather, Virginia. His responsibilities are lecture and exercise control duties dealing with hazardous materials and consequences of terrorism. Specialty areas include chemical and biological agent releases and exposures.

Dr. Wagner currently is Assistant Professor of Environmental Health Science at Salisbury University, a member institution of the University System of Maryland. He resides on the Eastern Shore of Maryland.

Chapter 1

The Worldwide Threat*
George J. Tenet, B.S.F.S., M.I.A.

INTRODUCTION

As we face a new century, we face a New World, a world where technology, especially information technology, develops and spreads at lightning speed -- and becomes obsolete just as fast, a world of increasing economic integration, where a US company designs a product in Des Moines, makes it in Mumbai, and sells it in Sydney, a world where nation-states remain the most important and powerful players, but where multinational corporations, non-government organizations, and even individuals can have a dramatic impact.

*Excerpted from Testimony Before the Senate Foreign Relations Committee, March 21, 2000. Mr. Tenet is the Director of the CIA.

This new world harbors the residual effects of the Cold War -- which had frozen many traditional ethnic hatreds and conflicts within the global competition between two superpowers. Over the past ten years they began to thaw in Africa, the Caucasus, and the Balkans, and we continue to see the results today.

It is against this backdrop that I want to describe the realities of our national security environment in the first year of the 21st century: where technology has enabled, driven, or magnified the threat to us; where age-old resentments threaten to spill-over into open violence; and where a growing perception of our so-called "hegemony" has become a lightning rod for the disaffected. Moreover, this environment of rapid change makes us even more vulnerable to sudden surprise.

TRANSNATIONAL ISSUES

Bearing these themes in mind, I would like to start with a survey of those issues that cross national borders. Let me begin with the proliferation of Weapons of Mass Destruction (or WMD).

We have witnessed continued missile development in Iran, North Korea, Pakistan, and India. Add to this the broader availability of technologies relevant to biological and chemical warfare, nuclear tests in South Asia, as well as continuing concerns about other nuclear programs and the possibility of shortcuts to acquiring fissile material. We are also worried about the security of Russian WMD materials, increased cooperation among rogue states, more effective efforts by proliferants to conceal illicit activities, and growing interest by terrorists in acquiring WMD capabilities.

Our efforts to halt proliferation are complicated by the fact that most WMD programs are based on dual-use technologies and materials that have civil as well as military applications. In addition, a growing trend toward indigenous production of Weapons of Mass Destruction-related equipment decreases, to some extent, the effectiveness of sanctions, interdictions, and other tools designed to counter proliferation.

Although US intelligence is increasing its emphasis and resources on many of these issues, there is continued and growing risk of surprise. We focus much of our intelligence collection and analysis on some ten states, but even concerning those states, there are important gaps in our knowledge. Our analytical and collection coverage against most of these states is stretched, and many of the trends that I just noted make it harder to track some key developments, even in the states of greatest intelligence focus.

Moreover, we have identified well over 50 states that are of concern as suppliers, conduits, or potential proliferants.

THE MISSILE THREAT

Let's look first at the growing missile threat. We are all familiar with Russian and Chinese capabilities to strike at military and civilian targets throughout the United States. To a large degree, we expect our mutual deterrent and diplomacy to help protect us from this, as they have for much of the last century.

Over the next 15 years, however, our cities will face ballistic missile threats from a wider variety of actors -- North Korea, probably Iran, and possibly Iraq. In some cases, this is because of indigenous technological development, and in other cases, because of direct foreign assistance. And while the missile arsenals of these countries will be fewer in number, constrained to smaller payloads, and less reliable than those of the Russians and Chinese, they will still pose a lethal and less predictable threat.

North Korea already has tested a space launch vehicle, the Taepo Dong-1, which it could theoretically convert into an ICBM capable of delivering a small biological or chemical weapon to the United States, although with significant inaccuracies. It is currently observing a moratorium on such launches, but North Korea has the ability to test its Taepo Dong-2 with little warning; this missile may be capable of delivering a nuclear payload to the United States.

Most analysts believe that Iran, following the North Korean pattern, could test an ICBM capable of delivering a light payload to the United States in the next few years.

Given the likelihood that Iraq continues its missile development, we think it too could develop an ICBM capability sometime in the next decade with foreign assistance.

These countries calculate that possession of ICBMs would enable them to complicate and increase the cost of US planning and intervention, enhance deterrence, build prestige, and improve their abilities to engage in coercive diplomacy.

As alarming as the long-range missile threat is, it should not overshadow the immediacy and seriousness of the threat that US forces, interests, and allies already face overseas from short and medium-range

missiles. The proliferation of medium-range ballistic missiles (MRBMs) --
driven primarily by North Korean No Dong sales -- is significantly altering
strategic balances in the Middle East and Asia.

THE BIOLOGICAL AND CHEMICAL THREAT

Against the backdrop of this increasing missile threat, the
proliferation of biological and chemical weapons takes on more alarming
dimensions. Biological and chemical weapons pose, arguably, the most
daunting challenge for intelligence collectors and analysts. Conveying to
you an understanding of the work we do to combat this threat is best dealt
with in closed session, but there are some observations and trends that I
can highlight in this unclassified setting.

First, the preparation and effective use of biological weapons (BW)
by both potentially hostile states and by non-state actors, including
terrorists, is harder than some popular literature seems to suggest. That
said, potential adversaries are pursuing such programs, and the threat that
the United States and our allies face is growing in breadth and
sophistication.

Second, we are trying to get ahead of those challenges by
increasing the resources devoted to biological and chemical weapons and
by forging new partnerships with experts outside the national security
community.

Third, many of our efforts may not have substantial impact on our
intelligence capabilities for months or even years. There are, and there will
remain, significant gaps in our knowledge. As I have said before, there is
continued and growing risk of surprise.

About a dozen states, including several hostile to Western
democracies -- Iran, Iraq, Libya, North Korea, and Syria -- now either
possess or are actively pursuing offensive biological and chemical
capabilities for use against their perceived enemies, whether internal or
external.

Some countries are pursuing an asymmetric warfare capability and
see biological and chemical weapons as a viable means to counter
overwhelming US conventional military superiority. Other states are
pursuing BW programs for counterinsurgency use and tactical applications
in regional conflicts, increasing the probability that such conflicts will be
deadly and destabilizing.

Beyond state actors, there are a number of terrorist groups seeking
to develop or acquire biological and chemical weapons capabilities. Some

such groups -- such as Osama bin Laden's -- have international networks, adding to uncertainty and the danger of a surprise attack.

There are fewer constraints on non-state actors than on state actors. Adding to the unpredictability is the "lone militants," or the ad hoc groups here at home and abroad who may try to conduct a biological and chemical weapons attack. Nor should we forget that biological weapons attacks need not be directed only at humans. Plant and animal pathogens may be used against agricultural targets, creating both potential economic devastation and the possibility that a criminal group might seek to exploit such an attack for economic advantage.

One disturbing trend that numbers alone do not reveal is that BW programs in particular are becoming more dangerous in a number of ways.

First: As deadly as they now are, BW agents could become even more sophisticated. Rapid advances in biotechnology present the prospect of a new array of toxins or live agents that require new detection methods, preventative measures, and treatments. And on the chemical side, there is a growing risk that new and difficult-to-combat agents will become available to hostile countries or subnational groups.

Second: BW programs are becoming more self-sufficient, challenging our detection and deterrence efforts, and limiting our interdiction opportunities. Iran, for example -- driven in part by stringent international export controls -- is acquiring the ability to domestically produce raw materials and equipment to support indigenous biological agent production.

Third: Countries are taking advantage of denial and deception techniques, concealing and protecting BW and CW programs. BW in particular lends itself to concealment because of its overlap with legitimate research and commercial biotechnology. The technologies used to prolong our lives and improve our standard of living can quite easily be adapted to cause mass casualties. Even supposedly "legitimate" facilities can readily conduct clandestine BW research and can convert rapidly to agent production, providing a mobilization or "breakout" capability.

Fourth: Advances are occurring in dissemination techniques, delivery options, and strategies for BW and CW use. We are concerned that countries are acquiring advanced technologies to design, test, and produce highly effective munitions and sophisticated delivery systems.

NUCLEAR PROLIFERATION

Turning now to nuclear proliferation, the growing threat is underscored by developments in South Asia, where both India and Pakistan are developing more advanced nuclear weapons and moving toward deployment of significant nuclear arsenals.

Iran also aspires to have nuclear weapons and Iraq probably has not given up its unclear ambitions despite a decade of sanctions and inspections.

Nor dare we assume that North Korea is out of the business just because the Agreed Framework froze Pyongyang's ability to produce additional plutonium at Yongbang.

NUCLEAR SECURITY AND SMUGGLING

I would like to turn now to a discussion of the problem of nuclear security and smuggling. We are concerned about the potential for states and terrorists to acquire plutonium, highly enriched uranium, other fissile materials, and even complete nuclear weapons. Acquisition of any of the critical components of a nuclear weapons development program -- weapons technology, engineering know-how, and weapons-usable material -- would seriously shorten the time needed to produce a viable weapon.

Iran or Iraq could quickly advance their nuclear aspirations through covert acquisition of fissile material or relevant technology.

The list of potential proliferators with nuclear weapons ambitions is not limited to states, however. Some non-state actors, such as separatist and terrorist groups, have expressed an interest in acquiring nuclear or radiological weapons.

Fortunately, despite press reports claiming numerous instances of nuclear materials trafficking, we have no evidence that any fissile materials have actually been acquired by a terrorist organization. We also have no indication of state-sponsored attempts to arm terrorist organizations with the capability to use any type of nuclear materials in a terrorist attack. That said, there is a high risk that some such transfers could escape detection and we must remain vigilant.

Similarly, we have no evidence that large, organized crime groups with established structures and international connections are as yet involved in the smuggling of nuclear materials. It is the potential that such involvement may occur, or may be on-going -- yet undetected -- that continues to be a concern.

SUPPLIERS OF WMD TECHNOLOGY

Let us now look at the countries which are the suppliers of WMD-related weapons technology.

Russian and Chinese assistance to proliferant countries has merited particular attention for several years. Last year, Russia announced new controls on transfers of missile-related technology. There have been some positive signs in Russia's performance, especially in regard to transfers of missile technology to Iran. Still, expertise and materiel from Russia has continued to assist the progress of several states.

The China story is a mixed picture. China has taken steps to improve its nonproliferation posture over the last few years through its commitments to multilateral arms control regimes and promulgation of export controls, but it remains a key supplier of WMD-related technologies to developing countries.

There is little positive that can be said about North Korea, the third major global proliferator, whose incentive to engage in such behavior increases as its economy continues to decline. Successes in the control of missile technology -- for example, through the Missile Technology Control Regime -- have created a market for countries like North Korea to exploit illicit avenues for conducting sales activities in this area. Missiles and related technology and know-how are North Korean products for which there is a real market. North Korea's sales of such products over the years have dramatically heightened the missile capabilities of countries such as Iran and Pakistan.

While Russia, China, and North Korea continue to be the main suppliers of ballistic missiles and related technology, long-standing recipients -- such as Iran -- might become suppliers in their own right as they develop domestic production capabilities. Other countries that today import missile-related technology, such as Syria and Iraq, also may emerge in the next few years as suppliers.

Over the near term, we expect that most of their exports will be of shorter range ballistic missile-related equipment, components, and materials. But, as their domestic infrastructures and expertise develop, they will be able to offer a broader range of technologies that could include longer-range missiles and related technology.

Iran in the next few years may be able to supply not only complete Scuds, but also Shahab-3s and related technology, and perhaps even more-advanced technologies if Tehran continues to receive assistance from Russia, China, and North Korea.

The problem may not be limited to missile sales; we also remain very concerned that new or nontraditional nuclear suppliers could emerge from this same pool.

POTENTIAL FOR SURPRISE

This brings me to a new area of discussion: that more than ever we risk substantial surprise. This is not for a lack of effort on the part of the intelligence community; it results from significant effort on the part of proliferators.

There are four main reasons:

First and most important, proliferators are showing greater proficiency in the use of denial and deception.

Second, the growing availability of dual-use technologies is making it easier for proliferators to obtain the materials they need.

Third, the potential for surprise is exacerbated by the growing capacity of countries seeking WMD to import talent that can help them make dramatic leaps on things like new chemical and biological agents and delivery systems. In short, they can buy the expertise that confers the advantage of technological surprise.

Scientists with transferable know-how continue to leave the former Soviet Union, some potentially for destinations of proliferation concern.

Plugging this "brain drain" and helping provide alternative work for the former Soviet Union's WMD infrastructure and key scientists are key goals of US nonproliferation policy, as well as a variety of US and international cooperation programs with Russia and other former Soviet states.

Finally, the accelerating pace of technological progress makes information and technology easier to obtain and in more advanced forms than when the weapons were initially developed.

We are making progress against these problems, but I must tell you that the hill is getting steeper every year.

TERRORISM

Let me now turn to another threat with worldwide reach -- terrorism.

Since July 1998, working with foreign governments worldwide, we have helped to render more than two dozen terrorists to justice. More than half were associates of Osama bin Laden's al-Qa'ida organization. These renditions have shattered terrorist cells and networks, thwarted terrorist plans, and in some cases even prevented attacks from occurring.

Although 1999 did not witness the dramatic terrorist attacks that punctuated 1998, our profile in the world and thus our attraction as a terrorist target will not diminish any time soon.

We are learning more about the perpetrators every day, and they are a diverse lot, motivated by many causes.

Osama bin Laden is still foremost among these terrorists, because of the immediacy and seriousness of the threat he poses. The connections between bin Laden and the threats uncovered in Jordan, Canada and the United States during the holidays are still being investigated, but everything we have learned recently confirms our conviction that he wants to strike further blows against America. Despite these and other well-publicized disruptions, we believe he could still strike without additional warning. Indeed, Osama bin Laden's organization and other terrorist groups are placing increased emphasis on developing surrogates to carry out attacks in an effort to avoid detection.

For example, the Egyptian Islamic Jihad (EIJ) is linked closely to bin Laden's organization and has operatives located around the world -- including in Europe, Yemen, Pakistan, Lebanon, and Afghanistan. And, there is now an intricate web of alliances among Sunni extremists worldwide, including North Africans, radical Palestinians, Pakistanis, and Central Asians.

I am also very concerned about the continued threat Islamic extremist groups pose to the Middle East Peace Process. The Palestinian rejectionist groups, HAMAS (Islamic Resistance Movement) and PIJ (Palestine Islamic Jihad), as well as Lebanese Hizballah continue to plan attacks against Israel aimed at blocking progress in the negotiations. HAMAS and PIJ have been weakened by Israeli and Palestinian Authority crackdowns, but remain capable of conducting large scale attacks. Recent Israeli arrests of HAMAS terrorist operatives revealed that the group had plans under way for major operations inside Israel.

Some of these terrorist groups are actively sponsored by national governments that harbor great antipathy toward the United States. Although we have seen some dramatic public pressure for liberalization in Iran, and even some public criticism of the security apparatus, the fact remains we have yet to find evidence that the use of terrorism as a political tool by official Iranian organs has changed since President Khatami took office in August 1997.

We remain concerned that terrorist groups worldwide continue to explore how rapidly evolving and spreading technologies might enhance the lethality of their operations. Although terrorists we have preempted still appear to be relying on conventional weapons, we know that a number of these groups are seeking chemical, biological, radiological, or nuclear (CBRN) agents. We are aware of several instances in which terrorists have contemplated using these materials.

Among them is bin Laden, who has shown a strong interest in chemical weapons. His operatives have trained to conduct attacks with toxic chemicals or biological toxins.

HAMAS is also pursuing a capability to conduct attacks with toxic chemicals.

EDITOR'S NOTE:

One of Osama bin Laden's former close associates testified in a trial in New York in February 2001 that bin Laden's organization, al-Qa'ida, is set up like a corporation with members assigned to such tasks as military training, religious studies, investments and public relations. He said members are constantly trained and are given advice on how to avoid suspicion. They are taught to shave their beards, wear western clothes, avoid discussing Islam and to carry cigarettes and wear cologne. He also testified that bin Laden had tried to acquire material to use in making a nuclear bomb.

Chapter 2

Terrorism and Public Policy
By Lawrence J. Hogan, A.B., M.A., J.D.

Policy makers play a more important role in terrorism than in any other crime because there are more important policy decisions to be made before, during and after a terrorist event and because one of the main goals of terrorists is to influence government policy.

Terrorism is a multi-faceted problem: It is a police problem, a military problem, a public safety problem, a political problem and a public policy problem.

Americans have been inclined not to take terrorism seriously as a local threat. News coverage about nuclear materials smuggled out of former Soviet bloc countries and sold to the highest bidder has not phased them. (Between 1990 and 1997 European officials documented 477 incidents of nuclear material trafficking, including weapon grade uranium and plutonium from Russia.) They have not seemed worried over newly formulated gases that can kill thousands in minutes, or Stinger missiles now in the hands of terrorists and the rouge governments which sponsor them -- all have seemed like scenes from a James Bond movie and remote from our everyday lives. But the World Trade Center bombing and the Oklahoma City tragedy were our wake-up calls.

All experts agree that terrorism attacks will increase in the years ahead and we all now know that no community in America is immune from terrorism.

Amazingly, we have more than 1,000 bombings in this country every year. The FBI states that it receives about 30 threats per week. Dale Watson, head of the Bureau's counterterrorism division said that fighting terrorism is like being a soccer goalie. "We can block 99 shots, but you miss one and you lose the game."

International terrorist groups have a support infrastructure within the United States, giving them the capability to attack us virtually anywhere they choose any time they choose.

There is rarely a terrorism event which affects only one area. The World Trade Center case illustrates this. That terrorist gang, which was also plotting to blow up the UN, the Lincoln and Holland tunnels, and the federal building in New York City, and to assassinate then Senator Al D'Amato and a Jewish leader, were active in several jurisdictions. The leader of the group was a Jersey City, New Jersey, Muslim clergyman. Fuses for bombs were recovered in Brooklyn. The group had a terrorist training camp in Pennsylvania. When some members of this group were arrested, they were stirring a bomb brew in Jamaica, Queens, New York. They tested the power of their explosives in Connecticut. The attackers trained for awhile in Perry County, Pennsylvania.

The perpetrators were from Egypt, Pakistan, Kuwait, Iraq and the United States. They are typical of the modern-day terrorists inspired by Iran's 1979 Islamic revolution.

They are linked internationally with guerrillas who fought and networked in Afghanistan. In that war they developed -- with help from the United States government -- expertise in weapons and explosives. Religion rather than nationalism is the glue which binds them together.

Nine terrorists (one of them the brother of the mastermind of the World Trade Center bombing) were arrested in Manila with an extensive cache of weapons and explosives. They were planning to disrupt the Asia Pacific Economic Cooperation Forum. They held passports from Iraq, Sudan, Saudi Arabia and Pakistan. A Philippine official said they were part of a global movement to promote establishment of an Islamic empire.

These transnational Islamic terrorists are active all over the world in a holy war against all who oppose them: adherents of other religions, artists and intellectuals, and the "Great Satan," the United States.

The fact that these terrorists are adherents of Islam should not lead to the conclusion that all Muslims are involved in these activities. Most Muslims deplore these activities as vehemently as anyone does.

While there are signs that some government officials in Iran might be softening the nation's hostility toward the United States, just a few years ago, the Iran parliament set up a special fund to attack so-called US conspiracies against Islamic countries. More than 200 deputies responded to the legislation by chanting, "Death to the United States!"

China and other countries have been shipping a variety of sophisticated weaponry, including cruise missiles, not only to Iran but to other rogue governments as well.

Every other year, when the US State Department issues its list of nations which sponsor terrorism (see Appendices A-K, page 279), we find virtually the same countries on every list. These sponsoring governments and other angels provide terrorists with money, logistics, explosives, intelligence information, false identification documents and safe harbors. The State Department also has files on over 55,000 suspected foreign terrorists in a program called "Tip-off." Visa Viper committees in US consulate offices throughout the world collect the names.

These governments which sponsor terrorists, could not win an all-out war against the United States, but they can and do wage terrorism through the use of primitive nuclear devices, bombs, and chemical and biological weapons.

The US Federal Government has information-gathering sensors in antennae, satellites, planes and unmanned aircraft which are valuable tools against international terrorism, but it is much more difficult to gather intelligence information concerning urban and domestic terrorism.

Following the World Trade Center bombing, the FBI opened 600 new investigations of Islamic terrorists.

Anyone who is still complacent about terrorism should remember the 168 innocent people killed in the Oklahoma City bombing and invoke images of a firefighter cradling a lifeless infant in his arms, or the Tokyo subway strewn with bodies of commuters killed from gas by religious fanatics, or the Unabomber's letter bombs which killed and maimed innocent people in 14 cities and on and on.

In a free country such as ours it is easy for terrorists to operate and extremely difficult to cope with them.

In addition to international terrorists, we need to be concerned about white supremacists, anti-government military groups, environmental terrorists and free lancers, etc. All present problems for governments at all levels.

As Peter Lejeune points out in Chapter 13, environmental terrorists are targeting tourism. In October 1998 the Earth Liberation Front admitted setting fires that caused more than $12 million in damages at Vail, Colorado, one of the nation's busiest ski resorts. They destroyed a restaurant, ski patrol headquarters and a picnic area. They wanted to halt expansion of the resort because they feared it could harm a potential habitat for the lynx, a threatened species of mountain cat. On March 14, 2001, an e-mail alert was sent by the Earth Liberation Front urging its followers to attack federal offices and engage in demonstrations and other militant action on April 5, 2001, the same day Frank Ambrose, an accused ELF saboteur who is charged with spiking trees to thwart logging in an Indiana State Forest, was scheduled to appear in an Indiana Court. The ELF, which targets enterprises which it accuses of profiting from destruction of the natural world, has claimed responsibility for 19 arsons and four other major crimes from Oregon to New York since 1996.

A band of ecoterrorists set a fire in late May, 2001, that destroyed the University of Washington's horticultural center, a complex of greenhouses where botanists grow rare flowers and study plants in the urban environment. Another blaze which was set simultaneously destroyed an Oregon tree farm. A graffiti message signed "ELF" was left behind which said, "You cannot control what is wild." An ELF spokesperson admitted that his group is probably responsible and they probably did it to protest genetic research on poplar trees. He added that any entity "that is involved in exploiting the natural environment can be considered the next target."

Radical vegetarians and animal rights advocates are also resorting to violence to punish those who kill animals for food, clothes or medical research. The ELF and a sister group, the Animal Liberation Front, have been responsible for most of the terrorist acts committed in the United States over the past two years. ELF's Web site calls on interested individuals to form cells to "inflict economic damage on those who profit from nature."

Policy makers must decide whether or not police agencies will be authorized to monitor the activities of these and other domestic terrorist groups in an effort to get advance warning so potential terrorists' acts can be thwarted.

Will these organizations be investigated? Will they be infiltrated with informants? Will they be kept under surveillance? These questions have civil liberties overtones and could become politically embarrassing for the local government and its policy makers. However, having a terrorist incident, which might have been prevented by sound intelligence information, would be even more embarrassing. In counterintelligence activities success is measured by what does not happen!

The basic purpose of government is to protect lives and property. Everything else springs from that fundamental duty.

Regarding terrorism, government has a two-fold mission:

PREVENTION -- Intelligence gathering.

REACTION -- Responding to and investigating acts committed by terrorists.

Keep uppermost in mind that when a terrorist incident happens the local first responders will be first on the scene. Federal personnel might not arrive for several hours. Acts of terrorism, like all crimes, are primarily local.

Recognizing that fact, the Federal Government is committing a considerable amount of money to train and assist local governments in this effort.

Congress has appropriated a significant amount of money to guard against chemical and biological attacks as well as assaults on computers and other important infrastructures.

Because state and local governments are charged with the primary enforcement and public safety responsibilities related to terrorist attacks, there must be a close working relationship between policy makers and operational people and with other government agencies at all levels.

There are more than 50 so-called patriot, anti-government militia groups in more than 25 states. It behooves you to know if your state is home to one or more of these groups.

These groups are becoming much more prone toward violence and they are well organized, well financed, well armed and they have expertise in all types of weapons, explosives and high tech communications.

Among the groups which present problems to local policy makers are: religious fanatics, hate groups, environmental terrorists, zealots such as the Unabomber, and mentally deranged people.

Possible incidents to be guarded against include: Chernobyl-style nuclear power plant problems (remember Three-Mile Island), danger from trucks transporting nuclear waste or weapons, and accidental launch of nuclear missiles.

In addition to other international terrorists, you may have in your area American organizations which have strong ethnic or nationalistic ties to foreign countries. These groups might pose a terrorist threat, but investigating them might be politically embarrassing for your government's policy makers. Strong and bitter rivalries between nations or ethnic and religious groups within other nations are frequently reflected in sympathetic US-based organizations. These domestic groups might be made up of former nationals of those countries and their descendants or American citizens with shared cultural, religious or ideological affinity, or foreign students.

In this context, in April 1999 the FBI warned the US military to be alert for possible Serb-led terrorist attacks inside the United States. Several Serbian Orthodox churches in the Sacramento, Milwaukee, Chicago and Indianapolis areas had received faxes urging Serbian-Americans to kill as many American soldiers in the United States as possible to stop NATO's attacks against Serbia. And this was not the only Serb-related terrorist threat being investigated by the FBI.

Visits by foreign dignitaries might also pose a danger. Assassinations, bombings, kidnapping and other acts of violence against official or unofficial representatives of the rival country or group while visiting the United State constitute serious terrorist problems, even though the United States itself might not be the target of the hostility. But, if it happens in your jurisdiction, it is your problem.

There have been a number of conferences on terrorism in the past several years and there has been one consistent theme running through each case which was studied: the need to develop a cooperative partnership among local, state and federal law enforcement agencies and other emergency response agencies, along with a coordinated incident command system.

Normally in emergency management, we prepare for situations. With terrorism, we must prepare for people which is much more difficult and much more unpredictable.

What should policy makers be doing in the face of these threats? First of all, make sure your emergency operating plan includes an up-to-date annex on terrorism.

Policy makers should ask themselves many questions:

Do you have the right kind of team in place to cope with a terrorist attack? Are your personnel properly trained? Does this team include: trained hostage negotiators; public information specialists, (the Oakland Hills fire used over 100 visiting Public Information Officers); incident response forces for hostage seizures, bombings and bomb threats; biochemical experts; cooperative links with other jurisdictions (police, fire, medical, search-and-rescue etc.) under up-to-date mutual aid agreements to share intelligence, training, equipment and personnel; computer experts to monitor the Internet and guard against viruses. (Terrorists use the Internet to propagandize, raise money, and recruit new members and we all now know how vulnerable our computers are to crippling attacks.); a coordinator to conduct liaison with federal and state authorities; and employees or outside consultants with the foreign language capabilities you might need.

Convene your top people to revise this plan to assess your vulnerabilities and capabilities with respect to terrorism. Study the problem as it specifically relates to your community.

Where are you vulnerable? What facilities might be targets? Airports, hospitals, federal buildings, military bases, water supply facilities, dams, government facilities, electric power plants, transmission lines for oil and gas, theaters, conference halls, sports arenas and stadiums, embassies, consulates and other diplomatic facilities... all are potential targets for terrorists.

What events are planned for your area which might be tempting targets for terrorists: sports tournaments, political conventions, world fairs, World Trade Organization, International Monetary Fund, World Bank meetings, etc.?

Technology has been developed to aid law enforcement in coping with terrorism at large-audience events. At the 2001 Super Bowl cameras were used to scan the faces of all those who entered the Tampa, Florida, stadium as well as those entering bars, restaurants and movie theaters. As each person passed through the gates, a camera recorded dozens of images which were then transmitted to computers. The computers then compared the portraits against a database of terrorists and other criminals which had been assembled from law enforcement agencies. Digitized images were constructed using 128 facial characteristics, including the width of a nose and the angles of cheekbones. Each apparent match was flashed side by side on a computer screen at a stadium command post where a police officer determined whether the faces were of the same person.

Software makers claim the technique will improve security at concerts, amusement parks and schools as well as athletic events.

What visits by VIP's or foreign dignitaries are scheduled in your area which might tempt terrorists?

Federal officials are increasing security at the 475 federal dams, including 58 large electricity-generating dams in the western part of the country which could be tempting targets for terrorists.

What groups or individuals in your specific area pose threats?

What equipment and training do you need to be adequately prepared?

If an infectious disease epidemic breaks out and health department officials decide to quarantine the affected people, how will you enforce the quarantine? Do you have adequate police to enforce it?

Congress has directed the Department of Justice to administer a $75.5 million grant program for local first responders to enable them to buy equipment to respond more effectively to a terrorist attack. These grants will be made by the Justice Department's Office of Justice Program. Decisions as to what equipment to acquire will be made by local authorities after conducting a needs assessment. Acquisitions then will be made from a standard equipment list.

For more information about these grants, contact the Office of Justice Programs Office for State and Local Domestic Preparedness Support at 202-305-9887 or at its web page, <www.ojp.usdoj.gov/osldps>.

From 1998 to 2000 the Federal Government trained and equipped 57,000 emergency response personnel in 69 cities, nearly half of the cities targeted for training, to respond to biological, chemical or nuclear weapons.

The Federal Government has also established throughout the country eight secret stockpiles of medicines and antidotes to chemical attacks.

The Defense Against Weapons of Mass Destruction Act of 1996 also provides resources to train state and local personnel.

US ARMY REPORTS

The US Army has released six reports to assist state and local governments to respond to terrorist attacks:

1) "Improving Local and State Agency Response to Terrorist Incidents Involving Biological Weapons," which covers medical response, hazard assessment and mitigation, population control, fatality management, emergency management operations, resource and logistics support and continuity of infrastructure. It also lists federal points of contact for planning assistance. (http://dp.sbccom.army.mil/fr/bwirp_interim_planning_guide.pdf).

2) "Guidelines for Mass Casualty Decontamination during a Terrorist Chemical Agent Incident." (http://dp.sbccom.army.mil/fr/cwirp_guidelines_mass_casualty_decon.pdf).

3) "Chemical Protective Clothing for Law Enforcement Patrol Officers and Emergency Medical Services when Responding to Terrorism [involving] Chemical Weapons." (http://dp.sbccom.army.mil/fr/cw_irp_cpc_lepo_ems_report.pdf).

4) "Use of Positive-Pressure Ventilation (ppv) Fans to Reduce the Hazards of Entering Chemically Contaminated Buildings Summary Report." (http://dp.sbccom.army.mil/fr/cw_irp_ppv_summary_report.pdf).

5) "Guidelines for the Incident Commander's Use of Firefighting Protective Ensemble with Self-contained Breathing Apparatus for Rescue Operations During a Terrorist Chemical Agent Incident." (http://dp.sbccom.army.mil/fr/cw_irp_final_incident_command.pdf).

6) "Biological Warfare and Terrorism Issues and Response." (www.biomedtraining.org).

Experts say that we are especially vulnerable to chemical and biological attacks. These weapons are cheap, easy to make, easy to conceal and difficult to cope with. A great deal of research is underway to develop effective vaccines, primarily for the military, but policy makers should explore ways of acquiring these vaccines for vulnerable first responders.

Some promising strides are being made in providing protection against bioterrorism. University of Michigan scientists have created a drug to protect soldiers from biological warfare. Microscopic drops protect patients from germs and viruses by fusing them with the dangerous bugs, causing them in effect to explode. These drops are so small they have been dubbed nanobombs. They act almost immediately. While they are still highly experimental, scientists think one day they will not only treat infections, but will also provide protection against them. Nanotechnology is a high research priority of the Federal Government. (See also EDITOR'S NOTE after Chapter 5.)

The Federal Emergency Management Agency, under the sponsorship of the US Department of Justice's Bureau of Justice Assistance, has prepared an "Emergency Response to Terrorism Self-Study" course for men and women of the nation's fire and other emergency services. This program is a National Fire Academy-certificate training program designed for first responders. For copies of the course, contact the US Fire Administration Publications Office at 1-800-238-3358 extension 1189 or 301-447-1213 or e-mail usfapubs@fema.gov. The course can also be downloaded from the Internet at http://www.usfa.fema.gov.

Your plans should also include educating citizens about the potential threats and alerting them to suspicious things to be on the lookout for. As citizens we need to become more alert and more suspicious than we used to be. We should be alert to an unattended suitcase in an airport, a suspicious package coming through the mail, a neighbor who accumulates a large cache of weapons or has an inordinate hatred of the government, or a strange car or truck parked near a building. These plans should also include conducting research about terrorism and the various groups in your area which you might have to cope with, and setting up a system for gathering intelligence information about groups which might pose a threat. We do not want to infringe on the constitutional rights of citizens, but it is essential that we know what these terrorists are planning.

Public opinion generally supports strong measures to cope with terrorism, but there are limits. When Israel uses Mossad agents to exterminate a terrorist or bombs a nuclear facility under construction, Israelis usually don't get too upset, but in the United States civil libertarians get very upset about anything resembling extra legal activities, even when terrorism is involved. We do not want to abridge freedoms, but on the other hand, terrorists also threaten those freedoms. It is a very perplexing dilemma for policy makers to wrestle with.

The National Commission on Terrorism addressed these issues in its June 2000, report. (See Appendix M.) The Commission concluded that current efforts to detect, prevent and prepare for chemical and biological attacks are inadequate.

Among other things, the Commission feels that coping with the threats from terrorism requires that human rights concerns be dropped in investigations; paying for legal help if agents overstep their bounds; monitoring foreign students studying in the United States; frequently updating the list of foreign terrorist organizations; standing firm against Syria and Iran; adding Afghanistan to the list of state sponsors of terrorism; designating Pakistan and NATO-ally Greece as "not fully cooperating" with the United States; expanding federal authority and considering designating the Department of Defense as the lead agency for responding to catastrophic terrorist incidents in the United States.

Needless to say, the Commission's recommendations are controversial.

The Commission was highly critical of current intelligence agencies, stating that US Intelligence services are "overly risk adverse," "excessively dependent on foreign intelligence services," and have procedures that are "both intricate and burdensome." It also criticized "bureaucratic and cultural obstacles," "lack of clarity," and "considerable confusion." It recommended clarification, simplification, streamlining of procedures, modifying the adversarial posture that prevails, making sure that agents on the ground know what they can and cannot do and offering assistance rather than criticism when they seek guidance.

Most controversial was the Commission's recommendation to drop the guidelines that restrict the recruitment of unsavory informants who might have committed human rights abuses. Reality tells us that the best information about terrorist plans will come not from choirboys, but from terrorists themselves who are not likely to meet our high standards of behavior. In order to learn about a planned terrorist attack, would we not try to recruit one of its members as an informant, even knowing that he or she had participated in previous terrorist attacks?

To improve our chances of preventing a bioterrorist attack, the Commission recommends that the United States develop an ambitious international-monitoring program to provide early warning of infectious disease outbreaks and possible terrorist experimentation with biological substances. Had such a system been in place, it might have picked up information that the Aum Shinrikyo sect was experimenting with anthrax before it later resorted to using Sarin in the Tokyo subway attack.

In the case of a catastrophic terrorist attack, the Commission recommends that the Department of Defense be designated the lead federal agency instead of the FBI and the Federal Emergency Management Agency because there may be need for the specialized capabilities which the armed services have available. It recommended that a federal panel be established to identify the circumstances and carefully set the rules before the Pentagon replaces the civilian agencies in major disasters.

On December 14, 2000, the Commission sent a report to President-elect George W. Bush, warning that the United States is vulnerable to terrorists wielding weapons of mass destruction. The panel reiterated its view that restrictions on CIA agents which prevent them from recruiting confidential informants who have committed human rights abuses, be lifted.

Virginia Governor Jim Gilmore, chairman of the commission, said, "The United States has no coherent, functional national strategy for combating terrorism. The terrorist threat is real, and it is serious." He said the responsibility for counterterrorism is diffuse and should be consolidated in a national office. The proposed agency would have a director appointed by the President and would give Congress a single point of contact on terrorism issues and would focus on counterterrorism planning. The new agency would not have operational control over the Justice Department, the FBI, the Department of Defense, the CIA, the National Security Agency or other entities currently engaged in fighting terrorism.

Gilmore reiterated the suggestions listed above. The report stated further: "We are impelled by the stark realization that a terrorist attack on some level inside our borders is inevitable and the United States must be ready. It is truly a national issue that requires synchronization of our efforts."

While the report to President-elect Bush emphasized the need to protect privacy, it did reiterate the Commission view that human intelligence must be enhanced by rescinding the prohibition against using "certain foreign intelligence informants who may have previously been involved in human rights violations." It continued, "Certain procedures, well-intentioned when implemented, are now hampering the Nation's ability to collect the most useful intelligence." The study emphasized that technology alone is not sufficient for keeping United States officials informed of threats.

Among the panel's other recommendations to Bush was establishment of mandatory reporting requirements on the domestic sale and purchase of certain equipment which can be used to make and deliver cyber, chemical, biological, radiological and nuclear weapons. The group also called for substantially enhancing the readiness of health and medical organizations at the federal, state and local levels to respond to a terrorist attack.

The report said, "The continuing challenge for the United States is first to deter and, failing that, to detect and interdict terrorists before they strike. Should an attack occur, local, state and federal authorities must be prepared to respond and mitigate the consequences."

While these recommendations are important, there are some more mundane and immediate things local governments and companies can do to better prepare for terrorism. Do you have adequate security at your buildings and other vulnerable facilities such as factories, airports, auditoriums, stadiums, train depots, sewer and water plants etc. Various tests have demonstrated how vulnerable we are to security breaches at airports and government buildings.

Do you have a bomb-sniffing dog, an armored personnel carrier and a robot to facilitate safely approaching barricades? Such a vehicle might enable you to deliver a telephone to a hostage taker for negotiation, attack a building with minimum danger to police officers, or to rescue a hostage.

If you don't have these things, you should know where you can borrow them.

Have you considered giving inoculations for anthrax and other biological agents to personnel who might be placed at risk? As the US Army discovered, this program is very controversial.

Are your personnel alert for a possible link between terrorism and collateral crimes such as robberies, vehicle and explosives thefts etc. Terrorist groups often commit robberies and other crimes to finance their operations. A pattern of suspicious crimes could indicate a terrorist connection. There is also often a link between terrorism and the drug trade -- growing, manufacturing and distributing.

What policy decisions should govern a hostage-barricade situation? Your policies should be flexible. Every government has a policy that it will not negotiate with terrorists, but when a hostage's life is in jeopardy, the government will negotiate with terrorists and rightly so.

Your government might have a policy to transport injured to the nearest hospital, but the terrorist incident may have so overcrowded the nearest hospital that the injured must be taken to wherever there is capacity available. Obviously, the policy will be ignored in that instance.

Make sure your policies are coordinated with and well known to everyone affected by it, including officials in the Executive Branch.

Policy makers should make sure they appropriate a sufficient amount of money for operational people to be adequately prepared.

As you set policies, you must be very careful. Responding to terrorism in a democratic society is difficult. Repression plays right into the terrorists' hands. Response must be measured so we don't infringe on the freedoms, which we cherish and which are such an essential aspect of our society.

In addition to up-to-date mutual aid agreements with neighboring jurisdictions, local government policy makers should set up Memoranda of Agreement with military bases in the area. Posse Comitatus, of course, does not permit the military to actively engage in local law enforcement activities unless expressly authorized to do so. However, this does not prohibit the military from being observers and reporting to the Department of Defense; preparing contingency plans; giving advice to civil authorities; sharing intelligence with local civil authorities; using military personnel to deliver and maintain equipment for civilian use; and training civilian law enforcement in the use of equipment.

Policy makers should make sure provisions for succession of power are adequately addressed.

Make sure also that the government's essential records are safeguarded -- tax and land records and other documents -- which the government needs to continue operating. There should, of course, be back-up computer files for these essential records.

Ensure that provisions are made to delegate to appropriate officials the authority they need to carry out their duties.

Do you have laws in place to give your top officials the authority to invoke martial law, rationing, price controls, curfews, anti-hoarding and anti-black marketing programs?

Have you provided for relocation of the seat of government if that should become necessary?

Some other policy decisions to consider:

What is your policy on the use of deadly force? (While you may have an on-going policy on this, circumstances in a specific terrorist incident might require it to be modified.)

Policy makers often face very difficult decisions. During the Three-Mile Island crisis, the US Secretary of Health and Human Services was urged by the National Institutes of Health, and by the Surgeon General and his staff to send in a million doses of potassium iodide to be prepared in case the plant exploded. The head of civil defense in Pennsylvania said,

"No. Don't send it! It will cause panic and a mass exodus, riots, confusion and public fear."

What was the proper thing to do? Government policy makers are frequently faced with choosing between two bad alternatives. Would you have given this story to the media or would you have tried to keep a lid on it?

Ronald Ray Decker, a former FBI Agent, has written a book, "Bomb Threat Management and Policy," published by Butterworth-Heinermann of Woburn, Massachusetts. The book addresses the growing problem of large corporations receiving multiple bomb threats. The book will assist businesses in determining what the corporate policy should be and what manpower and money should be committed to the problem of bomb threats. The book emphasizes that existing corporate assets and facilities should be used for coping with the problem. The book contains flow charts to illustrate the decision-making process; score cards for companies to assess their risks; schedules for evaluating the dangers associated with returning to work; event reporting forms to aid in the event analysis; and illustrations of quickly recognizable emblems for decision makers.

Another former FBI Agent has co-authored a book entitled, "Practical, Tactical and Legal Perspectives of Terrorism and Hostage-Taking." (*Criminology Studies*, Volume 9, January 2000, published by Edwin Mellen Press, P.O. Box 450, 415 Ridge Street, Lewiston, NY 14092, telephone 716-754-2266, Hardcover, $89.95.) Mike McCrystle, now a criminal justice professor at California State University, Sacramento (CSUS), and CSUS Professor James Pollard have written an in-depth examination of hostage negotiation and rescue. The book discusses the options for dealing with criminal, political and mentally ill hostage takers, discusses their motives and offers police strategies for coping with them. It also covers the legal duty to negotiate, the use of force, application of high tech devices and the legal aspects of post-emergency crime scene investigations. They stress the need for a coordinated response to hostage crisis incidents based on science, practice and law. They speculate about future hostage situations, including possible nuclear terrorism. The authors also give advice to the victims of hostage situations, offering tips on how to survive the trauma. Federal policy makers are wrestling with the problem of what to do about Osama bin Laden, if and when, his involvement in the October 12, 2000, bombing of the US Navy ship USS Cole is proven. (His organization circulated a recruitment video among

Muslim militants which boasted that the group had bombed the USS Cole.) Following that terrorist attack in the harbor at Aden, Yemen, in which 17 sailors were killed, investigators learned that a previous attack had been planned against a United States ship in January 2000 but failed when a small boat loaded with explosives sunk before it could reach the ship.

Investigators believe Osama bin Laden, mastermind behind the two 1998 US Embassy bombings in Kenya and Tanzania in which 224 were killed, is also behind the bombing of the USS Cole. There are definite links. Bin Laden, apparently anticipating a US attack, moved his mountain headquarters in Afghanistan. A few days following the bombing a previously unknown group calling itself "The New Unified Fighters Group" issued a statement to the Jordanian newspaper Al-Biad, repeating bin Laden's demands that US forces withdraw from the Persian Gulf. It said that American, British and Israeli planes and ships would become military targets unless the demands are met. Other evidence pointing to bin Laden's involvement in the attack include a coded electronic communication shortly before the attack in which he gave the "go order" to activate one of his terrorist cells. One of the suicide bombers responsible for the attack against the Cole is believed to have been a member of Egyptian Islamic Jihad, which has close ties to bin Laden. A joint US-Russian strike force of helicopter gun ships, combat aircraft and special forces commandos were poised to strike bin Laden's terrorist training camp in Afghanistan. The Muslim fundamentalist Taliban, which controls most of the country, has been highly protective of bin Laden. Because the Taliban has consistently refused to cooperate in bringing bin Laden to justice, the US, the Russians and the United Nations have imposed sanctions against Afghanistan. Following the US Embassy bombings in East Africa, US cruise missiles were launched against bin Laden's Afghanistan base, but they missed him.

In conclusion, we should be constantly alert to the threat from terrorism which all our communities face. Oklahoma City, which heretofore might have been considered an unlikely target for terrorism, will never be the same after the tragic bombing there which killed 168 men, women and children.

At the first anniversary of the bombing, a memorial was on display at the Murrah Federal Building. It reads:

"We come to remember those who were killed, those who survived and those who were changed forever. May all who leave here know the impact of violence. May this memorial offer comfort, strength, peace, hope and serenity."

Adequate preparation to cope with terrorism might eliminate the need for some future, similar memorial in your community.

Chapter 3

Chemical and Bioterrorism
By Vaughn E. Wagner, Ph.D., B.C.E., M.E.[1]

Terrorists by definition create fear and panic. Their motivations are legion and one rarely recognizes, until an incident happens, that the terrorist is in our community. Driven by ideology, grievance, anger and other sociological issues, they attempt to make their presence felt by sudden and dramatic means. Injury, disruption, and death are their goals. Other objectives include media attention, publicity for their cause and retribution for real or imagined grievances. Terrorist activity is a type of guerrilla warfare. A terrorist may be part of a highly organized, well-funded unit or may be a single, disgruntled employee. Potential for terrorism exists in every community. Public awareness, education, and training will help foil some incidents and mitigate others.

This chapter will examine chemical and biological terrorism in light of increased incidents in the United States as well as globally. The purpose is to answer some very important questions for the first responder community. These are: what types of chemical/biological (CB) agents are out there?[2] How would they be obtained? What delivery systems would be used? What inherent CB agent characteristics would pre-dispose terrorists to use them? What kind of expertise is required? Once these questions are answered, emergency managers will be in a better position to evaluate the likelihood of future attacks in their local community. More importantly, the response community will recognize and be alerted to incidences of possible terrorist-initiated theft or clusters of "illnesses" that suddenly appear.

Understanding the nature of CB terrorist incidents can be challenging to those charged with the responsibility for response and mitigation. It is the goal of this chapter to shed some light on this controversial and misunderstood facet of emergency response. In order to understand the potential threats, consequences, and vulnerabilities resulting from the intentional releases of chemical and/or biological agents, a basic review is needed of environmental and agent components affecting toxicity/infectivity. Also, the terms toxicant and toxin as used in this chapter mean two different things.

The first relates primarily to those synthetic chemicals produced by man (insecticides, solvents) while toxin refers to chemical metabolites produced by living organisms (T-2 mycotoxin, botulinum toxin). An understanding of toxicological and microbiological principles, choice of CW or BW agent, ease of acquisition, efficient aerosolization and dissemination, are key ingredients of the terrorist equation for effecting mass casualties and emotional trauma.

Bioagents most likely to be used in terrorist attacks are anthrax, botulinum toxin, and ricin.[3] Chemical agents may include cyanide blood agents; mustard gas-type vesicants; and organophosphate nerve agents. Less toxic substances could be used, however, to cause large scale injuries to the community. Examples are off-the-shelf insecticides such as malathion or diazinon (cousins of the nerve agents). Carbamates such as carbaryl are also good candidates.

One of the principal advantages of chemical and bioterrorism agents is their extreme toxicity in small quantities. These agents must have the ability to form and be delivered in respirable aerosol concentrations (10 μm or less) to result in mass casualties. The settling rate of aerosol droplets of this size proceeds very slowly and will drift for enormous distances at low wind speeds.[4] Consequently, the ability of CB agents to generate aerosol droplet clouds is a necessity in order to be effective.

Examples of efficient bioagents are the botulinum neurotoxin and anthrax. The former is effective at microgram levels while the latter is a spore bioaerosol that can result in mass casualties. The botulinum toxin causes disruption of nerve conduction between the peripheral nervous system and muscle receptors. It takes only an extremely small dose of this toxin to kill by respiratory paralysis. Entire families were poisoned by eating small amounts of green beans which became contaminated with botulinum toxin through unsanitary canning procedures. The toxin's LD_{50} is approximately 0.001g/kg of body weight. An anthrax dose, consisting of at least 8,000 spores, constitutes a lethal dose for humans. Exposure to at least 20 anthrax spores per cubic liter of air for a half-hour can result in a lethal dose.

Another biological agent of notoriety is the infamous yellow rain, T-2 mycotoxin, obtained from certain species of *Fusarium* fungi. These mycotoxin agents were allegedly used as a BW agent in Southeast Asia. Certain *Fusarium spp.* are common contaminants of agricultural commodities such as corn. They cause on-going health problems for agricultural workers in the grain handling/storage industry.

An attack using chemical weapons, while generally on a more limited scale, is quite destructive and can cause immediate and severe mass casualties. The most lethal of these chemical agents are the nerve gases, especially the organophosphates. A small quantity of a nerve agent, such as Sarin or soman, can produce an aerosol vapor cloud that can kill an individual in minutes. The nerve agent VX is even more toxic at lower doses.

CHEMICAL WARTIME AGENTS/PEACETIME EQUIVALENTS

While most civilized countries currently do not use chemical agents in wartime conditions (Iraq being the major exception), there are peacetime situations where a terrorist could, through low-tech formulation and easy accessibility, use similar compounds. Also decomposition products can be utilized quite effectively in intentional release scenarios.[5]

Of major concern is the accessibility of specific compounds such as the organophosphate (OP) insecticides (cousins of nerve agents) and the use of peacetime delivery systems such as insect sprayers, dusters and ULV foggers to disseminate the agent. Target delivery systems would be heating/ventilation/air conditioning (HVAC) systems and/or water reservoirs in high use areas (governmental buildings, shopping malls, or community centers).

The modern use of CW agents for warfare and terrorist activities dates back to World War I. The US military classification developed during that period is used to identify the CW agents along with their peacetime equivalent counterparts. The latter compounds are currently in use either as chemical manufacturing components/intermediates or have a peacetime use by specific end users. These compounds are most likely to be considered by terrorist groups as chemical agent candidates. They are accessible either commercially, by theft, or sabotage.

BLOOD AGENTS

The chemical agents in this classification all possess cyanide (CN). Cyanide (odor of bitter almonds) in gaseous form is a rapid-acting poison with death occurring within seconds to minutes. Cyanide inhibits cellular respiration. Common signs and symptoms of exposure include: mouth and throat irritation; headache, nausea, vomiting, convulsions and coma. Cyanides also react with moist tissue lining the respiratory tract.

Wartime Use: Previous formulations were used during World War I. The British Army's use of the JL mixture was primarily a prussic acid gas mixture. The delivery system was a chemical artillery shell color coded with two red bands.

Peacetime Equivalents: Cyanide products have numerous peacetime uses and are easily accessible to terrorist groups. Hydrogen cyanide (HCN gas) and the cyanide salts (KCN) are ingredients of pesticides, metal polishes, photographic chemical solutions and metal extraction's. Cyanide is also used in the manufacture of plastic polymers.

Other compounds that result in a similar type of cellular respiration inhibition are the sulfur-containing hydrogen sulfide (H_2S) and the alkyl thiol (mercaptan) compounds. They are equally toxic and, in addition, quite nauseous at odor-threshold levels. Hydrogen sulfide smells like rotten eggs and the thiols have skunk-, garlic-, and cabbage-like odors. The former is a gas and is commonly associated with petroleum/natural gas well fields, sewer gas, paper plant emissions and leather tanning processes. The thiols (methane and ethanethiol) are odorant additions to natural gas transport lines and storage tanks as well as pesticide intermediates.[6]

BLISTER AGENTS

Lewisite, mustard, nitrogen mustard (Agent HD) and phosgene oxime (Agent CX) are included in the blister agent group. These agents cause an immediate (Lewisite) or delayed blistering (mustard) effect when in contact with human tissue. They are also known as vesicants. Typical odors associated with the blister agents are geranium-like (Lewisite) and mustard/garlic-like (mustard gas). These chemicals act on the human cellular level.

Symptoms of exposure include severe respiratory and dermal irritation, corneal injury and blindness, anemia (Lewisite), chronic bronchitis, CNS depression, and cardiac arrest (mustard group).

Wartime Use: Blister agents were used extensively in World War I, especially the sulfur mustard agents. Although Lewisite was considered as the best arsenical-based war agent, it was never used during World War I. The average concentration of mustard gas on battlefields ranged from 3 to 5 ppm. Artillery units of the United States and German army utilized color-coded artillery shells containing mustard gas: US - three red bands; Germany - Yellow Cross (80 percent mustard, 20 percent solvents). CX or phosgene oxime was one of the original chemical warfare agents and was once stockpiled in the Soviet chemical arsenal. More recently, Iraq utilized a mustard gas formulation in the war with Iran. Mustard gas is no longer manufactured in the United States; however, stockpiles may have existed as recently as 1974.

Peacetime Equivalents: Mustard gas is used in small quantities for biomedical research and organic synthesis. It was also used as a topical agent for psoriasis treatment. While Lewisite is of historical interest and does not have a peacetime use, a precursor compound, arsine, does. Arsine is currently used in the manufacture of electronic components (semiconductors), glass dyes, fertilizers and in tin galvanization. It is one of the most powerful hemolytic poisons encountered. Major effects include hemoglobin binding, red blood cell lysis and anemia.

Individuals may be exposed to this dangerous toxicant through acid solution (used to clear drains) interaction with arsenic compounds previously placed in the drain system. Arsine is also evolved when acid solutions are placed in containers storing sodium arsenite weed killers. Any one of these scenarios could prove fertile ground for a terrorist group needing a low-tech and easily accessible agent.

CHOKING AGENTS/LACRIMATORS

The choking agents are primarily chlorine, chloropicrin, and phosgene-type compounds. Chlorine gas is a greenish-yellow gas with an intense, penetrating odor. Chloropicrin is an oily colorless/pale yellow liquid with an intense odor. Phosgene is a colorless liquid with a smell of newly mown hay. They are all strong irritants and corrosive to mucous membranes. Respiratory symptoms may be immediate (chlorine) or delayed (phosgene). Health effects include burning chest, coughing, and pulmonary edema.

Wartime Use: Choking agents were used in the largest quantities during World War I. Various types and combinations were used in artillery shells; mortar projectiles; and metal canisters. Phosgene accounted for 80 percent of all gas fatalities. Concentrated chlorine gas was quite corrosive to mucous membranes. Secondary irritation occurs from acids formed during tissue reaction. Increased airway reactivity has been described for up to 12 years following an acute exposure. Potential for secondary contamination is considered low because the gas is not carried on contaminated clothing. Chlorine is not environmentally persistent.

Chloropicrin (vomiting gas, pepper gas) is an oily, colorless or pale yellow liquid with an intense odor. Exposure causes coughing, mucosal edema, and lacrimation. Fatal pulmonary edema has been reported. Major mode of action is combination with cellular chemical groups. An additional toxic effect is the interference with oxygen transport. Chloropicrin can be transferred from a contaminated individual. It is not decomposed by water, and may be hazardous if it enters water intakes (a favorite target of terrorists). It is relatively stable in the environment.

Phosgene (Agent CG) is a colorless gas with odor of mown hay or green corn. It hydrolyzes in water and forms hydrochloric acid. Phosgene causes irritation at concentrations below the odor threshold. Initial effects include lacrimation, coughing, chest tightness, dry throat, nausea, vomiting, and headache. Toxicity may be delayed up to 24 hours. Irritant effects are due to the breakdown into hydrochloric acid. Phosgene is considered nonpersistent. Rain or fog reduces high concentrations.

Peacetime Equivalents: Chlorine is currently available (and easily accessible to terrorists) either in gas or liquid formulation. It is in wide use and is easily accessible throughout the United States. It is one of the highest volume chemicals produced in the US. Chlorine is used in the manufacture of bleaching agents for fabrics and wood pulp. Other uses include synthetic rubber and plastic manufacturing, water purification and disinfection. Dry formulations (granular or tablet) of chlorine-containing compounds are also available.

Chloropicrin, available in a ready-to-use concentrate, is currently manufactured in the US by the action of steam and hyprochlorites on calcium picrate.[7] It is used in soil and non-deciduous fruit fumigation; as a rodenticide, cereal and grain disinfectant and soil insecticide.

Phosgene was first prepared in 1812 and currently its major uses are in the preparation of organic chemicals. Included are aniline dye and isocyanate production, acid chloride manufacture and insecticide and pharmaceutical production. Phosgene may also be formed spontaneously during hazardous material incidents.

NERVE AGENTS

Nerve agents are organophosphorus (OP) compounds initially developed in 1936 by Dr. Gerhard Schrader, a German chemist with I. G. Farben Industrie. His findings led to the development of the nerve gases such as the G agents (tabun, sarin and soman).

The British primarily developed the V agents (VX). Tabun and the other G agents are liquids whose physical properties allow evaporation and dispersion and are considered environmentally nonpersistent. VX is an oily liquid that is persistent for weeks in the environment after being dispersed.

These compounds inhibit the normal activity of an enzyme that is used by the body's nervous system. The result is a prolonged stimulation of certain glands and muscles, as well as the central and peripheral nervous system. Signs of poisoning are chest tightness and wheezing as well as increased salivation and lacrimation. The muscle and respiratory systems are also involved.

The military nerve agents differ from other OPs in potency and rapidity of "aging" of the OP-enzyme complex. Nerve agents in general are moderately water-soluble and have a high degree of lipid solubility. They are slowly hydrolyzed in the environment to less toxic or nontoxic substances. Tabun and the other "G" agents are generally considered nonpersistent in the environment.

Wartime Use: The Germans stockpiled tabun during World War II as bomb and shell fillings, but it was never used in combat. Sarin and soman remained in the experimental stage due to technical production problems. During the cold war period, the United States and Russia investigated nerve gases as CW agents. In Russia, large-scale Sarin and soman production was initiated in the 1950s and 1960s; VX in 1972.[8] By the 1980s, binary artillery shells containing sarin were being produced by the US.[9]

TABUN (AGENT GA)

Tabun is a fruity-smelling (like bitter almonds) combustible, colorless to brownish liquid. It may also undergo hydrolysis in the presence of acids or water, forming hydrogen cyanide. Tabun is particularly toxic following inhalation exposure. The vapor does not readily penetrate the skin, but the liquid is rapidly absorbed following dermal contact. Tabun has high potential for secondary contamination.

SARIN (AGENT GB)

Sarin is a colorless liquid or vapor with almost no odor. Lethal effects result from an aerosol exposure of 2 to 10 minutes.[10] Sarin produces cholinergic overdrive due to inhibition of the acetylcholinesterase enzyme with accumulation of acetylcholine and excessive stimulation. Sarin's potential for secondary contamination is high.

SOMAN (AGENT GD)

Soman is a colorless liquid with a fruity odor. It is an extremely potent nerve agent with a human lethal dose as low as 0.01 mg/kg. It undergoes "aging" within minutes making poisoning with this agent much more difficult to treat. Like Sarin, lethality can occur in several minutes.

VX

VX is a persistent nerve agent that is a nonvolatile, amber colored, odorless liquid. Both the USA and Britain declassified the formula for making VX nerve gas. Liquid droplets do not evaporate quickly and result in systemic absorption. VX is 100 times as toxic to humans as Sarin (GB), and is better absorbed through the skin at higher temperatures. Symptoms include hallucinations, distorted perceptions, elevated blood pressure, and GI hypermotility with nausea, vomiting, and diarrhea. Unlike the "G" agents, VX is an oily liquid that is considered "persistent".[11] Dermal absorption of one drop can result in death within 15 minutes.

Peacetime Equivalents: Third generation OPs are in use today as biodegradable pesticides. Included in this group are parathion, malathion, chlorpyrifos, diazinon and dichlorvos. A group of insecticides with similar nerve agent effects are the carbamates including carbaryl, aldicarb, bendiocarb, and propoxur.

While most of these pesticides are not as toxic as the CW nerve agents, they are prime candidates for terrorist use against susceptible target populations.[12] In fact, parathion's toxic mode of action and poisoning are similar to those of nerve warfare agent, tabun. While parathion (and its analogues) are restricted pesticides and not available to the general public, they are accessible (by theft) from farm and agricultural insecticide storage warehouses.

Organophosphates such as malathion and diazinon are readily available over-the-counter to the general public. In the right doses and through the use of readily available insecticide spray equipment, a motivated terrorist can cause substantial injury and harm in enclosed areas such as a shopping mall or government facility.

RIOT CONTROL AGENTS

Agent CN causes intense pain and lacrimation and inhibits nerve endings in ocular mucous membranes. Agent CS is a strong irritant and is metabolized to cyanide in peripheral tissue.

Wartime Use: CN is a clear to yellow-brown solid with an apple-blossom odor and is dispersed as an aerosol. Symptoms include upper respiratory tract irritation, pulmonary edema, skin vesicle formation, and visual impairment. CN inhibits SH-containing enzymes at sensory nerve endings, resulting in pain and lacrimation. It is more likely to cause permanent corneal eye damage than CS. CN is non-persistent.

CS is a white, crystalline solid with a pepper-like odor. It is delivered as a fog of suspended particles. CS, when mixed with CS1 or CS2 (silicone water repellent), can remain active for weeks. This is especially true when dispersed on soil. Exposure symptoms include a burning sensation/pain in the throat, trachea, and lungs, followed by a suffocating sensation. Exposure to high concentrations can cause pulmonary edema and heart failure. Adult mortality was as high as 10 percent in confined space areas during the Vietnam War. CS is rapidly hydrolyzed by water. CS1 remains active for up to 5 days and CS2 up to 45 days in the presence of water.

Other agents in the Riot Control group include: Agent CR, a pale yellow, crystalline solid with a pepper-like odor. It has limited solubility in water. It is used in a liquid dispensing solution. Initial symptoms include a burning sensation and pain in the throat, trachea, and lungs, followed by a suffocating sensation, sneezing, and fatigue. Residual CR can be transferred from contaminated individuals. CR is more persistent in the environment and on surfaces than CS.

Members of the Adamsite Group (DM, DA, DC) are crystalline solids and are dispersed as aerosol smokes. They are organic-arsenical agents (see Lewisite; Blister Agents). The odor may not be noticeable, but can still have an irritant effect. They are all non-persistent agents. Particles fall to the ground following dispersion and are ineffective unless re-suspended. These agents are also referred to as vomiting agents.

Peacetime Equivalents: These types of agents are used primarily in law enforcement for apprehending uncooperative criminals and crowd control when rioting occurs. Related types of agents can be purchased by private citizens for personal protection. The attraction for terrorists is that these crystalline solid compounds can be dispersed as undetected aerosols to contaminate surfaces and food products. They also have the advantage of being re-suspended from hard surfaces.

BIOLOGICAL WARTIME AGENTS

Unlike CW agents, BW agents have not been routinely or traditionally used in warfare. However, there have been exceptions, which include testing, evaluation and unscheduled release scenarios:

Japanese dispersal of pathogenic organisms (including plague) against China and Manchuria during the 1930s and 1940s; British testing of anthrax spores as a BW agent on Gruinard Island, off the coast of Scotland;[13] United States army evaluation of bioagent "simulants" in US cities (post-World War II) and testing of offensive biological munitions in the Pacific during 1969; "Super Power" testing and evaluation of botulinum Type A and E toxins during the 1960s and 1970s; Asian-belligerent use of the infamous "yellow rain"; *Fusarium*-produced T-2 mycotoxin, during the Vietnamese war era; Bulgarian Secret Service-sponsored assassination (aided by the Russian KGB) in London, September 1978, through the use of a castor-bean-obtained toxin, ricin; Russian "accidental" anthrax release during 1979 in Sverdlovsk from a classified biological weapons facility; and Iraq's capabilities in biological warfare with bioagents including anthrax during the 1980s and 1990s.[14]

"Low-tech" formulation and/or easy accessibility of bioagents have resulted in the manufacture (actual or attempted) of crude botulinum toxin by terrorist groups. In the 1980s a Red Army Faction "safe house" in Paris was found to contain quantities of botulinum toxin. In 1984, a religious cult put *Salmonella* bacteria in the salad bars of a number of Oregon restaurants.

Other more recent attempts (1990s) by terrorist cells or radical activists included attempted purchase of plague bacteria from biological-type culture collections, alleged "anthrax-seeded" envelopes mailed to specific target populations and attempts to develop genetically engineered strains of *Escherichia coli (E. coli)*.

Terrorists would be more likely to choose a bacteriological or fungal rather than a viral or rickettsial agent. This is because viral and rickettsial agents usually require an invertebrate vector (mosquitoes, lice, ticks, and biting flies) to transmit the disease to humans. Also viruses are more difficult to isolate and grow and often do not live outside a host. This makes them more difficult to disseminate effectively. Bacterial and fungal toxins have the advantage of being more stable, relatively simple to manufacture and extremely toxic. Anthrax and certain fungal spores are "attractive" for their relative hardiness against adverse environmental conditions.

BIOLOGICAL AGENT CHARACTERISTICS

Examples of the bioagents that will be reviewed belong to the bacteria, fungi, viruses and rickettsiae. The specific biological organisms chosen fulfill the following criteria:

Used or investigated for use in wartime, sabotage and/or guerrilla activities; endemic/enzootic in the United States; available through type/research collections for biomedical experimentation; produce virulent toxins and are involved in human hypersensitivity reactions; present as bioaerosol contaminants in indoor air environments; meet "low tech" formulation and ease of accessibility.

Effective biological warfare agents should also be highly selective to the organ system they invade. Production of a virulent toxin is also important.[15] A final advantage is the ability of specific microbes to form spores (anthrax, fungal agents) that are highly resistant to adverse environmental factors and thus able to survive for long periods of time.

BIOAGENT CATEGORIES -- BACTERIA

In the bacterial category, the primary concerns are anthrax, botulism and plague. While not usually considered biological warfare agents, cholera and Legionnaire disease are included. This is due to cholera's alleged use in guerrilla warfare and Legionnaire disease's excellent capabilities for growth in and dissemination from domestic HVAC and water reservoir systems.

ANTHRAX

Anthrax is a good candidate for biological warfare. *Bacillus anthracis* is a highly virulent gram-positive spore-forming nonmotile rod. Spore stability and size are excellent and aerosol droplet nuclei are easily formed. Laboratory isolation and growth can be accomplished on ordinary media. A dose of at least 8,000 spores with a mean diameter of less than 5 μm is required for an infectious dose.[16]

The bacillus, *B. anthracis*, is endemic in the Middle East and it is an occupational disease in Iran among rug weavers. It is also known as malignant pustule, splenic fever, woolsorters's disease, and Charbon. Infection is caused by anthrax bacillus or spore-contaminated animal products. Conventional transmission is by contact with contaminated animal tissue or spore inhalation during hide tanning and wool/bone processing. Mechanical transmission can be by biting flies (deer/horse flies). Anthrax is not known to be transmitted from person to person, although cutaneous lesion discharge may be potentially infectious. A vaccine against anthrax is currently available from Bioport Corporation in Lansing, Michigan, and is administered as a series of individual vaccinations.[17] The United States is conducting (and has conducted) an anthrax vaccination program for military personnel.

The bacilli or exotoxin may spread locally or systematically through blood or lymph. The disease progresses to a hemorrhagic swelling of the lymph nodes, sepsis and death. The reported annual incidence rate for anthrax is usually: 1 or less in the US; 100 cases in Turkey, Iran, Iraq; and 1,000 cases in Haiti. Certain portions of Africa have experienced epidemics (greater than 100,000 cases).

Ideal terrorist-initiated release scenarios would be in confined spaces in subways or air-conditioning ducts in shopping malls.

BOTULISM

Clostridium botulinum produces one of the most powerful exotoxins known to man. It is an anaerobic, spore-forming, gram-positive rod. Only a few nanograms of type A botulinum toxin can cause severe toxic effects.[18] The ingestion of preformed toxin in contaminated food or water results in food-borne botulism. Toxin is usually produced through improperly processed, canned, low-acid or alkaline foods (like the infamous green-bean episode mentioned previously). Also incriminated, are lightly cured foods that have not been refrigerated. This is especially relevant for food products in airtight packaging. Occurrence is worldwide. Actual incidence is unknown. Untreated cases usually have a fatality exceeding 60 percent.

The toxin reaches susceptible nerve cells (neurons) at neuromuscular junctions and peripheral autonomic synapses by way of the bloodstream. It binds to pre-synaptic terminals. Symptoms usually develop in 12 to 36 hours. They consist of blurred or double vision and a dry, sore throat. Other symptoms include strabismus and respiratory failure. Due to the extreme potency of botulinum toxin, care should be taken when handling blood, gastric contents and feces. A trivalent ABE antitoxin is available from the Centers for Disease Control in Atlanta, Georgia.

Botulism toxin can be disseminated through bioaerosols or contaminated water/food products. Past terrorist activities have been to produce a crude form of the toxin for introduction into drinking water systems. Favorite and easily accessible targets are water reservoir standpipes.

PLAGUE

Plague is an acute infectious, highly fatal disease of wild rodents caused by the bioagent, *Yersinia pestis*. It is a gram-negative, nonmotile and nonspore-forming bacillus that grows in anaerobic and aerobic conditions. It is transmissible to man, and also from man to man. Plague is also known as Black Death, bubonic plague, pneumonic plague, and septicemic plague. Primary pneumonic plague and primary septicemic plague are usually fatal forms of the disease (57 percent fatalities). Pneumonic plague is highly contagious with good aerosolization properties. It is an especially effective terrorist agent under crowded conditions found in a subway system or other high use, confined areas.

Bubonic is the most common form, affecting about 84 percent of United States cases. Septicemic plague affects about 14 percent of cases, while pneumonic plague affects about 3 percent. Cases in the United States have ranged over the previous decade from 40 in 1980 to 1 in 1991. Thirty-one were reported during 1984. Most of the global activity was in Africa. Current research is centered in four western states: California, Arizona, Texas and New Mexico. In New Mexico, activities also include surveillance and Integrated Pest Management (IPM) programs for the flea vector.

Transmission can be by bioaerosol, water, food, fomites, and insects (fleas). As was mentioned previously, only the pneumonic (respiratory) plague is likely to be considered and used as BW agent. Antibiotics of choice are tetracycline or chloramphenicol.

CHOLERA

Cholera in the United States averages 10 reported cases per year of the 01 serotype. Endemic in the Louisiana and Texas area where cases usually are due to ingestion of shellfish from polluted water. *Vibrio cholerae* secretes an extremely potent enterotoxin that acts on cells of the small bowel. A chloride and bicarbonate hypersecretion occurs with fluid accumulation in the intestinal tract. Cholera transmission is usually by water and/or food.

Cholera usually does not make a good BW agent due to the necessity to ingest contaminated products. However, there has been alleged use of cholera in the 1970s by the South African government's Chemical and Biological Warfare program. Two instances were a suspected release of cholera into water sources of South African villages and the provision of cholera organisms to the Rhodesian government. The purpose was for use against rebel soldiers engaged in an on-going guerrilla war.

LEGIONNAIRE DISEASE

Legionnaire Disease, caused by *Legionella,* is not usually considered a BW agent. However, it has the necessary criteria for a good terrorist agent. This is due to its proclivity for growth in man-made systems including: cooling towers, evaporative condensers, humidifiers, potable water heaters, shower heads, faucet aerators and whirlpool baths. All strains should be considered pathogenic. There are 34 known species and 50 serogroups.

It is estimated by the Centers for Disease Control (CDC) that 25,000 to more than 100,000 cases of legionellosis occur annually in the United States.

The diseases caused by *Legionella spp.* are currently recognized to occur in two distinct clinical forms, Legionnaire disease and Pontiac fever. The former type is more serious, causing pneumonia and death in 15 percent of the cases. Pontiac fever is a non-fatal, flu-like disease of short duration that does not cause pneumonia. Approximately 95 percent of exposed individuals develop this disease, usually within 2 to 3 days.

FUNGAL AGENTS

Of all the bioagents, fungal agents are the cause of the majority of indoor air problems in the US.[19] Since a variety of symptoms can be produced by a number of fungi, specific clinical incidences are vague. However, airborne fungi can result in hypersensitivities, immune system suppression and systemic infections. When fungal agents overcome the body's defenses, brain abscesses, corneal ulcers, endocarditis, fungal cysts, liver and respiratory disease can occur. Fungal agent exposure also plays an important role in asthma attacks (affecting 5 percent of the US population).

TOXIC EFFECTS

Currently, there is widespread concern about the relationship between chemicals produced by fungi (mycotoxins) and their severe toxic effects. In many instances, mycotoxins (metabolic by-products) mimic man-made chemicals in their health impact.

Fungal agents of concern belong to the genera *Aspergillus*, *Fusarium, Penicillium*, and *Stachybotrys*. Mycotoxins of concern include aflatoxins produced by *Aspergillus* and tricothecenes produced by *Fusarium* (the infamous T-2 Toxin). These mycotoxins are associated with a variety of human ailments including cancer, hemorrhage, infection, and inflammation. Other fungi such as *Penicillium* can produce a variety of mycotoxins that can cause toxigenic effects, especially in penicillin-allergic individuals.

Fungal agent growth and transmission occur during unexpected (and prolonged) water intrusion into buildings and high humidity associated with HVAC systems, humidifying units, and whirlpool baths. Fungal agents would be prime candidates for terrorist use in shopping malls, government centers, and indoor recreational centers.

Wartime Use: T-2 toxin, a mycotoxin of a *Fusarium* species, has been implicated as a chemical warfare agent in Southeast Asia. While tricothecene mycotoxins are not produced commercially in the US, they can be readily prepared in gram quantities by culturing *Fusarium tricincitum* on corn. Humans and animals can be exposed orally, topically and by inhalation. Clinical effects include cytotoxic effect on the spleen, testes, bone marrow and gastrointestinal tract. Primary damage is to the gastrointestinal tract and hematopoietic system. Acute toxicity resembles (and can be confused with) damage done by chemicals such as nitrogen mustard. Symptoms can occur within minutes to hours after exposure, depending on the route.

Oral exposure results in a burning sensation in the mouth, tongue and throat. Vomiting, diarrhea and abdominal pain can also occur. Dermal exposure is accompanied by severe itching, tingling, and burning sensation of the skin. Other signs of T-2 exposure include visual disturbances and nasal bleeding. Mortality is high.

Tricothecene toxins have good environmental persistence and may exist for over a month. Moisture may dilute concentrations to below detectable amounts.

VIRAL/RICKETTSIAL AGENTS

Primary viral agents of concern are smallpox, Ebola and Marburg, hantavirus, and the arboviruses (AB). Rickettsial agents incriminated as BW agents include Q, Rocky Mountain Spotted and Typhus fevers. These agents would probably not be the first choice of terrorists due to the following requirements: development in invertebrate vectors such as mosquitoes, ticks and lice (smallpox is the exception), difficulty of isolation and growth outside the host and susceptibility to adverse environmental conditions.

SMALLPOX

The infectious agent is the variola major virus with inhalation being the major entry site. Incubation period is approximately twelve days. The virus needs to spread continually from person to person to survive. The smallpox agent multiplies in the lymphoid tissues and is identified by its unique skin lesions. The papules evolve into vesicles within two days then progress to pustules. There is vomiting, malaise, headache and a macular rash. Infected persons are able to transmit infection only from the first appearance of the rash until the scabs have separated. Transmission is from person to person. Lesion discharge is potentially infectious.

The last case of smallpox occurred in October 1977 and global eradication was certified two years later by the World Health Organization. The defense community's concern about possible clandestine stocks of the smallpox virus led the World Health Organization's Executive Board (1995) to defer a decision on complete destruction of laboratory stocks. The laboratories are located at the Centers for Disease Control in Atlanta, Georgia and the State Research Center of Virology and Biotechnology in Koltsovo, the Russian Federation.

EBOLA-MARBURG VIRAL DISEASES

These viruses are non-segmented, enveloped negative-stranded RNA virus, which are maintained in the environment as zoonoses (disease of nonhuman primates). They are also known as Ebola, Marburg, African hemorrhagic fever, and filoviridae. Mortality rates in man can range as high as 90 percent.

An incubation period lasts approximately one week for Ebola infections and 3 to 9 days for Marburg infections. Symptoms are flu-like with fever, headache, joint pain, and sore throat. Other symptoms include vomiting, diarrhea and abdominal pain. A skin rash often appears 5 to 7 days later. A hallmark of these types of viral fevers is gastrointestinal hemorrhage.[20] High fever and delirium can also occur.

Transmission has been shown to occur from non-human primates to humans. Viral transmission via bioaerosols does not appear to be an important exposure route. Due to uncertainty of stability outside of animal hosts, the Ebola virus may not be desirable as a biological warfare agent.

HANTAVIRAL DISEASES

Hantaviruses infect rodents on a global scale. The disease is also known as Andes virus, epidemic hemorrhagic fever, and Korean hemorrhagic fever. The pulmonary infection that occurs follows an exposure to aerosolized virus originating from rodent feces. Aerosol infectivity has been demonstrated experimentally.

Hantaviremia is an acute respiratory illness developing about two weeks after the initial exposure. Symptoms may include fever, headache, and cough followed by a cardiopulmonary phase. Fatality may be as high as 50 percent. Person-to-person transmission has not been documented.

ARBOVIRUSES (ABS)

ABs are found everywhere in the environment. An example is Eastern Equine Encephalitis (EEE), a disease of animals and birds transmitted to man by mosquitoes. In man, it can produce serious central nervous system (CNS) destruction with a high death rate (greater than 50 percent) or crippling effects. Artificial vaccines are reserved for high-risk personnel. Currently work on ABs in the US at Fort Detrick in Frederick, Maryland, is purely defensive. Areas of research for EEE include improved methods for diagnostic testing.

Q FEVER

Of all the agents in this category, Q fever would be the best candidate for terrorist use. It is an acute rickettsial disease whose onset may be sudden with chills, weakness, malaise and severe sweats. Pneumonitis and chronic endocarditis can occur. Unlike the other members of this group, Q fever's infectious agent, *Coxiella burnetii*, can be transmitted through airborne dust dissemination from areas that are contaminated.[21] These include facilities that process infected animals or their by-products. Airborne particles containing these infectious organisms can be disseminated downwind for considerable distances.

Q fever, like anthrax, is quite stable in the environment and can reach high concentrations. It is also resistant to many disinfectants. Due to its two antigenic phases, the resources to produce and maintain the organism would be considerable.

ROCKY MOUNTAIN SPOTTED FEVER

Rocky Mountain Spotted Fever is an acute infectious disease caused by *Rickettsia rickettsii* and transmitted to man by infected ticks. It is also known as North American tick typhus, New World Spotted fever, and tickborne typhus fever. Though the disease is recognized as being one of the most severe of all infectious diseases, its course is quite variable. It can be confused with enteroviral infection and meningitis. The disease is characterized by a rash that appears from the second to the sixth day. Convulsions and tremors may occur. The fatality rate can be as high as 25 percent.

EPIDEMIC (LOUSE-BORNE)/ENDEMIC (MURINE) TYPHUS

Epidemic (louse-borne) typhus is caused by *Rickettsia prowazekii* and is transmitted person to person by the body louse. Symptoms include a rapid onset of chills, headache and general body pain. A rash appears on the fifth or sixth day. Toxemia is pronounced and fatality rates (in untreated cases) can be as high as 40 percent. It occurs in colder areas where individuals are living in unhygienic conditions and are louse-infected. Historically, the disease is associated with wartime conditions. Epidemic typhus is rarely transmitted by aerosol inhalation of airborne organisms.

Endemic (murine) typhus is caused by *Rickettsia typhi*. It is transmitted to man from the rat by the rat flea and is, like epidemic typhus, rarely transmitted by aerosol inhalation. Occurrence is worldwide and is found where humans and rats occupy the same niche. Infective fleas defecate the rickettsial agent while taking a blood meal; the bite site is subsequently infected. Case fatality is low (1 percent or greater).

BIOLOGICAL WARFARE AGENTS/PEACETIME EQUIVALENTS

Peacetime equivalents that would intentionally expose citizens to biological agents are discussed in this section. Included in this group are disease organisms that are not recognized as human toxicants but are closely related to BW agents and are applied to the environment in large quantities (such as agricultural and public health use). Also peacetime equivalents include hazardous material incidents involving biomedical material (including medical wastes) and common carrier shipments of Class III pathogenic organisms.

Bioaerosol development and dissemination via man-made delivery systems

Specific bio-agents such as bacterial and fungal agents are ubiquitous in the environment and routinely develop in man-made delivery systems. These systems include HVAC systems as well as water displays and reservoirs. Terrorist development and dissemination of bioaerosols containing anthrax, botulinum toxin or fungal mycotoxins are feasible. High-use community areas such as domed stadiums, shopping malls, subways, and governmental complexes would be prime targets.

Hazmat incidents involving biomedical materials

This category would include the intentional discard of medical wastes and infectious tissue material into or onto a target site. These substances would be of a human and/or animal tissue/blood sample type utilized in drug/medical research. The health effect of these types of terrorist-initiated releases would be limited. The basic impact would be more of an emotional nature.

Shipment of Class III pathogens

Packaging containing Class III pathogens (anthrax, *C. botulinum*, and plague are examples) are routinely shipped throughout the country from type collection laboratories to medical and microbiological research facilities. It is estimated that 10 percent of the approximately 80,000 shipments of microorganisms throughout the United States are Class III pathogens.

Shipment is by common carrier.[22] Shipments involving 50 ml (or less) may be by passenger aircraft or ground transportation. Shipments that are 4 liters (or greater) must be by cargo aircraft.

The concern for emergency responders is that a terrorist group, disgruntled graduate student or angry medical researcher might target a shipment; intercept the package containing the bioagents; and use the contents as seed stock for BW production. Even if this is not the case, the placement of the stolen container at a high-use area would result in citizen trauma and panic. Intensive media coverage would also be a goal of the terrorist group.

Use of biological agents for agricultural pest or public health pest control

Bacillus thuringiensis (BT) strains have wide use as an agricultural and public health (mosquitoes, black flies) insecticide. The BT organism and its delta-endotoxin toxin adversely affect the targeted insect and effectively control the pest. BT is not a human pathogen. However, BT is closely related to the anthrax organism, *B. anthracis*. BT is also a spore-former whose parasporal bodies are cuboid or diamond shaped as opposed to anthrax's cylindrical or oval spores. BT is mass-produced in the US by a fermentation process. The resultant crystalline spores and delta-endotoxin are formulated as liquid concentrates, powders, or granules.

The concern from a terrorist standpoint is that spray and granular equipment designed for BT dispersion could be easily adapted to a bioaerosol dispersion of anthrax spores. Also BT formulations could be contaminated by anthrax and applied by air or ground spray equipment used in mosquito control and agricultural pest activities. This is particularly relevant to populated areas, as mosquito control is usually conducted in highly urbanized or recreational areas.

Low-tech production and availability of bioagents

The manufacturing ease and availability of BW weapons stems from the widespread access of materials and technical knowledge (Internet). Also, a single disgruntled employee or a terrorist cell with limited expertise is capable of producing and using bioagents. Manufacturing a lethal fungal or bacterial disease agent requires little more than a food source and a place for amplification (growth). Food sources are quite varied and can range from cellulose (wood products) to chicken soup. Growth sites can be as varied as on a plastic vapor diffusion retarder or a square whiskey bottle containing suitable media.[23]

CONCLUSION

This overview for CB agents is by no means conclusive. The categories and examples are guidelines as to what may be available and easily accessible. Terrorists are limited only by their imagination and creativity. They could manufacture CB agents, purchase them directly from legitimate businesses, or steal them from agricultural, chemical, and/or research facilities. Any number of hazardous materials can be used as chemical or biological weapons and, like insecticides, are commercially available. Biological agents may occur naturally or be obtained from culture collection laboratories in the United States.

The effective dispersion of CB agents can be accomplished in a variety of ways. Chemical or bioaerosol dissemination over widespread areas is feasible through aircraft-mounted aerosol generators used in insect control. In a confined space area such as a HVAC system or a discrete water supply, a more limited assault involving hand-held motorized spray application equipment would be highly successful. Direct contamination of food products and food preparation areas would be the easiest target for the terrorists.

Considering all the factors and the uneasy political times we live in, there is a very good possibility of terrorist attacks utilizing CB agents in the future. Most of the emergency response community agrees that this threat has to be taken seriously. Obviously, monitoring and responder training is most effective prior to an incident. Serious consideration should be given to the development of "real-time" biological sensors; establishment of tighter regulations dealing with the acquisition and use of CB agents, as well as the equipment used for aerosol dissemination. Also, high on the priority list are increased public awareness and education as to the threat posed by BC agent assaults, coordination between all intelligence, training, and military communities and increased training of local emergency managers.

On a more practical note, vaccine, antibody and antidote research and development need to be adequately funded. The responder community also needs the development of adequate and "user friendly" protective equipment. Finally, creation and maintenance of regional biological/chemical task forces would go a long way in assisting the local responders in mitigating "agents of mass destruction" incidents.

EDITOR'S NOTE:

Iraq's dictator Saddam Hussein has used poison gas on Iranians and nerve gas on his own people. He has no compunction in using whatever weapons he possesses in his various military adventures. He invaded Iran in 1980, began the Gulf tanker war in 1984, and bombed and rocketed Iran's cities in 1985. He stopped fighting against Iran in 1988, but then he invaded Kuwait. He has slaughtered Shiites and Kurds. In all of these exploits he used biological and chemical weapons.

When Saddam's son-in-law, who had supervised Iraq's unconventional weapons program, defected in 1995 he said Saddam's most lethal poisons had survived the Gulf War. Saddam has weapons carrying anthrax and botulinum toxin. Iraq had thousands of liters of anthrax. Inhaling one-ninth of a millionth of a gram of anthrax is usually fatal. Iraq has also stockpiled four tons of VX, the nerve gas referred to above, which can kill when one-hundredth of a gram is ingested. Iraq has the ability to produce more of these toxins which can be delivered on missiles to put hundreds of thousands of people in danger. Even before he banned UN inspectors from his country, Saddam had declared 60 square miles off limits. Satellite photographs have revealed stockpiles of biological and chemical weapons within this 60-square mile area. Anthrax can be smuggled into any American city in a suitcase.

CHAPTER 3 ENDNOTES:

1 Assistant Professor of Environmental Health Sciences, Department of Biology, Salisbury University, Salisbury, Maryland.

2 The terms CB, CW, BW are accepted for use in describing Chemical/Biological Agents; Chemical Warfare Agents, and Biological Warfare Agents, respectively. They will be used throughout this chapter.

3 In London, September 1978 the Bulgarian Secret service, aided by the Russian KGB, assassinated an opponent of the Soviet-backed government. The delivery system was the sharp tip of an umbrella and a small metal pellet containing the ricin toxin.

4   The successful effect of a terrorist-initiated aerosol on a target population is dependent on aerosol behavior. Aerosols are defined as colloidal suspensions of matter in air and, unlike gas molecules, cannot diffuse. What makes an aerosol cloud attractive to a terrorist is that small diameter droplets (less than 10 μm) will settle at extremely slow rates and have the potential to drift over long distances.

5   While conducting air monitoring during hazardous material releases, it has been the author's experience that chlorinated organic compounds evolve hydrochloric acid gas vapors when involved in fire and explosion scenarios. Occasionally, phosgene is produced when oxidizing materials are present.

6   Thiols are good candidates for a terrorist-initiated release into ventilation systems as these chemicals are effective at low concentrations and can result in intense nausea. The author was involved in an event where a non-related chemical, butyric acid was released into an abortion clinic by a radical anti-abortion group. Like the thiols, butyric acid is foul smelling and effective at low concentrations. Pregnant women are especially vulnerable to these types of compounds.

7   It was first produced over a hundred years ago from the interaction of picric acid and bleach powder.

8   David Wise in his book, "Cassidy's Run" (2000), interviewed Vil Mirzayanov (a scientist involved in Russia's nerve-gas program) who stated that a new super nerve gas called Novichok was perfected in 1973. Mirzayanov was quoted as saying that Novichok was eight to ten times more toxic than any nerve gas in the United States arsenal. According to Mirzayanov, a binary form was also developed. Although signing the Chemical Weapons Convention in 1992, the Russians did not list Novichok among the types of nerve agents possessed by them.

9   The binary concept is that in utilizing an artillery shell delivery system, the chemicals forming the nerve gas are kept separate in two different compartments. On approach to the target, the configuration that separates the chemicals is ruptured, the chemicals mix, and the nerve gas is produced.

10   On March 20, 1995, the Japanese Aum Shinrikyo religious sect released Sarin in the Tokyo subway system killing 12 and injuring over 5,000. The fatalities and injuries would have been much greater had the Sarin been of higher quality (or substituted an easily accessible peacetime equivalent insecticide, parathion) or the delivery system had

been better (a gasoline-operated handheld insecticide spray unit instead of punctured small canisters).

11 Apparently a cloud of VX being test-evaluated in 1968 by the US Army at Utah's Dugway Proving Grounds was responsible for a sheep kill in excess of 6,000. The US Army has never officially taken responsibility for this event.

12 The techniques for making nerve agents are similar to those used for insecticides. Intermediate products or OP insecticides can be commercially purchased, and by a further chemical reaction, production of a nerve agent is possible.

13 The uninhabited island is still believed to be infected with viable anthrax spores since the dispersion of this agent 40 to 50 years ago.

14 In 1986 Iraq succeeded in obtaining seed cultures of anthrax from a culture collection laboratory in the United States.

15 Cholera or botulism are caused by the production of toxins that effect the intestinal tract and nervous system, respectively. Specific fungal agent species of *Aspergillus, Fusarium, Penicillium, Stachybotrys* can produce highly toxic mycotoxins that are specific for the respiratory, immune, and circulatory systems.

16 An efficient substitute is *Francisella tularensis*, the causal agent for tularemia (Rabbit fever). The infective dose is much less, at 10 spores. However, *F. tularensis* is much less stable in the environment.

17 An FDA advisory committee recommended in July of 2000 that ciprofloxacin (manufactured by Bayer Corporation) be approved for the treatment of individuals exposed to anthrax. This action is part of the organized effort by United States federal agencies to respond to biological attack.

18 Botulinum toxin (especially types A and E) is a favorite candidate for use as a BW agent. The toxin is attractive to biological-warfare researchers throughout the world and was the subject of investigations by the two super powers during the 1960s and 1970s.

19 Most of the author's work over the past two years has been participation in indoor air studies to determine the causal agent of human health problems ranging from hypersensitivities, inmunosuppression, respiratory, and irritant problems. In a majority of these studies, fungal activity was the culprit. Pathogenic species that belong to the *Aspergillus* and *Penicillium* genera were the agents most commonly encountered and certain species are known producers of virulent mycotoxins.

20 A research team lead by Zhi-Yong Yang and Dr. Gary Nabel, National Institutes of Health, reported (*Nature*; August 2000) that a glycoprotein on the Ebola virus' surface was responsible for the hemorrhaging effects. When the researches made protein forms without the sugar component (the glyco- component) blood vessels were no longer destroyed.

21 Q fever has been reported from all areas of the world. It is endemic in areas where host animals are present. At-risk professions include veterinarians, meat workers, sheep workers, rendering plants, diagnostic laboratories, and medical research centers.

22 Type III Pathogenic Organisms are currently shipped in the US by either FedEx or the US Postal Service. Other common carriers such as UPS do not ship these bioagents. FedEx does have a hazmat capability at its headquarters in Memphis, Tennessee, in case of an incident involving one of its shipments.

23 The author has observed substantial quantities (greater than 3,000 Colony-Forming Units; - CFUs) of *Aspergillus spp.* in a crawl space existing on fire/water damaged wood joints. A plastic liner material on the soil floor acted as a vapor diffusion retarder and contributed to long-standing, water saturated conditions.

Chapter 4

Medical Aspects of Terrorism
By David W. Siegrist, B.A., M.S., M.S.

The vast majority of terrorists use guns and bombs as weapons. These inflict traumatic injuries on victims. Bombs typically create crush injuries from blast or falling objects, but most casualties tend to come from flying glass. Hospitals with shock-trauma centers are the best equipped to handle victims of traditional terrorism. Full shock-trauma centers have a fully integrated set of advanced life-saving systems, including Computer Tomography (CT), 3-D radiological scanning that rapidly identifies internal injuries. Unfortunately, the number of such centers is low and their size is limited. According to a recent report by the Department of Health and Human Services (DHHS), only five states have fully equipped shock-trauma centers.[1] DHHS has set a goal of one center per state by 2010. A major impetus for the development of shock-trauma centers was the Vietnam War.

There the US pioneered new methods to save critically injured patients, significantly increasing the ratio of wounded to dead in that conflict over historical standards. Up to 98 percent of treated patients survived. Modern technology has further accelerated that capacity to save lives. This includes the critical provision of skilled emergency care in the vehicle that brings the victim to the center for definitive care.

Less well equipped, but more plentiful, are hospitals with intensive care units (ICUs). ICUs are available most often in large urban hospitals. ICUs typically have respirators, which are often necessary to perform supportive care to trauma victims. The number of respirators is limited, with even major hospitals typically renting additional ones regularly or in times of high demand, e.g., flu season. ICUs, like shock-trauma centers, are staffed by a new medical specialty, trauma specialists and "intensivists," who work well in that high-pressure environment.

Emergency Departments (EDs) are less well-equipped than ICUs, but are also important for prompt care of victims of traumatic injury. There are almost one hundred million patient visits to over 4,000 EDs in the US annually.[2] The number of visits has increased as the number of EDs has declined, in part because EDs are viewed by some as portals into the health care system for the uninsured. US law guarantees the right of patients presenting at hospitals to have their condition stabilized, if not definitively treated. As cost containment pressures increase, excess bed capacity is being wrung out of the US hospital system, and EDs are being eliminated, even relative to the decrease in numbers of hospitals. Many EDs go for long periods at capacity, such that ambulances with emergency cases will be directed to other hospitals. For instance, in Philadelphia several years ago, addicts received a bad shipment of heroin. 100 victims fell ill, basically saturating the city's ED capacity. The specifics vary from location to location and time to time, but the trend is a disturbing one. Mass casualty terrorism could generate enough patients to quickly saturate one locality's ability to respond effectively.

Many cities consider a mass casualty event to be one with over a dozen victims. In addition to strictly medical resources, urban search and rescue (SAR) means are also limited. For instance, the Oklahoma City bombing taxed the SAR resources of the nation as a whole. Treating shock/trauma victims requires skilled practitioners in a labor-intensive process. Shock also typically denotes loss of blood. Fresh whole blood is also typically in short supply, especially around the holidays. There is no substitute for it, although plasma expanders such as colloids obviously are very helpful in stabilizing patients.

Patients in ICUs are often suffering from shock (hypotension), defined as loss of blood pressure due to loss of blood volume, impaired pumping capacity of the heart, or septicemia (e.g., acidosis of the blood).[3] In general, hypotension leads to loss of oxygenated blood flow to the extremities and organs. Anaerobic metabolism leads to an oxygen deficit in the tissues and a buildup of lactic acid. Increased oxygen deficit and acidosis of the blood is often associated with septicemia and poor prognosis. Infection or hemorrhage may set off the inflammation cascade and cause septicemia. This is the overreaction of a normally healthy response, in which the body recognizes insult, and activates T cells, which in turn release cytokines, cellular messengers that include the Interleukins, Tumor Necrosis Factor, and Interferon, among others. This complex cascade leads to the release of Nitric Oxide (NO), which dilates blood vessels in the organs (further lowering blood pressure). NO is also cytotoxic; in quantity it kills cells and probably accounts for significant damage to the tissues.

Significant research has gone into trying to modulate the inflammation cascade, for instance directly against toxic shock, as well as developing monoclonal antibodies against arthritis, an autoimmune disorder. However, progress has been limited due to the relative novelty of cytokine research and the complexity of the inflammatory process. (Cytokines were only relatively recently discovered, and new ones continue to be identified).

However, there appear to be some hopeful research signs in directly targeting NO, an end product of the inflammation cascade. One way is by introducing NO scavengers into the bloodstream. Another promising research approach is to inhibit the enzyme that, when it is stimulated by the cytokines, produces NO from L-arginine, which is common in the blood.

Most conventional terrorism features guns and bombs, which produce trauma in the body and kills through shock, that is, induced hypotension. Hypotension leads to increased acidity in the blood as the product of anaerobic respiration, followed by overreaction of the body through inflammation, which increases tissue damage through sepsis. Tissue damage becomes critical with brain involvement or multiple organ (especially kidney) failure. Rescue efforts normally end with the onset of brain stem death.

Victims of shock and trauma stand a better chance of survival if they are near a modern medical center with advanced ICU capabilities. However, large catastrophic events can overwhelm even advanced facilities through saturation of skilled staff time, blood supply (some individual patients can expend 50 units), and respirator availability, among other factors.

One of the simplest effective precautions to take if one is specifically concerned about the possibility of conventional terrorism is to apply a mylar-type film to one's windows. This minimizes the possibility of glass shards from a bomb blast, one of the major lethal mechanisms of explosives terrorism. The US Government has also done work on preventing structural failure in buildings, including preventing potential terrorists from gaining proximity to their targets. (Blast effects dissipate as the cube of the distance from the explosion, so this is a relatively very effective expedient). However, more survivable buildings are expensive to construct, slow in becoming available, and often enough tend to look like bunkers.

WEAPONS OF MASS DESTRUCTION TERRORISM

Many experts are concerned about the possibility of mass casualty terrorism using unconventional means. Walter Lacquer has called this phenomenon the "New Terrorism."[4] Unconventional means include nuclear, radiological, chemical and biological weapons. Nuclear and radiological weapons are considered less likely, although possible, threats compared to chemical and biological ones. These agents do not require special nuclear materials, which are comparatively difficult to obtain, while still being capable of inflicting mass casualties.

NUCLEAR AND RADIOLOGICAL TERRORISM

Nuclear weapons produce blast, heat, radiation, and fallout. The leading cause of prompt fatalities (deaths within 30 days) is expected to be blast overpressure, measured in pounds per square inch (psi). Humans theoretically can withstand up to 30 psi. However, only 2 psi can produce winds well over 100 mph. Such hurricane winds produce flying glass and debris that are expected to be the major killers. In describing nuclear blasts, casualty prediction models often assume that everyone within the 5 psi ring will be killed outright, with most within the 2 psi ring dead as well. Such damage expectations can be measured in miles for strategic nuclear weapons, but may be significantly reduced for improvised terrorist devices.[5] Prompt radiation and heat are expected to have a lesser radius of prompt fatalities.

Fallout often originates as material on the ground that is vaporized by the blast, taken up in the mushroom cloud, and then deposited downwind. Big pieces tend to fall out sooner and closer. It is possible to take shelter against fallout, especially of a small device. Short half life radioisotopes are the most deadly, but expend their force the quickest. Even four days after an attack, the radiation in some fallout should start to "cool." Dosimeters are needed to check particular locations for safety.

If terrorists lack the skills to make a nuclear device and cannot obtain one from a military source, they may still conduct radiological terrorism by attacking a nuclear power plant with conventional explosives or sabotage. However, US power plants have sturdy containment domes to guard against even most worst-case attacks. Terrorists may also obtain radiological materials from hospitals or power plants and perhaps spread them by explosive or other means as part of an area denial or other terrorist campaign.

Nuclear radiation kills epithelial cells, such as those that line mucous membranes and the gut. However, the most lethal damage of radiation is destroying bone marrow cells and weakening the immune system, with secondary infection actually taking the victim.[6] The focus of therapy is often to protect the patient from infection while his surviving bone marrow recovers. There are steroids and developmental means to help accelerate recovery. Many victims have been treated successfully who have been exposed to high levels of radiation (up to 500 rads/five grays). However, victims who show early neurological damage may be unlikely to recover.

Ionizing radiation attacks the cell, including disrupting DNA. Most cells that are significantly damaged tend to die and be sloughed off as part of radically accelerating an ongoing process within the body. Cancer may be promoted if tumor suppressor genes, for instance, are destroyed in the attack. Another way may be if polymorphisms are induced in DNA that are close enough to reproduce, and are not eliminated or repaired by the body's own machinery. As a laboratory curiosity, the Radiodurens bacteria can suffer high levels of radioactive exposure, and then repair its own DNA and reproduce itself despite incredibly adverse environment. It may teach us more over time about radiotherapy. Radiodurens is also being tested on bioremediation of some radiological wastes.

CHEMICAL TERRORISM

Chemical threats include choking agents (e.g., phosgene and chlorine); blood agents (e.g., cyanide); blister agents (e.g., mustard gas); and nerve agents (e.g., tabun, Sarin, soman and VX).

Blood agents such as cyanide and choking agents such as phosgene and chlorine may be the most likely chemical mass casualty threats. They are industrial chemicals with widespread application and relatively widespread availability. A terrorist may choose to redirect legitimate sources of such chemicals to criminal terrorist purposes. Indeed, there are several examples of such diversion. It is now considered by some that the lethal chemical spill at the Union Carbide plant in Bhopal, India, was intentionally precipitated by one or more persons who released water into the methyl isocyanate, creating a vast poison cloud of cyanide gas. The Tamil Tiger guerrilla group in Sri Lanka is said to have targeted a chlorine storage facility in order to attack a Government army base (the results were relatively ineffective, but disturbing). Recently in Pleasant Hill, Missouri, someone appears to have deliberately caused a chemical leak of about 200 gallons of anhydrous ammonia that turned into a dangerous vapor cloud on February 28, 2000.[7] No one was hurt in that incident.

Cyanide was misleadingly labeled a "blood agent" since it appeared to affect the whole body through the blood of the victim, as opposed to other chemical agents that impact the lungs or skin.[8]

Cyanides were ineffective battlefield weapons in WW I, in part because they are lighter than air and tend to rise. However, they might still be very effective terrorist weapons inside buildings. Cyanides poison cellular metabolism by binding with iron in the cytochrome oxidase complex in the mitochondria[9] (cellular energy source), inhibiting that enzyme. Cyanides act extremely rapidly, causing death in minutes. Intravenous therapy may prove effective, but it is relatively unlikely to be available in time unless there is advanced warning and preparation for the attack. Treatment requires fixation of the cyanide ion. Drugs such as intravenous thiosulphate and DMAP (4-dimethylaminophenyl-hydrochloride) are needed to achieve this cure.

Pulmonary agents such as phosgene may not cause serious initial discomfort. However, over time (hours), they produce pulmonary edema and acute respiratory distress. Phosgene releases hydrochloric acid as it breaks down in the body. Its major medical impact, however, comes from its acylation reactions in the lung at the alveolar/capillary membrane.[10] This leads to leakage into the interstitial portion of the lung.

This area is normally drained by the lymphatic system. Phosgene is treated with supportive respiratory therapy, to battle hypoxemia (unoxygenated blood from fluid in the lungs) and hypovolemia (due to the internal blood loss). Although pulmonary agents are not considered priority battlefield threats, their use by terrorists on a large scale would most likely saturate available respirators.

BLISTER AGENTS (VESSICANTS)

Mustard gas was one of the first chemical warfare agents, and remains a staple in many arsenals today. Even in WW I, only a small minority of victims died from exposure. However, they required long periods of treatment before recovery. Sulfur mustard agent does not irritate the skin, but rapidly penetrates it. Within hours, it can cause blistering, alkylation of DNA, and bone marrow suppression. Mustard dissolves rapidly to form extremely reactive ions that bind to intra- and extracellular enzymes and proteins.[11] This leads to cellular death and inflammatory reaction, including protease digestion of anchoring filaments in the skin and the formation of blisters. Vessicant exposure requires extensive supportive therapy such as may be provided by a hospital intensive care unit.

NERVE AGENTS

Acetylcholine is a biochemical neurotransmitter that links nerve cells to muscle and organ cells inside the body. When nerve cells are stimulated, they release acetylcholine into the space (synapse) between the different types of cells, stimulating muscle cells, for instance, to contract. Routinely, an enzyme called acetylcholinesterase rapidly breaks down (hydrolizes) the active acetylcholine, permitting its "reuptake" to the nerve cell. Chemical agents known as nerve gases prevent the acetylcholinesterase in the synapses from neutralizing the active neurotransmitter, thus assuring that the muscles or organs continue to be stimulated, leading to convulsions and death. Nerve gas was invented in the 1930s in Germany. It is based on organophosphates. Various insecticides, such as Malathion, can be considered a weak form of nerve agent. That is the way they kill insects.

Therapy for nerve agents is atropine and an oxime such as 2-PAM Chloride[12] (2-pyridine aldoxime methyl chloride, also called pralidoxime chloride). Even after surviving challenge, patients may enter an epileptic state in which they require anxiolytics such as diazepam (valium). Oximes attach to the nerve agent inhibiting the cholinesterase and break the bond with the agent, enabling the enzyme to resume normal activity. Once atropine and oximes are given, supportive respiratory therapy may be needed for recovery. A large attack would require more respirators than are likely to be available at most hospitals.

Sarin is one of the most widely feared nerve agents because it is relatively simple to synthesize, as well as having high lethality. VX, which is considerably more powerful, is commensurately much more difficult to make. VX use would tend to indicate a state sponsor of an attack, while an individual or small group might make Sarin. As a further example, the Aum Shinrikyo cult was trying to create a Sarin factory in Japan. The factory had several leaks and experienced at least one fatal accident before its development was discontinued by the cult.

The factory included a tall distillation tower to improve agent purity, indicating a level of sophistication in planning, even if the implementation of the nerve gas plant did not work out. For their attack on the Tokyo subway, the cult used a desktop synthesizer from Switzerland to rapidly create tactical quantities of Sarin. However, they did not purify it, leading to lower levels of effectiveness. In addition, Sarin is not a gas at room temperature, so its dissemination by evaporation was relatively ineffective. The only casualties who died appeared to have encountered drops of the liquid agent. So Sarin could have created many more casualties if the perpetrators had increased its quality to levels they knew how to accomplish, and had disseminated it more efficiently. Nevertheless, they did not, despite having considerable resources and expertise available to them. One hopes that would continue with any future terrorists.

Treatment for nerve agent poisoning requires rapid administration of atropine to counteract the agent. However, an overdose of atropine can also mimic the effects of nerve gas; thus, there would be the danger of overmedicating patients in a confusing operational context. Valium may also be administered as an anti-convulsant. Pyridostigmine Bromide (PB) is an interesting pre-medication. In effect, it acts as a relatively mild, reversible nerve agent. PB is a carbamate that temporarily binds to the molecular sites at which nerve agent also would attach. This makes those sites unavailable if nerve gas is used soon after. Later, the PB comes unbound, and the cell maintains normal function.

A recent meta-study by the Rand Corporation could not rule out that PB may be responsible for some manifestations of Gulf War Illness. Rand reviewed over 400 studies of PB, and found that it tended to be taken up by the body at different, largely unpredictable levels, and could have unintended deleterious effects, some of which were compatible with Gulf War Illness. In the face of a nerve gas attack, taking previously issued PB could significantly increase troop survival rates in a military context. However, absent credible warning of an impending attack, individuals may well wish to avoid taking PB because its health risks are not well understood.

BIOLOGICAL TERRORISM

Leading biological agents include anthrax, tularemia, plague, viral hemorrhagic fevers and smallpox. Toxins are usually classed as biological agents, although they are often chemical products of biological organisms. Toxins may be considered as powerful poisons, but they do not reproduce in the host's body, as bacteria and viruses do. This enables biological weapons to have such high lethality from a small initial exposure. The major categories of true biological agents are bacteria, viruses, and toxins. (To narrow the topic, we omit here Rickettsiae, fungi, prions, etc. that may also be used as biological weapons, since these are less likely, and share some similar features to bacteria and viruses). From a medical perspective, one may be vaccinated against either a bacterial or viral illness and build up immunity to it over weeks or months. However, bacteria are small living organisms that may be treated by antibiotics. Viruses, on the other hand, will run their course and are not susceptible to antibiotics. (Viruses are intracellular parasites that hijack healthy cells and destroy them to reproduce themselves). Viruses are also contagious from person to person, while many bacteria are infectious but not contagious. One has to be directly exposed to get the disease. Although there is much less that medical science can do to treat viruses, they are also much harder for potential terrorists to make. For instance, they need to be grown in eggs, animals or a bioreactor, since they cannot survive and reproduce independent of a host. Bacteria, on the other hand, may be simply fermented in a growth medium and produced in quantity.

The most worrisome release of biological agent would be as an aerosol, although it could also be done through food or water contamination. Food contamination would tend to be detected as the victims fell ill, and the source tracked down before a great deal was consumed.

Water contamination is harder than some people think. Airborne dissemination is one way to infect a great many people quickly. To be the most infectious, biological aerosols require a 1-5 micron particle size. This is small enough to remain airborne for a long period and be taken deeply into the lungs, without being so small that it is rapidly expired again.

If one has a mask that filters such small particles, or is effectively sheltered from the passing threat, one is not likely to be infected by the biological weapon. Contamination avoidance in this manner is much easier and safer than medical treatment to counteract the disease. The difficulty, obviously, is knowing when to protect oneself.

BACTERIA

Anthrax is often considered the leading biological threat agent because of its unique combination of high lethality, relative accessibility, and relative ease of covert employment. There is no cure for anthrax; it has a mortality rate of over 90 percent once the infection sets in and symptoms are present. However, there is a vaccine to make one immune to anthrax. In addition, if one knows one has been exposed to anthrax, one can start treatment with antibiotics to prevent the onset of symptoms. This may be done while also getting vaccinated, so that natural immunity is achieved before discontinuing the antibiotic regimen (about eight weeks).

Anthrax is a disease of herbivores that goes back to biblical times. (It may have been the plagues visited on the Egyptians in Exodus, once for animals and once for humans.) It was the first microbe imaged by Robert Koch. It was the first vaccine created by Louis Pasteur. Yet there is no cure for it once its infection has colonized a host. Working assumptions are that 90 percent of those who present symptoms will die. However, there are few cases of inhalational anthrax on which to base this assumption. The outstanding example was the inadvertent release at Sverdlovsk in 1972, in which perhaps 62 people died, closer to 70 percent of those infected.

Anthrax forms a spore that is very robust and endemic around the world. Animal outbreaks are usually associated with dry weather, when dust containing old spores is then inhaled or ingested by animals. About 8-10,000 spores are considered the minimal infective dose. Although that may seem like a lot, and it is compared to some other disease threats, that number of spores is so small as to be invisible. Anthrax can manifest itself in cutaneous or gastrointestinal forms if it infects cuts on the skin or is ingested. However, inhalational anthrax is considered the most deadly.

Spores in the 1-10 micron particle size are inhaled deep into the alveoli of the lungs. There the spores may germinate and become vegetative. They are identified by the immune system and transported to lymph nodes in the mediastinum, the area around one's heart and lungs. They are ingested by white blood cells known as macrophages (macro = large, phage = eat). The macrophage engulfs the anthrax. However, instead of dying, the anthrax has a capsule that protects it and permits it to reproduce even inside the macrophage. It effectively releases toxins from host cells, leading to edema and septic shock (and meningitis in about half the victims). Once the infection takes hold, even antibiotics cannot cure it, since the major impact is from the toxins released. Tissue cells just break down.

The incubation period of the disease is considered to be 1-6 days by the experts at USAMRIID. However, victims at Sverdlovsk developed symptoms up to two months after exposure. Why this was so is not clear. It is considered unlikely that the late presentation was the result of reaerosolization of the original spores. The Army has conducted research with protected troops exercising on ground with a generous covering of anthrax spore simulants. After several hours, the troops' gas masks were collected and the filters analyzed. The spores collected were well below the infectious dose of anthrax. On the other hand, medical testing has revealed that nonhuman primates may develop symptoms up to two months after lethal challenge by an aerosol if they are removed from antibiotic prophylactic therapy.

Even at late onset, the course of the disease is similar. The first symptoms are nonspecific and flu-like. Then there may be an "anthrax eclipse" during which the patient feels better. Within a day or so later, breathing becomes extremely difficult (dyspnea) and the patient dies within a day, basically similar to septic shock. It is the start of this second stage when most patients would probably seek hospitalization.

Since there are virtually no cases of respiratory anthrax, emergency room doctors will probably recognize it right away. With dispnea, they will probably order a sputum culture and an x-ray.

The sputum culture will come back negative, since the disease has taken hold in the lymph system rather than the lungs. The negative finding will probably trigger significant curiosity, since influenza or pneumonia, for instance, would come back positive, and are more likely to be found in the Emergency Room. However, the x-ray will reveal an enlarged mediastinum due to the anthrax edema, which impacts negatively on breathing and heart function.

It is at this point that aware critical care specialists may suspect anthrax, and move to preventively treat those with similar symptoms while they await the results of dispositive tests. Such tests have to be done in special facilities and may take 24 hours. Other evidence for a differential diagnosis may be drawn from autopsies. As noted, about half the victims will have meningitis, destructive inflammation of the brain.

During that day, waiting for positive confirmation from the laboratory, up to 20 percent of the victims who were originally exposed may present with symptoms. As noted above, the prognosis for symptomatic patients is poor. This is the time, as Frank Young has noted, that one realizes one is in a race with the grim reaper. The race has started with no pistol shot or puff of smoke. One only knows one is in a race when the grim reaper is in the first turn. That is, when the first victims start to die and the disease is recognized.

At that time, the race is to provide doses of antibiotic to all those who are believed to have been exposed. However, that will not be clear except in retrospect. One may assume that all persons in the impacted area will demand antibiotic prophylaxis. The antibiotic of choice is ciproflaxacin, until sensitivity tests on the microbe determine if it is sensitive to the tetracycline family or even ampicillin (oral penicillin). In general, antibiotics have a limited shelf life (about 3 years) and are purchased by health facilities at the rate that they are expected to be used. There are few stockpiles of large amounts of antibiotics, especially ciprofloxacin or other fluoroquinolones, and limited surge capacity. The US Centers for Disease Control is working on the stockpile problem.

However, at about $5 per day per victim over two months, the numbers significantly exceed CDC's budget for the project thus far. New York City, for one, is also arranging for a significant stockpile of its own.

This possible shortage may stoke civilian concern shortly after a large release by a bioterrorist, especially once they learn that medicine is needed before symptoms present, and there is no clear way to determine who has been exposed. For this reason alone, developing a treatment for anthrax should be a high priority. One novel way to approach this may be through bacteriophages ("eaters" of bacteria). Bacteriophages are viruses that attack bacteria, very small living organisms. Bacteriophages attach to the cell, inject their DNA and reproduce. When the cell bursts, up to 200 new bacteriophages are released, which pursue the same type of host cell and repeat the process.

In the gut, bacteriophages quickly dissipate shigella, for instance. A commercial product was developed by the Germans in WW II and issued to its troops against dysentery. The Russians did a great deal of research on bacteriophages. US work lagged with the success of antibiotics.

There are bacteriophages that are specific to anthrax. Some bacteriophages have been tried against sepsis and have survived and reproduced in that environment in a living host. It may be possible to develop bacteriophages that are able to attack anthrax even when they are engulfed in the macrophages. Current research is considering them against multi-drug-resistant tuberculosis, which is typically enclosed in fibrous tissue, presumably tougher to penetrate than macrophages would be.

If one is specifically concerned about the anthrax threat, obtaining a prophylactic supply of ciprofloxacin may be of interest. Anthrax vaccine is not released to civilians unless to veterinarians or others with a documentable need for it.

On the vaccine, this author believes it is fundamentally a good vaccine, with relatively very few side effects. However, it is based on old technology. A new cell culture vaccine is being developed. Once that is available, perhaps it could be made available to first responders and their families.

During any anthrax attack, one would not want the first responders, essential personnel, to be worried about their own susceptibility or that of their families. However, that distribution should be on a strictly voluntary basis.

BUBONIC PLAGUE.

Bubonic Plague is the disease that devastated Europe in the 14th century, killing perhaps one-third of the population. Plague is still endemic around the world, including the southwest US. However, it is susceptible to antibiotics. Bubonic plague is spread by fleas on rats that then infest humans. However, after the disease spreads from the buboes (certain lymph nodes) to the lungs, it becomes pneumonic plague. The pneumonic form can be spread by droplets, as by coughing, from human to human and is highly contagious.

The Soviets developed plague during the Cold War in order to make it resistant to most antibiotics. It was intended to be a strategic weapon used in conjunction with a nuclear exchange.

VIRUSES

Smallpox is one of the most prolific killers in history. Over 100 million died in this century alone before smallpox was declared eradicated by the World Health Organization around 1972. Currently, the only legally declared stocks are held by the US and Russia. The destruction of the last samples has been postponed at the request of the US, so that work may be done to find a medical treatment for the disease. This may be important if additional stocks have been withheld and remain viable, and if they are released by terrorists or others. (It is currently believed by some in the intelligence community that Iraq and North Korea, for instance, may possess the smallpox virus.)

Historically, smallpox kills about one third of those infected by it. Survivors may be physically scarred or blind afterwards. Ancient peoples created deities to ward off smallpox. The British used it against the Indians in 1763 in the French and Indian War. Later, General Washington insisted that all of his troops be "variolated," exposed to attenuated but live virus culture from pustules of recovering victims. This procedure conferred immunity, but carried the small but nonzero risk that those exposed to it would get the disease and die. However, Washington considered this was necessary, in that the British troops were relatively "hardened" to smallpox, whereas the colonists were more immunologically naive.

Smallpox is almost as communicable as chicken pox. In Yugoslavia around 1972, an epidemic broke out, spreading from one Kosovar who had inadvertently brought an infection back from the Middle East. Reportedly, one of the people he spread it to was a visitor to the hospital where he was being treated. The visitor had only stopped in the lobby downstairs from the patient to ask directions. (For diseases like smallpox, negative pressure treatment facilities are needed, so the germs won't escape. However, remarkably few treatment facilities such as this are still available.) Even though Yugoslavs were routinely vaccinated against smallpox at the time, they inoculated 18 million people in about ten days. Those potentially exposed were quarantined against their will in public buildings and hotels for over a week. Yugoslavia's neighbors and the airlines closed all international borders until it was seen the epidemic had passed.

The US has stopped vaccinating against smallpox since shortly after its formal eradication was declared. We retain about 16 million doses of vaccine (basically vaccinia or cowpox pustules scraped from purposelyinfected calves).

However, these stocks are failing quality control checks as they age, and moisture appears to be penetrating the package seals. Nevertheless, authorities believe the vaccine is still effective. They have not used it lately, however, since an antidote supply has also become questionable. The US Food and Drug Administration (FDA) insists that vaccinia immunoglobulin (VIG) be available to anyone who takes the vaccine, especially since the strain of the vaccine is very reactinogenic. However, all the VIG has turned pink in storage. Authorities also believe that the VIG is good, but they don't want to risk it.

A new smallpox vaccine and VIG are being created for the military. Sometime after 2005, it is hoped that a civilian supply will also become available. Smallpox vaccine is very important, in that it can prevent the onset of symptoms even if one has recently been exposed to smallpox. In that sense, it is somewhat like having a treatment for the disease. Victims are considered to be contagious from the time their symptoms start to appear until their pustules scab over.

Former Soviet scientist Dr. Ken Alibek has claimed that the Vektor organization, which is now the official Russian repository for smallpox, used to do research on turning smallpox into a weapon of war. It was a strategic weapon, which would be used against ports and airfields. Perhaps dissatisfied with its relatively low lethality rate, Alibek claims the Soviets were also trying to graft the smallpox virus together with Marburg, an Ebola-like virus. Like Ebola, Marburg tends to have a very high lethality rate, but is relatively fragile. The former Soviets were trying to obtain both the stability and lethality of a virus super weapon. However, Alibek left Kazhakstan before this "chimera" virus was perfected. It is not known if anyone succeeded in the effort.

TOXINS

Toxins are in effect the poisons that biological agents produce. Small quantities can cause fatal damage. However, most toxins will not penetrate the skin (the exception being mycotoxins; think "yellow rain"). So using toxins as a mass casualty weapon may be challenging. They do not reproduce themselves in the host, as biological agents do, and so multiply their numbers and pathological effect. Botulinum is one of the most potent toxins on earth. Interestingly, it tends to work in an opposite way to nerve gas. It prevents the uptake of the neurotransmitter acetylcholine. Thus patients have a characteristic lethargy and drooping eyelids.

Death occurs when the diaphragm no longer contracts, and breathing stops. Availability of artificial respirators is key to overcoming a botulinum attack. The effect wears off if breathing can be maintained. However, full recovery may take quite some time.

Ricin is another potent toxin, which can be derived from the common castor bean. Booklets and video tapes are available over the Internet to teach one how to do so. Ricin does permanent damage, even if the victim does not die. Ricin appears to have been procured with the intent of creating a weapon by a number of individuals and groups. This includes one case in which a man crossing the border from Canada was intercepted with a large amount of ricin, as well as thousands of dollars. He hanged himself in his cell before he revealed his intent. Another man had ricin and a nicotine compound presumably intended to facilitate uptake through the skin. However, a broad aerosol attack on a population does not appear to have been contemplated in known cases.

CONCLUSION

Advanced medical technology can be extremely effective in countering the effects of terrorism, from conventional to WMD. However, medical resources are limited in number and may be expected to quickly saturate out for a mass casualty event, especially if medical staff is also the victim of the attack. Biological terrorism threatens the greatest adverse medical impact. However, promising medical research is being conducted which may neutralize a broad array of pathogens, whether naturally occurring or deliberately disseminated.

CHAPTER 4 ENDNOTES

1   DHHS. "Healthy People 2010," Section 1-11.
2   American College of Emergency Physicians. "Defending America's Safety Net," Dec 99, p. 20.
3   R. L. Souhami, J. Moxham, eds. *Textbook of Medicine*, 3e. Churchill Livingstone Publishers; Edinburgh, Scotland; 1997; pp. 598-614.
4   Walter Laquer, "The New Terrorism," *Foreign Policy*.

5   Office of Technology Assessment, "Effects of Nuclear War," Washington, D.C.

6   Col. David Jarrett, "Medical Management of Radiological Casualties," Armed Forces Radiobiology Research Institute, Bethesda, MD., July 26, 2000.

7   Reuters, "Hundreds Flee Deliberate Poison Cloud in Missouri," Monday, February 28, 2000, at 2:41 PM ET.

8   Col. Jonathan Newmark, "Chemical Warfare Agents," US Army Medical Research Institute of Chemical Defense, Aberdeen, MD. July 26, 2000.

9   *Medical Management of Chemical Casualties Handbook*, 3Ed. US Army Medical Research Institute of Chemical Defense. Aberdeen, MD, August 1999, pp. 46-47.

10 Ibid., p. 27.

11 Ibid., pp. 66-69

12 Newmark, op cit

Chapter 5

Biological Agents as Natural Hazards and Bioterrorism as a "New" Natural Disaster Threat*

By Eric K. Noji, M.D., M.P.H.

Biological weapons represent a unique "natural" hazard. The pathogens involved are natural in the sense that they are risks that naturally occur in our environment. However, they are unnatural in the way in which they are inflicted upon society.

This article was originally published in the Natural Hazards Observer, November, 2000, 482 UCB, University of Colorado, Boulder, CO 80309-0482; 303-492-6819.

NOT A NEW HAZARD

Despite their current notoriety, biological weapons are not new. Two of the earliest reported uses occurred in the 6th century B.C., when the Assyrians poisoned enemy wells with rye ergot, and Solon used the purgative herb hellebore during the siege of Krissa. In 1346, plague broke out in the Tartar army during its siege of Kaffa in the Crimea. The attackers hurled the corpses of those who died over the city walls and the plague epidemic that followed forced the defenders to surrender. Some infected people who left Kaffa may have started the Black Death pandemic that spread throughout Europe, killing one-third of the population.

BIOLOGICAL WEAPONS
AS MODERN INSTRUMENTS OF WAR

In 1972 the United States and many other countries signed the Convention on the Prohibition of the Development, Production and Stockpiling of Bacteriological [Biological] and Toxin Weapons and on Their Destruction, commonly called the Biological Weapons Convention. This treaty prohibits the stockpiling of biological agents for offensive military purposes and forbids research into offensive employment of biological agents. The former Soviet Union and the Government of Iraq were both signatories to this accord, but despite this historic agreement, biological warfare research continued in both countries.

Since 1972, there have been several cases of suspected or actual use of biological weapons. For example, in late April 1979, an incident in Sverdlovsk (now Yekaterinburg) in the former Soviet Union appeared to be an accidental release of anthrax in aerosol form from Soviet Military Compound 19, a microbiology facility. Residents living downwind from this compound developed high fever and had difficulty breathing, and a large number died. The final toll was estimated to be 200 to 1,000.

In August 1991, the first United Nations inspection of Iraq's biological warfare capabilities was carried out in the aftermath of the Gulf War. On August 2, 1991, the Iraqi government announced to leaders of the United Nations Special Commission that they had conducted research into the offensive use of Bacillus anthracis, Clostridium perfringens (presumably one of its toxins), and botulinum toxins. This was the first open admission of biological weapons research by any country in recent memory, and it verified many of the concerns of the international community. Biological agents were tested by the Iraqis in various delivery systems, including rockets, aerial bombs, and spray tanks.

Despite the Biological Weapons Convention of 1972, the threat of biological warfare has actually increased in the last two decades, with a number of countries continuing to conduct research on the use of these agents as offensive weapons. The extensive program of the former Soviet Union is now controlled largely by Russia, and the Russian government has stated that it will put an end to further biological research. However, the degree to which the program has been scaled back, if any, is not known. A senior bioweapons program manager who defected from the former Soviet Union in 1992 outlined a remarkably robust biological warfare program. There is also growing concern that the smallpox virus -- eradicated in the late 1970s primarily through the enormous efforts of the US Centers for Disease Control and Prevention (CDC) and the World Health Organization and now stored in only two laboratories at the CDC in Atlanta and the Institute for Viral Precautions in Moscow, Russia -- may have been "bargained" away by desperate Russian scientists seeking money. An attack with an agent such as smallpox could pose threats to large populations because of the potential for person-to-person transmission, enabling spread to other cities and states. Such a disease would quickly become a nationwide emergency, with international involvement sure to follow.

Not surprisingly, there is currently intense concern about the proliferation or enhancement of offensive programs in several countries due to possible hiring of expatriate Russian scientists as well as a number of other conditions, including neglected security systems and unpaid and unemployed technical personnel with access to and knowledge of weapons of mass destruction. Reportedly, in January 1998 Iraq sent about a dozen scientists to Libya to help that country develop a biological warfare complex disguised as a medical facility in the Tripoli area. In a report issued in November 1997, former US Secretary of Defense William Cohen singled out Libya, Iraq, Iran, and Syria as countries "aggressively seeking" nuclear, biological, and chemical weapons.

BIOLOGICAL WEAPONS AS INSTRUMENTS OF TERRORISM

In addition to biological agents as weapons of war, there is also increasing concern over the possibility of terrorist use of biological agents to threaten civilian populations. There have already been cases of extremist groups in the US trying to obtain micro-organisms to use as biological weapons. Until recently, an attack on civilians with a biological agent was considered very unlikely; however, now it seems entirely plausible.

Recent events indicate that neither arms control treaties nor the moral repugnance long associated with the use of biological weapons will deter their use as terrorist weapons. Some experts have stated publicly that it is no longer a matter of if, but when, such an attack will occur. They point to the accessibility of information on how to prepare biologic weapons (e.g., on the Internet) and to activities by groups such as the Japanese terrorist group Aum Shinrikyo, which, in addition to releasing nerve gas in Tokyo's subway system, experimented with botulism and anthrax and vigorously sought to obtain the Ebola virus.

A NEW HAZARD

Unfortunately, a disaster caused by the intentional release of biological weapons would be very different from other natural or technological disasters, conventional military strikes, or even attacks with other weapons of mass destruction (e.g., nuclear, chemical, or explosive). For example, when people are exposed to a pathogen such as plague or smallpox, they may not be aware of their exposure, and they may not feel sick for some time, even though they would be contagious. Indeed, the incubation period may range from several hours to a few weeks, and, consequently, an attack would not become obvious for a similar period. By that time, modern transportation could have widely dispersed the pathogen and greatly expanded the population of victims, perhaps exponentially.

Moreover, unlike an explosion, a tornado or an earthquake, in a biological event it is unlikely that a single location or cluster of people will be identified for traditional first response. The initial responders to a biological disaster will most likely include county and city health officers, hospital staff, members of the outpatient medical community, and a wide range of response personnel in the public health system and not the traditional first responders such as police, fire, rescue, and ambulance services.

Few American physicians have ever seen a case of smallpox, or anthrax, or plague, and diagnosis of an epidemic is certain to be delayed. Laboratory capabilities for diagnosis and measuring antibiotic sensitivity of organisms are similarly limited and would cause further delays.

Few, if any, recent disasters on American soil have resulted in the large numbers of patients needing immediate and sustained medical care that would probably result from an epidemic due to an intentionally released virulent biological agent.

It is hard to identify a modern disaster that has tested the capacity of the US health care system to deal with something comparable to an attack on a US city with an aerosolized anthrax weapon. Clearly, should such an attack occur, hospitals would be front-line response institutions, with hundreds, thousands, or perhaps even tens of thousands of people requiring immediate and/or intensive care. Yet, hospitals in the US are already overburdened, over-occupied, and understaffed, and thus ill prepared to deal with a mass disaster. In addition, in any event involving biological weapons, the number of people actually ill and in need of hospital care would likely be exceeded by the number seeking care because they were fearful of being sick. (The Scud missile attacks on Israeli citizens during the Gulf War produced large numbers of people seeking medical care for acute anxiety symptoms that closely mimic the early effects of nerve gas.)

Additionally, in their initial stages, many of the diseases delivered by biological weapons resemble common illnesses. Rapid diagnostic tests for smallpox, anthrax, etc. would be most helpful, but even their availability would not obviate the need to distinguish the truly sick from the worried well. Hence, triaging affected individuals in order to best deploy limited drugs and equipment will require significant hospital resources and skilled staff. Moreover, in the event that a bioterrorist attack employs a contagious pathogen, health professionals must be protected from the diseases afflicting their patients, and patients must be prevented from infecting others. Yet most hospital infection plans are capable of managing only a handful of infectious patients.

No one knows how people would react to a disaster caused by a deadly pathogen, but it is likely that some health care workers would leave their jobs to care for their families and others would leave for fear of their own safety. Maintaining security at hospitals, health care centers, and pharmacies would pose great challenges since many hospital security staff are off-duty police officers who would presumably be needed elsewhere during the crisis.

At the same time, media coverage of modern epidemics (as has occurred with the West Nile Fever, Hantavirus, Swine Flu, Legionnaire's

Disease, etc.) will have a profound influence on the response to a biological attack. It is easy to imagine the opportunities for misinformation or contradictory interpretations by various self-appointed or media-anointed "experts."

The situation could certainly lend itself to fueling public mistrust, whereas providing the public with accurate, timely information which people would not only believe, but would act on, could literally save lives.

Planning a response to terrorist attacks or biological disasters must not neglect the social consequences of epidemics. Unlike most "natural disasters," deliberate epidemics may continue to produce victims over a period of weeks or months, and additional attacks must be anticipated. If the biological weapon is a contagious disease, fellow citizens may represent ongoing threats to public safety, or be perceived as such. Thus, the attack would exact a physical and emotional toll on the whole population, but, again, especially on health care workers and family caretakers. Normal routines and commercial activity would likely be seriously disrupted, possibly on a city-wide or regional basis and for an extended period. Proper attention to the psychological needs of people in crisis will be essential.

Historically, some disease-control measures taken in times of public health emergencies have been at odds with, or perceived as violating, certain democratic principles and processes. For example, mandatory quarantine, enforced vaccination in order to limit disease spread, and imposition of martial law have been perceived as threats to individual freedom and the right to privacy, or as discriminatory actions against certain groups. During a crisis, communication failures among different communities and between government officials and citizens can create suspicions and resistance to public health response measures.

Moreover, differing ideas of what constitutes proper response can also have long-term political consequences, contributing to distrust of government institutions and disengagement from the processes of representative democracy. A bioterrorist attack would undoubtedly raise many important political, legal, moral, and ethical issues involving civil liberties, the authorities of state and federal health officials, and liability in the event mass vaccination is necessary. An effort to identify and better understand such issues is important.

In conclusion, the best public health measures to protect, respond to, and defend against the adverse health effects of biological terrorism or disasters due to deadly pathogens are the development, organization, and enhancement of life-saving public health tools. Planning and training involving all organizations potentially involved in responding -- from emergency managers to public health officials to hospital administrators and staff--is essential.

Expanded public health laboratory capacity, increased surveillance (disease monitoring) and outbreak response capacity, and health communication and training, with focused public health preparedness resources at the state and local level, are necessary to ensure that we will be able to respond effectively to this unique "natural" disaster.

EDITOR'S NOTE:

Medical researchers are hopeful that a vaccine currently under development might eventually be effective against Ebola. Four monkeys that were injected with a dose of the experimental vaccine were exposed to lethal doses of the Ebola virus and felt no ill effects. Normally such a dose would have been fatal. Four other monkeys who were exposed to the virus without having had the vaccine injection died within six days. Gary Nabel of the National Institutes of Health wrote an article about the findings of this research in the Nature *journal. It could be years before experiments on humans could begin because of concerns over safety and how to deal with varied strains of Ebola for which there is no current known cure. Victims die agonizingly by bleeding out of every orifice.*

Claims have also been made that compounds found in a plant used by West African faith healers stopped the spread of Ebola in laboratory tests and may be effective against that virus. Maurice Iwu, founder of the London-based Bioresources Development and Conservation Program, told the International Botanical Congress in 1999 that the Garcinia kola plant, which grows wild in Africa, contains compounds with two flavonoid molecules fused together that scientists believe halted the spread of Ebola in tests. It is hoped that these compounds from the plant can be used to form the basis of drugs in a few years.

In the Fall of 2000 in Gulu, Uganda, an outbreak of Ebola occurred. More than 100 people were infected. An outbreak of Ebola in 1995 in the Democratic Republic of the Congo (formerly Zaire) killed 81 percent of its 315 victims.

Chapter 6

SLA-C4I Multifunctional Cross-Border Airport Security System
By George H. Balestrieri

In this chapter a long-range strategic concept for sea, land and air cross-border multifunctional control/security systems, including the management of national revenue sources, will be discussed.

OVERVIEW
The primary purpose of a cross-border station is to process passengers, their baggage and freight by methods that will ensure the maximum speed of movement with the minimum of inconvenience, an art that has earned itself the descriptive term "facilitation." However, this highly desirable aim must be achieved safely and "facilitation with

security" is essential in meeting the threat of contraband, hijacking, armed assault and sabotage.

Commercial cross-border stations require a rapid, effective and efficient means to screen and correlate passengers, luggage, and freight through security checkpoints. The new and advanced concept of a comprehensive Multifunctional Cross-Border Management System based on the integration of state-of-the-art subsystems offers the real-time management of a cross-border station. Such system provides comprehensive, precise security measures and causes no interruption to passenger cargo flow, thus maximizing security screening.

Analyses of cross-border security problems reveal deficiencies resulting from overworked security staff served by a collection of single-purpose devices such as access control monitors, baggage x-ray equipment and personnel scanners. Today's cross-border systems are a diversity of free-standing loosely related devices that are both defensive in application and expensive to operate.

Tomorrow's cross-border security systems must present an integrated, interrelated, interdependent network of devices and information services to drive security to the offensive.

The multifunctional management of important commercial cross-border structures and their associated free trade zones demand computer-based data processing and telecommunications that will include state-of-the-art data-handling techniques, artificial intelligence technologies, and image processing and matching methodologies. Expertise both in the military and industrial security systems culminated in suggesting a common approach and standards for a National Sea, Land & Airport Cross-border Systems project.

The SLA-C4I system represents the integration of state-of-the art telecommunications and security systems already produced by the international industry and has its basis or starting point in an "electronic corridor" which is the foundation for all future developments.

The advantages of such a project fall into two key categories: technical solutions to cross-border security problems and a host of economic advantages supported by unique management and business elements.

TECHNICAL SOLUTIONS

The system collates the movement of cargo, passengers and their luggage, and provides a continuous accounting of their movement through the process culminating in border crossing of cargo and passengers. The system allows for local and central authorities to control, monitor, and manage special situations when non-correlated events cause different levels of alarm.

Furthermore, the system allows the integration of state-of-the-art subsystems and devices ranging from perimeter security, access control for employees and suppliers, explosive and narcotics detection, cargo manifest checks, visa and passport controls, and non-invasive inspections at several points to many other capabilities specified to meet cross-border needs.

The multifunctional security system must be structured on a modular basis for two primary reasons:

1   Existing systems (or subsystems) must be kept in place if they perform certain functions satisfactorily. Interfaces will be provided for working subsystems with the Security Communications Command and Control Center.

2   Due to advances in technology and the fact that subsystems' implementation may be best achieved in stages, a modular approach is the most rational. A modular design permits flexibility in packaging various combinations of subsystems while preserving their integration capabilities.

ECONOMIC ADVANTAGES

The advantages of the SLA-C4I model are quite significant.

1   A multifunctional integrated system for cross-border security will assist the country authorities in the management and generation of Customs revenues as well as control of cargo and people through the country's international gateways.

2   The implementation of the system will require NO expenditure on the part of the taxpayers. A levy on passengers or cargo will pay for the installation and subsequent operation and maintenance.

3   In order to implement the project, local operating companies must be employed, thus maximizing local content and contributing to the regional economic development.

MANAGEMENT AND BUSINESS ELEMENTS

A key factor in marketing cross-border systems is worldwide knowledge and business relationship with major manufacturers and vendors of state-of-the-art ready available communications and security subsystems.

Human resources are also very important and this section briefly addresses some of the business elements supporting SLA-C4I. Specifically, the team is supported by an adequate organizational structure necessary to implement such a nationwide project.

Security Planning Teams must be ready to perform in major task areas such as:

♦ Surveys and studies
♦ System design and specifications
♦ Evaluation, test and procurement of subsystems
♦ Training and procedures in support of a contractor selected by the national authority with the necessary security clearances to implement the system.

STRATEGIC PLANNING FOR AIRPORTS AND PORTS

Security belongs to governments and safety belongs to the transportation industry.

International airports and ports are most dramatically affected by the increasing threat of narco-terrorism and now cyberterrorism. These airports and ports, representing a major market, are in most cases owned and operated by the state or local government. In order to facilitate a rapid penetration of the international marketplace airport security experts need to enter into a business relationship with a corporation in each country/state in which the Security Planning Team recognizes a need.

COUNTRY/STATE PARTNERS AND CONSULTANTS

Corporations (country/state partner and consultants) will be selected based upon their ability to work with state and local port authorities in securing the contracts, as well as their ability to provide (or arrange for) the engineering services required in the preparation of the airport site and the subsequent installation of the SLA-C4I equipment.

A jointly owned company would be created with the country/state partner (partnership) which is tasked with selling, installing and maintaining the system to be operated by expert and law enforcement officers.

Through the partnership, the Team members will perform that work best suited to their individual capabilities, contract for outside services when required, collect the SLA-C4I revenues, pay bills and participate in the profits generated by the effort.

The country/state partner should have available system engineering and technical assistance (SETA) in the town area in which an airport and/or port is located sufficient to support the sales efforts. If the country/state partner does not have all the necessary support, support would be generated through one or more companies or individuals (engineers and consultants). To be successful in the international marketplace, it is necessary to screen and select "qualified" country/state partners, engineers and consultants. To do this, it is necessary to:

♦ Identify large successful organizations that are currently qualified and involved in building airports, ports, installing systems, or are service contractors.

♦ Identify the organizations that have considerable political influence to enact legislation to mandate cross-border enforcement to the appropriate law enforcement agency not to the private sector.

♦ Within the above, to identify organizations that are interested in airport security, and are willing to enter into joint venture agreements on a profit-sharing basis.

♦ Work with each partner to close targeted contracts.

It is important to note that use of words "country/state partner," "engineers and consultant," and "partnership" do not imply any specific type of legal relationship between a major system integration/prime contractor, the security planning team and a foreign corporation or individual.

Each country and state has unique laws, which govern the creation of such entities. The words "security planning team," "system integrator/system developer," and "country/state partner" "engineers and consultants/host country/state contractor" and "partnership/airport-harbor franchise" are only used to convey the nature of the business relationship.

KEY MARKETING STRATEGY ELEMENTS

A key element in our marketing strategy is the fact that the SLA-C4I is not sold to the port authorities. Instead services are provided to the port authorities on a fee per passenger/cargo basis.

1   The SLA-C4I is paid for by the individuals who use its services.

The partnership charges a service fee to the port authority, which as the landlord of the facilities that include the system operated by the law enforcement agency, in turn charge the airlines and/or shipping agencies, who charge their customers/passengers/importers/exporters of goods. (Today the passengers pay a small security surcharge, which is collected by the airline. Typically in the USA $10 is included as a surcharge in a round-trip fare. The airport authority will collect these fees from the airlines.)

2   The cost for site preparation, engineering hardware, software, installation of the SLA-C4I and training of personnel are financed on a ten-year basis.

Funds derived from the passenger/cargo service fee are used to repay the ten-year loan along with sales acquisition costs and operating expenses. This financing plan is designed to eliminate the need for capital investment on the part of the airport/port owner/operator, thereby facilitating their ability to acquire the system.

3   The country/state partner (host country/state contractor) is responsible for securing a ten-year service contract with the port authorities assisted if necessary by a local engineering and consulting firm.

Technical sales support will be provided and assistance in writing proposals. Any additional effort needed to support the sale is the responsibility of the country partner. If the consultant is responsible for the acquisition of the contract it will receive compensation as a percentage of the gross revenue from the service contract of the Host Country Contractor.

4   Once the service contract is secured, the partnership must arrange for contract financing, prepare the airport/port site, install the SLA-C4I equipment, hire and maintain maintenance and operational staff, conduct a final acceptance test and cut over the system to full operation.

5   The partnership will continue to train the operators and maintain the SLA-C4I System once it is in place and operational. The operational training and maintenance staff would be employed by the partnership and report to the general manager of the partnership.

The partnership would collect the passenger/cargo service fee from the port authority, and monthly pay the installment on the original financing note, pay any fees which may be owed to the system developer, the airport/port franchisee the country partner/consultant (host country contractor services), pay operating and maintenance expenses and set aside the remaining balance for a "National Airport/Port Funding Program" after taxes to the local and central governments.

MANAGEMENT OF REVENUES

The SLA-C4I System will allow the orderly management of cross-border revenues (customs fees) and the control of movement and security of all passengers and cargo at Sea, Land and Airport Cross-Border Stations and their related free trade zones. It can evaluate data well before an aircraft arrives using the ABACoS the visa and passport border access and control subsystem of SMI (see the description of the Automated Border Access Control System in our web page at http://www.securitymanagementint.com). The System incorporates "EDICS" (the "Explosives and Drugs Interdiction and Control Subsystem) for non-invasive inspections with full computer control to cross-check manifest with other associated financial data for the identification and tracking of contraband and the illicit drug-related activities, production facilities and substances.

The design of such a multifunctional integrated cross-border security system has evolved to the actual C4I stage, reflecting today's information revolution and the roles of communications, intelligence and computer systems in support of the command and control function.

The SLA-C4I International Airports Airport Security (Passenger-Luggage Subsystem)

The system's capabilities must provide the means of implementing a totally integrated system including a database that contains pertinent data on each passenger who had recently used the airport, or is scheduled to use it in the immediate future. This data provides the foundation for an expert system to profile each passenger. The process starts with the airline information concerning its frequent fliers, courtesy club members, and other repeat passengers, and current reservation and ticket holders.

The SLA-C4I is connected to the ABACoS, performing the visa and passport security control and has the capability to search its "persona-non grata" database for a match on any suspicious individual, stolen passport, or similar abnormality. This data is subjected to analytical procedures to produce a recommendation to airport security control. Prior to flight departure, the PNR (Passenger Name and Record) information is obtained from the airline's PNR system. At the check-in, a unique control number is assigned to each passenger. This number -- the address of the passenger's file in the computer -- is printed on bar coded labels which are attached to the boarding pass, carry-on articles and checked luggage.

The bar code labeled boarding pass is used to authorize entry through the EDICS (Explosives and Drugs Interaction and Control Subsystem) an electronic corridor leading to the departing area. At the moment of authorization to enter and before passport/visa verification, the passenger is also photographed and the image is stored in the computer. In this electronic corridor, by utilizing the passenger profile, the controls can reach the maximum security screening authorized by local laws before law enforcement officer intervention. Since bar-code readers at strategic locations permit the system to track passengers' luggage, based on the passenger profile and screening results maximum or routine checking can be applied to the checked-in items. At the boarding gate, the boarding officer can confirm, by viewing the electronically stored image, that the person who checked the luggage is the passenger boarding the flight. Luggage loaded on the plane without the matching passenger is detected and off-loaded before departure.

The telecommunications subsystem of the SLA-C4I provides for notification to the destination airport authorities of data concerning all passengers and luggage, including passport and visa status. This data can be used to expedite immigration and customs clearances at arrival and concentrate security efforts on high risk passengers.

Other subsystems integrated in the SLA-C4I are:

♦ Access control for airline employees, contractors and visitors.
♦ Perimeter fences covered by IDS (Intruder Detection System), supported by CCTV (Closed Caption TV) utilizing ULLL (ultra low level light) and/or TI (thermal imaging) cameras.

Cargo areas and aircraft parking areas, as well as other sensitive parts of the airport such as the fuel farms, must be similarly protected.

For passengers, the system classifies threat, potential threat, or no threat by applying artificial intelligence to the rules established by airport security officials and the information contained in the database. The system also provides the means of ensuring that passengers and baggage are routed through the airport in accordance with the passenger's security classification.

THE SLA-C4I SYSTEM STRUCTURE

The system contains a number of security subsystems connected to the airport security command, communication, computer, control and intelligence center:

♦ Airport C4I Center
♦ Each subsystem serves a different aspect of security management. A building block approach allows stations and terminals for new or mixed applications to be assembled quickly and economically.

The subsystems are:

- Passenger Control
- Baggage Control
- Landside/Airside Access Control
- Aircraft Control
- Perimeter Control
- Cargo Control
- Area Access Control.

The modular design permits flexibility in packaging various combination of subsystems while preserving their integration capabilities. Implementation begins with the installation of the passenger and baggage control subsystems. This basic configuration may be expanded through the addition of other subsystems as the airport's needs dictate. All subsequent additions enjoy the full benefit of the modular integrated design.

INTEGRATION

The following subsystems are assumed to exist:

- Perimeter
- Aircraft Control
- Cargo Control
- Area Access Control
- Landside/Airside Access Control

Monitoring and controlling functions of these subsystems will be connected and performed by the Airport C4I Center.

An airport's existing security subsystems may range from nonexistent to adequate. This adequacy of an airport's perimeter cargo area and aircraft security control subsystems is assessed as part of the planning and design process. The decision to retain an existing, but obsolete subsystem, or to upgrade to a new state-of-the-art one, ultimately rests with the airport authorities.

TYPICAL AIRPORT SCENARIO:
(1) and (2) Check In

The name of the passenger is retrieved from the database system, a bar code label is applied to the check luggage, carry-on luggage and boarding pass.

(3) Access to the International Area

The passenger enters the security-control station after the boarding pass is introduced into the appropriate reader. During the security controls, a compressed video TV image of the passenger is stored in the system. Passengers without luggage who already have boarding passes may go directly to this station where a bar-coded label is produced for carry-on items and the boarding pass.

(4) International Area (or "Sterile Area")

If the passenger goes through the duty free shop or other facilities reserved to the international departing passengers, the system will acknowledge the passenger's presence. (The cashier of the duty free shop will introduce the boarding pass into the appropriate reader and will register that the passenger bought some duty free merchandise before boarding.)

(5) Boarding Area

The passenger gains access by his bar-coded boarding pass being checked by the airline agent. The CRT shows the picture of the passenger, flight information, and seat arrangements can be made if not already done. The security status of the passenger and his carry-on and checked-in luggage is evidenced to the airline agent.

(6) Boarding Gate

The passenger gives the boarding pass to the boarding officer, the boarding pass is placed on the reader. If all the necessary security elements are cleared, the passenger is allowed on the aircraft.

(7) Luggage Check-In

The checked-in luggage goes through the cargo area, and after all the necessary security measures (ion detectors, x-rays etc.) are automatically ousted by the system that reads the tags with laser scan, bar-code readers.

(8) Luggage Loading Area

As luggage is loaded into containers, the system records in which container each passenger's luggage is stored.

(9) Aircraft Loading

The system acknowledges that the luggage is stored on board and the position of the container in the aircraft. Upon correct completion of the operation of passenger boarding and luggage loading through points (6) and (9), the flight is cleared and the manifest is printed within seconds.

(10) Arriving Passengers

At the arrival, where the airport is the final destination, the passenger clears immigration. Customs and immigration services will use a subsystem such as the EDICS, in a configuration for arriving passengers in order to detect illicit materials such as drugs, and a subsystem such as the ABACoS (the visa and passport security control) to screen all incoming passengers.

(11) Customs Checking Station

The customs officer checks his/her database, matching the checked-in luggage sticker number to the explosive and drugs inspection carried out on the arriving luggage and clears the passenger.

(12) Transit Passengers for National Flights

The passenger in transit for a national destination first clears customs and then proceeds to national flights, checking through the transit transfer desk.

(13) Transit Passengers for International Flights

The passenger in transit for an international destination does not clear customs. However, the checked-in luggage is routed into the new flight only after going through the security system. This passenger receives a boarding pass with the required bar-code number at the international transfer desk, and the sticker number of his checked-in luggage is matched to the new boarding pass number. The passenger in transit then goes through security like any other departing passenger.

(6) & (9)

IF PASSENGER AND LUGGAGE ARE NOT ON BOARD THE SAME FLIGHT, THE SYSTEM WILL ACKNOWLEDGE THE ABNORMAL SITUATION AND DISPLAY IT AS AN ALARM.

(3) EDICS:

Explosives and Drugs Interdiction and Control Station

EDICS "a user-friendly electronic corridor" uses the latest technology in explosive and aromatic detection, combining sensors and subsystems. Access to this control station occurs after the passenger has received both labels for boarding pass and carry-on luggage, and after luggage has been checked-in.

TYPICAL EDICS CONFIGURATION
FOR DEPARTING PASSENGERS

(1) Entrance marked TO GATES (Only Passengers Beyond this Point)

The system records that the passenger is about to transit from landside to airside through the security control station when the boarding pass is introduced into the reader. The first sliding glass door opens and the passenger enters the screening room.

(2) Air Screening Station

After a sample of air is stored by one of the aromatic detection units, the second sliding door opens (analysis of the air is now in process, the number of analysis is matched to the passengers' unique bar-coded boarding pass number). The passenger exits the room and leaves the carry-on items on the x-ray screening conveyer belt.

(3) & (4) X-Ray/Metal Detector and Picture Taking Stations

As the passenger goes though the metal detector screening device, it is the only time the passenger is obliged to go through a fixed point and does not have anything in hand. At that point a picture is taken and stored in the computer. The picture and results of the screening will be matched to the passenger's unique bar-code boarding pass number that is also the address of the passenger's file in the computer.

(5) & (6) Portable Devices Screening Station and Table

If necessary, the passenger may be asked to be screened with portable screening devices and to open his carry-on luggage for an additional visual search and aromatic screening with portable explosives detectors.

(7) Passport Control and Security Clearance Station

The passenger's boarding pass is introduced into the reader and the result of the screening will appear on the CRT, along with the inputs generated by all security personnel and the passenger's flight information. The personnel in charge of the passport control and security clearance station will control passport, visa and boarding pass, verify that the passport picture matches the image taken and stored into the computer and the passenger, and then issue the clearance to cross the landside/airside line directing the passenger to the designated boarding gate. From that moment, the boarding pass with the unique passenger/luggage matching number and passenger image is a positive identification of the passenger in the sterile area.

(8) Personal Search Room

If necessary, before clearing the passenger, a body search can be carried out in such a room.

(9) To the Gates

All cleared passengers will proceed to the designated boarding gates.

(10) PASSENGERS WHO DO NOT CLEAR THE SECURITY SCREENING ARE ESCORTED BY THE LAW ENFORCEMENT OFFICERS FOR FURTHER INVESTIGATION.

IMPORTANT NOTE:

Much of the hardware and software which could be used in the SLA-C4I System currently exist, and a total security system can be rapidly customized, built and tested in a specific airport and country. It, however, needs to be implemented in stages (starting with the optimization of security checkpoints, using a combination of in-place system and existing state-of-the-art technology) so that it will not disrupt current operations and gain maximum utility from current hardware and software already procured for that specific airport or country.

EDITOR'S NOTE:

The February 19, 2001, issue of U.S. News & World Report published an article emphasizing how vulnerable US airports are to terrorist attacks. Former Federal Aviation Administration Special Agent Steve Elson strolled through a screening station at New Orleans International Airport with a hunting knife hidden in his pants and was not detected. He later went behind counters at Delta Airlines, in plain view of passengers and employees, looking for unused baggage tags. He sent these tags to members of the US Congress, making the point that terrorists could easily take such a baggage tag, attach it to a suitcase containing a bomb, leave in near a jetway and the bag would likely be loaded onto a plane.

Following the 1988 bombing of Pan Am Flight 103 over Lockerbie, Scotland, the FAA promised to revamp its security system by requiring computer-coded identification cards for airport workers, add new x-ray equipment and match passengers to their bags. Elson and other experts claim there has been little, if any, improvement in airport security. Elson was quoted in the article as commenting, "Virtually anyone can put bombs on planes at any major airport with minimal chances of being caught."

FAA officials disagree and point out that the agency has spent $100 million a year on new hardware alone, including sophisticated devices now in place at 130 airports and planned for 279 more, that scan checked and carry-on baggage.

In May 2001 the FAA was scheduled to assume direct authority over screening personnel who heretofore have been poorly paid, largely transient contract workers only loosely supervised by the airlines.

An audit by the US Department of Transportation's Inspector General disclosed that too many airport employees of unknown or questionable backgrounds have access to secure areas. The audit showed that 16 percent of the employees had been given incomplete background checks and 19 percent had been given no background checks at all.

A senior FAA special agent told US News & World Report that the new security apparatus is more show than substance. He added that during testing at major airports in 1998 and 1999 FAA agents gained access to secure areas 95 percent of the time, breaching computer-controlled doors and gates. The FAA special agent said, "Rarely did anyone respond to the alarms. Even when they did, it was so long after the fact it was irrelevant."

Robert Spence, a former FAA headquarters official who performed covert surveillances at airports throughout the country, believes too much attention has been paid to gadgetry and not enough to inattentive airline employees, rapid turnover of screening personnel etc.

Chapter 7

Public Works and Terrorism
By Richard J. Evans, B.S.

Not many years ago public works people were seldom, if ever, concerned about terrorism. However, events such as the bombing of the Federal Building in Oklahoma City, the assassination of the Mayor and a Supervisor in San Francisco, anthrax scares in a number of cities, and other incidents have pointed out the need for public works and building management people to become involved in building and system security matters.

Building security is a mixed bag at best, especially for public buildings which, by their very nature, must be open to the public on an almost unlimited basis. This is even more true when the buildings are populated by elected officials. The issue of how to provide access and yet maintain a level of security is complicated.

To begin with, you cannot accomplish these goals by yourself, nor can you do it by using local law enforcement people. Not that they are not competent, far from it, but they are often too close to the matter to be totally objective. Nor can you just go out and buy magnetometers, x-ray machines and hire a couple of security guards and think that the job is finished. Although this might be what you end up doing, you should first make a serious effort to analyze the problem, review the alternatives, seek the advice of trained professionals and then refer to the body politic the range of solutions and your recommendation for the preferred alternative.

You might want to visit your local airport, jail or courthouse to see the levels of complexity in equipment, operations and management of security systems. During these visits you need to discuss with the people in charge of the facility issues relative to maintenance, operations and management of their systems. You might even enlist these people to serve on an advisory board during the decision making process. This will, of course, depend on the level of confidentiality you need to maintain.

There is a wide range of cost and of quality for the various pieces of equipment that are available. However, it can only function to the level of the people who are hired to operate it. Again, there is a wide range in the cost and quality of the people that you might hire. With all of this in mind, it is now time to begin the quest for a security system for your building(s), including the people to manage and operate it.

There are several sources that might offer a high level of expertise for your project. These include utility company security employees (retired or on loan), retired FBI or Secret Service employees, retired law enforcement officers, and retired military personnel to name a few. If you are in a time crunch, you may be able to get some pro bono help from any of the above to help you get started. Remember, check their qualifications before accepting any help -- free or not.

The first thing that you should do is try to find an expert in the field. You might circulate a "Request For Proposal" (RFP) that asks for interested parties to apply and bring with them a list of their accomplishments, experience, background, training, and whatever else that might support their qualifications for the project. At some point in time you should have the candidates develop a cost figure for their services, but you may want this to be delayed until you have developed a "short-list" of bidders for consideration.

An RFP allows you to select the party that is most qualified, rather than the one with the lowest bid. After all, you are not building a sewer, but you are developing a security system. Whatever the process, the experts need to include with their proposal, recommendations regarding management and operation of the system. Also, you might want to limit your list of consultants to firms that do not have any connections with manufacturers of security equipment. Further, you do need to include in your RFP their recommendations for operation, repair and maintenance of the system(s). This should also include training for the operators when they are selected. Finally, they should be willing to appear with you when you present your recommendations to the decision makers. They will be the best people to answer technical questions regarding the equipment, etc. They should also be of value when you are developing recommendations for how the system is to be operated and by whom.

Depending on who the occupants are of the building that you are trying to protect, you may want to make them aware of the process. You may also want to make your local law enforcement people aware of what you are doing, especially if they are going to be charged with the ultimate responsibility for supervision or operation of the system.

Now we come to a significantly different part of the process: selecting the people to operate it. There are a number of alternatives. These include hiring a private security firm, using local law enforcement officers (police or sheriff personnel), retired law enforcement or retired military people or using building and grounds patrol people. Once again, discussions with others, such as those you visited, will give you a lot of help in selecting alternatives. Once again, cost will be a significant part of the equation in your decision making process.

No matter who is selected, they need to be fully trained, not only in the operation of the equipment, but in the way they conduct themselves, deal with problem people, diversions, questions, etc. These are often the first contacts visitors have with City Hall or whatever the facility is. This means the security people need to make sure that this is a good contact, one that is not confrontational, but one that tries to maintain a secure building.

The vendor of the equipment should be involved in the training. Further, your consultant may be able to advise you relative to training the security people regarding their duties and how best they are performed. The performance of your security people need to be monitored on a regular basis.

By now most people are familiar with the security provided at airports and the way it is managed so that security for public buildings need not be a threat. However, tenants and visitors alike must not be lulled into a false sense of security. Just because there is a guard at the gate does not mean that the place is totally secure. Therefore, you may want to maintain an internal security system that will provide additional protection.

There are a number of ways to provide internal security. These include keyed or keyless entry systems, closed circuit television systems, roving patrol people or any combination of the above. All of them have cost impacts, and depending on conditions, have liabilities. Building configuration may make closed circuit television difficult if not impossible.

Keyed or keyless entry may be very expensive. And roving patrols likewise have their limitations. In fact you may need to develop different levels of security for various areas inside the building. This may require some special effort and perhaps some relocation of some offices but this should not be very difficult to do. Having occupants of the building involved in the planning process should facilitate any relocation issues.

The issue of intruding on people may also affect your decisions. This is an area where your agency's legal staff may be able to advise you. Actually, your agency's legal staff should be involved in the entire process, from consultant selection through the RFP and the conclusion of the project. This is another area in which your consultants may be able to help. Again, on your visits to other facilities, discuss internal security with your hosts.

So far, we have dealt with building security. However, public works and general services people need to be aware of security needs for other facilities and systems under their jurisdiction. Sewage and water collection, distribution and treatment facilities, sports complexes, arenas, theaters, museums, transit stations, schools and hospitals are all potential targets. Condition assessment analysis is a good tool for determining the condition of these facilities and systems that are needed to serve the people. These analyses look at structural conditions, life-safety and code compliance, maintenance history, usability and a number of other items that need to be reviewed on a regular basis to insure that the money spent on the operation and maintenance of the infrastructure is done so wisely.

Likewise, a vulnerability assessment could and should be included in the analysis. This would use some of the same people listed above and help clarify decisions that need to be made, especially with regard to use, repair with upgrades and/or replacement. But now that you are considering vulnerability, you need to bring in experts who are qualified to assist you in this part of the process.

We have moved past the use of chainlink fences, barbed wire or razor wire. Granted that these things will keep out many, determined people can easily get past such low-tech devices. And you cannot use these devices to protect public buildings, although they are somewhat effective for protecting operational facilities (treatment plants, transit stations, etc.), especially when used in concert with closed circuit television, high intensity lighting and fences equipped with motion sensors. A vulnerability analysis will assist you in ultimately selecting the optimum way that you might protect your facilities.

A vulnerability analysis looks at what might be done to damage the operation of a facility or system, what is located nearby which, if damaged, might have an impact on the quality of life or the health or economy of adjacent parts of the city, and what alternative systems might exist to replace those that are damaged or destroyed. Is it practical to protect these facilities or should or could they be relocated to reduce or eliminate the risk? Finally, how would your city recover if the subject of your study was damaged or lost to use?

A number of factors will complicate your work. These include the age of your infrastructure, who has jurisdiction (public or private), existence of redundancy, the practicality of replacement or redesign, and the availability of funding to complete the necessary work. A half completed project is probably worse than no project at all.

You cannot keep people out of a subway system nor can you build a wall around a watershed. Transportation facilities, railroads, airports and highways allow the movement of thousands of people and millions of pounds of goods daily. It is impossible to keep out those who are intent on doing damage, yet we must do all that we can to make conditions as safe as possible. Look at the risks and try to develop answers to the following:

♦ If we cannot eliminate the risk, can we develop a warning system that will activate a response that will minimize it?

♦ Have we established and tested evacuation routes?

♦ What can be done to mitigate the risk? Relocation, etc.?

♦ Is there, or can you develop, a recovery plan?

Regardless of the complexity of your buildings and facilities, some very basic steps need to be followed. These include key control, attention to keeping windows closed and locked at night, alert security staff, evacuation plans that are tested on a regular basis, and a building population that participates in the same way a "Neighborhood Watch" group does. And, no one is allowed to by-pass the security devices. No one, no favorites. Just provide the same level of scrutiny for all. No exceptions shall be allowed. Once again, you should not try to convince the tenants that they are perfectly safe, because they are not. A false sense of security is the most dangerous environment that you can provide.

EDITORS' NOTE:

One of the problems with x-ray equipment at building, seaport, border and airport checkpoints is that it is virtually worthless against plastic guns, plastic explosives, drugs and contaminated fruit. New tools are now available from four companies to cope with this shortcoming. American Science and Engineering makes a patented x-ray system called Z Backscatter that flags organic material and plastics. It works in conjunction with transmission x-rays. In Vision Technologies and L-3 Security Systems, a division of L-3 Communications, sell CT scanners which spot plastic explosives in baggage. Vivid Technologies makes a product which does the same thing with an X-ray machine.

To increase security at airports, consider eliminating curbside check in, prohibiting unattended vehicles within 300 feet of the terminal, using bomb-sniffing dogs and searching all vehicles larger than sedans.

As reliable as fingerprints are, iris scanners which digitally analyze a person's eyes are also effective tools for keeping certain people from certain areas. Japan used these devices to clear Olympic competitive shooters carrying guns to make sure they were not terrorists.

Chapter 8

Terrorism and Technology: Threat and Challenge in the 21st Century*
By Oliver "Buck" Revell, B.A., M.A.

The rather abrupt end to the Cold War was expected to bring about a substantial improvement in international cooperation, and a concordant change in the manner in which governments dealt with transnational issues such as terrorism and organized crime. However, the expected improvements in overall safety and security of US citizens and interests have not materialized except at the strategic level.

This presentation was originally delivered in Orlando, Florida, on May 26, 1999, before the Conference on Technologies and Tools for Public Safety in the 21st Century, sponsored by the National Institute of Justice, US Department of Justice.

Terrorism remains a constant and viable threat to American interests on a global basis, even though the sources of the threat may be evolving into heretofore unknown or undetected elements/organizations.

The threat is changing and increasing due to the following factors:

1.) The philosophy, motivation, objectives and modus operandi of terrorist groups, both domestic and international, have changed.

2.) The new terrorist groups are not concerned with and in many instances are trying to inflict mass causalities.

3.) Terrorist groups now have ready access to massive databases concerning the entire United States infrastructure, including key personnel, facilities, and networks.

4.) Aided by state sponsors or international organized crime groups, terrorists can obtain weapons of mass destruction.

5.) The internet now allows even small or regional terrorist groups to have a worldwide C3I (command, control, communication and intelligence) system, and propaganda dissemination capability.

6.) Domestic anti-government reactionary extremists have proliferated, and now pose a significant threat to the Federal Government and to law enforcement at all levels. Militia organizations have targeted the Federal Government for hostile actions, and could target any element of our society that is deemed to be their adversary.

7.) Islamic extremism has spread to the point where it now has a global infrastructure, including a substantial network in the United States.

Terrorism has been a tough political, analytical and operational target for years. Nonetheless, twenty years ago, analysts could agree on several "tenets of terrorism." First, terrorists were viewed as falling into one of three categories: those that were politically motivated, and used violence as a means to achieve legitimacy, such as the IRA or PLO, or; those that used violence as a means of uprising; or finally, those that were state-sponsored whose violence was manipulated by foreign powers to achieve political leverage. Second, terrorists were generally thought to calculate thresholds of pain and tolerance, so that their cause was not irrevocably compromised by their actions. While US officials worried about terrorists "graduating" to the use of weapons of mass destruction, especially nuclear, we believed that most terrorist groups thought mass casualties were counterproductive.

This was because mass casualties seemed to delegitimize the terrorists' cause, would certainly generate strong governmental responses, and erode terrorist group cohesion. In essence, we thought a certain logic and morality line existed beyond which terrorist dared not go. The different types of terrorist groups had a wide range of motives.

The extreme left's motivation for violence has been significantly diminished by the disenchantment with communism on a global scale. These groups find that their message is out-of-fashion, and they can no longer mobilize the public to their causes. This loss of motivation is a major reason for the recent downward trend in international terrorist incidents, as documented in the State Department's report, "Patterns in Global Terrorism." (See Appendices.)

The threat level of all leftist groups globally, once rated high, is now considered moderate. Of the twenty-two known groups, three have denounced violence altogether. Indeed, high collateral casualties are inconsistent with the fundamental message of leftist terrorists who profess their goal to be the betterment of the masses.

State-sponsored terror has seen a notable decline in the last several years for three primary reasons. First, the Middle East peace process has given previously violent groups and states a motive to refrain from terrorism in order to gain leverage and bargaining power at the table. Second, post Cold-War geopolitical realities have brought about many new agreements and growing cooperation among nations in countering terrorism. One of the largest sponsors of terrorism in the past -- the former communist East European countries -- are now aggressively supporting counterterrorism initiatives.

However, several state sponsors remain who continue to fund, motivate, support, and train terrorists. Iran is by far the most active of these state sponsors, with the greatest long-term commitment and worldwide reach.

Iraq remains of concern, but has a more limited transnational capability. However, attacks within Iraq's own backyard, such as the attempted assassination of former President George Bush in 1993 during his trip to Kuwait, and the assassinations of dissidents in Jordan, are more likely to threaten the peace and stability of the region.

Syria is a more pragmatic sponsor, by providing supplies in transit, but has refrained more recently from terrorism in order to enhance its negotiating position in the peace talks. Its loss of USSR patronage has meant a decline in financial and logistical support, but it nevertheless allows some rejectionists to maintain headquarters in Syria. Hizballah still receives supplies through the Damascus airport and operates openly in parts of Syria and Syrian controlled territory. The newest sponsor on the list is Sudan, which was added in 1993 because of its provision of safe haven and training for a variety of terrorist groups. Sudan has hosted Osama bin Laden's facilities.

Libya, a notorious state sponsor, has also refrained lately from terrorism in order to obtain some sanctions relief. It continues, however, to target dissidents, fund extremist Palestinians, and provide safe haven for Abu Nidal, all while attempting to avoid accountability for the Pan Am 103 bombing, the surrender of the Pan Am 103 suspects came only after crippling sanctions by the United Nations. For state-sponsored terrorism, the value of deterrence retains credibility, and America should not relinquish this capability.

Radical Islamic groups are now the most active in terms of the rate of incidents. Many of these groups are considered separatists, and desire a seat at the recognition and negotiation table. Others, considered extreme Islamic zealots, operate as loosely affiliated groups, as in the World Trade Center and East African bombings. For these groups, deterrence has less effect. And, in fact, many have stated that they wanted to maximize casualties to punish the United States, which they have demonized as the "Great Satan."

Ethnic separatist terrorism, as old as mankind, can be temporarily sidetracked by a few contemporary geopolitical developments, but generally, it is impervious to such developments because its root cause is invariably long-lived. Most of these groups seek world recognition and endorsement. To date, they have not resorted to the use of weapons of mass destruction.

The "new" terrorist presents new problems. The argument has been made that while traditional terrorism -- in terms of motivations -- is still a large segment of the terrorist population, there is a new breed of terrorist for which the old paradigms either do not apply at all or have limited application. These groups -- cults, religious extremists, anarchists, or serial killers -- must be regarded as serious threats, and perhaps the most serious of the terrorist groups operating today. These "new" terrorists are driven by a different set of motivations: they seek an immediate reward for their act, and their motivations and objectives may range from rage, revenge, hatred, mass murder, extortion, or embarrassment, or any combination of these.

They may desire mass casualties, or at least not care about how many people are killed in their attacks. As such, they do not make traditional calculations of thresholds of pain or tolerance within a society. These groups tend to be loosely affiliated both internationally and domestically, and may have no ties at all to state sponsorship. They change affiliations and identities as needed, and are extremely difficult to detect. Where traditional groups want publicity to further their cause, many "new" terrorists do not desire attribution. This is particularly true of the religious extremists. In their view, God knows, and will reward. Religious extremism is growing in numbers, and is not limited to the Islamic faith. While the "new" terrorist may have a variety of motivations, some single issue groups, such as, extremists in the animal rights, environmental, and anti-abortion movements, may also pose a significant threat, and can not be overlooked. Many terrorist groups, both traditional and "new," have privatized their practices through a few standard business techniques (fund-raising, use of technology, etc.).

Some of the most difficult groups to track today are the domestic militia-type extremists. While much is not known about these groups, some commonalities prevail. Many of these groups have substantial expertise. They communicate on Internet chat rooms about dosage levels of various biologicals needed to cause the greatest lethality. They have also exhibited a fascination with poisons and high explosives, along with more standard military weapons. Contrary to some popular opinion, these types of groups are growing, even after the devastating attack in Oklahoma City, and they are building skills, developing international connections, and are exhibiting growing political sophistication. Of great concern is that they have in their ranks both military and law enforcement personnel. Their targets are diverse: they may attack Federal buildings, specific racial groups, corporate icons, or multinational companies. They capitalize on and heighten paranoia of the growing fear among some Americans of big, intrusive government.

Terrorists have shown a propensity to mimicry, the so-called copycat syndrome, as we are now seeing in the tragic violence in our schools. So it is with alarm that analysts today view the chemical attack precedent set by the Aum Shinrikyo in 1995 in Japan because it shattered the paradigm that "terrorists don't do Weapons of Mass Destruction." In fact, the B'Nai Brith incident in Washington, along with several others, has shown that terrorists are watching, reading, and learning.

They are motivated by government actions or, in some instances, inaction. The World Trade Center bombing was an attempt at mass casualties, and the actual mass killing within the Federal Building in Oklahoma City was an equally alarming precedent, in that terrorists demonstrated a desire to inflict mass murder in our homeland.

Also new today, is the proliferation of knowledge and technology among many criminal, terrorist, and narcotics groups. Many of these groups are building skills in state-of-the-art communications and weaponry. They are achieving new global links and support from one another in cooperative ways. The barriers to inflicting mass casualties seem to be falling.

Twenty years ago, intelligence specialists viewed proliferation of Weapons of Mass Destruction primarily through the lens of nation states seeking the ultimate weapon. Chemical and biological weaponry was only a minuscule afterthought of the whole nuclear problem.

Organized crime and narcotics trafficking organizations, while scourges twenty years ago, were not among primary intelligence targets. They, by and large, fell within the domain of law enforcement agencies. Crime groups jealously guarded their turf, and tended to view one another as competitors rather than allies. Today, each of these categories is a priority intelligence target, with a wide array of government participants working on the problems.

The traditional characteristics of organized crime groups remain relevant today. Generally, familial, ideological or ethnic ties that instill loyalty and reduce the likelihood of law enforcement or intelligence infiltration affiliate them. The purpose of their activities has remained unchanged: they seek money and status or power. They will often seek to provide government-like services so that the local populace will learn to rely upon them. Finally, criminal organizations will almost always seek to establish respectability and legitimacy, often through philanthropic acts, the controlling of local businesses, and provision of local employment opportunities.

One of the outcomes of the globalization of economies and technologies, the phenomenon that former President Bush termed the "New World Order," is the relatively new linking and intermingling of disparate crime and narcotics organizations with terrorists.

Analysts have been dismayed to find that even the most notorious crime groups with global reach, such as the Italian Mafia, the Russian

Mafiyas, the Nigerian criminal enterprises, the Chinese triads, the Colombian and Mexican cartels, and the Japanese Yakuza, are developing new working relationships. They are developing cooperative arrangements, and networking with one another and with insurgent and terrorist organizations to take advantage of one another's strengths and to make inroads into previously denied regions. This has allowed terrorists a new means to raise money as well as to provide them with a marketplace to purchase sophisticated weaponry and other high-tech equipment. This cooperation, for example, has long been seen among Colombian drug lords and Italian crime groups in exploiting the West European drug market, but now is seen in New York City and in Eastern Europe with drug and financial crime networks linking Russian and Italian groups. As organized crime groups become increasingly international in the scope of their activities, they are also less constrained by national boundaries. The new lowering of political and economic barriers allows them to establish new operational bases in commercial and banking centers around the globe. The willingness and capability of these groups to move into new areas and cooperate with local groups is unprecedented, magnifying the threats to stability and even governability. All of these transnational groups are becoming more professional criminals, both in their business and financial practices and in the application of technology. Many of them use state-of-the-art communications security that is better than some nation's security forces can crack.

Chapter 9

Dignitary Protection
By Sean Carr, BA

When the public thinks of terrorism, the image that very often comes to mind is the weapons of mass destruction type attacks on targets where the results are likely to have a large number of casualties. The terrorist attacks with the use of ammonium nitrate and fuel oil on one of the World Trade Center Buildings in New York City or the Oklahoma City bombing are prime examples. The Sarin gas release on the Tokyo subway system or the use of an in-flight aircraft, small arms, and explosives on the many highly publicized aircraft hijackings are incidents that are often thought of first. It generally isn't until the discussion has been going on for quite some time before it dawns on someone that one of the most effective tools of the terrorist is the abduction or murder of individuals who represent or give the perception of representing something contrary to the attacker's cause.

Since the beginning of history, there have been numerous accounts of assassinations, attempted assassinations and kidnappings, as well as attacks on dignitaries, heads of state, representatives of private enterprises, tourists, and other people because of differing ideals. In the United States this tactic is not as common as it is in the Middle East, Europe, and South America. However, any discussion or text about terrorism would be incomplete without including the topic of dignitary protection.

The objective of a good dignitary protection program should be to plan to avoid situations that needlessly put the protected person at unnecessary risk. This is often difficult for people experienced in law enforcement to grasp since their day-to-day practices and their training are designed toward an effective and efficient reaction to the demands of the variety of calls for service that they receive. This statement is not by any means meant to imply that law enforcement personnel are not good candidates for a dignitary protection program. That same experience and training make them ideal candidates, but it is necessary to realize that a transition is in order. It is, therefore, imperative that certain traits be considered as desirable when assembling a dignitary protection team.

The first is that each person should have demonstrated self-reliance and self-confidence in past situations that were highly stressful. These individuals should present an assertive, yet confident appearance. They should be able to keep their composure during chaotic times and continue to act in a disciplined, team-member manner. They should be in excellent physical shape with the ability to go from an almost relaxed state to a highly stressful state without adverse physical effects. They must be able to maintain a high degree of alertness and yet still be able to respond quickly to emergencies, even though many fatiguing hours have passed.

These protectors should be proficient at hand-to-hand, defensive tactics with emphasis on the ability of rendering an armed attacker harmless, quickly and effectively. Participation in a good physical conditioning program should be mandatory to meet the demands of the position. The persons under consideration should be highly skilled in the use of firearms, especially under highly stressful life-threatening conditions and be able to quickly determine whether the risk to innocent bystanders permits the use of a firearm.

It would also be very helpful if candidates for this team had additional field training or previous experience that endowed them with expertise in such topics as business or home security systems, audio and visual electronics, including all the means of maintaining, employing, detecting, and eliminating mechanical and electronic surveillance devices. The recognition of explosive devices and munitions accompanied by knowledge of safe methods of minimizing their destructive potential is desirable. A high level of proficiency in the administration of first aid is extremely beneficial. Specialized training in the foot and motor vehicle movement of protected people is also a plus. The driver during protected motor vehicle travel should have experience and training that increases his or her defensive, evasive, and escape driving skills.

When taking into account the above qualifications, one might mistakenly fall into the trap made popular by the entertainment media, the use of "bodyguards." This method of protection, even though well meaning, is perhaps the most misused and misunderstood method employed today, particularly if a threat of real significance exists. The very theatrical and flamboyant look of having a protected individual surrounded by muscle-bound people who throw intense stares into the crowd while on the lookout for potential threats provides minimal protection at best. The "bodyguard" method of protection fails to address the attacker's greatest advantage, the use of surprise and a well-thought-out assault plan.

Terrorists study their targets as well as their target's vulnerabilities to determine the most optimum time and place to strike. Unfortunately, when employing this method of protection, the bodyguards frequently die along with the person they were supposed to be protecting. History has shown that a reactive plan to dignitary protection is not effective. Even after stating this, it is still important to have all of the people assigned to a dignitary protection program trained and capable of responding and confronting a life-threatening ambush in a quick, effective manner in case the need arrives. However, the emphasis of the program should be on effectively avoiding situations of this nature.

The protected person should have the opportunity to meet, interview, and gain confidence in the people chosen for this assignment; after all, his or her life may depend on them. If the protected person has serious objections to an individual, someone else should probably be given the assignment.

The first step to designing any protection program is to perform an honest threat assessment. A complete evaluation of the protected person's potential exposure to threat is necessary. The problem with this is, there is no exact science to ascertaining one's potential exposure to threats. Unless the protected person has received threatening messages from known hostile groups or individuals, this assessment will be based on the characteristics and capabilities of possible hostile parties in comparison to the defined vulnerabilities or exposed positions of the protected individual. The assessment will be flexible, ongoing, and forever changing in order to meet the day-to-day changes and trends that affect the protected person's lifestyle.

Begin by studying the home and work environment of the protected person. After all, if you were an attacker, where would you begin? Get to know all of the habits of the person to receive protection. Is there a hobby or recreational activity that puts this person at a certain place at a predictable time? Time should be taken to learn that person's daily routine, such as the routes most often traveled, and vehicles he or she uses.

Put yourself in the attacker's position, be imaginative, and look for activities that put the protected person in a position of disadvantage. Take action to minimize or negate that threat. Learn what personal and home security systems are already in place. Do they have to be improved, and if so, how can they be modified to help reduce or eliminate potential threats? Determine the strengths and weaknesses of those systems and how they can best be utilized.

Whenever vulnerabilities appear, they must be examined to see if they pose a significant threat, and corrective action must be taken. A realistic profile of the protected person is also needed. Determine how this person sees himself, his position, and how he or she interacts with others. How does the protected person feel about having a protective detail? Does he or she want an obvious display of personal protection while shopping, dining, or out in public? Is he or she inclined to rearrange scheduled plans without warning, to embark on a hand-shaking session whenever opportunities arise? Is there any type of security equipment that is not acceptable to the protected person? How well does he or she accept advice from others or, more particularly, from a security detail? What intrusions are acceptable into his or her life? Is there a particular person who acts as an informal counselor and, therefore, has influence over the decisions that the protected person makes? Is his or her personal life consistent with his or her public image?

Are there any groups or causes that he or she will pay particular attention to or which will seek him or her out? These, and many more, are all questions that will need answers. Some can be answered now; some will have to be answered later as the team interacts with the protected person. The objective is to avoid as many surprises as possible that may happen because of the style, attitude, and the psychological predisposition of the protected person.

After completing an exhaustive study of the protected person's lifestyle and environment, equally exhaustive intelligence reports on people and groups of people that pose a potential threat to the protected person must be made. A general evaluation of the threat presented by the group or individual should include physical descriptions, photographs, criminal histories, methods of operations and other profiling information. This intelligence will also be an ever-changing report requiring constant revision as conditions affecting it change.

As you can see, this is a long and laborious endeavor. However, the scope of this threat assessment will be based on the conclusions derived from this information. The greater the threat, the more detailed and precise the information must be. The level of protection should be determined by the results of this assessment.

After gathering this information, it should be put to use to decide what protective measures are appropriate. Experts in this field of dignitary protection should be consulted to help make decisions on the identification, selection, and implementation of counter measures. The experts should have knowledge of the most state-of-the-art, ever-widening variety of measures in the field of security. They will also need all the information gathered thus far in the threat assessment, including the identified strengths and vulnerabilities. Decisions have to be made as to which security precautions should be implemented and which ones are not necessary. Will a perimeter intrusion system be adequate or do you need a protection program including a physical security system with surveillance and electronic listening device countermeasures? Does a security team have to be with the protected person around the clock? Your threat assessment and the guidance of your expert consultants provide answers to all of these questions. As these decisions are being made, the cost of the implementations deserves a great deal of consideration. Protection programs require large operating costs with substantial outlays of personnel and resources. State-of-the-art equipment is also very expensive. What will the budget allow?

Is it more cost effective to do this within your agency or to capitalize on the experience of other agencies by obtaining the assistance of specialists in protection services? Remember the end game is to develop a methodical, efficient, and exhaustive process to keep the protected person out of harm's way.

It is obligatory to brief the protected person on all proposed security operations and procedures before implementing them. If any out of the ordinary events take place, causing a change in plans, he or she should be advised again. The protected person must have a realistic idea of the level of threat he or she is facing, along with the proper explanation for the security measures being recommended, if the security team is to gain his or her support. If recommendations are overruled, it should be noted and made a matter of record.

It is imperative that members of the protected person's family and staff understand how important their roles are in the overall protective mission.

Another matter that should be discussed at this point is how will this protection team coordinate with other agencies. There will be times when the protected person will enter areas in which the protection team has limited or no jurisdiction. What coordination efforts can alleviate this very serious problem? This is something that must be resolved before the operation commences. Most organizations do not have complete intelligence resources; they rely on the assistance of other private, city, county, state, or federal agencies. Intelligence is something that must be constantly updated and changed if it is to be effective. Every operation performed by the protection team will be relying on the accuracy of the intelligence reports received prior to and used for planning. Efforts must be made to create a constant liaison between agencies to keep each other abreast of new and changing information. Planning has to include methods of locating, obtaining, tracking and coordinating the implementation of special equipment and special skills that are not normally available to the protection team when needed for a particular operation.

After all, very few agencies maintain the full range of specialists, materials, and support capabilities needed to maintain an intensive or prolonged dignitary protection operation. These are just a few of the instances requiring the aid of other agencies or services. It is a necessity to identify other situations and scenarios that will require help from outside of the protection detail.

Resolutions to these issues must be made in the planning stage so as not to distract field personnel from their regular duties. Coordination and implementation of these issues must also be handled in advance whenever possible, again so that field personnel can maintain their focus without unnecessary distractions.

The issues of command and control must be addressed before any protective operation can be put into action. These operations can easily become complex endeavors. Command and control is essential to get all of the personnel from the varying agencies, jurisdictions, and disciplines to work in unison under a tight timetable. The use of a Command Post and a Command Structure like that of the Incident Command System can effectively direct normal operations. It is equally effective in the redirection of support troops and equipment in the event of an emergency situation. The most trained and experienced dignitary protection personnel should man the Command Post. It will be their responsibility to monitor all transmissions concerning the movement, activity, observations and status of the protected person. They must also keep track of the location of the protected person, direct the activities of all of the support personnel and maintain a record of everything that is going on for review, critique, and training purposes.

The Command Post should be equipped with a status board to maintain control over assignments, available resources, out-of-service resources, the location of those resources, crowd and traffic conditions, weather conditions, the position of the detail in relation to the timetable, and anything else pertinent to the mission. There should be contingency plans, maps, checklists for tracking pre-planned actions, maintaining schedules, as well as checklists for assuring routine functions are completed at hand. A complete and specific itinerary will be there. The Command Post should also have a directory with emergency and other telephone numbers that may be needed. Stationery, other supplies and forms that may need to be completed should be handy. Complete intelligence files on individuals and groups, including photos and other pertinent data, should be available.

After all these matters have been completed, it is time to get to work on an operational plan. It is important to understand the concept of what are known as protective screens. Most operational plans are derived through inner and outer perimeters (or protective screens) that can appear as two concentric circles.

The outer perimeter can consist of the posts on exterior entrance and exits, hallways, stairwells, rooftops, and possibly the top floor and ground level of an elevator shaft when protecting someone in a building. Some protective programs may use electronic sensing devices, motion or other alarm systems, closed circuit television or even barriers to make it physically impossible to enter these areas. Others may assign posts to isolated floors or rooms of buildings and elevators restricted from public access. This perimeter is designed to identify people seeking access to the protected party. It also works as an advanced warning buffer zone to transmit alarms, report unusual activity and provide some time in order to mount a tactical reaction to any threat or emergency before it reaches the protected party (threat reaction). This outer perimeter provides an initial screening to people wishing to enter the general area around the protected person.

The inner perimeter is designed to serve as a second level of screening and further shield the protected person from people who desire to enter his or her immediate area. A more unyielding enforcement policy is mandatory for inner perimeter assignments as reaction time for countermeasures to any threat is decreased as the proximity to the protected person is reduced. The only people who should breach this perimeter are known consultants, staff members, family and those with specific permission of the protected person, when on high-security operations. The inner perimeter on a building detail could consist of personnel assigned to posts immediately contiguous to the protected person such as his or her office, lodging, or inside his or her home.

Having determined an overall plan by deciding on the locations of the inner and outer perimeter posts, it is time to put the plan on paper. Only those who need to know its contents should see this plan.

Once the overall plan is documented, a more specific plan must be made. One that shows who is assigned where and contains briefings for each assignment on a task-by-task basis. Assignments must be given with specific instructions describing all of the responsibilities pertaining to them. Each member of the security detail must understand the responsibilities connected to his or her post and how that post fits into the overall plan.

Now is the time to develop contingency plans. I don't think anyone has ever been able to develop plans that could be executed without a hitch. Conceivable problem areas can often be located early in the planning stage.

When the advance team tests different motor vehicle routes, potential traffic congestion areas should be noted and alternate routes identified. A listing of the locations of recommended hospitals and doctors along the routes that could be traveled should also be present in case the protected person succumbs to illness or injury. A listing of personnel either assigned close to the protected person or at fixed locations throughout the route who are fully trained in first aid should be available in case of an automobile accident.

Plans should be in place in case the protected person unexpectedly changes the itinerary or is delayed for some reason. Protected places or safe houses have to be identified with directions indicating what routes to take to get to them. After all, they are not safe havens if they cannot be found. Plans for possible evasive or escape tactics and ambush countermeasures near areas (bottlenecks) that are conducive to possible ambush must be made. Identify points along the route where vehicle inspections can be made without interfering with scheduled events. Plans have to be made for emergencies that result from non-hostile acts as well as ones from hostile acts.

What you have just read is a pretty basic outline describing the bare bones minimal requirements of a dignitary-protection program. Security programs such as this are expensive and complex, but the alternative of ignoring a threat of terrorism is much more costly. The key to a successful protection program is imaginative planning. Allow the planners to look at terrorism from the terrorists' perspective and design countermeasures for every conceivable attack they can imagine.

EDITOR'S NOTE:

If the dignitary will be in a parade, consideration should be given to sealing manhole covers along the parade route. Anyone who will have personal contact with the dignitary should be subjected to a file check. The dignitary should be interviewed, inquiring if he or she has received any threats. The dignitary should always travel in an armored vehicle and similar vehicles should be used as decoys. Routes of travel should be varied and changed frequently. In advance of the dignitary's arrival, the protection team should test the plans to expose vulnerabilities, with some members of the team posing as terrorists.

Chapter 10

Local Law Enforcement Preparation For and Response To a Terrorist Act*

By John Kane, B.A., M.A.

INTRODUCTION

A terrorist act is defined as: "The use, or threatened use, of force to achieve a political or social goal." The person(s) who instigate these acts can be from either foreign or domestic sources, and unfortunately terrorist acts in America are increasing in frequency. We can count on the fact that these attacks will continue, that anyplace in our country can be a target, and that the local law-enforcement officers, firefighters and emergency medical personnel will be called on to handle the first response to these acts.

It is a frightening reality of these incidents that within the last two years we have begun to use the term WMD -- Weapons of Mass Destruction -- in referring to large-scale terrorist incidents. With the advent of cheap and easily constructed explosives, such as Ammonium Nitrate Fuel Oil (ANFO), and the abundant material available on biological weapons such as ricin, we need to have a focused and well-coordinated plan on how to respond to these incidents.

The actions that are taken by these first responders are of paramount importance. These initial actions will determine the safety of the innocent civilians involved and the ultimate successful outcome of the prosecution of the suspects.

The first twenty to sixty minutes of an incident are the most critical. The policies and procedures that we follow during this initial stage of response will set the tone for the entire incident. It will determine whether or not we have organized and focused resources on scene, or whether we are fighting from behind the power curve during the entire incident.

It is with this principle in mind that we set forth some basic guidelines in this chapter, to assist local law enforcement officers in their first response to these incidents.

PRINCIPLES OF RESPONSE

There are several principles we need to be aware of prior to our actually discussing how we respond to a terrorist incident. Once we have these principles taken care of, we can then move into the actual actions that need to be followed in a priority order by local law enforcement as the terrorist incident begins to unfold.

These principles are: Preparation, Site Surveys, Use of an Expert, Team Building, Clear Speech and Unified Command.

PREPARATION FOR A TERRORIST ATTACK

One of the "carved-in-stone" principles of emergency response and disaster operations has always been: your level of success is in direct proportion to your level of preparation. The more time you spend on preparation and drills the higher your success rate; the less time you spend on preparation, the lower your chances for success. This is the equivalent of the famous military expression: "The more you sweat in training, the less you bleed in battle."

I like to paraphrase Gary Brown, the Emergency Manager during the Flight 232 disaster in Sioux City, Iowa, who correctly said that when a major event occurs, and it will occur, we won't have time to sit down, open up a book and read the plan on what we are supposed to do. When the tornado comes over the hill, or a DC-10 lands in your backyard, or when a terrorist bomb goes off in your town, you're going to respond that minute, as best as you can.

Local law enforcement's response is more a factor of what we know about the other major players such as the Federal Bureau of Investigation and the fire department. We have to know what their needs and concerns are, and how they are going to respond, so that we can work as a cooperative and complete team.

The only way that's going to occur is if we take the time in advance to prepare. We need to meet and train with the other members of these groups, so when we come together on a major event, we will have the ideal coordinated response.

SITE SURVEYS

Pick the top 10 terrorist targets in your area and conduct a site survey. Physically go to each site and examine such things as: possible points of attack, staging areas, traffic flow patterns for ambulances and other emergency vehicles, preset routes to the local trauma center, locations for the Emergency Operations Center (EOC), field incident command post, medical triage location, casualty collection points, etc.

To get focused on potential targets and threats, the local law enforcement officers need to contact the local office of the FBI. The FBI's job is to conduct counterterrorist operations and gather intelligence on these suspects and groups. The local FBI office will have Special Agents assigned to counterterrorism and weapons of mass destruction (WMD), and they can be excellent sources of solid information about current trends, possible threats and targets.

Remember these sites don't have to be critical government buildings. Today, any place where there are large numbers of people can be a potential target. Look at places such as: sports arenas and stadiums, convention centers, and transportation centers such as bus stations, railroad stations and airports.

Make sure you include targets in your area of high current interest. In certain areas of the country abortion clinics might be targets of current interest. In others it may be a political party's headquarters, or religious locations such as a church, or a religious leader's home.

These sites should be evaluated and upgraded every six months. These locations will change in their physical appearance and surroundings, and these changes have to be included in your planning. Additionally, locations will change due to the issues and threats that are current, such as the staff of the Serbian Embassy in the US. This is one of those "living" projects that have to be maintained.

THE EXPERT

I firmly believe that each local law enforcement agency needs an "expert" in terrorism issues. Most people find terrorism to be somewhat complicated, and because it deals with several cross-boundary issues such as intelligence, emergency response, hazmat, training, etc., it can get overwhelming. Select an individual who is really interested in this topic, someone that is fired up, who will devote the time and effort, which is required to create a quality program. Rank should be immaterial in the selection of the right person, and that person should keep the assignment if he or she is promoted or transferred within the agency.

This person has to have above average intelligence and public relations skills, along with an ability to work with such divergent groups as politicians, media, and law enforcement across the federal, state and local levels. This person has to show an interest in fire and medical emergency services and be willing to learn their systems and how they operate in a major event.

Each agency needs a "point of contact," a "guru" if you will, whom the other agencies will recognize as our in-house person who is up-to-speed on these issues and whom they can contact to seek and convey information. This information exchange works both ways because field officers can also come upon potentially excellent information about a possible threat, and they need a person to hand the information off to. The expert can then act as the conduit for the information so that it can be directed to the proper people who have the need to know, such as the Department's local FBI contact for terrorism issues.

This person should also be picked for his or her willingness to train others on how to respond and to keep others informed on the "hot button" issues and trends. This expert will have to conduct drills and exercises to test the Department's state of readiness, along with keeping the listing of site surveys up to date.

Lastly, the agency must make a commitment to give this person adequate support. Whether this assignment is full or part-time, the expert will have to go to schools, seminars and take trips to stay current and he or she will then come back with training ideas and new procedures that need to be implemented by the agency. Nothing will burn a person out faster than thinking he or she has critical information and no one in the department wants to act on it or spend the time, effort and funds to be adequately prepared.

TEAM BUILDING

I cannot say enough about the positive effect of personal relationships in the emergency response organizations such as local law enforcement, local fire department, and the local office of the FBI. As soon as possible, begin meeting and training with all of the major players in these organizations. There is an urgent need to meet these counterparts, discuss, plan and drill on what to do before an actual incident. The friendships and allegiances that are built up by working closely with each other can overcome significant problems and obstacles such as "turf battles." This is very easy to say, but not so easy to implement.

During an actual incident no one is going to have the time to sit down and read the book with the plans in it. At best, there might be time to consider a checklist. We, therefore, have to know what the other agencies are going to do, and have our coordinated effort ready before the event.

There is nothing like knowing the abilities, skills and actions of other first responders prior to a major incident unfolding. You'll know exactly what the other responders are doing and what their needs are and you'll be able to act more confidently because the confusion of the moment will be lessened. The only way that this is going to take place properly is not on the battlefield, so to speak, but during peacetime conditions where all agencies can talk about problems and train together.

Discuss problems, talk about resources, understand communications issues such as radio frequencies and cell phones, and really learn what each group is trying to accomplish at the event before a terrorist event happens.

Start regular meetings with all the first responders at the supervisory levels. At a minimum, this should include the Law Enforcement Watch Commander and Field Supervisors, the Fire Department's Battalion Chiefs, the supervisory staff at the local trauma center, and the FBI Special Agents and Supervisors from your area who are responsible for terrorism response.

Try to locate all the players who will be on scene in the first critical hour. Start meetings to identify each other's needs and concerns first, then work into a few short tabletop exercises built around some possible local targets. These exercises make great icebreakers, and help to identify operational problems early on when no lives are at stake.

At subsequent meetings include the representatives from the local media, local city or county managers, public works personnel, utilities companies such as phone and electric services, and local elected officials. It's important that they are reassured that the government is aware of these problems and how it will be responding to them. They also need to advise the first responders what information they will need and how it should be managed during a terrorist event.

The personal and professional relationships we build during these early stages will help to cement our cooperative efforts during the real event. The knowledge of the various jobs and agencies gained by including all of the principal players will streamline our response in a time when, truly, seconds count.

One of the best examples regarding the worth of team building is the use of public works personnel to staff an outer perimeter. Most jurisdictions of small-to-medium size cannot have the immediate ability to put police officers in an outer perimeter position to restrict access by the curious and others attempting to get into the terrorist scene. This is the classic example of how other local employees such as public works, parks and recreation, utilities and parking control, can be a significant help. However, this requires a high level of coordination and prior briefing that has to occur in the team-building phase.

CLEAR SPEECH

Clear communications and standardization of terminology is an important issue. The time wasted trying to figure out an acronym can hurt operations in an emergency. In California we learned these lessons the hard way in the Oakland Berkeley Hills Fire of October 1993. The lack of communication with each agency using its own particular terms, led to lost time and a lack of coordination between emergency responders. It is important to understand that, once the incident expands beyond your own agency, you must begin using the principles of clear speech, or clear text.

Simple terminology that is utilized every day by one emergency responder might not be familiar to other agencies. As an example, almost all of six hundred police officers in Sacramento, California had never heard the common Fire/Medical term " MCI" that stands for Mass Casualty Incident. Most believed this term referred to the phone company. Make sure all understand these terms, and that clear speech is used in these events and that everyone on the response team knows what these terms mean.

The coordination meetings between the first responders are an excellent time to bring up this issue, conduct some practice, and finally put it to rest. Within the City of Sacramento we have three different sets of radio codes, and more than 160 possible radio channels. Considering we're going to be listening to each other on the radio and scanners, there is little room for miscommunication and error when a terrorist attack occurs.

We need to be very specific when requesting various items. Simply asking for a generator is not sufficient. We need to specifically tell people whether we need a small Honda generator capable of powering a television set, or a 400 kw monster that can power a hospital. We cannot say, "I need gas." Are we asking for unleaded gas in five-gallon cans, a tanker truck full of diesel fuel for larger vehicles, or CS tear gas in canisters? In time of crisis, we cannot tolerate any kind of confusion and simple tabletop exercises and meetings before the event will help professionalize the response.

INCIDENT / UNIFIED COMMAND

The task of Incident Command during a terrorist incident is a cooperative effort between the three main players: the local Fire Department, local Law Enforcement, and the Federal Bureau of Investigation.

In the past there have been incidents where these three groups did not work cooperatively. This is not the case today. Old style inter-agency rivalry has given way to an era of better sharing of responsibility and cooperation. Today, faced with shrinking budgets and manpower, and a media that are highly critical of emergency response agencies, this most destructive behavior must be eliminated.

The progression of incident command responsibility at a terrorist act will pass through these three significant groups, following the order of what is needed most as the incident unfolds. In order, the Incident Command will rest with:

1. **LOCAL FIRE DEPARTMENT** To assume command during the initial fire, rescue, medical response to the incident.

2. **LOCAL LAW ENFORCEMENT** To assume command after the fire-rescue-medical threat has been neutralized and to conduct preliminary investigation until the FBI is prepared to assume command. During the time that the Fire Department is in command, local law enforcement will follow the Mass Casualty Incident (MCI) Protocol for Law Enforcement while it is preparing to assume command.

3. **The FBI** Pursuant to the Federal authority of Presidential Decision Directive 39, the FBI is the lead agency in any act of foreign or domestic terrorism, and will assume command of the incident and subsequent criminal investigation. It will take some time for the FBI to have sufficient resources on the scene to assume command. It is critical that local law enforcement remains on scene to assist and support the FBI in this mission after the role of local Incident Command has passed to the FBI.

UNIFIED COMMAND

The Incident Command System (ICS) will be discussed at length later, but it is important in the context of "who's in charge" to talk about the ICS concept of Unified Command.

Unified Command speaks to the issue that all of the major players in an incident need to get together to share information, resources, and responsibility for the smooth delivery of effective service. But, as in all events, there can only be one boss, one "shot caller," directing the focus of the group, and setting the group's goals.

The image of a triangle helps to convey this concept. In our terrorist incident, there are three major players: local fire, local law enforcement, and the FBI. There could certainly be others, such as public works for heavy equipment and major infrastructure damage, but let's stay with the main three for now.

This whole system of "who's in command" and unified command only work if all agencies are aware of each other's primary needs. The Fire Department must have crowds kept back and clear streets to move in heavy equipment. Law enforcement needs to have evidence preserved and witnesses identified. The FBI needs to have extensive cooperation and support for many days and even weeks from both the local fire and law enforcement to preserve the scene and collect evidence.

As the three main players come together on the scene, they will form a unified command group. The first priority will be to handle all of the fire, rescue, and medical problems. The Fire Department will move to the top of the triangle and set the goals for the operation. Once the fire, rescue and medical efforts have ceased, the local law enforcement agency will move to the top of the triangle and assume incident command.

UNIFIED COMMAND
WITH FIRE AS INCIDENT COMMANDER

This does not mean that law enforcement sits around waiting until fire has relinquished command. Local law enforcement will be responsible for following the principles that are outlined in the next section during the time that the Fire Department is in charge.

When Incident Command passes to law enforcement, the law officer in charge will then set the goals for the operation, and begin full conduct of the preliminary criminal investigation. This will include identifying and taking initial statements from potential witnesses and victims, along with crime scene preservation and any emergency actions or evidence collection.

When the Fire Department begins to wind down its functions of fire-rescue-medical response, the fire and law commanders will agree when incident command will pass to law enforcement. When this occurs, simultaneous broadcasts should be made on both the fire and law enforcement channels so that all personnel understand that incident command has passed from the fire service to law enforcement.

Also at this time, the specific location for the law enforcement command post should be repeated via radio so that there is no mistake as to where the command post is located.

It is essential that a Fire Department command-level officer remain in the command post. This will insure continuity of information, and also provide an officer who can direct fire resources if they are needed during this time.

Remember, until someone makes the call that the incident fits our definition and is an act of domestic or foreign terrorism the event is basically the local jurisdiction's homicide, assault, vandalism, bombing, etc.

The FBI will usually dispatch an initial Special Agent as soon as the incident occurs, as a direct result of just being in your town and monitoring radio frequencies. If you even slightly suspect that you are dealing with a possible terrorist event that fits our definition, call the FBI out immediately. Depending on your location, it may take a few minutes to a few hours to get a Special Agent at the scene, and the lost time for coordination can be harmful to later efforts.

It is always better to have the FBI on scene as soon as possible. In the event the incident is a terrorist act, the Bureau will be up-to-speed and be able to assume command responsibility without any loss of information. If the incident develops, and it is a local crime such as a homicide or bombing, the FBI's presence will give you another well-trained investigator on scene as a valuable resource for both investigative ideas and evidence-collection issues.

The FBI also provides both technical support and special resources you may not have at your local level. However, it can be several hours before the FBI has assembled a full command team and is ready to take over the incident. During the interim, the local law enforcement agency will assume the position of Incident Commander, while coordinating in the Unified Command with the Fire Department and the FBI staff on scene.

When the FBI team has been assembled and is in place, the Bureau then will assume command of the incident. The FBI might be able to respond its evidence collection teams to the area fairly quickly to assess the evidentiary problems and get a handle on how much staff they will need and what specialized equipment they should bring. The FBI has its own policies on evidence collection, so if you believe this is a terrorist event, it is better to seal the area and let their evidence technicians collect the evidence rather than filling up your property warehouse and creating major chain-of-custody issues. If some evidence needs to be preserved on an emergency basis, this should be done for later transfer to FBI custody. Since almost all of our response to an act of terrorism will be after the fact, evidence collection issues will be crucial for the arrest and conviction of the suspect(s).

UNIFIED COMMAND
WITH FBI AS INCIDENT COMMANDER

The important thing to understand at the local level is that once the FBI Agents have assumed command, they will still need continued support and assistance from the local law enforcement and fire agencies. They will need help with traffic control, body and evidence recovery, scene security, and a host of other critical tasks.

The FBI, in order to better coordinate the federal response to an act of terrorism, will establish its own version of the Emergency Operations Center called a Joint Operations Center or JOC. This is the location where all federal agencies will first report and work out of for the duration of the incident, and it corresponds to local government's EOC.

In recent discussions with Special Agents of the FBI, they indicated that they would try to co-locate the JOC near the local agencies' EOC. At a minimum, they will try to provide a command-level officer to stay in the local agency EOC to facilitate direct communication between the groups involved in the unified command, and to facilitate the sharing of resources, personnel and information.

In order to better function together it would be helpful to work out of one central EOC. The FBI's establishment of a separate JOC is based on the large numbers of agencies and support staff that could be called in to help at a major terrorist event, which is a legitimate concern. In the event the incident is a large one, the Incident Commander should be looking for an area large enough to accommodate these priorities so that both facilities can be at the same location.

As the local agencies' involvement winds down, fewer staff will be necessary, until finally the JOC will become the only coordination point for the incident. When on-scene activity ceases, all follow-up investigative activity will be the responsibility of the FBI.

As you can see, during each of these phases, a different group will be moving to the top of the triangle. But all will still be together working on the issues, and sharing concerns and information in the Unified Command concept.

THE LOCAL LAW ENFORCEMENT RESPONSE
THE PLAN

The Local Law Enforcement response to a suspected terrorist attack will encompass four major areas. In priority order they are:

1.) Locate -- Isolate -- Evacuate (LIE)
2.) The Mass Casualty Incident Protocol for Law Enforcement (MCI)
3.) The Emergency Checklist
4.) The Incident Command System (ICS)

| **L – I – E** |
| MCI |
| Checklist |
| ICS |

LOCATE -- ISOLATE -- EVACUATE

During any major event such as an explosion, large-scale shooting incident, or a terrorist attack, there will be many different things going on simultaneously. The initial calls from citizens will be extremely confusing, and they will need to be verified by our first emergency responders on the scene.

In law enforcement the large percentage of major incidents revolves around barricaded gunmen, shootings or hostage takings. The procedure practiced by the first arriving officers: Locate -- Isolate -- Evacuate, will not change in a terrorist event.

It is imperative that these actions be taken in the order listed. The job of the first responding officer(s) is to alert other emergency personnel and fix the exact Location of the problem, Isolate that location so that the bad guy(s) cannot escape and to prevent innocent people from walking into the danger zone, then, begin Evacuation of the two primary groups affected -- injured persons and those in the line of fire.

The critical nature of: Locate -- Isolate -- Evacuate, is that these steps must be followed in this priority order. If we begin to evacuate people who may be in the line of fire before we have located the suspect and isolated him, law enforcement officers can become targets.

If the suspect is free to move around the area while we are evacuating wounded or persons in the line of fire, he is free to escape or continue to harm the officers and innocent civilians in the area. Once the situation is effectively located, and the movements of the suspect are isolated, safe evacuation can begin without making police officer's part of the problem.

LOCATE

At the onset of a major incident there is tremendous confusion. Numerous calls are coming into the communications center from civilians describing pieces of the incident, and officers arriving are contributing valuable intelligence about what is happening. It is imperative that the exact location of the incident be found. These incidents have a tendency to become highly fluid, increasing the area affected. It is the duty of the first responding officer(s) to fix the accurate location of the incident as best as possible, and to direct other officers to the scene. It is extremely dangerous if officers are directed to the wrong locations, or are wandering around the area unaccounted for, searching for suspects.

In the event the incident takes place in a large building or complex, the first responding officer(s) must locate a building representative and use this person as a guide. Most large facilities have internal building management staff or security personnel. It is imperative that the first-arriving officers contact one of these individuals and guide others into the scene. Often calls come in saying that the incident is at a location known only to "insiders"-- the people who live or work at the location.

In one example in Sacramento, California, a gunman walked into a large computer-assembly plant with more than two thousand employees.

He went to a specific work area and began firing at his co-workers. When the first call came in from a security officer, he kept yelling at the dispatcher that the gunmen were in "Building 1- Bay 1." This meant nothing to the dispatcher, and all the heroic efforts on her part couldn't get the security officer to calm down and give directions that were "police" appropriate.

The first-arriving officer was able to grab one of the security officers who had an internal company radio. He then took the security officer in the patrol car as a guide to the exact location where the suspect was still firing.

Once the officer arrived at the proper location, he was able to advise other officers that the building was located in the North/Eastern end of the complex and to access the complex from a specific city roadway. In the event of a similar circumstance, a local, knowledgeable person should be kept with the first responding officer(s) until the Locate task has been accomplished.

ISOLATE

It is imperative that as soon as possible the incident should be isolated, along with any suspects who may be present. In the best terms, the bad guys should be locked down and prevented from moving. This means that if the terrorists are still on the scene, a team of officers must be assembled who can penetrate a facility, Locate these individuals and then Isolate them so that they cannot escape and to prevent them from moving around and harming more potential victims, including the responding officers.

If the incident involves a large facility, such as a high-rise office building or a college campus, an immediate four-officer team should be sent into the area or structure to pin down the suspects. Four officers are a minimum team, consisting of a team leader, two officers with shotguns or patrol rifles, and one officer with a handgun. The team leader directs the officers, the rear guard officer covers the rear and the two long-gun officers lead the advance. This configuration works best because it takes three officers to cover a corner with maximum firepower, one prone, one kneeling and one standing.

If the facility is large enough, several teams may be needed, but with sufficient communication so that they can operate safely. Once they have locked the suspect(s) down, evacuation of the wounded and people in the line of fire can begin. As SWAT resources get on scene, equipped and available, they should be moved up and replace the four-officer Isolate team and to become the inner perimeter.

Again, it is critical that this process be accomplished in strict order. If the officers get bogged down evacuating wounded people before the suspects have been Located and Isolated, the suspect(s) are free to move around killing and injuring more victims and possibly the law enforcement, fire and medical responders. Once Isolation is successful, then Evacuation can begin.

If the first responders are satisfied that no suspects are on scene, and then in order to Isolate the area, they will establish inner and outer perimeters. There are severe restrictions on the number of officers available in smaller jurisdictions, so the inner perimeter should be the first priority for sworn officers, and other city or county workers or even volunteers could man the outer perimeter.

In a major event such as a terrorist attack with injuries, these perimeters have added responsibilities under the Mass Casualty Incident (MCI) Protocol that will be discussed more fully later. But for now, the inner perimeter doubles as a crowd-control device to keep the bystanders from getting in the way of the emergency personnel and the outer perimeter is used as a traffic control device to allow access only to proper emergency vehicles.

EVACUATE

At this stage, our priorities in order are to:
♦ evacuate anyone who may have been wounded, and
♦ evacuate anyone who is in a potential line-of-fire.

WOUNDED

In order to evacuate wounded people, it may be necessary to enter into a potential danger zone. Each agency has to evaluate its ability to conduct these operations. Are ballistic shields available to protect officers and civilians? What is the first-aid capability? Are extra vests and helmets available for firefighters in case it is necessary to take a medical team into the area?

Most fire / medical policies are for personnel to stage outside the area until law enforcement says the area is stable, and they can enter safely. This is a critical point that needs to be taken care of in the preparation and training stage before the reality presents itself.

If fire and medical resources won't come into an unstable area to treat and evacuate the wounded, can the law enforcement officers be taught how to get the wounded out of the area and to a triage point using backboards, following proper c-spine and other medical precautions?

What about officers escorting fire and medical staff into the danger zone after putting vests and helmets on them? Has this type of operation or rescue with medical personnel been practiced and have they agreed to it? Or, will law enforcement personnel bring the wounded to triage? Is there a vehicle that can be used for a medical evacuation under fire, such as an armored car? These questions need to be asked, answered, and trained for, prior to the incident. Not made up as the incident unfolds in the street.

With over 80 percent of terrorist events perpetrated through the use of explosives, the issue of evacuating the wounded from collapsed or demolished buildings must be confronted.

Law enforcement officers are not equipped or trained for evacuation operations inside a collapsed building. These skills and equipment in police work are very limited and almost non-existent. In any area where serious danger still exists, such as from a building collapse, this is actually a rescue event. Police should stay clear and let the persons with the expertise in this field, namely the firefighters, handle it.

Each Officer has to conduct a risk-vs.-benefit analysis before proceeding into a danger situation and ask: "Is the risk to my person -- and the possible compounded rescue of me by other officers -- worth the benefit I will receive?"

By entering into a more hazardous environment the officer could actually create more of a problem for other officers. If an officer is injured inside a collapsed building, such as in the Oklahoma City bombing, that is a circumstance where even more officers will risk their lives to rescue that trapped officer.

If an officer enters a smoke-filled building, or a hazardous material scene, or a collapsed structure, and disappears -- what are his or her fellow officers going to do? In every law enforcement agency in this country, officers would run in to try to get that officer out of harm's way. They would never leave an officer in a hazardous situation without doing everything possible to rescue the officer.

The individual officer must think of the extreme jeopardy those rescuing officers would be placed in.

Another way to view this issue is that police handle evacuations, fire handles rescue. If the operation leans toward a rescue of people in a collapsed structure, it is almost always better left to the rescue experts. No one would criticize an officer who made a decision to enter one of these structures if he or she had made a proper risk-vs.-benefit analysis, knew of the above factors, and still decided that his or her help was necessary to save lives. It must always be kept in mind that the desire to help can lead into a situation where the rescuer becomes a victim.

LINE-OF-FIRE

The line-of-fire evacuations have to be conducted with respect to the threat that is faced. A gunman in a high rise office building armed with a .22 caliber pistol is a threat that will produce a different evacuation than a gunman in the same building armed with a hunting rifle with a scope. In a terrorist incident, a decision has to be made almost immediately how large an area has been affected -- or will be affected - and a commensurate evacuation has to be undertaken.

If the weapon, such as a large explosion, has influenced a great area, it will be necessary to call out as many officers as possible to deal with the line-of-fire issues due to the potential for a secondary explosion. In the event of a Weapons of Mass Destruction (WMD) threat, such as a chemical or biological weapon, the area considered to be in danger could be even larger.

It is always better to have too many officers at the scene, and have to send some of them home, than to get caught behind and be fighting the power curve during the entire incident. Law enforcement resources take time to gear up and arrive on scene, especially mutual aid from other departments. Considering the large area that could be affected for a line-of-fire evacuation in a terrorist incident, it is important to get organized as quickly as possible and call for resources as fast as possible.

Think big. The possible evidence from an explosion can travel hundreds of yards from the scene. Additionally, secondary explosions may occur or suspects intending a second act could be in the area. The larger the evacuation area, the better the chances are of not losing evidence, apprehending suspect(s) and protecting the innocent people who could be hurt.

LOCATE -- ISOLATE -- EVACUATE / TACTICAL CONSIDERATIONS

Below are two potential scenarios, which demonstrate how the Locate -- Isolate -- Evacuate functions would occur in a practical situation. Both are similar to potential terrorist actions.

SITUATION #1 –
RESIDENCE OR BUSINESS LOCATION, SINGLE GUNMAN

A 30-year-old male individual with a rifle goes crazy inside his house and begins shooting into the street. Officers are called, and upon arriving on the scene, several shots are fired at the officers. The officers obtain a very good look at the suspect and are able to describe not only his clothing but also the weapon he is carrying. One of the officers knows this individual from a prior call, and knows that he lives alone.

The first responding officer assumes command and confirms the location of the suspect. Once this officer has identified the specific house, he then directs the other officers into the area so that the gunman can be isolated. The officer in charge positions the other responding officers so that the house is covered, and the suspect cannot escape without encountering an officer. As sufficient manpower becomes available, multiple officers are placed in these isolation positions.

Once this is accomplished and the suspect is sufficiently isolated, the officer now begins the evacuation of the neighborhood. The next group of responding officers is sent to the various houses near the suspect location, to locate residents and escort them out of the area.

The first responding supervisor will assume Incident Command from our first responding officer. SWAT resources are called for, and begin arriving on the scene. The first arriving SWAT Officer becomes the Scout. This officer moves forward and assesses the positions of the inner perimeter / isolation team around the house. A radio broadcast is made to all personnel that the Scout will be moving forward to assess the inner perimeter so as not to create a potential gunfire situation.

Once the Scout has completed the survey he or she returns to the command post area. At this location the full SWAT team will assemble and the Scout will present the diagram of the house area and the team will decide where to place its various members and weaponry. When the SWAT team is fully ready, another radio broadcast is made and the SWAT team will move forward, replacing the inner perimeter / isolation team. Once SWAT personnel have replaced these inner perimeter patrol officers, the latter return to the command post for debriefing and further assignment in the operation.

SITUATION #2 –
LARGE AREA LOCATION, ACTIVE SHOOTER(S)

Numerous calls are received regarding shots fired at a local high school. The initial information is that two gunmen have entered the school grounds and are roaming the hallways shooting faculty and students. The first officer arrives on scene and reports that many students are running out of the school and into the surrounding neighborhood. This officer also reports hearing gunshots coming from the interior area of the school near the cafeteria.

Many officers from allied jurisdictions are responding code 3 to the scene. The first arriving supervisor puts together a four-officer Locate / Isolate team. As soon as the team is properly equipped, it enters the school grounds to locate and isolate the gunmen.

The other officers who are immediately available to the supervisor are sent to form an outer perimeter team. The supervisor then establishes a staging area three blocks away in a supermarket parking lot. All other officers responding are told to go to the staging area. A second supervisor assumes the role of staging-area manager.

The supervisor at the school calls the staging-area manager and requests a second four-officer Locate / Isolate team. The staging-area manager assigns four officers to move forward and meet with the supervisor at the school. Approximately five minutes after entering the school, the second team locates the two gunmen in the library with approximately 10 hostages.

The team leader at the library requests six more officers to reinforce his team. The supervisor at the school has the first Locate / Isolate team respond to the library and then obtains two more officers from the staging area manager. These officers all meet with the team leader at the library and a complete inner perimeter is established around the library building.

The supervisor at the school then requests five two-officer teams to move forward from the staging area and help with the collection of wounded students. The supervisor working with the Fire Department Battalion Chief determines a triage area and all of the casualties are moved to this area.

The supervisor appoints an Intelligence Officer in Charge (OIC) and has all of the students that have been evacuated from the school brought to this officer's position so that possible intelligence on the gunmen can be obtained. In addition, officers are assigned to the triage area to obtain information from the wounded students.

As you can see, both of these situations are dramatically different. The first situation is of a more static nature. The gunman / terrorist has been located inside his residence, and other than the panic caused by the neighbors, the situation is fairly manageable with a medium-size number of officers.

In the second school-shooting scenario, we have a circumstance known as an "active shooter." This is a circumstance where either single or multiple gunmen/terrorists are moving through a large complex and actively shooting people or trying to escape. This kind of a circumstance requires immediate action to preserve life.

The supervisor put together a four-officer Locate / Isolate team to find the active shooters and to lock them down so that they were not free to create more victims or to escape. Most SWAT personnel are assigned to other duties, and take a prolonged period of time to arrive on scene. If these officers are immediately available, they are, of course, the best choice for the Locate / Isolate team. These officers train extensively, and are accustomed to working together as a close-knit team.

If, however, a field Supervisor is confronted with an "active shooter" scenario, he or she needs to understand how to put together a four-officer team and conduct this kind of Locate / Isolate operation. There are many lesson plans available from such organizations as the FBI, the California Tactical Officers Association and the National Tactical Officers Association. It does not matter which of these methods you choose. It matters that you have explained this concept to your officers, and especially to the law enforcement mutual aid first responders who could be coming into an "active shooter" circumstance to help your agency.

The four-officer Locate-Isolate team concept with a team leader would basically follow the format below:

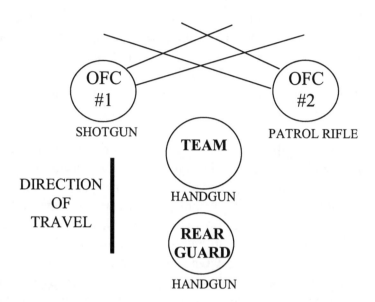

In a large facility such as a high school or multi-story office building, the supervisor may need to appoint several Locate / Isolate teams to cover the entire area. No team should be allowed into the danger area without clear communication ability to both the other teams and to the Incident Commander.

In a case such as the Columbine, Colorado, high school shooting, a very large number of mutual aid officers responded. It is imperative that we organize these officers through the use of a staging area so that we conduct a systematic search without putting the officers responding in the line-of-fire. Emphasis should be placed on the point that the suspect is located and isolated before we begin evacuation of the wounded or people in the line of fire.

```
L - I - E
MCI
CHECKLIST
ICS
```

MASS CASUALTY INCIDENT
PROTOCOL FOR LAW ENFORCEMENT

Since almost all terrorist acts injure significant numbers of people, it is important that local law enforcement has a plan on how to respond to these events. There is a limited capability for preventing these kinds of acts and almost all response will be after the fact. Before discussing the specific jobs and roles for local law enforcement associated with a Mass Casualty Incident, it is important to understand how an MCI unfolds and is handled, both in the field and at the local trauma center hospital.

Understanding how these events unfold will afford a better perspective on how law enforcement actions should mesh with the fire / rescue / medical response.

A Mass Casualty Incident is usually defined as five or more seriously injured persons. By definition, these events usually have many severely injured people, and the valuable seconds and minutes of the medical response can mean the difference between life and death. These events are most often large traffic crashes with multiple vehicles, explosions, bus crashes, train derailments or even plane crashes.

In order to organize and have the most efficient response to these traumatic scenes, the medical community joined with the fire departments and ambulance providers across the country to develop a standardized plan. From some very hard work, their MCI protocol was born. The plan is enforced by the group that sets medical standards and issues accreditation to hospitals. By regulation, each county is supposed to have a full scale Mass Casualty Drill every year to test its response plans.

In a simulated explosion, an MCI response would unfold as follows:

Many calls are received at fire and police dispatch regarding the explosion and a rough estimate of the number of injured. Responding units begin to arrive on scene and the first estimate of casualties is 65 injured people. There are roughly 25 severely injured and the rest are equally divided between serious injuries and walking wounded with minor injuries.

The Fire Department dispatcher will take the best estimate of the number of casualties and send a corresponding number of ambulances, trucks, engines and supervisors that would be needed to handle that number of casualties.

This is a fire / rescue / medical event and so a fire department command officer will become the Incident Commander. He or she will appoint a Medical Director who will have responsibility for treatment of the injured and setting up a temporary morgue if needed.

During an MCI response, the first-in ambulance will assume triage duties and will become the source of the medical supplies for the injured. In a large event, there may be several ambulances at triage with the responding firefighters and medical personnel using all the supplies in these vehicles.

It is imperative that law enforcement officers understand that these triage ambulances will remain stationary and will not go to a hospital. If you are trying to help injured persons don't put them into a triage ambulance. Just bring the injured to the triage point, and the staff there will assess the injuries and effect proper treatment and transportation.

All firefighters are trained to the Emergency Medical Technician (EMT) level, and the real need is for people who can do the actual medical treatment on scene. The responding fire trucks and engines will park their vehicles in a nearby street and not drive them near the actual scene. This parking area is known as "base" and they will leave a firefighter on scene to guard the vehicles. They will then take whatever first-aid supplies and equipment they have on their vehicles and walk into the triage area. At the triage point, they will deliver their supplies and they will then be assigned specific patients to treat.

At triage, the patients will be divided into specific categories depending on their injuries. The severely injured 25 people will be classified as "immediate treatment," which means they need to be treated right away as a matter of life and death.

The next 20 who are severely injured but not life threatened are put in the "delayed treatment" category. They will be treated as soon as possible in accordance with their injuries and the staff available.

Our last 20 people form the "walking wounded," people who have received minor injuries such as cuts, inhalation of smoke, or bruises, but are still getting around under their own power. They are held in an area for first aid. Medical personnel like to use transit buses for this purpose. A bus has wide aisles where a single first aid person can administer to large numbers of people, and the bus is safely out of the elements.

A colored tag placed on their front identifies every person in each group. Red tags designate "immediate treatment," yellow tags designate "delayed treatment," and a multi-colored tag designates "walking wounded." A black tag is used to designate a deceased person. Regardless of the color, the tag also contains information regarding the specific injuries and medicines or treatment given, along with the patient's name if it is known.

The immediate treatment area near triage is marked by a red colored tarpaulin placed on the ground. The "delayed treatment" area is marked by a yellow colored tarpaulin also placed on the ground adjacent to the immediate treatment red tarp. The responding firefighters and medical workers use these tarps for ready identification of the critical treatment areas.

Ambulances used for transportation of patients from the scene will start a taxicab-like queue, near the "immediate treatment" area. This is the area where the most critically injured are positioned. As soon as these critically injured patients are stabilized, they will be transported from this area to nearby medical facilities. As an injured person is cleared for transportation, the next ambulance pulls up to the "immediate treatment" area and takes on the next patient(s). As ambulances return from the hospital, they get back at the end of the line, waiting to receive another patient or patients.

As the fire dispatcher is starting this field response, another fire dispatcher will call the designated trauma center. The dispatcher will alert the trauma center staff of the MCI in progress, and try to give a rough estimate of the number of casualties. The trauma center is connected to the other hospitals in the county by a ring-down phone line or radio system that connects to all the emergency departments in these hospitals.

The trauma center uses this system to declare an MCI and then polls all of the other hospitals. Each hospital emergency department reports back to the trauma center with the number of critical care beds available, and the number of physicians and nurses available on site. They will also report any specialists available such as neurosurgeons, cardiac surgeons, etc.

The trauma center then logs all the staff and facilities available on a large board. As ambulances leave the explosion scene, they call into the trauma center and detail the injuries of the patient(s) on board. The trauma center staff then analyzes these injuries and matches them up with the hospital that is best equipped and closest to handle that patient or patients. In essence, the trauma center acts as a traffic cop, directing the injured to the best possible hospital to get the most out of the trauma care system. This scenario continues until all of the patients are clear of the explosion scene and accounted for in the hospitals.

MCI SCENE DIAGRAM

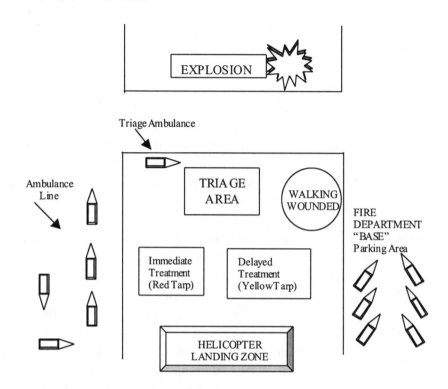

THE FIRE DEPARTMENT ROLE

At its initial stage, a terrorist act will require some kind of a fire / rescue / medical response. This job falls to the local fire departments and they are very proficient in the handling of Mass Casualty Incidents. Most fire departments hold frequent MCI drills, and have extensive equipment and supplies to handle numerous casualties.

As discussed above, the Fire Department will have Incident Command during the first stage of a terrorist act because it is responsible for handling the initial fire-rescue-medical problems at the scene. These scenes will usually meet the definition of an MCI considering the potential for many casualties. Law enforcement will be working for the fire Incident Commander in a unified command at this point.

The law enforcement protocol in this response would be the same for any initial law enforcement response to an event such as a bus crash, plane crash or any large industrial accident where many people are injured.

The first calls received by local law enforcement will usually be as a simultaneous response with fire and medical personnel. In over 80 percent of terrorist acts the weapon of choice is an explosive device. The initial calls received by fire, police and medical will usually be to a large explosion. This does not preclude the possibility that a reported terrorist act could be first reported to the emergency responders as a normal call for service.

In the Tokyo subway Sarin gas attack, the first calls to the emergency responders consisted of "man sick in the subway," a fairly common radio call. When the first emergency responders arrived, they also became part of the problem because some of them were affected by the poison gas.

With the new trend toward Weapons of Mass Destruction (WMD), we are seeing potential threats from biological, chemical and even radiological weapons. With their highly developed hazardous materials capability, the Fire Department becomes an even more significant resource in these events.

The fire service is very aware of the critical significance of its role as the first responders to a terrorist incident, and have received training regarding the proper preservation of evidence, and how to guard against potential secondary devices. Firefighters also have received training in how to deal with chemical agents, radiation dangers and biological weapons that can be threats to first responders.

With their training and equipment, firefighters are the logical Incident Commanders in any fire-rescue-medical event. Added to its ability to operate in the dynamic area of a possible terrorist or WMD incident, the Fire Department is the logical "shot caller" at this first stage as the event unfolds.

CRISIS MEDIA RELATIONS (See also Chapter 11, page 179)

Normally, most departments have a press or public information Officer. This person usually has a fairly small staff and is in charge of all of the media releases conducted by the department. Sometimes this person is augmented by a designated relief person, but this main PIO handles for the most part all daily public information issues.

The system works very well for almost all of our contacts with the media. However, it becomes totally inadequate to handle what I like to refer to as Crisis Media Relations. When a crisis or major event has occurred in your jurisdiction, all the rules of normal contact with the press seem to change and we need to go to a configuration that can handle these problems.

In this new 24-hour crisis time of hurried communication the normal person handling public information can sink very quickly in a sea of media problems. When a crisis occurs in your agency, you need to go into a specific format to handle these media problem. In time of crisis the format for media relations changes to the following:

- **Press briefings times 100**
- **VIP Tours**
- **Manning an Information Room**

Press briefings times 100 – The media is now a 24-hour operation. During a crisis the entire world, state, or community could be focusing on your jurisdiction. You must, therefore, be prepared to conduct "100 times" more press briefings and releases than during a normal day. In order to handle this problem, you must have an increased number of people who are comfortable in front of the camera and who can represent your department in a professional manner.

If you do not have a significant number of people who can assist with the PIO function, the single individual who normally handles this job will drown very quickly under a flood of media inquiries. The more people that you train to handle media information the better off you're going to be when a large event strikes your department. We'll discuss how to do this below.

VIP Tours – In a major event your department is going to be flooded with significant amounts of VIPs. All of these personnel are going to want to see the disaster area and to be outside talking with the people affected by your event. It is a fact of life that there is a significant connection between VIPs and the presence of the media.

Regardless of the reason why these VIP's show up, you have a significant obligation to accommodate them. These people control your budgets, and have a significant impact on your department. They can often times be a significant help utilizing their political clout to cut through red tape that is slowing up relief to your department.

It is important to understand that the Incident Commander cannot show these people around. The Incident Commander will be far too busy managing the recovery and the emergency problems that can come up. A distraction of this nature on a repetitive basis for the Incident Commander could actually delay emergency response in your department. You, therefore, need to acquire a fairly large group of department personnel who are capable of conducting tours of the affected areas for these critical VIPs. The staff that you choose to fulfill the role of "tour guide." can have a critical impact on how your department is viewed. Again, we'll discuss the training of these individuals below.

Manning the Information Room – Each law enforcement agency has some kind of a 911 communications center. This communications center will be overwhelmed under the weight of inquiries by phone. All of the relatives of the people affected by the incident, along with department personnel and a host of other people, will be trying to get information from this central point in your department. Under the weight of this huge number of inquiries your department communications center could totally shut down and become ineffective.

In order to stop this problem, you need to have a designated information room within your department. This room would have a central phone number that would have "ring down" capability. In other words, by calling one specific number the same number could potentially be answered by 10 separate phones in a designated room. By having this capability, you will be able to free up your communications center so that they can return to some kind of normal activity.

When they receive an inquiry they'll be able to say "Yes, please call 264 – 8000, and people of that location will be able to help you with your inquiry." By giving your communications center this capability, you will return to a normal activity as quickly as possible. You'll also provide better service to the people who are asking legitimate questions regarding your operations and the people that they're concerned about.

Staff training – Your next job, therefore, is to come up with three separate groups of people. A group who can do stand up press releases, a group who can conduct tours for VIPs, and a group who can staff an information room, handling over the phone, all of the problems people may have.

This is no small to ask to come up with this large number of people. In my agency we found out that the best way to come up with a group of people capable of fulfilling these tasks was to actually train everybody in the agency how to do Crisis Media Relations.

We taught a four-hour Crisis Media Relations class to everyone within my agency. Then, when we needed to have someone conduct a tour or conduct a stand up for the press, we found we had a fairly well trained cadre to draw from. In order to obtain this group of people you need to give them hard practical experience in conjunction with the class. In order to do that, there is no substitute for actual contact with the real people of the media.

We gave our people a solid class and then at every opportunity we took people from the ranks and had them handle press contacts and tours during our day-to-day operations. This gave us a large group of people who were familiar and capable of handling all three of these significant changes to our daily media routine. We have utilized these people on an almost daily basis, and it has helped us immeasurably to cope with Crisis Media Relations.

We also learned a valuable lesson in that the media does not want to talk to the normal press spokesperson during a crisis event. They want to talk to the person closest to the event who can give them real-time information regarding what's happening. By training our entire patrol division on how to cope with these three major activities, rewriting the general order that clearly allows them to speak with the press, and then encouraging them on a daily basis to talk to the press, we developed a solid cadre of officers capable of fulfilling these roles in Crisis Media Relations.

The big step forward was that we had to realize that we needed to relax control over our field Supervisors and Officers, and encourage them to talk to the press on a daily basis. Not only did we find that they did an admirable job in a very timely fashion, but we also found out this timely action prevented two serious other problems. While waiting for the normal PIO to arrive it would sometimes take an hour or more. During this time, the media is constantly filming our officers and this has led to some embarrassing moments. Additionally, during the long wait for the PIO to arrive, several citizens in the area would hold impromptu press conferences and say things that were inaccurate or even inflammatory. Both of these problems were decreased when we had our people on the scene with all the proper information talk to the press right away. We have even received praise from the media regarding our helping them to do their job in a timely manner.

In the following pages I have attached the 20 significant points that we utilized as a lesson plan during our crisis media relations class. Please feel free to utilize these same points when you return to your department to organize your media staff.

THE CARE AND FEEDING OF THE MEDIA MONSTER

Dealing with the press can be stressful. Cameras and lights surround you. Suddenly you realize what you say is going to be heard and seen by a lot of people. Relax. It's not as bad as it seems. Reporters and their editors are looking for one or two brief quotes. Contrary to popular opinion, they're not looking for the one sound bite that will make you look like an idiot. They will almost always overlook your little missteps.

Remember these are sharp people who feed their kids and pay their mortgages with their ability to come back with some footage. So we want it to be good footage that gives a good image of the Agency. Here are some simple things to keep in mind that will make your dealings with the press more effective and less stressful.

1. TELL THE TRUTH. If you follow only one suggestion, make it this one. If you bluff and are caught, the damage is irreparable. There is a big difference between making an honest mistake and trying to float a half-truth.

2. STICK TO WHAT YOU <u>KNOW</u>. Incorrect information, once out, is hard to get back. There's nothing wrong with admitting you don't know the answer to a question. You should, however, tell the reporter where to find the answer or attempt to find out the answer.

3. JUST BECAUSE THEY ASK, DOESN'T MEAN YOU <u>HAVE</u> TO ANSWER. Some kinds of information can't be released. It's very helpful, though, to explain <u>why</u> you can't answer a question. "That would be speculating on my part" or "That could be an important part of our investigation strategy", go a long way to letting reporters know you're not just stonewalling.

4. NONVERBAL COMMUNICATION IS IMPORTANT. Shifty eyes or looking off camera every time a tough question is asked can make you look less than truthful. Look at the reporter, not the camera.

5. KEEP IT SHORT. Reporters are writing a news story, not a book. They can't use long-winded or technical explanations. If you're concise, they'll get it the first time and leave you alone to do the rest of your job.

6. FORGET THE JARGON. We sometimes speak in a language particular to only our area of expertise. Often, though, it reinforces the idea that you aren't "regular people." Instead of "We're

attempting to develop investigative parameters that will help us arrest the perpetrator", try "We're trying to find the person that broke into the Jiffy-Lube."

7. DON'T BE DRAWN INTO AN ARGUMENT. Take the high road. If the reporter is rude and you maintain a calm, professional demeanor, you'll come out the winner.

8. DON'T ACCEPT AN UNFAIR CHARACTERIZATION. Just like in any situation, don't let someone color your remarks. "So you're saying this rapist will strike again?" "No, that's not what I said. I said we're trying everything we can to get this guy into custody."

9. IF THERE'S A CAMERA AROUND, IT'S ON. The same goes for microphones. Take a cue from President Reagan. Getting funny or careless with recording equipment will lead to trouble. Assume it's rolling at all times.

10. "OFF THE RECORD" MEANS NOTHING. This is one of the most commonly misunderstood aspects of journalism. Everybody has a different definition of OTR and not one of them will hold up in court or when the chips are down. If you don't want to read it in the next day's paper, don't say it. It's that simple.

11. DON'T SAY "NO COMMENT." There are times when you can't answer a question or address a difficult issue. This phrase, though, makes you sound like you have something to hide. Instead, try something like, "I can't comment on that because it's privileged by law/etc."

12. BE CAREFUL WITH SPECULATION. In general, it's best to stick with the Jack Webb approach. Just the facts, Ma'am. If you do engage in a bit of guessing, be very clear that it is just that.

13. AVOID OFFERING A PERSONAL OPINION. There is a big difference between a personal opinion and a professional one. If you do offer your opinion, "I guess kids just aren't scared of the system these days," be sure you label it as such. Otherwise it'll come out as department policy with plenty of confusion attached.

14. YOU'RE NOT A NETWORK CENSOR. Blocking the camera's view of a crying victim may feel right at the time, but it's a mistake. They're there to look and see. Most editors won't use the grisly stuff anyway, but they will hand out pink slips for cameramen who come back with poor footage. Do your job and let the cameraman do his.

15. AVOID HORSEPLAY OR ANY SEMBLANCE THEREOF. We all know a sense of humor is key to survival in any job. The viewers of the evening news, however, won't understand this if they see you laughing it up as you stand there at a serious event.

16. TREAT ALL REPORTERS IN THE SAME WAY. Playing favorites will come back to haunt you. Giving some better access than others, regardless of your personal feelings for the individuals involved, is unprofessional and wrong.

17. NOTHING FUELS THE FRENZY LIKE A LACK OF INFORMATION. This is a lock. The less the press knows, the more excited they get. If you <u>want</u> them to pepper you with questions and make you miserable, tell them nothing. If you want them to go away and let you do the rest of your job, tell them something they can use. As long as it's true, of course.

18. <u>REMEMBER THE 20-SECOND RULE.</u> The most in-depth TV story will last about 2-3 minutes. Of that, your comments will last about 20 seconds. Prepare your statement to that time frame and then keep your answers to the follow-up questions brief and to the point.

19. <u>NOTHING GETS THINGS ORGANIZED LIKE A SCHEDULE.</u> News organizations run by the clock. Be familiar with their deadlines and try to accommodate them. If the story is so big as to be covered by many different news organizations, telling everyone a set time and place for a briefing will have them together so you do not have to go through a dozen of the same interviews.

20. <u>FINALLY, RELAX.</u> Many times, dealing with the press is about as stressful or combative as you make it. A smile or explanation will work wonders. Put them at ease and they'll be less agitated and/or difficult.

THE LAW ENFORCEMENT ROLE

With the Fire Department having the initial Incident Command responsibility, the senior law enforcement officer will immediately respond to the Fire Command Post and take up law enforcement command duties in the Unified Command structure. This will ensure that the law enforcement Incident Commander is completely up to speed on the progression of the event when it becomes his or her time to assume control of the Unified Command.

After insuring that the Locate - Isolate - Evacuate functions have been accomplished or are in progress, it will be the local law enforcement Incident Commander who will carry out law enforcement's actions in response to this terrorist event. All of these actions will be occurring at the same time the Fire Department is handling its fire / rescue / medical duties.

Our next challenge will be to begin the MCI protocol for law enforcement agencies.

The jobs in the MCI protocol for law enforcement dovetail with the Locate - Isolate - Evacuate function, and carry law enforcement's response one step further.

They are: crowd control, traffic control, coroner liaison, and criminal investigation.

CROWD CONTROL

During the initial stages of an MCI, the Fire Department will have its hands full dealing with the fire / rescue / medical response. Firefighters have very little contact with civilians. They mostly handle all of their coordination with fellow firefighters and very rarely get to significantly interact with the public during an event. They are dependent upon law enforcement to handle the crowds and keep these crowds from interfering with their duties.

It's very common for law enforcement to handle this problem on an almost daily basis. Officers frequently tell agitated and concerned people: "No sir, I'm sorry you can't go in there. Yes, I know that your son is injured, but you have to stay outside and allow the medics to treat him. Yes sir, we will try and get you to the hospital as fast as we can, but you have to stay outside here and let the medics treat your son."

Because of its familiarity with handling crowds and its almost constant interaction with people, it falls to law enforcement to handle the crowd control problems at the scene.

The Law Enforcement Incident Commander (IC) should take charge, and have the immediate goal of setting up both an inner and outer perimeter around the scene. The inner perimeter's purpose is to control the crowds so that the law enforcement officers can allow the firefighters to do their jobs with the least amount of interference.

The outer perimeter's goal is to permit access by vehicles that are involved in the emergency response and to deny access to vehicles of people who want to just view the event. The outer perimeter also functions as a secondary line of containment in the search for suspects.

As you can see, this is an extension of the Isolate function from the initial response of Locate -- Isolate -- Evacuate. The IC should not get bogged down with the actual assignment of units to specific locations. Instead, he or she should appoint a specific OIC (Officer In Charge -- the generic, rank immaterial term for a law enforcement team leader). OICs are needed for both the inner and outer perimeters, and the IC should give them personal guidance on the areas to be contained.

The OIC will then position the officers, mutual aid forces, and even volunteers in the specific locations to accomplish their missions.

TRAFFIC CONTROL

There are two major parts to traffic control:

♦ SCENE - Traffic management of the actual scene; and
♦ ROUTE - Clearing a path to the nearest double access freeway ramp for the ambulances leaving the scene.

SCENE

Traffic management at the scene is a critical element. The confusion created by the large numbers of first responders, along with the self-dispatched off-duty personnel and other volunteers can create chaos at the scene. Without effective scene management of traffic, needed rescue and medical vehicles will not be able to get to the scene.

A traffic team with a designated Officer in Charge (OIC) must be formed as soon as possible. There are too many tasks involved in traffic control that could overwhelm the Law Enforcement Incident Commander, and one person must be in charge of controlling and setting up the traffic plan with valuable input from the Fire Department Incident Commander. Then the plan has to be broadcast to all responders, giving the entrance and exit routes and the locations of selected parking areas.

In order to handle this problem, think big. Take over nearby streets and turn them into emergency vehicle parking lots with officers present who can handle the parking of these vehicles properly.

The first priority is to put officers at the key intersections to restrict access to facilitate emergency traffic. The second priority is to turn streets that are nearby, but out of the danger zone, into an emergency vehicle parking lot.

Normally it won't be possible to get emergency vehicles directly up next to the scene, and for several reasons it's not a good idea to do so anyway: There may be huge amounts of evidence close to the scene and vehicles driving over it can damage or destroy critical items.

With the recent problems of secondary devices at blast scenes such as in Atlanta and Fulton County, Georgia, emergency responders or vehicles that park too close to the scene could be in jeopardy. The incidents in Georgia have led to the policy that triage and other medical aid points should be well out of the potential area for a secondary device. This philosophy has been represented as a 1,000-feet safety area (3 football fields), both horizontally and vertically, around the blast site to protect first responders from a secondary explosion. These concepts are critical to managing the scene and lessening the confusion of vehicles parked all over the place and blocking each other.

The key issue is to get as many emergency vehicles into the nearby side streets -- properly parked -- so that the responding personnel can get to the scene. In a fire, rescue, or medical response, the number of vehicles parked close to the actual scene will usually be minimal. The fire service will only require a few key vehicles parked near the scene. What are required will be the responding firefighters and medical personnel to effect medical treatment and begin rescue of the injured. The emergency vehicles they arrive in will be parked on these side streets / staging area, and the firefighters and rescue personnel will walk into the scene to keep the area as clear as possible and to lessen the confusion.

The best possible way to get the maximum number of vehicles into a given street is to angle park them. Using this technique will insure that the maximum number of vehicles can be parked in the street and that no vehicle will be blocked in by another vehicle. A common fire service term for this parking lot is "base."

Again, the key is to have the traffic control officers block off access points so that only emergency vehicles are permitted into the parking area, as illustrated in the diagram below:

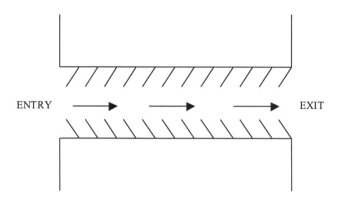

ROUTE

The second half of traffic control consists of getting the emergency ambulances to the hospital. This requires law enforcement officers to be positioned at the critical intersections needed to get an ambulance to the nearby hospitals. Again, in smaller jurisdictions other workers such as parking enforcement or public works staff can fulfill this role.

Almost all hospitals are accessed by freeways. This concept requires rapid travel access to the nearest freeway ramp. The critical point is that the freeway ramp must have double access (East/West or North/South) so that an ambulance can have the best access to as many roadway combinations as possible.

As each ambulance clears the scene and begins to travel to the freeway, it must pass through intersections that could slow it down and also present a risk for accidents. Position police cars at these critical intersections. As each ambulance approaches, the officer will hear the siren, pull the patrol car into the intersection, and stop traffic in all directions. This will permit the ambulance free travel through the intersection quickly with as much safety as we can provide.

These two traffic-control tasks can be significant operations involving a large number of officers. With some training and practice with fire and ambulance personnel, police officers can provide a significant benefit to the overall care of the people involved in the incident and lessen the confusion at the scene.

An excellent training and practice event for the traffic-control function can be performed at an MCI drill. This would be an excellent opportunity to meet key players in an MCI operation and to establish law enforcement's helping role in traffic management at a major event.

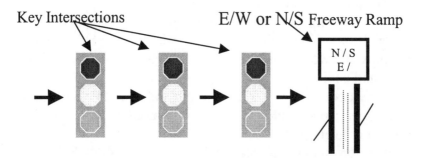

CORONER LIAISON

The job of coroner or medical examiner throughout the United States can fall to any number of people. In large metropolitan areas the job can fall to a formal medical examiner, or deputy coroner. In some rural areas, the duties of coroner fall to specific deputy sheriffs. In some smaller communities and rural counties, the duties of the coroner can fall to the local undertaker or a local physician.

Regardless of which situation exists in your local area, the casualties present at a terrorist act can quickly overwhelm the coroner function. In order to assist the local coroner with the collection and preservation of evidence, and the protection of the remains of the people killed, local law enforcement officers must assist. The area of most need will be the collection of personal possessions and the proper recovery of the bodies.

Most coroner mutual aid plans are sufficient to handle these problems if the number of fatalities is low. However, in the event of a mass casualty incident with many fatalities, the coroner function could be overwhelmed. Dead bodies cannot be left exposed at a given location for the many days that it would take for a few coroners to effect the proper personal property collection and body recovery.

In this case local law enforcement officers, because of their familiarity with evidence collection and preservation at homicide scenes, would be the only trusted personnel that the coroners could utilize to assist them in their functions. Normally, homicide investigators, who are familiar with the problems and have had experience in this work, will be the first officers used in this capacity. However, your agency may not have sufficient homicide investigators to handle all of the casualties produced at a large terrorist act. In this event, regular officers will be assigned to handle coroner liaison, and the amount of preparation now will determine the success of this critical operation.

This would entail assigning a group of from two to five officers to one coroner deputy. The officers would work under the direction of the coroner deputy and would assist that deputy with the collection of personal possessions and bodies.

This task could be extremely foreign and stressful to officers. This means that supervisors would have to closely monitor personnel for signs of trauma and critical incident stress.

Law enforcement must plan on how to deal with the post traumatic stress associated with these events so officers will not be overwhelmed psychologically.

Review plans for post traumatic stress debriefings and update them to handle the possibility that large numbers of officers might need debriefing. Can current plans handle 100 officers needing counseling in a timely manner? Is your agency prepared for handling group debriefings for some of the officers and civilian staff such as dispatchers, and making referrals for specific officers? Have your supervisors received any training in recognizing these problems among the staff and how to refer them in a confidential and caring manner that will inspire organizational trust?

If you have trouble answering these questions, take a look at your program and begin working toward a solution. These horrifying events can do serious psychological damage to officers. With some advanced preparation, the effect of these incidents can be dramatically lessened.

With regard to coroner liaison, the earlier that officers are educated as to their duties in this role, the better. The officers will see this as a logical extension of their job if it is presented properly before any incident occurs so that it is not demanded of them at the scene of a critical occurrence without advance training.

In a terrorist act, an FBI Agent would most likely be Incident Commander by this point and would be providing command direction on how the Bureau wanted to conduct coroner operations. Even if a full FBI response is delayed, no coroner operation should proceed without the Bureau's input. All actions need to be thoroughly coordinated to minimize any possible loss of evidence.

Also, because of the very specialized nature of this work, an Officer in Charge for coroner operations should be appointed to ensure that all information is directed to one central point. This person can be any mutually agreed upon expert, but should be fully aware of the hazards of a high profile event such as a terrorist attack and have a staff sufficiently skilled and sized to handle media and family inquiries with the diplomacy required.

CRIMINAL INVESTIGATION

At any MCI, responders can never assume that it was simply some kind of an "accident." Most MCI events may appear to be some kind of an "industrial accident" or "transportation accident" in which people are injured. Law enforcement officers normally just direct traffic and keep the curious at bay. They can no longer do this. A criminal investigation should be conducted.

In many recent examples, local law enforcement has responded to scenes that were originally believed to be accidents only to find out later that criminal activity was the cause of the incident. A crash involving a bus driver who was drinking, or a train derailment with a rail that was intentionally pried loose, are two incidents that may appear initially to be "accidents" but in reality are criminal acts.

If several hours are allowed to pass, evidence might be destroyed, and critical firsthand statements might be lost.

Regardless of first impressions of how the MCI was caused, officers should be immediately detailed to begin potential criminal investigations during the first few minutes of the law enforcement response.

The first critical issue will be to take statements from eyewitnesses at the scene. It is imperative to lock these witnesses down in their statements as to exactly where they were positioned when the incident occurred and what they saw from that position. Many individuals surface after a critical incident and give false or misleading testimony as to their participation in the incident. Their motivation can be to intentionally mislead the police, or to simply gain their moment of fame.

Officers identifying and locking these people into a specific statement at the beginning of the event can avoid many lost investigative hours following false leads.

In the confusion of the first response to a large incident, we can lose valuable physical evidence. The immediate fire, rescue, medical response can put a tremendous number of people into the potential crime scene. Adding to this confusion can be large numbers of media, civilian responders, and concerned relatives and friends of the injured people.

Crime scene investigators should immediately begin taking photographs and videotape, which will be invaluable in recreating what will become an ever-changing scene as the emergency response continues for hours and sometimes for days.

They can also be used to take photographs and videotape of the crowds, in the hope of identifying potential suspects or their vehicles remaining at the scene. Perpetrators often remain on the scene to "enjoy" the commotion their action has caused.

Investigators must be detailed immediately to begin criminal investigation at the scene of an MCI to insure that valuable criminal leads and statements are not overlooked during the confusion of the initial response. Remember, these initial stages of an MCI, the fire, rescue, medical response, can continue for quite some time. As an example, the response during the Oklahoma City bombing on the part of the fire, rescue, medical agencies continued for many days.

Responsibilities for evidence collection cannot be ignored during these critical continuing days of an event. In the Oklahoma City case, the FBI was able to put representatives in with the various rescue teams searching for survivors. As the teams proceeded through the building, these law enforcement observers were able to identify potential pieces of evidence and collect and preserve them. It's important to understand that this was an exceptional incident, and that in most cases, the fire, rescue, medical response will be over fairly quickly.

Local law enforcement officers' role will be limited to the emergency collection and preservation of evidence, specifically those items that could be destroyed if not preserved immediately such as a muddy footprint or a weapon left out in the open.

As discussed earlier, if the event is declared an act of terrorism, the FBI will assume command. They will bring in their evidence-collection teams and will begin processing the evidence according to their policies. Any items seized by local law enforcement officers will have to be transferred to FBI control, setting the stage for possible chain-of-custody issues.

It is, therefore, the best policy to freeze the scene and await the decision on who is going to assume ultimate command of the criminal investigation. Remember, until such time as the call has been made on who is going to handle the investigation, this is still a local area homicide or bombing. It can take many people to process a complicated scene. With this in mind, an early call out of all the available crime-scene staff can alleviate manpower problems with the emergency preservation of evidence and having enough people to handle the scene if incident command ultimately remains with the local law enforcement agency.

```
┌─────────────────────┐
│  L - I - E          │
│  MCI                │
│  CHECKLIST          │
│  ICS                │
└─────────────────────┘
```

MCI CHECKLIST; ICS CHECKLIST

During the initial stages of a response to a suspected terrorist incident, it is important that a call be made for additional resources and equipment that will be needed to set up and begin dealing with the problem as fast as possible. These resources take time to arrive (a SWAT team could take several hours to be set up and deployed in the best of circumstances) so the earlier they are ordered the faster they will be on scene.

It is impossible for one person to be able to recall all of the items that are necessary to assist in the proper containment and investigation of a terrorist incident. Given the high emotional state of these incidents, it's also impossible for one person to remember all the various items that he or she may have initially thought to order, but lost track of during the heat of the incident. Officers can actually be overwhelmed by the situation, and need a solid starting point to get focused and back on track.

To properly order resources that will be needed at a terrorist incident, it is imperative that there be an organized checklist to follow. The following checklist which the author has developed will assist the first on-scene supervisor and Incident Commander in major calls critical incidents - the barricaded gunman, hostage taking, etc. This checklist is also readily adaptable for a terrorist incident to assist in ordering the proper resources for the incident and to remain focused while lessening the sense of panic and confusion that grips us all.

The checklist is printed on several pages and is double-spaced so that officers can take notes directly on the pages to keep material all in one place. Officers can write directly on the checklist the unit number or name of the officer assigned to handle a particular task. Printing this checklist on bright yellow paper makes it stand out among all other white paper, and seems to help with finding items on the list. Copies should be issued to all officers and supervisors and be placed in all patrol cars.

It is important to understand that all of the items that are listed might not be needed at a specific incident. They are listed on the checklist so that the first-on-scene supervisor or Incident Commander can consider them and either disregard or order them, depending upon the circumstances of the incident.

While the law enforcement Incident Commander is still in the MCI protocol stage, the checklist should be started and a staging area be established immediately as detailed in the checklist, so that all personnel and resources can be sent to one specific location.

At the staging area, equipment carried by officers can be checked, as they are committed to the event to insure they are properly protected. Such critical items as ballistic helmets, armored vests, and chemical protective suits need to be checked prior to personnel being committed to the event. Responding to the immediate area without a specific assignment creates more confusion and puts officers in peril.

This checklist is only a guideline. The local law enforcement agency can change and adapt it as appropriate. Take some time to go over this checklist with your command staff and determine which items are unnecessary or which items should be added to the list to provide a better response to a terrorist incident.

As the checklist unfolds and you begin to order resources, several of the items on the checklist are specific reminders for the Incident Commander to begin filling positions in the Incident Command System. There is also a blank ICS diagram page so, as people are assigned to these jobs, their names can be listed in their job positions. This method leads into the next phase of response to a terrorist incident: the establishment of the Incident Command System as a way to manage the operation for the long haul and to transition command to the FBI.

Additionally, there is a chart page that lists the main sections to be detailed in any tactical event. As the situation permits, this chart should be filled out. It must be completed during the first one to two hours. This will provide an immediate record of the event, and assist in the briefing of any new staff that comes on board after the start of the event.

The Incident Commander does not want to be put into the position of having to orally brief every new arriving officer or dignitary. By duplicating this chart, each new arrival will have a complete briefing document. This chart also makes up the foundation for the after-action report.

MAJOR CALLS / CRITICAL INCIDENTS
EMERGENCY ACTION CHECKLIST

- ❏ ***LOCATE / ISOLATE / EVACUATE***

- ❏ ***MCI PROTOCOL: CROWD CONTROL / TRAFFIC CONTROL CORONER LIAISON / CRIMINAL INVESTIGATION

- ❏ ***USE THE INCIDENT COMMAND SYSTEM***

- ❏ ADVISE RADIO -- REQUEST DESIGNATED CHANNEL AND DISPATCHER

- ❏ INNER PERIMETER -- COMMANDER

- ❏ OUTER PERIMETER -- COMMANDER

- ❏ DETERMINE INJURIES AND EVAC

- ❏ FIELDS OF FIRE FOR SUSP -- PROTECT AND EVAC

- ❏ REPEAT SUSPECT DESCRIPTION TO ALL OFFICERS

- ❏ POSITION OF PATROL RIFLE OFFICERS

- ❏ CALL OUT SWAT -- HOSTAGE NEGOTIATORS
- ❏ 1st SWAT Officer to scout the inner perimeter. When ready, SWAT replaces Inner perimeter, and these patrol officers report back to CP for debriefing.
- ❏ FIRE DEPARTMENT / AMBULANCE STANDBY -- NOTIFY BATTALION CHIEF TO CP FOR BRIEFING

- ❏ NAME ROUTES TO / FROM THE SCENE, AND STAGING AREA

- ❏ ESTABLISH COMM W/SUSP -- ASK TO SURRENDER

- ❏ OIC FOR NEIGHBORHOOD EVAC -- ACCOUNTABILITY -- Designate a Shelter Location

- ❏ DESIGNATE A PURSUIT TEAM -- IF SUSP CAN GO MOBILE

- ❏ LIMIT PHONE ACCESS TO SUSPECT -- Consider Call-out of Phone Co., Electric and Gas Utilities.

❑ NOTIFY ALLIED AGENCIES AS NECESSARY -- Sheriff, Highway Patrol, etc.

❑ RADIO NOISE DISCIPLINE

❑ DOUBLE CHECK YOUR LEGAL AUTHORITY TO PROCEED

❑ VOICE OR MDT AS LOGGING DEVICE -- TACTICAL DISPATCHER TO SCENE

❑ FILL OUT ICS DIAGRAM AND TACTICAL INCIDENT INFORMATION SHEET

❑ INTELLIGENCE OIC (USUALLY WITH HOST NEG) -DEBRIEFING NEIGHBORS, HOSTAGES, RELATIVES, ETC.

❑ PIO -- BROADCAST PRESS TO RESPOND TO A SPECIFIC LOCATION

❑ CONSIDER POOL VIDEO

❑ LOGISTICS OIC -- Staging areas, maintaining security and routes to and from, personal needs of officers. Call out for Red Cross / Salvation Army, etc. Logging of all assigned personnel

❑ CHAPLAIN CALL-OUT, BOTH COMMUNITY AND LAW ENFORCEMENT'S. CHAPLAINS -- to be Shelter Managers, and assist with displaced persons and victims

❑ CALL DETECTIVES TO THE SCENE -- Criminal follow-up, report writing, Intelligence on the suspect, statements from witnesses, etc. Work for INTELL OIC

❑ FLOOR PLAN -- ANY NEIGHBOR, BUILD MGR, ETC. -- PRACTICE ON SIMILARS

❑ AIR ASSETS -- BOTH HELICOPTER AND FIXED WING

❑ MARINE ASSETS -- Drowning Accident Recovery Team, PD BOATS, FD BOATS, ETC.

❑ MUTUAL AID DECISION -- LIAISON OFFICER IF NEEDED

❑ CORONER STAND-BY OR NOTIFIED

❑ SIGN-IN / SIGN-OUT ROSTERS FOR ALL ASSIGNED

- ❑ A/V CALL-OUT FOR DOCUMENTATION -- (CRIME SCENE INVESTIGATORS -- HOMICIDE ETC.)

- ❑ WHO IS PRIMARY REPORT WRITER (FINANCE/ADMIN OIC)?

- ❑ *****HOLD SCHEDULED MEETINGS WITH ALL ICS STAFF AND THE OIC's AS NECESSARY FOR HOSTAGE NEGOTIATORS AND THE SWAT TEAMS -- FOR STATUS AND DECISIONS TO CONTINUE THE OPERATION*****

- ❑ CALL OUT OF CIV STAFF -- PROPERTY ROOM, I.D. TECH, ETC.

- ❑ MAJOR CALLS / CRITICAL INCIDENT CHECKLIST CONT'D:

- ❑ LOCATION OF SURRENDER AND APPOINT TRANSPORT OFFICERS.

- ❑ NARCOTICS / GANGS FOR MOBILE INTELL GATHERING.

- ❑ CONSIDER SPECIAL SUPPORT ITEMS -- DOJ FOR HIDDEN TV CAMERAS AND LISTENING DEVICES, FBI CALL OUT FOR ELECTRONIC DEVICES AND SPECIAL SUPPORT FOR SWAT, HOSTAGE NEGOTIATORS, ETC.

- ❑ CSI AT SCENE (Video Camera, Evidence retrieval)

- ❑ K-9 (Use for Call, or CP Security)

- ❑ TRANSIT AGENCY FOR BUSES

- ❑ LOCATION FOR MASS PRISONER PROCESSING IF NECESSARY

- ❑ MEDICAL LIAISON OFFICER TO STAY WITH MEDICS/FIRE

- ❑ COMMAND OFFICER NOTIFIED

- ❑ UPDATES TO PRESS EVERY 30 MIN -- ADJUST AS NECESSARY

- ❑ UPDATES TO ALL OFFICERS AS FREQUENT AS POSSIBLE -- 20 Min

- ❑ PREPARE FOR THE NEXT SHIFT

OPERATIONS CONCLUSION

- ❑ APPOINT A RESPONSIBLE CLOSE-OUT OIC

- ❑ GUIDE FOR MEDICS / FIRE / CSI AS THEY MOVE IN

- ❑ CLOSING OF OUTER PERIMETER TO INNER AS SECURITY DEVICE --
  Maintain scene integrity -- log all who enter and leave -- prepare to turn over the
  scene to detectives

- ❑ SWAT RETRIEVES EQUIP AND LEAVES -- TAKE PHOTO/VIDEO OF
  SCENE PRIOR TO OUR LEAVING

- ❑ EVERYONE CHECK OUT (sign in/out rosters) -- THRU LOGISTICS
  STAGING AREA MANAGER

- ❑ FOLLOW -UP OFFICER FOR NEIGHBORHOOD BRIEFING AND THANK
  YOU

- ❑ ESTIMATION FOR DAMAGES -- CALL OUT OF RISK MGMT STAFF

- ❑ RED BORDER FORMS FOR CITY LIABILITY

- ❑ 1st REPORT OF INJURY FORMS

- ❑ WORKERS COMP FORMS

- ❑ CLEAN UP OF ALL AREAS USED

- ❑ DESIGNATE WHO WRITES THE AFTER-ACTION REPORT -- ADMIN
  OIC

- ❑ ARRANGE FOR POST-TRAUMATIC STRESS DEBRIEFINGS

INCIDENT NAME:
DATE / TIME START:
DATE / TIME END:

INCIDENT COMMAND SYSTEM

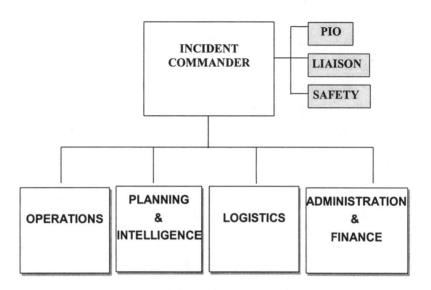

NOTES:

TACTICAL INCIDENT INFORMATION

CRIMINAL ACTS	SUSPECT(S) INFORMATION
THREAT CONDITIONS (Weapons and Demands)	INCIDENT SITE INFORMATION

```
L-I-E
MCI
CHECKLIST
ICS
```

THE INCIDENT COMMAND SYSTEM

Following "Locate-Isolate and Evacuate," the Mass Casualty Incident Protocol for Law Enforcement, and the Checklist, the Incident Command System should be addressed. ICS is a management-operational system that will help the responding forces to stay organized and focused for the long run.

The Incident Command System (ICS) provides a management structure and system for conducting on-site operations. It is applicable to small-scale daily operations as well as major mobilizations for such things as a forest fire, flood, or terrorist event. ICS, because of its standardized operational structure and command terminology, provides a useful and flexible management system that is particularly adaptable to incidents involving multi-jurisdictional and multi-disciplinary responses, such as a terrorist attack. It has been in use for many years by the fire and medical services and is a proven tool to manage these large events.

ICS provides the flexibility needed to rapidly activate and establish an organizational format around the functions that need to be performed in a major event such as a terrorist operation. One of the key principles of ICS is that the Incident Commander only activates the sections needed for a specific operation. He or she doesn't have to appoint all eight of the jobs right away unless the situation calls for it. Basically, the incident builds the organization needed to handle the incident.

The use of the Incident Command System has been mandated in California since December 1, 1996. All law enforcement agencies in the state have been trained in its use, and are now applying it in all major events. This application allows for the smooth integration of mutual aid into multi-jurisdictional incidents, such as a terrorist event that could cross the boundaries between a city and county. Everyone involved in the incident is using the same terminology according to ICS, which lessens the confusion and miscommunication created in these types of incidents.

It also makes an excellent pre-planning tool. If a major event such as a parade or a VIP visit is in the near future, the main division heads and team leaders in the Incident Command System are appointed weeks or months before the event. That way when any questions or problems arise in the planning stage, they are directed to the correct person. When the actual event arrives, the same person continues in that role during the event. Confusion and loss of information are greatly reduced.

By using ICS, the jobs detailed in this system are entirely adequate to handle any problem that could arise. Literally, there is no task that could occur during a major event that cannot be successfully assigned to one of the eight functional ICS jobs.

INCIDENT COMMAND SYSTEM

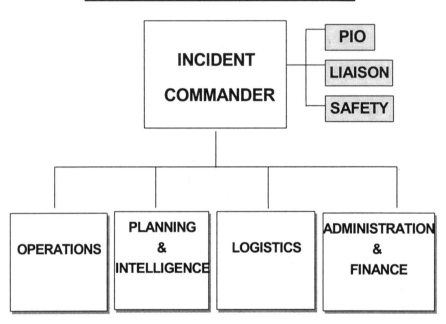

When the author teaches the Incident Command System, he tries to explain its structure as the "stack-of-dishes" theory. If you are going to have a large party with about 50 people, you're going to need all the dishes you have in your house. If you're going to throw a medium-sized party, you'll only need about half of your dishes, and if it's a small party perhaps just a few of them. So, for example, on a barricaded gunman incident that lasts only four hours, you may only need a medium-size structure that looks like this:

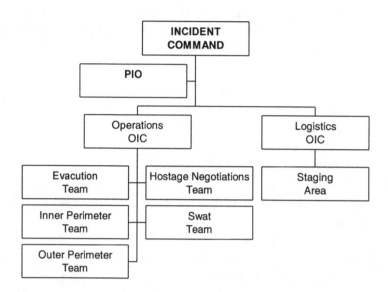

As the incident progresses, you may have to add other teams, branches or divisions as the situation dictates. The listing of all eight of the ICS positions is attached.

On the following pages there are written a brief description of the tasks assigned to each of the eight functional jobs in the ICS. This is not meant as a full explanation of the functions of ICS. There is still some debate going on between disciplines as to where some functions should be placed. For example, fire would like to see the staging area as a function of operations, while law enforcement sees it as a logistics function.

Emergency responders should have a class on ICS, and a complete working knowledge of the system. This system is gaining nationwide acceptance, and is the easiest way for all of the disciplines -- fire, law, medical and public works -- to be "on the same sheet of music" as they respond to these critical events under circumstances of high stress and confusion.

INCIDENT COMMAND SYSTEM ASSIGNMENTS

Incident Commander

The Incident Commander sets the priorities for the event. What does he or she want to see accomplished and in what priority order? The other division and section members conduct the follow-through. Frequent meetings between the IC and the other OICs (Officer in Charge -- the generic, non-rank, specific term for the commander of a division or team) of the various sections are necessary to keep everyone updated as the priorities change and to guard against duplication of effort.

The Incident Commander's Staff

The PIO -- one of the most critical functions, that is necessary all of the time. (See Chapter 11, page 179.)

Critical functions are:

1.) Conducting frequent media briefings,
2.) Handling VIPs, and
3.) Staffing a telephone reference point for the general public and the media.

Estimates for media: (anticipate what questions they will ask and have the answers ready ahead of time), estimate of money damages, exact number killed, exact number injured, estimated number of buildings lost or damaged. Need outside chalk board or briefing schedule to update press, Need rapid, factual information, as soon as possible. This will cut phone calls which jam lines. Just releasing the information that "only one person injured at," can reduce the number of phone calls into the communications center.

Liaison -- the locator of all the agency representatives needed for this incident and also has to keep all of the other agencies nearby informed as to the progress of the incident.

Safety Officer: has the authority of the Incident Commander, and is charged with operational safety. The job is to ensure that the mission is being accomplished in the safest possible manner by inspecting the area to check on safety issues. One thing that some agencies are looking into, is to assign the Safety Officer position the additional duty of acting as a mentor to newer Incident Commanders to have an experienced senior officer available for the newer person to discuss ideas with and to assist in formulating action plans.

THE FOUR MAJOR DIVISION ASSIGNMENTS

Operations: the teams in the field handling the mission. In a major incident -- the original Incident Commander in the field might hand off to a more senior officer who will then become the new IC. This new IC will be responsible for opening up the Emergency Operations Center (EOC) for the law enforcement operation. If the event is big enough, as in a terrorist explosion, all of the functions and their Incident Commanders -- fire, law enforcement, public works, medical command, etc., will co-locate in a central EOC.

The initial Incident Commander will become the Operations OIC, so that the drop of information is greatly reduced. This Operations OIC is responsible for naming the teams needed to handle the mission. Under the Operations OIC they might be such teams as: SWAT, hostage negotiators, evacuation teams, looter patrol teams, inner and outer perimeter teams, security, criminal investigation team, traffic management team, etc.

INTELLIGENCE / PLANNING: TWO KEY MISSIONS

1. To gather all intelligence on the scope of the occurrence and the people and things involved. This could require a large number of officers, depending on the size of the event. Both field information gatherers and staff working in the office may be necessary. This function also includes maintaining the status on all the manpower and resources committed to the event. Are they off-duty, committed to the field, or in reserve, etc.?

2. To plan for the future -- What will be needed in 2 hours? 12 hours? 48 hours? To come up with the lists of manpower and things needed to run the operation at these time lines and then forwarding them to logistics.

LOGISTICS:

The "bullets, bread, beans, and butter" people. They are charged with obtaining all of the needed items such as batteries, chain link fencing, rental cars, generators, toilets, food, etc. This includes finding the people needed for the operation by calling out off-duty staff or by using mutual aid. A good rule to follow is to replace all staff every twelve hours, including command staff and field personnel.

Logistics is also in charge of maintaining a staging area. This will be the central location for all supplies delivered and officers signing in, prior to their actual assignment. Once called for, the items and personnel leave the control of logistics and take up whatever assignment they are given under operations.

FINANCE / ADMINISTRATION: TWO KEY MISSIONS

1. Finance -- to pay for all the items purchased, rented, or leased during the incident, and to account for all time keeping and payroll issues.

2. Administration -- to account for all of the paperwork. Becomes
    the collection point for such items as: Injured-on-Duty forms,
    workers compensation documentation, city/county liability
    forms, crime and incident reports, etc. Accumulates all of the
    section and division logs, and writes the after-action report for
    the incident.

That is just a thumbnail sketch of the Incident Command System.
A detailed description would take up many more pages within this
document. The ICS model is a highly effective way to manage everything
from a multi-car accident to a multi-state forest fire. It has a proven track
record for simplicity and the ability to get the job done.

Consider adopting this system if you haven't already done so.
There are many excellent schools and train-the-trainer programs all over
the country that can help your agency become more proficient in the
Incident Command System. With a quick class and some table top
exercises, any agency can become proficient in a very short time. Then, as
the agency uses ICS on a daily basis and everyone gets familiar with the
duties of each job, working in the ICS format during a terrorist event will
be second nature.

As law enforcement agencies begin to rely on mutual aid more and
more in handling large scale incidents, we need this Incident Command
System that all can understand and adapt to. The sooner all are using the
same terms and operating system, the faster and more professional will be
the coordinated effort in these critical incidents.

THE WMD THREAT

One of the biggest problems that must be faced during the 1990s
and beyond is the threat that someone will utilize a Weapon of Mass
Destruction (WMD). These devices, whether improvised or manufactured,
have come to be known as "the poor man's atomic bomb." There are three
basic categories of these weapons: nuclear material, biological material,
and chemical material.

All these agents have specific ways they attack the human body,
and each has some sets that can have varying symptoms and effects when
released in a populated area. The task of product identification and the
planning of a specific approach belongs to the hazardous materials experts
in the fire department and public health fields. (See Chapters 3, 4 and 5,
page 27 et al.)

In considering a potential WMD threat, what will the role of local law enforcement officers be? As we already have discussed, response will almost always be after the fact of a terrorist incident. The device will already have exploded or have been released and the law enforcement officers' job is to respond into unknown circumstances. As pointed out above, the first calls into the police and fire services during the 1995 Tokyo subway Sarin gas attack were, "man sick in the subway," a very common call to the first responders in any major city with a transit system. Several of the initial casualties in Tokyo were police officers and firefighters.

Safety during normal operations depends upon the initial response and how observant and vigilant officers are. If they go walking into calls as if nothing dangerous is going to happen, sooner or later that attitude will injure officers. Real effort should be spent educating patrol officers how to recognize one of these incidents when they see it. As officers respond to one of these unknown trouble calls, they need to be as observant as if they were responding to any hazardous materials spill.

INITIAL RESPONSE:

Let's consider a possible scenario:

Officers arrive at the local convention center. They are confronted with 20-30 people down. There are no normal signs of violence such as gunshot wounds or explosive debris. People are showing signs of being very seriously ill such as vomiting, cramps and nausea. Once officers recognize the signs as that of an unknown agent, they need to effect the proper approach, withdraw from the scene, and warn the other first responders.

The best response in this circumstance is to react to this incident as officers would respond to any kind of a hazardous materials spill. There is basically no difference between a release of a chemical weapon, for example, and an accidental hazardous materials release of a large quantity of a lethal industrial chemical. As simplistic as this sounds, it is a very appropriate analogy.

Sometimes officers' fear can be their worst enemy. Reaction to the mention of a terrorist chemical release would predictably be different from reaction to hearing of a nearby hazardous materials spill. Officers must overcome this fear reaction and conduct the same appropriate response.

Officers also need to overcome their natural reaction to rush in and try to help people. Training programs emphasize the importance of recognizing warning signals and placards in hazardous materials incidents and this problem is no different. Say that officers arrive on the scene of an overturned tanker truck leaking a chemical. The placard on the truck reads, "1092," and the driver is unconscious in the cab of the truck. In this circumstance officers have been trained to know they cannot rush up to the truck and try to pull the driver out. Officers have been trained to know they would be risking their own safety without proper protective gear, and potentially making themselves victims.

Law enforcement officers are trained to the level of First Responder Awareness in hazardous materials incidents. This is the same training needed in the response to a WMD incident.

In the scenario at the convention center, the procedure would be the same as the law enforcement first responder to the overturned truck: Resist the impulse to run in without the proper protective equipment, withdraw from the area, call for the appropriate hazardous materials response and establish a protective perimeter.

Once the first responding officers have withdrawn from the immediate scene and notified the other emergency responders that a potential WMD or hazmat situation exists, an effective outer perimeter should be set up.

The minimum safe distance for response to circumstances of this nature should be 1,000 feet. The guiding rule in these circumstances is that "more is always better." The scene should be approached utilizing the same principles as in any hazardous materials response: uphill -- upwind -- upstream. This principle should be followed for establishing routes into the area along with our staging area and command post.

It is impossible to overemphasize the potential for a secondary explosion in terrorist events. Recent occurrences have shown that first responders to a terrorist explosion were also targeted by secondary explosive devices. This is another factor that reinforces the importance of maintaining a 1,000-foot perimeter. Don't forget that this perimeter includes vertical distance for responding helicopters and other air assets.

In the case of a street explosion, we would practice the concept of "load and go," the same concept that the Fire Department has utilized for many years when faced with injured people in a car accident when the car is on fire. They don't spend valuable time stabilizing the injured person, taking blood pressure, and checking someone's pulse. They will immediately grab the injured parties and move them as quickly as possible to a safe distance where they can begin triage and medical treatment. This concept should be followed in terrorist actions. The triage point should be located outside the 1,000-foot perimeter and patients should be brought there.

In the WMD incident at the convention center, the decision for movement of the contaminated casualties will rest with the Fire Department Incident Commander. As discussed before, the Unified Command model dictates that the Fire Department would be the first Commander in the Unified Command due to the fire, rescue, medical and now hazardous materials problems.

If it is an accidental release or a weapon or a hazardous material spill, people need to be decontaminated before they can be moved out of the area and medically treated. The worst-case scenario is for a contaminated person to be transported by ambulance to the local trauma center. Depending on the nature of the contamination, the ambulance, its crew and the local trauma center might become contaminated, forcing all of them out of service.

People might have already left the scene to seek medical care before the police even got set up. This means the media should be asked to alert these people and have them identify themselves so they can be decontaminated before they show up at a doctor's office or hospital emergency room. Officers might actually have to retain people at the scene until they are decontaminated and medically cleared to leave or put up a perimeter around the trauma center to prevent contaminated people from entering until they are decontaminated.

The same procedures followed in responding to "regular" terrorist events will come into place at this point. Law enforcement's main function once the Fire Department turns over command, is to establish scene security, preserve evidence, identify witnesses and take their preliminary statements.

Law enforcement officers also need to consider their capability for performing the important functions during a WMD event: the first is to engage any possible suspects left inside of the "hot zone." This task usually falls to SWAT officers who have been trained to neutralize potential armed suspects and have sufficient firepower to handle whatever the terrorists may throw at them. This means that SWAT officers must be trained to operate inside protective suits that afford protection in this WMD - hazardous materials environment. This is no small task. The mobility of the officers is extremely restricted inside this equipment and there is a communication problem between officers involved in any emergency action. Extensive training can overcome these problems, but it has to be conducted long before the incident.

The second law enforcement function is perimeter security. It needs to be accomplished with an emphasis on protecting individual officers who are all on the outer perimeter where a WMD has been released. Due to potential wind shifts or larger-than-anticipated affected areas, the officers on these outer perimeter positions should have a protective outer suit. The current military charcoal chemical suits (available through the Department of Defense property release program) or other appropriate outer attire is a must. When combined with a highly efficient mask that can filter out the potential weapons (such as the military M-17 with the 18 P. A. filters), the outer perimeter officers should be well protected. Regardless of which job is being conducted, there is a significant fatigue factor that arises utilizing the suits. Officers should be well trained in both their use and how the suit affects them personally over a prolonged period of time.

Local governments should obtain this equipment and train police officers how to use it. Officers should not be asked to perform their duties without the proper protective equipment and sufficient training to ensure their survival in this most hazardous environment. Because equipment is extremely expensive, consideration should be given to cost sharing and having this equipment centrally warehoused and available to many jurisdictions who can share costs.

One of the biggest problems in responding to this kind of event will be the panic created by the information that a terrorist weapon has been released. There will be overwhelming media involvement that needs to be dealt with immediately to lessen the panic. A Public Information Officer (PIO) should be appointed as soon as possible notwithstanding a manpower shortage.

The media can be critical allies in lessening panic and stopping misinformation and confusion but, it only works that way if the right person is out front with the media so that they can be constantly updated and have their questions answered. Remember, because this will be a visual event the media will want to go where the action is. They will try to get as close as possible to the action. If the PIO is at the scene, there will be someone present who can work with the Incident Commander and stop a lot of confusion.

It is rare that an actual media relations officer will be on scene or available within the first hour of the event. Most agencies do not have the luxury of having a full-time on-call media officer, and usually one of the executive staff handles this role in addition to his or her normal duties. Training senior patrol officers, corporals and sergeants in crisis media relations is very important. Immediately, someone should be available to work with the media. If the media is not given information from government representatives they will find their own sources. The media will interview people who sometimes provide wildly different accounts of the incident and outright misinformation. Additionally, to fill live air time, the media will often speculate and theorize among themselves as to the nature of the incident and its potential hazards. Both of these problems, along with the unavailability of an "official person," can cause serious problems with the public and allow it to think that the government is not dealing effectively with the crisis.

For example, a press release could stress the small area and minimal number of people affected. Also, the fact that one person has been influenced by a weapon of this nature, it would be almost impossible to spread the weapon to other people. For example, if a person received a normal exposure to the chemical weapon Sarin, that person would not be able to contaminate other people. Facts like these would help to greatly lessen panic, but they won't get out if the local law enforcement agency doesn't have a cadre of trained people to deal with the media at the start of an event. (See Chapter 11, page 179.)

As time goes on, governments will undoubtedly encounter more and more threats of this nature. Each one should be approached on a case-by-case basis with the same consistent plan to minimize the fear associated with the term "Weapons of Mass Destruction," and to prevent it from ruling over our common sense and tactical response to the incident.

CASE STUDY:

The April 25, 1995, Unabomber Attack, Sacramento, Ca.

At about 2 p.m. on April 25, 1995, an explosion was reported in the 1300 block of I Street in the City of Sacramento, California. This location is less than one block from the central fire station located at 1230 I Street. Numerous citizen calls were received, including several reporting casualties and possible fatalities.

Since police and fire radio broadcasts are monitored, a large number of media representatives arrived. This was fueled by the proximity of this event to the Oklahoma City bombing which had occurred six days before. The first responding firefighters encountered a one-story brick building with smoke coming out of the west side main entry door.

The first-in fire company was commanded by Fire Captain Jim Greene. Captain Greene immediately organized a response based upon a possible criminal action / terrorist event. Upon entering the building, the firefighters discovered a minor fire in the lobby area of the California Timber Association headquarters. After using the minimum amount of water necessary, they put out the small fire and discovered the body of a man, later identified as Gilbert Murray, the Timber Association's president, who had been killed by a bomb blast while opening mail in the central lobby/reception area.

Realizing the serious potential for this crime scene, Captain Greene set about preserving the scene and completing his fire-related duties until it was safe to turn the scene over to local law enforcement.

The third-arriving police patrol car officer on the scene was Sgt. Don Strickland. Sgt. Strickland immediately recognized the possible criminal / terrorist action after speaking with Captain Greene. After insuring that the "Locate, Isolate and Evacuate" functions had been accomplished, he realized that no Mass Casualty Incident (MCI) was present. Sgt. Strickland then set about utilizing his checklist to call for resources.

No other personnel had been injured by the bomb blast. Several of Mr. Murray's coworkers were traumatized by the event, as they had been in various nearby offices at the time of the explosion. Sgt. Strickland included a call-out from his checklist for a chaplain to help these victims /witnesses.

The author was in the fifth police car to arrive at the scene, and upon my arrival, I assumed the role of Incident Commander for law enforcement. Captain Greene explained that he had taken all of the potential witnesses out of the building and had them located in a specific area of a nearby parking lot. He had also isolated all of his fire personnel who had been inside the building, explaining that he knew law enforcement would need their boots and clothing for possible evidentiary value.

Captain Greene explained that he had secured the rear door to the building from the inside, and had placed two of his firefighters on the front door for security. They had been given explicit instructions not to permit anyone into the structure not authorized by Captain Green.

Captain Greene further explained that he needed more time to check on the structure following which he could turn over Incident Command to local law enforcement.

Utilizing his checklist, Sgt. Strickland continued to call for various resources. He also placed officers in critical inner and outer perimeters to prevent personnel from trespassing into the crime-scene area and interfering with the firefighters. While this was in progress, the author immediately began calling for more officers and established an Incident Command System on scene.

Approximately 20 members of the local media had arrived almost immediately following the announcements of a bombing. A PIO function was set up to handle the press by calling out our department PIO, Mr. Michael Heenan. While Incident Command was still with the Fire Department, all media inquiries were handled by the Fire Department PIO, Battalion Chief Jan Dunbar. After the arrival of the police PIO, the two worked together handling the large number of media inquiries. When Incident Command was transferred from fire to police, the PIO lead also changed to police.

The author appointed Sgt. Strickland as the Operations OIC, and had him continue setting up the perimeter teams to keep the large number of spectators out of the area. A criminal investigation team was established, utilizing the Captain who was the detective commander at the time. At this point it was not known whether or not the Unabomber perpetrated this attack. Several FBI agents from the local FBI office had arrived on scene and the possibility of a Unabomber attack was discussed.

The initial plan was to call for the Unabomber-task-force experts in the FBI's San Francisco office, and have them enter the facility with the Sacramento police bomb squad. They would determine whether or not there was sufficient evidence inside to label this an act of domestic terrorism by the Unabomber. Their analysis of the scene would determine whether it was to remain a local homicide investigation handled by the Sacramento PD or, whether the FBI would assume command based on PDD-39.

A large contingent of law enforcement agencies responded to the scene: Postal Inspectors, including the area Postmaster, Alcohol Tobacco and Firearms agents, State Fire Marshals, Arson Investigators, State Department of Justice Special Agents, Combined Bomb Squad members from the California Highway Patrol, Sacramento Sheriff's Department, Davis Police Department, and several other agencies. All of these agencies had a legitimate interest in this explosion and its possible link to the Unabomber series.

We had to maintain two distinct restricted areas within the inner perimeter one for all of these allied law enforcement officers responding to the scene, and the other inner perimeter for the media.

The media acted admirably. There were no incidents of improper conduct, even though we had numerous media arrive from outside the local area. At the height of the story, we had over 50 media representatives at the scene with at least another 50 scattered at various locations, such as Gilbert Murray's house.

The media's excellent behavior and cooperation was undoubtedly due to the policy of keeping them apprised of all of our actions with frequent briefings, and allowing them access to a specific "media only" area within the inner perimeter. We defined a walking path through the inner perimeter ending in a large circular area using cones and crime scene tape. A police officer was posted at the entrance to this "press bubble" to check press credentials before allowing access.

They were able to film all of the action from this location without interfering in the operation or compromising the crime scene. We told them that, if anyone was caught out of the "media only" area, we would close it down and move them to the outer perimeter. They understood the significance of this and took the responsibility of policing themselves. Overall, the media behaved admirably.

The problem with the allied law enforcement responders was that they all wanted access to the building prior to determination of whose case it was. We controlled this group with a second restricted area "For Law Enforcement Only" in the parking lot across from the main entrance to the building. Once this area was established, we were able to keep them out of the building itself and control the crime scene properly to preserve evidence. In order to allow all of these agencies crime-scene access, we agreed on a videotape plan.

We had one Sacramento Police homicide detective and a cameraman from our Media Services unit enter the building. They filmed the entire scene with the detective doing a narration. We then set up a television and video tape recorder in a nearby conference room for all of the investigators to observe the crime scene without actually entering it.

Approximately 30 minutes after the author's arrival, Captain Greene reported that the fire department was now ready to relinquish Incident Command to local law enforcement. Captain Green and the author made simultaneous broadcasts on our respective radio channels, telling all fire and police units that Incident Command had been transferred from the Fire Department to the Police Department and where the new emergency operations center (EOC), was to be located.

The FBI Task-Force experts arrived from San Francisco during the second hour of the event and, together with local bomb squad experts, entered the building. Shortly thereafter, they identified a trademark item of the Unabomber. The joint decision was then made that the FBI would assume Incident Command, with local police and fire in support in a unified command structure.

Up to this point, we had been giving press briefings through the PIOs every 15 minutes. These briefings continued for approximately three hours. We then informed the press that we would be scaling back the meetings to every half-hour due to a lack of new information. Approximately four hours into the incident we went to hourly briefings, and shortly thereafter we went to briefings only when significant events occurred.

We held a press conference when the FBI's Special Agent in Charge of the Sacramento office announced he was assuming Incident Command and confirmed that this was definitely a Unabomber attack. We also held a press conference when Police Chaplain Mindy Russell made a statement on behalf of Gilbert Murray's family. She was asked by the family to make a statement regarding their feelings over the death of their father/husband, and to ask the press to respect their privacy.

Once we confirmed that this was a terrorist incident, we began to work towards changeover of Incident Command to the FBI. Supervising Special Agent Don Pierce had now arrived on scene and was working with me in the Emergency Operations Center. We had worked on several past projects together and had developed a solid working relationship based on the same concepts we discussed earlier in the Team Building section.

Having discussed in advance the parameters under which who would be the Incident Commander, time was saved when it came to hand off command responsibility. Joint announcements on all radio channels advised all responders that command was being transferred to the FBI. This was then followed up by a press conference.

Even though command now fell to the FBI, both local law enforcement and the local Fire Department remained on the scene and continued to work in a unified command structure to provide support for the FBI. We provided logistical support along with personnel to perform such tasks as traffic control and crime scene security. Approximately 10 hours after the initial call, I left the scene leaving a detachment of police officers to work with Supervisory Special Agent Don Pierce and his combined team of FBI, ATF, and Postal Inspectors. This effort lasted for eight days while the crime scene was processed.

In reviewing my own performance in this case, I feel I did make a significant mistake in not checking for a possible secondary device. I made an assumption, almost from the start, that this event was linked to the Unabomber. All of the bombings in this series were single-device events and I did not take any precautions in case of a secondary device. In view of the recent secondary-device lessons, I should have evacuated the recommended 1,000 feet area and cleared the area with both bomb technicians and trained bomb dogs before allowing the investigation to proceed.

This incident is a good example of the kind of cooperative effort between the three key agencies of police, fire, and the FBI. Our various departments had had many conversations and participated together in training drills geared for this type of event. Most of the players had developed that critical personal relationship from working together on past training projects and real incidents.

The capital of the State of California is an inviting target for several reasons, and we realized we might have an incident similar to this. Even though this incident was relatively small in size, the cooperative efforts and smooth transition on the part of all the players was due to this prior association and planning.

All of the supervisors on the scene had received training in handling this kind of a terrorist incident, and we had participated in similar drills. We were all aware of each other's specific needs, and we were able to work successfully in a unified command so that all of our goals were met and the incident was handled in a professional matter.

I firmly believe that this kind of effort and success is a tribute to prior planning and training. Successful outcomes don't just happen as a matter of luck, they are the direct result of solid hard work, and a desire to see a terrorist incident well handled by all of the three key players.

<u>**Unabomber Crime Scene, 1315 I street, Sacramento, Ca.**</u>

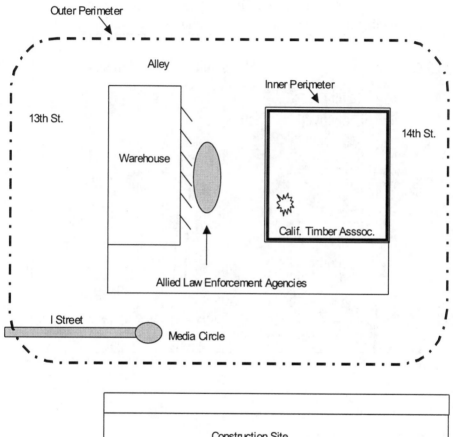

Outer Perimeter

Alley

Inner Perimeter

13th St.

14th St.

Warehouse

Calif. Timber Asssoc.

Allied Law Enforcement Agencies

I Street

Media Circle

Construction Site

OVERALL RESPONSE - SCENE DIAGRAM
Simulated explosive event in an urban area.

NOTE: This diagram details all of the locations and positioning of the major components of a Terrorist Incident response. The distances are approximate. Always take into consideration the

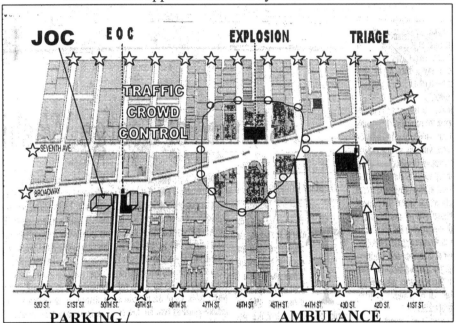

SUMMARY AND CONCLUSIONS

Remember: the goal of a terrorist may not be to kill a large number of people. The goal of the terrorist is to effect some type of change through the use of fear. The only thing that will conquer the fear brought about by acts of terrorism is the swift and efficient response of government.

Local law enforcement officers are not likely to ever get the chance to prevent an act of terrorism. The job of counterterrorism and penetrating these groups to stop their actions falls to the FBI.

However, there is always the potential of an unknown group or individual perpetrating one of these acts. These crimes are going to continue and, unfortunately, they are going to remain with us for a very long time. It will fall to the local law enforcement agency, the local fire department and the local office of the FBI to handle the initial response to these acts. The actions of these first responders will set the tone for the entire event.

The first responders will be responsible for the swift treatment of the injured, the preservation of the crime scene, and the ultimate arrest and prosecution of those responsible. Our goal must be to fulfill the citizens' need to see a coordinated and efficient response to justify the trust they have placed in government, and to stop the fear brought about by these acts. Using the program set forth in this chapter will get us to this goal.

EDITOR'S NOTE:

Law enforcement officers should be alert for possible links between routine police activities and terrorism. A routine traffic stop was the key to solving the Oklahoma City bombing incident, and the December 1999 border checks of terrorist suspects entering the United States from Canada was the key in aborting a New Year's terrorist attack. Also, terrorists often engage in other crimes such as robberies and drug trafficking to finance their activities.

Chapter 11

Media/Public Information and Terrorism
By Haven P. Simmons, M.A., Ph.D.

INTRODUCTION

The frequency and scope of recent terrorist attacks has magnified the need for rapid and responsible dissemination of public information. Terrorism is unique to emergency response because of its blatant criminal intent. Unlike natural disasters and some hazardous materials incidents, for example, the media and public follow criminal investigations.

Terrorism also creates a profound element of surprise and horror for the public and private sectors, victims and communities. These factors present daunting challenges to emergency response agencies, government officials, companies and spokespersons.

Opinion surveys consistently show a high degree of public skepticism and disdain toward the media. The relationship of media and government has frequently been adversarial, while some companies face increasing media scrutiny.

Unfortunately, suspicion and negativity can hamper response. It is easy to be defensive, forgetting that the media are the most pervasive and comprehensive vehicle for disseminating vital public information.

Needless to say, government agencies and companies invariably perform better under duress when they set a year-round precedent of positive, proactive rapport with the media. Protecting their domain and being accountable to the public is the toughest task confronting government and businesses when terrorism occurs.

PROFILING THE MEDIA

Television is widely considered the most influential news medium. Television markets range from small towns in North Dakota to New York City. ABC, NBC and CBS comprise the traditional television networks, but cable stations such as CNN and MSNBC are competing with them for viewers.

The most positive aspect of television is its ability to convey public information instantly through words and video. Television satellites transmit images around the world in a real-time basis.

A negative slant is the deluge of news trucks and camera crews at emergency scenes. Their mere presence can create turmoil, and video cameras have been known to compromise response or security with live depictions on television.

Emergency Alerting System (EAS) enables broadcasters, including cable television, to digitally convey the latest emergency information at the behest of the Emergency Operations Center (EOC) or the National Weather Service. Community and government access channels are also helpful public information sources.

Radio is a highly mobile medium, virtually monopolizing news for motorists around the nation. The amount of local radio news coverage, however, has actually declined in recent years.

Radio reporters require unobtrusive equipment and generally desire less information than their television contemporaries. Like television, radio's immediacy is critical to public information.

Newspapers usually seek more detail than electronic media. On this basis, they are most likely to annoy officials with an onslaught of questions. While lacking immediacy, the volume of public information in the oldest medium can be very useful to readers.

Newspapers also devote more time and resources to investigative reporting. Large newspapers such as *The Washington Post, New York Times* and *Chicago Tribune* assign reporters to major stories in the remotest parts of the country.

Magazines typically cover only the nation's largest government agencies and companies on a daily basis. During major incidents, they pursue in-depth coverage and extensive photos for weekly publication.

Like newspapers, they have a penchant for detail. *US News & World Report, Time* and *Newsweek* are generally considered the most credible news magazines.

On-line media present new challenges to government agencies and businesses. Their proliferation runs the gamut from the mainstream to the obscure.

Breaking stories sometimes appear initially on media web sites and requests for information are made via e-mail. Chat rooms, meanwhile, provide forums for public conjecture about the most publicized emergencies.

Tabloid media are typically of little consequence to businesses or government, preferring gossip about celebrities. A major incident, though, can attract every tabloid from *The National Enquirer* to Geraldo.

Tabloid media are especially willing to undermine investigations or humiliate officials. The television tabloids interview "experts" who consistently refute or question policies.

International media are converging more often on major incidents in the United States due to satellite and on-line capabilities. Organizations have actually employed translators to address questions in foreign languages. Their deadlines are diverse because they report to audiences in different time zones.

BUILDING POSITIVE MEDIA RELATIONS

It is incumbent upon government agencies and businesses to punctually release information mandated by public records laws, which vary among states and jurisdictions. They should be intimately familiar with the laws.

Government and businesses should be proactive, meaning the constant cultivation of contacts with reporters and editors in the media. This entails sharing positive and negative information in a forthright manner, while occasionally allowing media coverage of training regimens and innovations.

Spokespersons, known as Public Information Officers (PIOs) in the public realm and public relations specialists in the private realm, are vital to establishing a positive relationship with the media, which can only enhance the public image of the organization and the dissemination of information.

Spokespersons have become more prominent in recent years due to demands of media and citizens for public information and accountability. They typically handle media relations, public speaking, writing, editing, research, special events and website maintenance.

The role of spokespersons, many of whom have media backgrounds, should be fully defined and applied. They should not be compromised by administrative in-fighting, and must have direct access to top officials in government agencies and businesses.

Numerous spokespersons have learned the hard way that "No comment" and "I don't know" are ill-advised responses to media inquiries. They imply secrecy and ignorance, respectively. A genuine attempt should be made to track requested information, even if it is difficult to meet their deadlines.

All employees should receive media relations training, which normally precludes them from talking to reporters without the permission of spokespersons and/or superiors.

Savvy government agencies and businesses educate the public, their employees and other groups such as shareholders and consumers on the latest terrorism trends and safety tips via PSAs (Public Service Announcements), videos, brochures, newsletters, web sites and articles peddled to the media for publication.

In addition, government and corporate spokespersons should practice terrorism scenarios in concert with top officials, familiarizing themselves with one another and their resources.

MEDIA SYMBOLISM AND TERRORISTS

Terrorists understand that their actions are validated and magnified by media attention. Imagine the global impact of the terrorists at the 1972 Winter Olympics in Munich if they had been covered by today's astounding array of media. As it was, they terrorized a monumental event on an international stage by taking hostages and killing athletes.

In 1996, suspect Eric Rudolph apparently disrupted a much larger media venue when he allegedly detonated a bomb that killed one person and injured more than a hundred at the Summer Olympics in Atlanta.

Likewise, anarchists reached a global audience in 1999 at the annual World Trade Organization Convention in Seattle, with protesters challenging the police and hooligans brazenly looting stores, all of which was sent on live television.

A recent study shows that the Lincoln Memorial and Vietnam Memorial in Washington, D.C., are especially vulnerable to terrorists. The media have publicized ways the Federal Government intends to safeguard the symbolic memorials.

"Cyberterrorists" have launched attacks against corporations and on-line retailers. Yesterday's demonstrations, destruction of property and hostage crises could be today's seizure of financial records, blackmail and extortion on computer.

Government and media are likely vulnerable to on-line terrorists, too, setting up a potential public information nightmare that only cooperation and the most sophisticated computer technology can avert. It is disturbing to fathom the sheer horror of a terrorist attack that disables both government and media communications systems in the US.

Allegations rage that recent school shootings are really "copycat" crimes, committed by impressionable teenagers desiring fame and notoriety brought by television cameras. Indeed, school shootings are now at the forefront of the media and public conscience.

John Hinckley, Jr., was supposedly trying to impress movie star Jodie Foster when he attempted to kill President Reagan. The drifter probably realized she would be forced to acknowledge his existence through media coverage of the attack.

While some officials may lament the supposed media role in fomenting terrorism to build ratings, they should also understand the importance of news values such as prominence, impact and proximity to public information.

CONTROLLING THE MEDIA ONSLAUGHT

Chaos can evolve when the media disrupt the response, portray deployment of law enforcement officers, release conflicting information and fan premature, potentially damaging public conjecture about the incident. The situation worsens when organizations are paralyzed by indecision, bureaucratic haggling, information overload and inferior communications technology.

The media are driven by deadlines and competition. The media are resourceful and there is no way to stop them completely from preceding emergency personnel to the scene or renting apartments for better video angles, as they did following the bombing in Oklahoma City. Likewise, reporters on cell phones talked to students inside Columbine High School near Littleton, Colorado, and live cameras showed converging members of the SWAT team while the suspects were still at large. In the mid-90's, soldiers were caught live on camera as they approached a hostage crisis at the Japanese Embassy in Lima, Peru.

Even so, a recent hostage situation in Baltimore revealed media willingness to cooperate with the authorities by not violating the response perimeter and refusing to air a phone conversation between the suspect, who had killed four people, and a local television reporter.

There were no live portrayals of the SWAT team storming the apartment to locate the suspect. The media apparently agreed to temper their coverage because of the risk to the hostages. This arrangement was reportedly founded on trust developed between the media and police over the years.

The amount of media interest in the terrorist attack could surpass anything officials are even vaguely prepared for. The veracity of public information usually correlates directly with their comfort level and confidence in officials.

The key to maintaining some semblance of control over the media is to cordon off the area quickly and establish a media center. The center should contain adequate parking, sanitary facilities, cots, furniture, phone/computer hookups and, if possible, soft drinks and sandwiches.

The swarm of local, state and federal emergency response agencies requires outstanding teamwork. A Joint Information Center (JIC) should be convened, allowing officials and spokespersons to coordinate, formulate and disseminate information smoothly. Ideally, the JIC should be located at least three blocks from the media center. A JIC located separately from the EOC also requires accommodations similar to those at the media center.

Failure of affected government and corporate leaders to apprise each other and spokespersons of decisions and strategies invites the release of erroneous, destructive information. There must also be thorough understanding of jurisdictional responsibilities and statutes governing the response. Within minutes, law enforcement, fire, hospital and school officials were scurrying for information and trying to coordinate the response at Columbine High School.

"Feed the beast" is a useful adage regarding the media. Press conferences must be held regularly at the media center, or meddling reporters will seek information from other agencies, victims, witnesses and neighbors. These intervals are normally every three to six hours.

Spokespersons typically organize the press conferences and should be prepared to address the media when top officials and field commanders are occupied with the response. Spokespersons, however, should remember the importance of making their top officials accountable to the public.

Essential public information, such as casualties, hospital admissions, health precautions, closures, shelters and evacuations, or special phone numbers for citizen inquiries usually takes precedence in early press conferences and press releases, which are transmitted punctually in person, via computer or fax machine.

In the event of poisoning or contamination, it is generally better to tempt mass hysteria with public warnings about potential health risks than assuming blame for additional fatalities by remaining silent.

Spokespersons can also anticipate repeated media questions about investigative information pertaining to suspects, arrests, tactics and motive when terrorist attacks occur. In a sense, it is their job to "buy time" for investigators, keeping them out of the media glare.

Finally, conveying concern and compassion for the victims throughout the response frequently diffuses the more cynical media, some of whom perceive aloof, defensive behavior as a challenge.

UNDERSTANDING THE MEDIA SCRIPT

Reporters and editors frequently develop their own theories about the circumstances of a terrorist attack and who is responsible. These perceptions are based on past scenarios, personal leanings and observations, not to mention rumor and innuendo. They sometimes impose immense pressure on authorities to confirm their suspicions by completing the script.

Media questions regarding airplane crashes usually concern pilot error, weather, shoddy maintenance, faulty equipment, the elusive black box and, of course, terrorism.

The traditional stereotype of the Arab terrorist apparently applied in 1988 when a Pan American Boeing 747 exploded over Lockerbie, Scotland, killing everyone on board. (Two Libyans were prosecuted in connection with the crash and one of them was convicted.)

Early speculation focused on Arabs in the Oklahoma City bombing which, of course, was perpetrated by domestic terrorists. The media also speculated about Arab involvement in the TWA Flight 800 crash of 1996, but it was never substantiated. A similar specter hovered over the Alaska Airlines crash nearly four years later.

Officials should not be pressured prematurely into speculation according to the script. Nor should they allow the media to hasten the wrongful arrest of a suspect, as was purportedly the case with William Jewell in the bombing at the 1996 Summer Olympics in Atlanta.

One of the latest publicized trends in terrorism, heavily-armed militias in remote areas of the US, also tempts the media and authorities to co-author the script. The connection between Timothy McVeigh of the Oklahoma City bombing and a domestic militia in Arkansas, however, turned out to be much looser than initially suspected.

Intense coverage of white supremacist or "hate groups" such as World Church of the Creator probably ignited supposition that the Columbine shooters targeted minorities, even though many of the victims were white.

Perhaps most baffling to the media and authorities are terrorists like notorious "Unabomber" Ted Kaczynski, who make the script even more difficult to follow by purportedly acting alone.

ENDURING MEDIA SCRUTINY

The siege mentality is synonymous with persistence, something most media have a reputation for. Government and corporate officials should be ready for intense coverage long after the terrorist attack occurs. It is normally in the aftermath of terrorist attacks that the media ask difficult and probing questions: Could more lives have been saved? What is being done to ensure security in the future? Spokespersons and top officials will be interviewed for weeks, if not months, following the event.

The media often keep the attack in the public mind with the intense type of anniversary coverage that was devoted to the Oklahoma City and Columbine tragedies. In some instances, bereaved families and friends of victims solicit aggressive media scrutiny of the response.

Diligent government agencies and organizations schedule weekly meetings to discuss relevant policies, public education strategies and persistent media interest. They remain accountable by holding press conferences to update and reassure the public.

Media presence changes the complexion of communities like Andrews, North Carolina, where reporters hunkered down for nearly two years as Federal agents traversed the mountains for bombing suspect Eric Rudolph. They constantly asked local residents what they knew about the suspect, and he attained celebrity status in some circles with "Hide-and-Seek Champion" T-shirts and other memorabilia.

Although no arrest had been made when the search was scaled back, the media widely publicized Rudolph's background, description and possible whereabouts, which may have led to his apprehension.

CONCLUSION

The potential impact of terrorism on human life and America's infrastructure poses the ultimate challenge to government agencies and businesses: protecting their domain and guarding against premature release of investigative information to the media while being accountable to the public.

The challenge is met by employing consistent, comprehensive media relations and public information polices before, during and after terrorist attacks. After all, the performance of government and business officials is largely measured by public perceptions of media coverage, their primary source of information.

EDITOR'S NOTE:

You may have serious clashes with the media in terrorist situations. It is always a challenge to balance the public's right to know against the government's right to withhold information for public safety. As part of your advance planning, you should discuss this dilemma with the media in your area.

Some years ago, Ted Koppel moderated a discussion on the relationship between the American media and international terrorism.

Koppel said to his media guests that finding one of the most wanted men in the world who had promised to murder President George Bush may have been a major journalistic coup, "but when a television network agrees to keep [that terrorist's] whereabouts secret, is that journalism or aiding terrorism?"

Tom Brokaw replied that he thought it was journalism. He said NBC decided to keep secret Mohammed Abu Abbas' whereabouts "because we thought the news value outweighed" bringing him to justice. Brokaw said that Abu Abbas had admitted his role in hijacking the Achille Lauro ocean liner but had "made some very serious charges against the American people and the American president in the wake of the Libyan bombing."

Some years ago a man took over the IBM facility in Montgomery County, Maryland, which resulted in three deaths and injuries to more than 20 people. A news reporter telephoned into the IBM building, talked to the murderer, and injected herself into the negotiating process with the perpetrator. She made comments, which were very inflammatory, putting the hostages in great danger, both because of the manner in which she intruded and the comments she made.

That same year there was an incident at the Lake Braddock area in Northern Virginia in which hostages were held for over 12 hours. A radio station broadcast sensitive information about the hostage taker who was listening to the broadcast! He became very agitated and the hostages were clearly endangered by the radio station's actions. In both the IBM and the Lake Braddock incidents the media alerted the hostage taker to positions and movements of police personnel.

In the Atlanta prison riots, a SWAT team in full body armor and carrying automatic weapons was walking into the administrative building for a routine shift change. A local TV reporter spotted them. Without checking with anyone, she went on the air live, speculating that a government assault against the prisoners appeared imminent.

The prisoners, who were watching the TV broadcast, became extremely agitated. They threatened to kill the hostages if there was a rescue attempt. They screamed, "There will be rivers of blood! Heads will roll!" The prisoners assembled a group of hostages, poured inflammable liquid on the floor and set the open cans nearby. They held cigarette lighters over the liquid and said they were ready to incinerate the hostages. The FBI negotiators painstakingly explained that the TV report was in error.

Fortunately, they were able to defuse the situation. Clearly, the irresponsibility of the TV reporter put the lives of the hostages in jeopardy.

At Waco, when the ATF planned to raid the Davidians' compound, they made the mistake of notifying the media. The media, in turn, notified the Davidians. After a 45-minute exchange of gunfire, four ATF agents were dead and 15 were injured.

Another example of media irresponsibility occurred in St. Petersburg, Florida. Hostage negotiators, police and SWAT team members surrounded a gas station where a gunman was holed up with a hostage after killing three police officers. Suddenly, the telephone inside the gas station rang. A news reporter from Radio Station WFLA was calling to interview the murderer. At the same time police hostage negotiators were trying to get through to him. (A reporter from the St. Petersburg Times also called and interviewed him.) During the interview the subject said, "I can't see giving myself up to fry in an electric chair. If anything, I'll shoot myself." After a four-hour standoff, he released his hostage and shot himself to death.

Chapter 12

Trends in Terrorism*
By Ambassador Michael Sheehan, B.A., M.A. (2)

I want to [give]...a detailed description of a significant trend in international terrorism -- namely, the geographical shift of the locus of terror from the Middle East to South Asia. In our annual report to Congress, "Patterns of Global Terrorism 1999" (see appendices), we described this shift in some detail. In fact, this was one of the two trends we identified as the most important recent developments in terrorism, the other being the shift from well-organized, localized groups supported by state sponsors to loosely organized, international networks of terrorists.

Excerpted from testimony before the U.S. House of Representatives International Relations Committee, July 12, 2000. Mr. Sheehan is the US Coordinator for Counterterrorism.

The increased willingness and ability of terrorists to seek refuge in South Asia are disturbing developments, and they require us to re-focus our diplomatic energies and policy tools as well.

Why South Asia?

Let me begin by outlining why South Asia has become a new locus for terrorism. Understanding the causal factors at play is a fundamental step in developing an effective counterterrorism policy for the region.

REGIONAL INSTABILITY

To examine the role of regional instability in fostering terrorism, we can start with the Soviet invasion of Afghanistan and the decade-long civil war which followed. This war destroyed the government and civil society of Afghanistan, at the same time bringing arms, fighters from around the world, and narcotics traffickers to the region. The Soviet withdrawal left a power vacuum, leaving the country in the hands of warring groups of mujahidin as well as outsiders seeking to further their own interests. Many of the current leaders of Afghanistan came of age in training camps designed to create a generation of combatants to fight wars inside and outside Afghanistan. These camps in turn fostered relationships with Afghan Arabs and others fighting wars or involved with terrorism in the Middle East and elsewhere. Eventually, the Taliban, a radical group with a world-view informed by the experience of war, gained power over much of the country.

Fierce conflicts still flare up in South Asia. The Taliban continues to fight the Northern Alliance, and the border conflict over Kashmir causes instability and bloodshed. South Asia also finds itself serving as a support area for conflicts further afield, such as those in the Caucasus and in the Middle East. The proximity of terrorists to such sources of regional instability is a mutually reinforcing relationship. Terrorists can contribute to such instability by lending a hand to other terrorist groups intent on destroying peace processes. Conversely, instability draws more weapons into the region, increasing the chances that terrorists will get their hands on them. In addition, governments otherwise occupied with wars are less likely to root out terrorists operating within their borders.

IMPROVEMENTS IN THE MIDDLE EAST

Another factor in the shift of the locus of terrorism to South Asia is the progress we have made in reducing terrorism in the Middle East. In the Middle East, by designating state sponsors of terrorism, by criminalizing support to groups designated as Foreign Terrorist Organizations (FTOs), and through intense bilateral discussions with various states, we have stimulated other countries to confront terrorism within and across their borders. And even though terrorism remains a threat in the region, our efforts have brought results. Many Middle Eastern governments -- with some notable exceptions -- have strengthened their counterterrorist policy and improved international cooperation.

Jordan and Egypt are examples of Middle Eastern countries that took positive steps last year. Jordan remained particularly intolerant of terrorism on its soil, arresting extremists reportedly planning attacks against US interests, closing HAMAS offices and arresting some of its members, and responding vigorously to a variety of other terrorist threats. Egypt continued carrying out counterterrorism measures in 1999 by arresting, trying, and convicting a number of terrorists threatening its own interests and those of the US and our allies. Also in the Middle East, the Palestinian Authority mounted counterterrorist operations last year designed to undermine the capabilities of HAMAS and the Palestinian Islamic Jihad to use terrorism to disrupt the peace process.

We cannot take credit for all improvements in the counterterrorism sphere in the Middle East, but our diplomacy played a major role. Make no mistake, I do not mean to suggest we can let down our guard in the Middle East. Recent threats in Jordan both during the millennium and a few weeks ago demonstrate that continued vigilance is warranted. Of course, Iran remains an active state sponsor, and Syria, Libya, and Iraq remain on our list because they provide safe haven and material support to terrorist groups. But their direct sponsorship of terrorist acts has diminished. Unfortunately, as we work to neutralize terrorism in the Middle East, terrorists and their organizations seek safe haven in other areas where they can operate with impunity. South Asia is one of them.

IDEOLOGICAL EXTREMISM

There is, unfortunately, a misperception among some people that terrorism is driven by belief in Islam. In fact, terrorism is a perversion of the teachings of Islam. That being said, another factor contributing to the shift of the locus of terrorism to South Asia is the intersection of regional instability and weak political and economic systems with ideological and militant extremism. For instance, the Taliban practices an austere, extreme brand of Islam. While this is not threatening in and of itself, the Taliban has proven sympathetic to other radical groups, some of which distort religious ideas and principles to justify terrorist acts.

In addition, Pakistan's political and economic difficulties and the resultant damage to Pakistan's institutions have provided fertile ground for terrorism. One of the great failures has been in education. Pakistan's government-sponsored educational system has been unable to meet the needs of Pakistan's people. As a result, many poor Pakistanis are drawn to free education provided by madrassas, or religious schools. Many of these schools perform a needed service in imparting such education. Some schools, however, inculcate extremism and a violent anti-Americanism in their students. In these schools, a rigid condemnation of Western culture, coupled with the local conditions of failing societies, produces young men inclined to support the same causes championed by Osama bin Laden and other terrorists. The Government of Pakistan is aware of this problem and has stated that it intends to ensure that madrassas provide a proper education for their students.

FINANCING TERRORISM

When discussing the various causes of increased terrorist activity in South Asia, we must address the ability of terrorists to raise funds to support their activities. One of the most important ways to combat terrorism is to disrupt the financing of terrorist groups and activities.

We have already made this a priority and are working hard -- with unilateral and multilateral sanctions, bilateral diplomacy, and through the UN and G-8 -- to disrupt the financing of terrorism in South Asia. One notable success was the adoption by the UN General Assembly in December 1999 of the G-8-initiated International Convention for the Suppression of the Financing of Terrorism. Full implementation of this important new counterterrorism treaty by the largest number of governments is essential.

But we must keep up the pressure. The ability of terrorists operating in Afghanistan, for example, to obtain funds and other material support is a symptom of the other primary trend in terrorism.

This shift has profound implications for our policies in South Asia. The capabilities of Osama bin Laden's al-Qa'ida network, which has centered itself within Afghanistan, demonstrate why this is the case. Bin Laden's organization operates on its own, without having to depend on a state sponsor for material support. He has financial resources and means of raising funds, often through narcotrafficking or the use of legitimate "front" companies. He enjoys international financial support. Bin Laden and other non-state terrorists also benefit from the globalization of communication, using e-mail and Internet web sites to spread their message, recruit new members, and raise funds.

These capabilities allow bin Laden and other terrorists to extend their tentacles around the world. Terrorist networks outside the context of the international state system provide everything that is needed for groups such as the Egyptian Islamic Jihad (EIJ) to survive and become stronger, even when they are based in friendly states with vigorous counterterrorism policies. The threat posed by this group, a faction of which is closely allied to bin Laden, illustrates the challenges we face as non-state terrorism becomes more prevalent.

THE ROLE OF THE TALIBAN

The ability of groups such as al-Qa'ida to plan and carry out terrorist attacks with impunity brings us to the final causal factor in the shift of terrorism to South Asia: the Taliban's refusal to crack down on terrorists. Afghanistan has become the primary swamp of terrorism, harboring terrorists from the region and around the world. The Taliban, which controls most Afghan territory, provides safe haven for Osama bin Laden and his network. Because of the room which the Taliban gives him to operate, bin Laden has created a truly transnational terrorist enterprise, drawing on recruits from across Asia, Africa, and Europe, as well as the Middle East. The Taliban has also given logistic support to members of other terrorist organizations, such as the Egyptian Islamic Jihad, the Algerian Armed Islamic group, Kashmiri separatists, and a number of militant organizations from Central Asia, including terrorists from Uzbekistan and Tajikistan.

Chapter 13

History and Anatomy of Terrorism
By Peter H. B. Lejeune

Terrorism is not new having been used for centuries by individuals, groups and even states to alter the course of events through coercion and fear. Sometimes terrorism has been used by the weaker party to fight the stronger, sometimes it has been used to get a message from a single event to a global audience. It is almost always used to produce an effect disproportionate to the investment in the act, for terrorism traditionally has been intended to influence groups, rather than simply to inflict damage. As Brian Jenkins put it, "Terrorists want a lot of witnesses, not a lot of dead."[1]

Over time the practice of terrorism has evolved to optimize opportunities and react to pressures.

There have been organizational changes, an evolution in the number of casualties that may be inflicted, and now the looming specter of the possible use of Weapons of Mass Destruction (WMD) better defined as Chemical, Biological, Radiological and Nuclear (CBRN) weapons. In reaction to these changes in international terrorism, the United States has done a great deal to increase public awareness of the subject, and has introduced laws to broaden the scope of arrest powers with regard to terrorism.

TERRORISM DEFINED

In attempting to define the terrorist, we must take care not to fall into the trap of choosing a demonized image from an "evil empire." One man's terrorist may be another's hero for the application of the label "terrorist" depends upon one's point of view. George Washington and Menachem Begin were both terrorists to the British, and are now celebrated by their respective countries. This holds true whether the conflict is between states or ideologies for over the centuries many have rallied behind their religious leaders to fight the satanic opposition. Because the spectrum from liberator and freedom fighter to terrorist is so broad, and often subjective, we need to bring focus by means of a definition.

In the United States the FBI's definition of terrorism is "The unlawful use of force or violence against persons or property to intimidate or coerce a Government, the civilian population, or any segment thereof, in furtherance of political or social objectives." This definition dispels the belief that terrorists are "foreigners." Timothy McVeigh brought that fact home when he bombed the Alfred P. Murrah Federal Building in Oklahoma City. To be prepared to combat terrorists one must make an effort to understand what drives them, and how and where and if they will strike. To simply look at vulnerabilities as so many others have done is imprudent, leads to an unbalanced response, and can waste resources in addition to raising unwarranted fears. A more complete analysis requires thought regarding certain aspects of the threat.

"Who" are the terrorists? What drives them to be terrorists, and plan and execute attacks and what will the future hold? Being prepared is the best defense, and in a world of finite resources, it is essential that effort be expended where it is required.

Terrorism is as old as conflict itself. To quote the former Chairman of the Joint Chiefs of Staff, General Shalikashvili: "This isn't a new problem, it is simply an old problem getting worse. Those out to do us harm are no longer political zealots with a few sticks of dynamite. These are determined operatives, with access to very sophisticated information and technology. Unable to confront or compete with the United States militarily, they try to achieve their policy objectives by exploiting small groups to do the dirty work for them."

EARLY TERRORISTS

There is no first claimant to the term of terrorist, but a good example of an early terrorist approach would be the Zealots who were a Jewish religious-political faction, known for its fanatical resistance to Roman rule in Judea during the 1st century A.D. As with many terrorist organizations, the roots were political. They emerged as a distinct political group during the reign of Herod the Great (37-4 B.C.). In A.D. 6, when Judea was put under direct Roman rule and the authorities ordered a census for purposes of taxation, the Zealots, led by Judas of Galilee, called for rebellion in response. Acknowledging the authority of the pagan Roman emperor, they argued, would mean repudiating the authority of God and submitting to slavery.

Political resistance did not suit all members, and an extremist group of Zealots, called Sicarii "dagger men," adopted terrorist tactics, assassinating Romans and also some prominent Jews who favored cooperation with the Roman authority. The acts of this terrorist faction kept narrowing the negotiating space for solutions. It served to destroy the credibility of moderates on both sides, and expanded the conflict between the Jews and the Romans. When Jerusalem was taken by the Romans in A.D. 70, the last remaining rebels withdrew to the remote mountain top of Massad.

Under their leader, Eleazar bin Ya'ir, they withstood a two-year siege by the Roman Tenth Legion. When it became clear that the Romans were going to succeed in breaching the Jews' defenses, the Jewish leader Eleazar bin Ya'ir called the 960 Jews together and proposed, just as Josephus had in the Galilee, that everyone commit suicide rather than be captured by the Romans, and they did so. Breaking through the fortifications the next morning, the soldiers found that all but seven killed themselves rather than surrender when the besiegers finally captured the fortress in AD 73.

A thousand years later the Assassins functioned from the 11th to the 13th centuries. They came from the Ismailis, a Shi'a Islamic sect. For them, killings were a holy mission designed to frighten, weaken and ultimately overthrow the Sunni establishment.

In India the Thugs, claiming allegiance to the goddess Kali, garroted people to supply her with blood for nourishment, and themselves with money. They terrorized travelers, and also fought against British rule, until they were finally destroyed in the 19th century.

One of the first acts of state terrorism occurred in Europe during the 18th century when Maximilian Robespierre and his Committee of Public Safety, formed in April 1793, officially executed 15,000 French, although estimates rise as high as 40,000. More than 100,000 people were detained as suspects.

Robespierre and the Committee of Public Safety resorted to the Terror, not because they were blood-thirsty madmen, but because they wished to create a temporary dictatorship in order to save the Republic. Whereas the previous examples gave us words such as Zealot and Assassin, it was Robespierre who coined the word "Terror" as we use it in terms of [State] terrorism. To quote him: "If the driving force of popular government in peacetime is virtue, that of popular government during a revolution is both virtue and terror: virtue, without which terror is destructive; terror, without which virtue is impotent.

Terror is only justice that is prompt, severe, and inflexible; it is thus an emanation of virtue; it is less a distinct principle than a consequence of the general principle of democracy applied to the most pressing needs of the patrie."[2] On July 28, 1794, Robespierre was guillotined. -The sans-culottes made no attempt to save him and the Republic passed into a more moderate era. Now in the 21st century, we see recurrent echoes of the thoughts and methods of the Zealots, the Assassin, the Thugs and state-inflicted terror.

As we mentioned at the beginning of this chapter, America was born through terrorist struggle against the English crown, and soon after independence the United States became the recipient of terrorist acts while George Washington was still president. An arms-for-hostages deal, the price of which was estimated by the Treasury at $992,463.25, was executed in 1795.

To quote "A Treaty of Peace or Amity concluded this Present Day Jima artasi ye twenty first of the Luna Safer year of the Hegira 1210 Corresponding with Saturday the fifth of September One thousand Seven

Hundred & Ninety five between Hassan Bashaw Dey of Algiers his Divan and Subjects and George Washington President of the United States of North America and the Citizens of ye Said United States." It was this money and not any instrument of ratification, which made the treaty a reality[3].

This treaty and payment did not end the matter, and the lesson serves as an example of the sometime futility of "making deals" with terrorists. The treaties and negotiation continued through the presidency of Adams to Thomas Jefferson.

Jefferson, like other presidents after him, became embroiled in and distracted by the debate over how to counter this form of terrorism, and Congress even mandated the setting aside of money to pay ransoms. But this dealing with the terrorists did not help matters, and the Tripolitan war commenced in 1801, and it was in 1803, that President Thomas Jefferson sent the Constitution to the Mediterranean to protect American ships and seamen from attack by the Barbary pirates.

With Captain Edward Preble in command, the Constitution and other ships of the squadron bombarded Tripoli. Thanks to such determination, a treaty of peace was signed in June 1805 between the United States and Tripoli aboard the Constitution, not without further ransoms being paid, however. The Barbary story, however, has all the components of terrorism, hostages, failed negotiations, frustration, symbolic gestures, and a hold over the presidency and the people of America.

MOLLY MAGUIRES

It was in the 1860's that terrorism -- domestic terrorism -- appeared in the United States. To quote from *McClures'* magazine of 1894: "Some twenty years ago five counties in eastern Pennsylvania were dominated, terrorized, by a secret organization, thousands strong, whose special purpose was to rob, burn, pillage, and kill. Find on the map that marvelous mineral country, as large as Delaware, which lies between the Blue Mountains on the south and the arm of the Susquehanna on the north, and there you will see what was the home of these banded outlaws, the merciless Molly Maguires. Look in Carbon County for Mauch Chunk, with its towering hills and picturesque ravines, and from there draw a line westward through Schuylkill County and into Northumberland County as far as Shamokin. This line might well be called the red axis of violence, for it cuts through Mount Carmel, Centralia, Raven Run, Mahanoy Plane,

Girardville, Shenandoah, Tamaqua, Tuscarora, and Summit Hill, towns all abounding in hateful memories of the Molly Maguires. Now, on this line as a long diameter, construct an egg-shaped figure, to include in its upper boundary Wilkes Barre in Luzerne County and Bloomsburg in Columbia County, and on its lower to pass somewhat to the south of Pottsville.

Your egg will be about fifty miles long and forty miles across, and will cover scores of thriving communities that once were the haunts of the murderers and ruffians who polluted with their crimes this fair treasure garden of a great State." The Molly Maguires were an Irish group, linked with the ancient order of Hibernians, and worked for the Philadelphia Reading Iron and Coal company, a subsidiary of the Pennsylvania and Reading Railroad. In vain the officials of the Philadelphia and Reading and Lehigh Valley Railroads offered thousands of dollars in rewards for the apprehension of the criminals.

Archbishop Wood of Philadelphia fought the Molly Maguires with the whole power of the Catholic Church, issuing an edict excommunicating all members of the organization from the Church. In 1873 Mr. Franklin B. Gowen, then President of the Philadelphia and Reading Railroad, consulted Allan Pinkerton in regard to the matter. James McFarland, a young Pinkerton's detective, was given instructions to run down the Molly Maguire bandits, whether it took six months or six years, six hundred or six hundred thousand dollars. His orders from Allan Pinkerton were explicit:

"You are to remain in the field until every cut-throat has paid with his life for the lives so cruelly taken." From 1877 to 1879 nineteen members were hanged for their association with the Molly Maguires and their alleged acts.

LABOR VIOLENCE

Labor violence continued. Early in 1886 labor unions were beginning a movement for an eight-hour day. On May 1 many workers struck for shorter hours, but then matters worsened as an active group of radicals and anarchists became involved in the campaign. Two days later shooting and one death occurred during a riot at the McCormick Harvester plant when police tangled with the rioters. On May 4 events reached a tragic climax at Haymarket Square in Chicago where a protest meeting was called to denounce the events of the preceding day.

At this meeting, while police were undertaking to disperse the crowd, a bomb was exploded. Policeman Mathias J. Degan died almost instantly and seven other officers died later. Eight men were finally brought to trial and Judge Joseph E. Gary imposed the death sentence on seven of them and the eighth was given fifteen years in prison. Four were hanged, one committed suicide and the sentences of two were commuted from death to imprisonment for life. On June 26, 1893, Governor John P. Altgeld pardoned the three who were in the penitentiary.

On Sept. 16, 1893, in New York City a bomb planted in an unattended horse-drawn wagon exploded on Wall Street opposite the House of Morgan, killing 35 persons and injuring hundreds more. Bolshevist or anarchist terrorists were believed to have been responsible, but the crime was never solved. At Morgan's request the damage was never repaired, and the scars can still be seen on the Wall Street side of 23 Wall, the building which used to be J.P. Morgan's head office.

TERRORISTS COMMON THREADS

These brief sketches of past terrorist organizations and acts illustrate some common threads. The terrorist group often evolved from a parent political or religious organization to form a faction composed of those who felt that more militant, or violent, action was required. Sometimes these moves were sanctioned, sometimes not. Terrorist groups will themselves spin off more militant factions, especially when the members feel that the leadership is not fighting hard enough, or violently enough. In the group psychology of terrorism there is a drive for action. Therefore, sometimes a group may perform acts of terrorism because they must for the leadership to survive. If the leader does not originate these actions, others may. It should also be noted that the acts of terrorism did not necessarily succeed in helping the group achieve their goals. In fact in some cases, such as the Zealots, the terrorists' acts may well have polarized the two sides and made negotiations harder. These factors have not changed, and still affect today's environment.

The 1960s and 1970s saw what may be described as the heyday of terrorism in the United States.

THE EL RUKNS GROUP

One group, El Rukns, is an anomaly as far as most terrorist groups are concerned, for they were really a Chicago street gang, known as the Blackstone Rangers, which dated back to 1963 and had its genesis in drug trafficking. They were not idealists, but were a successful Southside gang controlling the area around Blackstone Street. The leader, Jeff Fort, combined his gang with 21 different black gangs to create the Black P. Stone Nation in 1968.[4] As they renamed themselves, they also felt that they represented the class struggle, and Fort was considered a legitimate black leader and even became involved in federal programs under the Office of Economic Opportunity. He was imprisoned in 1972 for making false statements to obtain federal funds. At this point Fort converted to Islam, and renamed his gang El Rukns in 1976.

The metamorphosis from gang to a group struggling against American imperialism continued, and the change to the terrorist cause was probably more or less complete when in 1986 four of Fort's top leaders flew to Libya and offered their services to Kaddafi in exchange for a promised payment of $2.5 million. This transition to terrorism as a state sponsored agent of a foreign government tested El Rukns' capabilities, and eventually they were arrested by the FBI during their efforts to obtain a Light Anti-tank Weapon. A 50-count indictment was handed down against Fort and his co-conspirators. This case is remarkable as the first conviction of US citizens conspiring with a foreign government to commit an act of terrorism.

The Government definitions of international and domestic terrorism would classify El Rukns as international terrorists:

Domestic: Groups or individuals based and operating entirely within the US and Puerto Rico without foreign direction whose violent acts are directed at the US Government or population

International: Groups or individuals with some connection to a foreign power or whose activities transcend national boundaries and whose acts are to intimidate the government or population.

El Rukns and other groups of the 1960s, 70s and 80s dispel the popular myth that terrorists are foreigners, or that foreign (enemy) states would not be able to find Americans willing to do their work. This capability of terrorists to create loose, small, cell-type organizations makes them a formidable foe to law enforcement. Although certain terrorist groups' or individuals' driving force is more criminal or mercenary than ideological, strong beliefs are a more common motivating factor. Although many would paint Islam as the root of terrorism, this is far from the truth, for in the United States we have also seen acts of terrorism inspired by right-wing beliefs, left-wing beliefs, Christian ideology, and other forces or beliefs where terrorism has been used as a means of expression.

PUERTO RICAN TERRORISTS

For example, the Armed forces of National liberation (FALN) a Puerto Rican group first surfaced in 1974 and was a very active movement, killing four in the Fraunces Tavern bombing in New York in 1975, and being responsible for at least 100 bombings during the next six years. FALN was the only Puerto Rican Independence group to operate primarily in the continental United Sates.

Five others, the Organization of Volunteers for the Puerto Rican Revolution, EPB Macheteros, Armed Forces of Popular Resistance Guerrilla Forces of Liberation and Pedro Albizos Campos Revolutionary Forces were primarily based in Puerto Rico. All these groups were leftist, pro-Puerto Rican independence from the United States and influenced by Castro's brand of Marxism-Leninism. They certainly benefited from offshore training. They were able to leverage their skills through the fact that some individuals belonged to more than one group.

Although the last terrorist incident involving Puerto Rican terrorist groups was a bombing in Chicago in December 1992, these groups continue to be of concern. Between 1982 and 1994, approximately 44 percent of the terrorist incidents committed in the United States and its territories are attributed to Puerto Rican terrorist groups. Efforts are continuing to locate fugitives still at-large from these incidents.

Puerto Rican terrorist groups believe the liberation of Puerto Rico from the United States justifies the use of violence to obtain that objective. These groups characterize their terrorism activities as "acts of war" against invading forces and, when arrested, they consider themselves to be "prisoners of war" who must be treated as such according to the Geneva Convention. Clandestine behavior and security are of utmost importance in these group's activities. The EPB-Macheteros has been the most active and violent of the Puerto Rican-based terrorist groups since it emerged in 1978. The FALN (Armed Forces for Puerto Rican National Liberation) is a clandestine terrorist group, based in Chicago, which emerged in the 1970s. The MLN (Movement of National Liberation) is the "above ground" support group and political arm of the FALN. The MLN is the major fund-raiser for the FALN.

The 1960s and 1970s saw the emergence, and in some cases the fall, of many ideological leftist groups. However there was a re-emergence in the 80's, and it would be unwise to assume that such terrorism could not re-emerge. It is safe to say that, where there is a cause, there may also be a radical ready to commit acts of terrorism. The Communist Party of the USA (CPUSA) dates back to 1919 as the Workers Party. In 1991 the Soviet paper Rossiya revealed that the Soviet Union provided annual funds in excess of $2 million to support activities of the CPUSA against the United States Government. There were many other left-wing groups in the United States during that time, including the Weathermen, Black Panthers, Black Liberation Army and May 19th communist Organization.

DOMESTIC GROUPS

Right-wing terrorism is as old as left-wing. In fact the Ku Klux Klan predates the CPUSA, and the Christian Identity (also known as Kingdom Identity) movement has its roots (peaceful) back in England of the late 19th century. The threat from right-wing extremist groups includes militias, white-separatist groups, and anti-government groups.

All right-wing extremist groups tend to encourage massing weapons, ammunition and supplies in preparation for a confrontation with federal law enforcement officers, as well as local law enforcement officers who are often perceived as agents for the state / Federal Government.

The supposed goal of the militia movement is to defend and protect the United States Constitution from those who want to take away the rights of Americans. The militia movement believes that the United States Constitution gives Americans the right to live their lives without government interference. Some of the rallying cries include the right to bear arms, resentment of state laws forbidding them to gather together to fire weapons; mistrust of federal law enforcement; taxes; and the United Nations which is perceived as an organization bent on taking over the world and destroying American democracy and establishing "the New World Order."

The FBI is not concerned with every single aspect of the militia movement since many militia members are law-abiding citizens who do not pose a threat of violence. The FBI focuses on radical elements of the militia movement capable and willing to commit violence against government, law enforcement, civilian, military and international targets (U.N., visiting foreign military personnel). Not every state in the union has a militia problem. Militia activity varies from states with almost no militia activity (Hawaii, Connecticut) to states with thousands of active militia members (Michigan, Texas).

Militia groups are often multi-racial, but they are predominantly white. Their members often view themselves as "sovereign citizens" who are exempt from the laws and regulations of the US Government. Many militia members subscribe to the theory that the Federal Government is in a conspiracy with the United Nations that would result in the creation of a one-nation world government, or "New World Order." This one-world government would use foreign troops in the United States to seize all privately owned weapons and imprison and execute patriotic militia members.

Many militia groups advocate stockpiling weapons and explosives and conducting paramilitary training as part of their preparation for what they believe will be an inevitable armed conflict with the government and the impending U.N. invasion. Some militia groups openly advocate the overthrow of the Federal Government.

Since 1992, the United States has seen a growth of militia groups. While the majority of militia members are law abiding citizens, there is a small percentage of members within militia groups who advocate and conspire to commit violent criminal acts. Of particular concern to the FBI is the potential for militias to be infiltrated by extremists who seek to exploit militias and their members in order to further their own violent terrorist agenda.

Militia members who engage in criminal acts commit a wide variety of criminal activity, such as bombings, bank robberies, and destruction of government property. They also file spurious lawsuits and liens designed to harass law enforcement, elected officials, and others, as well as to disrupt the courts. Militia members have engaged in fraudulent financial schemes to raise funds.

An example, is the FBI's investigation of the Mountaineer Militia. This investigation was initiated in August 1995. The group had obtained the plans to the FBI Criminal Justice Information Services facility in Clarksburg, West Virginia, and they intended to destroy the facility as part of their war on the US Government. The FBI began an undercover investigation and arrested seven key members of the group in October 1996. All seven have since been convicted and sentenced to lengthy jail sentences.

The American militia movement has grown over the last decade. Factors contributing to growth include:

GUNS

The right to bear arms is an issue with which almost all Militia members agree and most militia members believe a conspiracy exists to take away their guns. The national system of instant background checks for all gun buyers, mandated by the 1993 Brady Act and which actually was implemented on November 30, 1998, has further angered many militia groups.

These militia members see this new law as another example of how the government is conspiring to take away their guns. The banning of semiautomatic assault weapons has also angered many militia members.

STATE LAWS

Militias resent state laws forbidding them to gather together to fire weapons. Sixteen states have laws which prohibit all militia groups and 17 states have laws which prohibit all paramilitary training.

MISTRUST OF FEDERAL LAW ENFORCEMENT

Is frequently mentioned in militia literature and overall militia mythology. FBI and Bureau of Alcohol, Tobacco and Firearms (ATF) actions, such as Ruby Ridge, the Branch Davidians, and the Freeman standoff, are cited, engendering hatred and mistrust of these agencies.

TAXES

Militia members believe that they pay too many taxes and that those tax dollars are wasted by a huge, uncaring and inefficient bureaucracy in Washington, D.C. Since the Internal Revenue Service collects federal taxes, it is widely hated by militia members.

THE UNITED NATIONS

Is perceived as an organization bent on taking over the world and destroying American democracy and establishing "the New World Order." The New World Order theory holds that, one day, the United Nations will lead a military coup against the nations of the world to form a one-world government. United Nations troops, consisting of foreign armies, will commence a military takeover of America. The United Nations will mainly use foreign troops on American soil because foreigners will have fewer reservations about killing American citizens. Captured United States military bases will be used to help conquer the rest of the world.

Most of the militia movement has no racial overtones and does not espouse bigotry. There are some black and Jewish militia members. However, the pseudo-religion of Christian Identity, as well as other hate philosophies, have begun to creep into the militia movement. This scenario is currently being played out in the Michigan Militia, arguably the largest militia group in America. Lynn Van Huizen, leader of the Michigan Militia Corps, is currently trying to oust Christian Identity factions from his group. This pattern of racist elements seeping into the militia movement is a disturbing trend, as it will only strengthen the radical elements of the militias. Conceived by an Englishman, Richard Brothers, the Identity movement believes that Christ was an Aryan and the ten lost tribes of Israel eventually ended up in England and even the word British derives from the Hebrew berit-ish, man of the covenant. This was an intellectual concept of the late 19th century, but subsequently the "Israel of God" migrated to the United States where today the concept is finding a larger and more vociferous following.

Christian Identity adherents believe the Jews are predisposed to carry on a conspiracy against the Adamic seed line and today have achieved almost complete control of the earth. British-Israelism was brought to America in the early part of the 1920s, where it remained decentralized until the 1930s. At that time, the movement underwent the final transformation to become what we know as Christian Identity, at which time its ties to the original English movement were cut and it became distinctly American.

The Christian Identity belief system provides a religious base for racism and anti-Semitism, and an ideological rationale for violence against minorities and their white allies. Fundamentally, the Jews are considered the Children of Satan. Wesley Swift is considered the single most significant figure in the early years of the Christian Identity movement in the United States. He popularized it in the right-wing by combining British-Israelism, a demonic anti-Semitism, and political extremism. He founded his own church in California in the mid 1940s where he could preach his ideology.

In addition, he had a daily radio broadcast in California during the 1950s and 1960s through which he was able to proclaim his ideology to a large audience. With Swift's efforts, the message of his church spread, leading to the creation of similar churches throughout the country. However, it was not Swift, but Howard B. Rand (whose writings are published by Destiny Publishers) who first coined the term Identity.

According to James Coates, Rand's intention was to describe Hine's concept of Anglo-Israelism, in which Jesus was not a Jew of the tribe of Judah but an Aryan of the ten lost tribes of Israel and an ancestor of the present British, Germanic and Scandinavian people. In 1957, the name of Swift's church was changed to The Church of Jesus Christ Christian, which is used today by Aryan Nations (AN) churches.

The farm crisis is an important source for Identity propaganda. The farmers provided a classic recruitment pool, when during the 1980s foreclosures were common. Big businesses such as Cargill, Corn Agra, Archer Daniels Midland and the Federal Government were, and still are, perceived as causing the loss of more than one million small and medium-sized farms. The farm losses were real. Many farmers committed suicide, meetings and services led by farmers to rally around the concept that the government was behind their problems, and beyond that, that the government is dominated by Jews, the children of Satan. Some Identity teachers are suggesting that the Zionist Occupational Government or the Jews are behind the loss of the farms.

One action tied to this movement was the death of Gordon Wendall Kahl in 1983. He was a North Dakota farmer and a member of the "Posse Comitatus" who was charged with tax evasion and the murder of two federal marshals in Medina, North Dakota. In keeping with Posse doctrines recognizing no government authority above the county level, Kahl refused to renew his state driver's license in 1974. In 1977 he was charged with tax evasion on his 1972-74 taxes and was placed on five years' probation. After killing the marshals, Kahl escaped and a four-month search ensued. In June 1983 Kahl was discovered hiding out in an Arkansas farmhouse. He was killed in an ensuing shootout with law enforcement officers; however, he killed a local sheriff in the process.

Although Gordon Wendall Kahl became the martyr for the Sheriff's Posse Comitatus, and certainly brought it to the front page, it was actually founded in 1969 by Henry "Mike" Beach. The words "Posse Comitatus" mean power of the county, and as such had existed in England. For example, names were assembled in 1780 in Buckinghamshire for defense against possible French invasion. State laws allow for the sheriff to form a "posse comitatus." The organization Sheriff's Posse Comitatus stood this law on its head, and declared that no government above the county level had authority, -- including Federal and State government -- and if the sheriff failed to protect the citizens from threats including from higher levels of government, then they would. A convenient offshoot of this concept was the determination that taxes should not be paid to the Federal Government. As an extreme manifestation, James Wickstrom and Donald Minniecheske created a new township of Tigerton Dells in Wisconsin in 1985. This was, in fact, a paramilitary camp which was raided by Federal authorities who arrested the leaders. Wickstrom's sentence was commuted, but in 1990 he was arrested in Pennsylvania for conspiring to distribute $100,000 in counterfeit money.

The example of the Posse Comitatus demonstrates the altered sense of reality found in many groups -- in their case the county as the highest level of government -- and the ability to recruit people who feel themselves wronged.

Gordon Wendall Kahl provided a connection to another domestic organization when he hid in Arkansas on the farm of William Wade, an associate of the Covenant the Sword and the Arm of the Lord (CSA). Founded in 1971 by former San Antonio fundamentalist minister James Ellison, (CSA) was a paramilitary survivalist group which operated an Identity-oriented communal settlement in Arkansas. CSA is important for the fact that it demonstrates that large organizations, such as the Christian Identity movement, will spawn spin-offs who believe that the main organization is too soft, inactive or otherwise failing to meet its mission. Ellison was the absolute leader of CSA and members were aged 25-35, poor and many of them ex-convicts recently released from prison.[5]

After the killing of Kahl in June 1983, the CSA leaders attended the Aryan Nations Congress in Hayden Lakes in July. They returned and embarked on a series of violent acts, including the firebombing of an Indiana synagogue, the arson of a Missouri church, and an attempted bombing in Missouri of a pipeline supplying Chicago with natural gas. In April 1985, 200 FBI agents raided the CSA compound on the Missouri-Arkansas border and seized hundreds of weapons, bombs, an anti-tank rocket, and quantities of cyanide allegedly intended to poison the water supply of a city. This supply of poison constitutes one of the first incidents where the use of a Weapon of Mass Destruction was contemplated by a domestic terrorist group.

The foregoing is far from a comprehensive list of militia, sovereign and right-wing groups in the United States. There are many, some are short lived, and not all espouse violence, and even fewer actually commit violent acts. The driving force behind a group need not necessarily be religious beliefs.

SINGLE ISSUE GROUPS

Another category is special or single issue groups. Special interest or single issue extremists advocate violence and/or criminal activity with the goal of affecting change in policy vis-à-vis one specific aspect of society. The most recognizable single issue terrorists at the present time are those involved in the violent animal rights, anti-abortion, and environmental protection movements.[6]

Special interest terrorist groups engage in criminal activity to bring about specific, narrowly focused social or political changes. They differ from more traditional domestic terrorist groups which seek more wide-ranging political changes. It is their willingness to commit criminal acts that separate special interest terrorist groups from other law-abiding groups that often support the same popular issues.

By committing criminal acts, these terrorists believe they can force various segments of society to change attitudes about issues considered important to them.

The existence of these types of groups often does not come to law enforcement attention until after an act is committed and the individual or group leaves a claim of responsibility. Membership in a group may be limited to a very small number of co-conspirators or associates. Consequently, acts committed by special interest terrorists present unique challenges to the FBI and other law enforcement agencies.

Animal rights extremists target animal research laboratories and manufacturers that make use of the research and continue to pose significant challenges for law enforcement. Various arsons and other incidents of property destruction have been claimed by the Animal Liberation Front (ALF) and the Earth Liberation Front (ELF). Originating in England, ALF committed their first known act in the US in 1982.

They were designated a terrorist organization by the FBI in 1987 after causing $3.5 million in damage when they set fire to the new veterinary research building at the University of California at Davis. In 1989 they stole more than 1,000 animals from the University of Arizona and set fire to the Pharmacy Microbiology Building. They continue to maintain an active level of harassment by "liberating" laboratory animals. *Newsweek* on September 29, 1997, reported "The battle for animal rights is getting uglier.

The ALF fancies itself a kind of IRA for the animal kingdom. So far this year, its members have claimed responsibility for violent acts at a rate of almost one a day. Its crimes range from small-time vandalism (smashing windows at a butcher's shop in suburban Connecticut and spray-painting "McMurder" inside a Michigan McDonald's) to large-scale "rescue" operations (releasing 10,000 minks from a farm in Oregon). State and federal investigators thought they had shut the group down after a spree of bombings and break-ins ended with the arrest of an ALF leader in 1994. But now the violence is escalating again. Supporters brag that no one's ever been hurt in an ALF action, but investigators who have tracked the group say that's just sheer luck.[7]

Political scientist Kevin Beedy, writing in the March 1990 issue of Animals' Agenda, said: Terrorism carries no moral or ethical connotations. It is simply the definition of a particular type of coercion. ... It is up to the animal-rights spokespersons either to dismiss the terrorist label as propaganda or make it a badge to be proud of wearing."

More recently, on October 19, 1998, the Vail Ski Resort suffered a series of arson attacks that damaged or destroyed eight separate structures and resulted in approximately $12 million in property damage. In a communiqué issued to various news agencies in Colorado, ALF claimed responsibility for the arsons in retaliation for the resort's plans to expand its ski areas. The group claimed that the proposed expansion would destroy the last remaining habitat in Colorado for the lynx. Such organizations could be one of the waves of the future as the environmental and single issue terrorists become more numerous, more determined and more violent.

This form of terrorism is disturbing, and could well continue for some time. The animal rights and earth groups show little concern for human beings. The laboratory animals and buildings they destroy were being used for medical research, and aside from the dollar loss, the delay to research progress must be considered as a great loss. Nothing is too extreme it would seem.

In Portland, Oregon on June 6, 2000, a group calling itself the Anarchist Golfing Association claimed responsibility for the destruction of experiments on genetically altered grass being developed for use on putting greens. According to an e-mail the group sent to *The Oregonian*, members broke into two greenhouses owned by Pure-Seed Testing in a Portland suburb. They stomped on plots of experimental grass, spray-painted such slogans as "Nature Bites Back" and left golf balls embossed with the international anarchists' symbol, the letter "A" in a circle. Pure-Seed said the saboteurs destroyed five to ten years of work and caused up to $500,000 in damage. Pure-Seed was targeted because it is experimenting with a grass that has been genetically modified to resist a herbicide, the group said.

"The biotech industry usually hides behind the racist aura of 'feeding the Third World,'" the group wrote, "but ... it is quite obvious that these crops are grown for profit and the pleasure of the rich and have no social value."

The threat from domestic terrorists by no means supplants the threat from foreign terrorists. In fact, by demonstrating that the United States is a soft target, they may even encourage attacks. The first blow arrived with the assassination of two CIA employees outside CIA Headquarters. The second and most dramatic strike was the bombing of the World Trade Center which claimed the lives of six, injured more than 1,000, and severely disrupted business operations. The bombing of the Murrah Building in Oklahoma City showed an American can perform such an act on his own soil.

Ramzi Ahmed Yousef brought the threat of foreign terrorism and mass deaths to the nation's notice with the bombing of the World Trade Center in 1993 and conspiring to bomb a Philippines airliner in 1994 and other US airlines transiting the Far East. There are many terrorist organizations. The US Antiterrorism and Effective Death Penalty Act of 1996 authorizes the Secretary of State to make designations every two years as to which organizations are considered as terrorist. The Secretary of State may add organizations to the list at any time. In October 1999, the US Secretary of State designated 28 groups as foreign terrorist organizations. (See Appendix L on page 458)

The international terrorist threat can be divided into three general categories. Each poses a serious and distinct threat, and each has a presence in the United States.

The first category, state-sponsored terrorism, violates every convention of international law. State sponsors of terrorism include Iran, Iraq, Syria, Sudan, Libya, Cuba, and North Korea. Put simply, these nations view terrorism as a tool of foreign policy. In recent years, the terrorist activities of Cuba and North Korea have declined as their economies have deteriorated.

However, the activities of the other states have continued and, in some cases, have intensified during the past several years. For state-directed terrorist groups, the objectives are determined by the political needs of the state. They work within the parameters of the state and the targets are usually enemies of the state.

Targets range from political assassination of an opposition leader to attempts at eradicating the entire political body such as the Sarin gassing of the Kurds in Northern Iraq by Saddam Hussein. The aims are to create an environment of fear and intimidation in order to maintain the state rule. It should be remembered that a foreign state may direct actions overseas. These actions are reminiscent of those of France's Robespierre.

The second category of international terrorist threat is made up of formal terrorist organizations. These autonomous, generally transnational organizations have their own infrastructures, personnel, financial arrangements, and training facilities. They are able to plan and mount terrorist campaigns on an international basis, and actively support terrorist activities in the United States. The formal groups are still sponsored by states and these terrorist groups tend to be more transnational in terms of their operating area. Targets are determined by the sponsor's condition of support.

For instance, Iran's desire to further the influence of Islamic Fundamentalism sets the condition for terrorists to target any country or organization that oppose their goals. Iran is known to sponsor HAMAS which is responsible for suicide bombings against Israeli public transportation in an effort to derail the Middle East Peace Process. The ultimate goal is for Islam to be the only ruling party of the world. Iraq is also a State Sponsor of terrorist groups specifically aimed against targets that oppose the regime. Most of these attacks occur in the Northern Iraq area with poisoning of Iraqi National Congress members, attacks on UN convoys and relief personnel with the objective of frightening away support for the opposition. State sponsorship goes beyond the provision of money and a safe haven. It can include materials, such as biological or chemical weapons which are beyond the technological means of the group to produce.

We must bear in mind that most of the sponsoring states have these weapons in their stockpiles, and as such, can dramatically elevate the threat posed by the terrorist organizations to their enemies.

It must be remembered that state sponsorship is business activity, and the terrorist has business considerations and obligations. If the consequences of their act are so horrible as to draw revulsion and have adverse effect on the sponsor's mission, they will lose their funding. Extremist groups such as Lebanese Hizbollah, the Egyptian Al-Gamat Al-Islamiya, and the Palestinian HAMAS have placed followers inside the United States who could be used to support an act of terrorism here.

The third, and possible most worrisome, category of international terrorist threat stems from loosely affiliated extremists characterized by the World Trade Center bombers and rogue terrorists such as Ramzi Ahmed Yousef. These loosely affiliated extremists may pose the most urgent threat to the United States at this time because their membership is relatively unknown to law enforcement, and because they can exploit the mobility that emerging technology and a loose organizational structure offer. The FBI believes that the threat posed by international terrorists in each of these three categories will continue for the foreseeable future.

Non state-sponsored, international or domestic, groups pose a large threat to any country for they have absolute freedom to choose their targets. Narco-terrorists target wealthy individuals for profit and regional government officials in order to bypass laws through intimidation. Religious extremists will target anything or anybody who is not part of their faith.

Ethnocentric groups' targets are based on cleansing their area or the world of the other corrupting tribes. Anti-federal groups such as some militia groups will target any symbol of government oppression. Anti-abortionist extremists target abortion clinics as well as the personnel who work there. Environmental extremists who believe that the human race is destroying the world, target industrial operations such as the logging and oil companies.

There is no single label for the many and varied individuals who are or plan to be involved in acts of terrorism. Robespierre was well-educated and upper class; Lenin was born into a religious, middle-class background; Che Guevara was a doctor; the Weathermen were college graduates or students; many Black Panthers had little formal education and grew up in the ghettos; and many members of the various Palestinian terrorist organizations grew up in refugee camps and may also be college graduates. Obviously, there are no simplistic, common identifiers.

The profile of the terrorist changes from left wing, to right, to single issue and they are formidable foes to law enforcement. Terrorists come in all races, nationalities, ages, socio-economic status, educational levels, and genders. However, some demographic generalizations can be made. Much of the discussion below comes from an excellent study done by Russell and Miller (1978), who studied the demographic composition of 18 terrorist organizations from all over the world. They found that the terrorist in general was usually between 22-25 years old.

They noted that the age of the terrorist appeared to be falling, especially in Ireland, Latin America, Spain, and Turkey, where many of the terrorists were teenagers in secondary schools. Some Irish terrorists were as young as 12 years old. (Note: In the United States, this age pattern holds true for left-wing terrorists. However, the right-wing terrorist is usually much older, with many being in their 40s and 50s. In the United States, the left-wing terrorist leader is in the late 20s or early 30s. The right-wing terrorist leader is considerably older, late 40s to mid-60s. The age of right-wing terrorist leaders is consistent with the leader ages found by Russell and Miller.) The majority of terrorists are male and over 80 percent of the leaders are male. Females tended to be support personnel, with less than 16 percent in operational areas. The one exception was in Germany, where 33 percent of terrorists were female.[8]

Right-wing terrorists are almost exclusively male, with the few females involved serving as support for the males. According to Richard Butler, head of the Aryan Nations, the purpose of the female is to provide a well-run home to refresh and inspire her man.

In the United States, the right-wing extremists tend to be highly religious, rigidly following their interpretations of the Bible. As part of this system, the female is seen as being subservient to the male.[9]

Most terrorists are unmarried. Russell and Miller (1978) reported that 75- 80 percent of all terrorists in their study were single. The same figure likely holds true for the left-wing terrorist in the United States. The figure for single right-wing terrorists is probably much lower as was demonstrated in the survey of the CSA camp. Being older and religiously oriented, many right-wing extremists are not only married, but also have children. This is consistent with their beliefs that dictate a family life run by the male. Therefore, it is the obligation of the male to have a family.

Although not numerous, there are notable exceptions to the findings of Russell and Miller in terms of left-wing terrorist leaders. Ulrike Meinhoff led the Baader-Meinhoff Gang, Fusako Shigenobu the Japanese Red Army, and in the United States, Nancy Ling Perry the Symbionese Liberation Army (SLA), and Bernadine Dohrn the Weather Underground. As a rule, when females lead the terrorist organization, a male is appointed as a "front" appearing to the world to be the true leader. In the case of the SLA, everyone believed Donald DeFreeze to be the leader.

As pointed out by Russell and Miller, in the left-wing organization, women serve in support not so much because of chauvinistic attitudes by the males, but for security reasons. Law enforcement is not likely to consider three single females living together as operating a safe house. Women, because they are perceived as less threatening, might be able to enter areas males could not enter. The female can thus gather surveillance and intelligence information which a male would not be able to get. The female terrorist tends to be free lance, offering her services to a variety of organizations that share her ideals and philosophy. She is more overtly hostile, ruthless and displays little moral constraint. In addition, the female terrorist exhibits many male personality and physical traits (Georges-Abeyie, 1983).

In terms of socioeconomic background, most terrorists (66 percent) came from middle or upper-class backgrounds (Horowitz, 1973). Their parents were from professional disciplines, government service, police and military officers, diplomats, and the clergy. The one exception was the IRA, where the terrorists came from the lower classes. In the United States, most right-wing terrorists come from lower-class backgrounds, while the left-wing terrorist conforms to the findings of Russell and Miller (1978) and mostly come from middle or upper class urban backgrounds.

Most terrorists (66 percent) had a university degree. The high was in Germany (80 percent) and the low in Ireland (20 percent). About 75 percent of the terrorists in Latin American have university degrees. The degrees included economics, education, engineering, history, the humanities, law, medicine, philosophy, and the social sciences. The terrorist with an engineering degree is at a decided advantage over many law enforcement personnel, as terrorists have the knowledge of technology which can he used to construct sophisticated devices. In the United States, the left-wing terrorist typically does have a university degree or some university education (Demaitre, 1973). Right-wing terrorists typically do not have any university education (Blumberg, 1986). Many, in fact, do not even have a high school education. This lack of a formal education is offset by the fact that many have Special Forces military training. While many were in the military, the majority received training from ex-Special Forces members hired to conduct paramilitary training.

Many are well educated, dedicated to success, and motivated to the point of fanaticism. The average terrorist, leaders aside, has a history of being an outsider with a background history of being shunned and humiliated by his peers (and in many cases, by his family) and a long history of personal failure. This leads to a lowered self-esteem, social isolation, and a negative self-image. Low self-esteem places unrealistically high demands on him, feeling his life is controlled by external sources. He projects his self-hatred onto an external object and is drawn by feeling inadequate to the feeling of belonging.

The terrorist organization ends the social isolation. By defeating or humiliating others, the terrorist improves his worth as a human being, both as an individual and as a contributing member of the group. The reliance on other group members is also increased. The terrorist has learned and carefully nurtured a misperception of reality. Left-wing terrorists see themselves as the oppressed victims of an unfair society or system. The right-wing terrorists perceive themselves as the elite. There are no gray areas for compromise or negotiation. This leads to a lack of sophistication on the part of the terrorist. Thinking in simplistic terms, they tend to plan operations simplistically .

The ideologists need a cause, and are looking for guidance in finding this cause. They are naive, immature, and innocent in the ways of the world needing a Stalin (or Christ) to worship and die for. The terrorist is a mortal enemy of things as they are. The ideologist is often from an upper or middle class family whose parents were politically and/or religiously liberal.

Contrary to popular belief, all terrorists do not like to kill. After acts of violence, terrorists will employ several strategies to reduce their guilt. The terrorist tends to depersonalize and stereotype his enemies and victims to remove the human identity of the victim. The more depersonalized the terrorist can make the victim, the more likely the terrorist is to do violence to the victim. To even further distance himself from a victim's suffering, the terrorist may couch his actions in legalistic terminology. Victims are not assassinated, they are "executed after a trial;" victims are not kidnapped, they are "held in a people's prison." Using legalistic jargon also strengthens and reinforces the belief that true justice and right is on the terrorist's side.

One of the pressing questions is how many will be killed? Generally acts of terrorism have been limited by the weapon. However, weapons of mass destruction are now readily available. The most popular weapon remains explosives, and for mass destruction a truck bomb has proven most effective. Not only is the capability changing, but there are signs that the intent is also changing.

A US Secret Service Agent Brian Parr, recounting Ramzi Ahmed Yousef's admission to the World Trade Center bombing, said, "He related to us that during World War II, the Americans had dropped the atomic bombs on the cities of Hiroshima and Nagasaki, killing 250,000 civilians, and he said that the Americans would realize, if they suffered those types of casualties, that they were at war."

Since the end of the Cold War, a new, and very worrisome threat has begun to emerge, that is asymmetric threat. This is where terrorism is used as a new way of waging war. The United States is now a dominant super power and other nations cannot win a traditional battle using traditional means. Therefore, smaller countries must seek a new paradigm which would be to move warfare to the shores of the United States. The National Defense University wrote that put simply, asymmetric threats or techniques are a version of not "fighting fair," which can include the use of surprise in all its operational and strategic dimensions and the use of weapons in ways unplanned by the United States. Not fighting fair also includes the prospect of an opponent designing a strategy that fundamentally alters the terrain on which a conflict is fought.[10] The NDU continues: "Future opponents will have many options for attempting to deter, disrupt, or defeat US use of military power. Four broad options could be part of an asymmetric response to current and foreseeable US superiority in regional combined-arms warfare capability.

The first option is the acquisition of weapons of mass destruction (WMD) and long-range ballistic or cruise missiles. A future regional opponent could threaten US and allied forces with a dramatic form of military escalation. Even without operational use, the mere presence of such capability would act as a regional-strategic shadow and might weaken the commitment of key allies to any future US military response to regional aggression. The second is the selected acquisition of high-technology sensors, communications, and weapon systems. This is the strategy of the niche player.

The third, the exploitation of cyber weapons, could be used to disrupt the next generation of information-technology (IT) military logistics systems or to bring the war home by attacking the national strategic infrastructure (NSI), itself rapidly exploiting IT in the name of economic efficiency. And in the fourth, opponents could choose to fight in environments, such as large cities or jungles, that degrade the US capacity to find and attack militarily significant targets. This could include conducting acts of aggression that purposely blur boundaries between actions considered crimes and those viewed as warfare."

Clearly not all of these responses involve terrorism, however, the blurring of the boundaries is where acts of war become acts of terrorism. In his report to Congress, former US Defense Secretary William Cohen stated: "The likelihood of a state sponsor providing such a weapon to a terrorist group is believed to be low. It is possible, however, that groups, especially extremist groups with no ties to a particular state, could acquire and attempt to use such weapons in the future.

AUM SHINRIKYO

The March 1995 attack on the Tokyo subway by the religious group Aum Shinrikyo using the nerve agent Sarin was the most glaring example of terrorist use of these kinds of weapons. This attack crossed a psychological boundary and showed that the use of nuclear, biological and chemical (NBC) weapons was no longer restricted to the traditional battlefield. As a result of the Tokyo subway attack, government authorities became concerned about the potential use of NBC agents by non-state groups and have placed such groups under increased scrutiny. However, this increased scrutiny is no guarantee of thwarting a potential terrorist attack."

Aum Shinrikyo has been extensively quoted and used to demonstrate everything from the fact that the threat is high, to the fact that the threat is low, therefore this even bears some discussion.

The following summary as delivered by former Defense Secretary William Cohen:[11] Aum Shinrikyo was formed in 1987 by Shoko Asahara as an apocalyptic religious organization that prophesied an Armageddon-type conflict between Japan and the United States in the last years of the century. The group had intended to hasten the conflict by interceding with the use of chemical and biological weapons. Recruitment of members focused on socially disaffected individuals with technical and scientific backgrounds, many of whom also possessed or had access to substantive economic resources. Some worked for the Japanese government, including the military. All apparently were seeking spiritual fulfillment.

Aum Shinrikyo personnel involved in developing weapons were assigned to internal sub-elements that acquired materials, constructed production facilities, produced agents, and engaged in weaponization, storage, and operational training. The group established front companies for legal chemical acquisition, then closed them down when sufficient quantities of precursor chemicals had been purchased. The group researched, developed, tested, and practiced employment of lethal chemical and biological weapons.

Funding came from legitimate businesses that Aum Shinrikyo had established, as well as from funds generated from donations received when members turned over their bank accounts and properties to the group. At its height, the group's financial base may have had as much as $2 billion in assets. Japanese authorities were constitutionally restricted from investigating the group because Aum Shinrikyo was a religiously chartered organization. It was only when lawsuits were brought against the group by local communities and individuals that official concerns were raised.

Subsequent law enforcement plans to conduct searches of facilities apparently led to the group's decision to conduct the subway attack, revealing Aum Shinrikyo's capabilities and intentions. Until that time, little was known regarding the internal operations of Aum Shinrikyo.

Press coverage of Aum Shinrikyo's activities revealed that Shoko Asahara directed the organization to produce lethal chemicals in 1993 and that a plant became operational in 1994. Other group activities included: chemical tests on sheep on a ranch owned by the group in Western Australia; preparations to use lethal chemical agents against a large Japanese city; and acquisition of the means to disseminate lethal agents. Aum Shinrikyo had purchased a large Russian helicopter and two remotely piloted vehicles. All could have disseminated chemical or biological agents.

The group established chapters in a number of European cities and in the United States, and claimed membership in Russia of some 30,000, triple the Japan membership.

In addition to the March 1995 subway attack, the group had used the same chemical agent nine months earlier in Matsumoto, Japan. The alleged purpose was to halt or slow judicial proceedings in civil litigation brought against the group. Two of the three judges in that case were critically injured by the chemicals and the legal case remains unresolved.

Japanese police suspect that members of the group placed five cyanide-based devices in Tokyo subway facilities (subsequent to the March 1995 attack), in an attempt to force the release of cult leader Asahara, who remains under arrest.

Certainly, Aum Shinrikyo challenged the statement that terrorists are more interested in publicity than casualties. Their goal was to take over the Japanese Parliament, not simply gain publicity. The attack in Matsumoto was to interfere with the judicial process and in the Tokyo attack it was against the police, having been timed to kill as many policemen as possible. Their principal attack was to be against the government and would have used a variety of weapons. Aum Shinrikyo are not the first to have used biological or chemical weapons to effect the judicial process. In 1984 members of a religious cult led by the Bhagwan Shree Rajneesh contaminated the salad bars of ten restaurants in The Dalles, Oregon, area with salmonella bacteria, in the hope of debilitating the local populace and thereby rigging a key municipal election in the cult's favor.

Although their plot was unsuccessful in achieving the group's political aims, some 751 people reportedly became ill with salmonella gastroenteritis as a result of the attack. Publicity was certainly not an issue in this attack, for information regarding the attack was not discovered until later.

One conclusion drawn from the Aum Shinrikyo attack is that the use of chemical biological or nuclear weapons by terrorists is far harder than is assumed by most people. An excellent report to the President by the Gilmore Commission made this point. To quote from the report:[13] "Despite Aum's considerable financial wealth, the technical expertise that it could call on from its well-educated members, and the vast resources and state-of-the-art equipment at their disposal, the group could not effect even a single truly successful chemical or biological attack.

On at least nine occasions the group attempted to disseminate botulinum toxin (Clostridium botulinum) or anthrax (Bacillus anthracis) using aerosol means; each time they failed either because the botulinum agents they grew and enriched were not toxic or the mechanical sprayers used to disseminate the anthrax spores became clogged and inoperative."

Even the more successful Sarin attack on the Tokyo subway would almost be laughable, if not for the tragic deaths of twelve persons and harm caused to thousands more. For all its sophisticated research and development, the best means the group could find to disseminate the nerve gas was in plastic trash bags that had to be poked open with sharpened umbrella tips to release the noxious mixture.

Finally, the group's distinct lack of success in wreaking the mass destruction or mass casualties ascribed to these types of weapons, despite the considerable resources at its disposal, speaks volumes about the challenges facing any less-endowed terrorist organization. New research has revealed that, of the 5,000 persons who received medical treatment in the aftermath of the subway attack, the vast majority suffered from shock or emotional upset, or evidenced some psychosomatic symptom. Accordingly, the number of persons physically injured or affected by the attack may be much lower than previously reported.

In sum, Aum's experience suggests, however, counter intuitively or contrary to popular belief, the significant technological difficulties faced by any nonstate entity in attempting to weaponize and disseminate chemical and biological weapons effectively.

Although the Aum experience represents only a single point of reference, it provides a striking refutation of the claim about the ease with which such weapons can be fabricated and made operational. Public officials, journalists, and analysts, for example, have repeatedly alleged that biological attacks in particular are relatively easy for terrorists to undertake. According to one state emergency management official, biological weapons "are available and easy to make. . . . One does not need a degree in microbiology to make this work, being able to read is enough. . . . It's not like enriching uranium."

This is a correct assessment, but it should not be interpreted to say that there is no threat of the use of CBRN weapons by terrorists within the continental United States. Above we noted that when the FBI raided the CSA compound they discovered cyanide. More recently, on April 22, 1997, the North Texas Joint Terrorism Task Force (NT JTTF), in conjunction with the Wise County (Texas) Sheriff's Office, executed multiple arrest and search warrants for four members of the True Knights of the Ku Klux Klan.

The group had planned an elaborate scheme to rob two drug dealers of weapons and cash in order to outfit themselves for an armored car robbery. The armored car heist was to be preceded by the detonation of multiple diversionary bombs at a natural gas processing and storage facility, which could have caused the release of hydrogen sulfide into the air. The investigation also revealed that members of this group had detonated at least two "practice" explosive devices in preparation for the planned attack on the natural gas facility.[14] The release of the hydrogen sulfide would have constituted an attack using WMD, and an act of Domestic Terrorism by a group with no scientific capability using industrial chemicals.

The asymmetric threat brings to bear actions with state sponsorship, and there are approximately 25 countries with chemical and/or biological weapons capabilities, and some of these states could either use terrorist organizations and provide them with the weapons, or use the weapons themselves against the United States thereby greatly expanding the threat which can be classed as terrorism.

The threat against the United States was exemplified by the embassy bombings in Africa. The near simultaneous vehicular bombings of the US embassies in Nairobi, Kenya, and Dar Es Salaam, Tanzania, on August 7, 1998, were terrorist incidents costing the lives of over 220 persons and wounding more than 4,000 others. Twelve American US

Government employees and family members, and 32 Kenyan and 8 Tanzanian US Government employees, were among those killed. Both embassies withstood collapse from the bombings, but were rendered unusable, and several adjacent buildings were severely damaged or destroyed. These attacks, like those against the World Trade Center, the Alfred P. Murrah Building and other targets all used high explosives.

The choice of weapons, and the types of target are both driven by technology. As soon as new target types have been introduced, the terrorist has used them. Ships have provided targets from the times of the Barbary pirates, up to the unpremeditated, but nonetheless attention-getting seizing of the Achille Lauro. Planes soon presented themselves as targets for diverting, insurance fraud, and gaining attention. Skyscrapers and other large structures offer a concentration of people. Subways, trains, and planes all can be added to the list, for one thing is sure, the terrorist will adapt to the available targets, including the possibility of computer systems being the target of attack on the critical infrastructure. Knives and garrotes were replaced by guns, which are now eclipsed by bombs.

Improvement to fuses and detonators has made it easier for the terrorist to make their getaway, or plan for an explosive to detonate at a chosen time or place.

It is interesting to note that many terrorists prefer the "macho" weapon. Afghan guerrillas use women to plant land mines because they believe that it is not an activity for warriors. The indirect nature of some weapons of mass destruction may make them less appealing for this reason. Now we are threatened by the availability of weapons of mass destruction, and we would be denying history if we refuse to accept that terrorists will use whatever weapons technology is most suited to their objectives, including weapons of mass destruction.

The threat due to weapons, as we have seen in the discussion regarding the asymmetric threat, goes beyond the conventional explosives. According to FBI Director Louis Freeh, "There is now greater danger of nuclear attack by some outlaw group than there ever was by the Soviet Union during the Cold War."

A nuclear device could be small enough to be covertly transported to its intended detonation point by small truck, ship or small aircraft. Such a device could yield about the same as the weapons used in 1945. Certainly this is not news, and some good capabilities have been developed to search for and disable such a weapon, but these responses cover only a small part of the spectrum of threat scenarios. Such an attack requires significant skills and resources, and as such activities leave a signature: acquisition, a place to assemble the weapon, transportation, target surveillance, and so on. The track record of the United States and our allies has been considerably better than is commonly understood, and with their larger signatures, it is possible that nuclear threat operations could be detected for warning and interdiction. But, should an event occur, the effects would be unmeasurable, and the world would be changed forever.

Chemical warfare is not new. It was first recorded during the Peloponnesian wars when Spartan allies attacked the Athenian city of Delphi by directing smoke from lighted coals, sulfur, and pitch through a hollowed-out beam into the fort. Compared to nuclear weapons they are cheap and relatively easy to obtain. It is difficult to compute exactly how much it would cost to make some chemical agent, but figures suggest that a kilogram of Sarin would cost about $100.

Chemical weapons can be produced in a small covert laboratory or small-scale industrial facilities, and the technologies are dual use, giving the possibility of plausible denial.

In the late 1930s, a German industrial chemist, Dr. Gerhard Schrader, searching for more potent insecticides, synthesized tabun (GA), an extremely toxic organophosphorus compound. Two years later, he synthesized Sarin (GB), a similar but even more toxic compound. During World War II, Nazi Germany weaponized thousands of tons of these potent organophosphorus compounds that came to be called nerve agents. Why they were not used during the war is a matter of continuing discussion.

Hitler, himself a mustard casualty during World War I, did not favor their use; neither did his senior staff who had fought on chemical battlefields during that war.[16] This does not mean they may not appeal to the terrorist. Widely publicized reports of Iraqi use of chemical agents against Iran during the 1980s led to a United Nations investigation that confirmed the use of the vesicant mustard casualties and the nerve agent GA. Later during the war, Iraq apparently also began to use the more volatile nerve agent GB, and Iran may have used chemical agents to a limited extent in an attempt to retaliate for Iraqi attacks. Press reports also implicated cyanide in the deaths of Kurds in the late 1980s. They can be extremely lethal in small quantities, and the effects can be somewhat controlled.

They are likely to survive most dispersion techniques, be it an explosive or an aerosol. Their properties are well known and the terrorist can calculate how long the agent will remain active. Also, not all nerve agents produce immediate symptoms, giving the attacker time to make good his escape. Mustard is an extremely persistent agent as is exemplified by the case of the American freighter, the S.S. John Harvey, which was carrying 2,000 M47A1 bombs, each containing 60 to 70 pounds of sulfur mustard (H) bombs and an unknown quantity of high explosives when it was attacked during a German raid on Bari, Italy, on December 2, 1943, and sank in Bari Harbor, killing all aboard in the blast.

Shortly after the end of World War II, the United States dumped unspecified quantities of phosgene, hydrogen cyanide, and cyanogen chloride bombs in the Adriatic Sea off the Island of Ischia, near Bari. From 1946 to 1997, medical researchers at the University of Bari detected over 230 cases of exposure to mustard in the Adriatic Sea, most recently in June 1997. Most of the cases have been among Apulian trawler fishermen.[17] Phosgene, a lung-damaging pulmonary agent was used during World War I. Now Phosgene is a widely used chemical intermediate, primarily manufactured for the synthesis of isocyanate-based polymers, carbonic acid esters, and acid chlorides. It is also used in the manufacture of dyestuffs, some insecticides, and pharmaceuticals and in metallurgy. Large quantities are transported on the roads, and used in plants.

A chemical cloud released by the Rhone-Poulenc Ag Co. Institute plant on Friday night, October 15, 1999, was made up entirely of gas. Rhone-Poulenc used phosgene to make methyl isocyanate, or MIC, the pesticide ingredient that killed thousands of people when it leaked from a Union Carbide plant in Bhopal, India, in December 1984. At about 9:15 p.m. Friday, Kanawha County (West Virginia) emergency officials ordered people within two miles of the Institute plant to take shelter from a leak at the plant. The shelter-in-place was lifted at 10 p.m. for everywhere but the area immediately surrounding the plant. It was lifted for that area about 10:15 p.m.[18] The concern regarding terrorism is that use could be made of industrial chemicals, such as phosgene, without the attacker needing to go beyond destroying a storage facility or breaching a chemical tanker.

Biological weapons are the most discussed, and to some, the most worrisome. Biological agents are available and inexpensive and deniable. The difference between a small attack, and accidental release and a natural outbreak may be indiscernible. Note how Wayne Harris uses denials which could not have worked if he had been arrested with a large quantity of explosives.

There is one saving factor in all of this horror, and that is revulsion. There will be universal hate and revulsion directed at the perpetrator of a BW attack. In the case of a sponsored terrorist, or one attempting to make a point and gain something, this will be a very negative effect, and may be one of the reasons it has not been used as yet.

Because of the fear associated with the concept of a biological attack, and the fact that the initial effects are unseen the threat alone may be sufficient to the terrorists goal, and response plans should encompass this scenario. The biological weapon also presents another specific challenge to response planning - the actual event may not be detected, and the effects - victims - may not occur for hours or even days after the attack. The first responders will, in the absence of intelligence or a threat, be unaware of what they are dealing with. In fact the first responders will probably be hospitals and medical clinics.

Biological Weapons have followed a similar development pattern to chemical weapons. As early as 400 B.C., Scythian archers used arrows dipped in blood and manure, and in 1346 the Mongols catapulted plague infected bodies into Caffa, possibly initiating the spread of the disease throughout Europe. In 1650 the Polish artillery developed hollow spheres full of saliva from rabid dogs.

In 1915 the Germans initiated programs in the United States and the Western and Eastern fronts to infect horses and cattle respectively with glanders and anthrax. Other accusations have been made against the Germans and all were denied. One of the characteristics of a biological weapon is that "plausible deniability" is often applicable, for many outbreaks can be passed off as natural. This fact that an attack can be masked as natural adds to the requirement for security officers to be alert to medical anomalies.

The United States considered the development of biological (toxin) weapons in 1918, but in 1926 Major General Fries decided that the development of biological weapons was not practical.

In 1933 Major Leon Fox of the Medical Corps wrote, "Bacterial warfare is one of the recent scare-heads that we are being served by the pseudo-scientists who contribute to the flaming pages of the Sunday annexes syndicated over the Nation's press." One sees similar views expressed today, but, as he wrote, the Germans were testing using simulants in the Paris Metro. By 1940 Britain, France, Japan and other countries all had robust offensive biological warfare programs. The Japanese program, Imperial Unit 731, is estimated to have killed more than 1,000 prisoners while experimenting with anthrax, botulism, brucellosis, cholera, dysentery, gas gangrene, meningococcal infection and plague. In 1942 the United States created the short-lived War Research Service, and in 1943 Fort Detrick was activated and equipped with four biological agent production plants. The US program targeted agriculture in addition to people and eventually created the M114 4 lb. anti personnel bomb (containing 300 ml of Brucella Suis) and the 80 lb. anti plant balloon bomb. The United States offensive program ended at the same time in 1968 as the offensive chemical program, however, it is known that other countries continued to develop biological weapons into the 1990s, and some programs still exist. One of the more famous incidents of the use of a biological agent was when, in 1978, a Bulgarian exile named Georgi Markov was attacked in London with an umbrella which discharged a ricin-filled pellet into his leg. He died several day later, unlike a compatriot, Vladimir Kostov who was attacked in Paris using the same design of weapon. In Kostov's case the pellet did not release the ricin.[19]

After the Gulf War, Iraq disclosed that it had prepared 166 bombs containing botulinum toxin, anthrax, or aflatoxin; 25 scuds with the same agents and 122-mm rockets; spray tanks and artillery shells.

As was discussed earlier in this chapter there is great need to better calculate the threat, and not confuse "can" with "will" and "vulnerability" with "threat." How do motives and trends translate into threats and targets?

For a political act with the purposeful intent of influencing the political process or to insert the sponsor's own government, will terrorists target persons of the ruling government, government symbols, foreign residents, journalists and educators of the country? Economic damage may be intended and the targeting of commercial carriers in the seventies and eighties greatly affected the tourist trade globally. Economic terrorism can also strike at the heart of the economy.

Although the greatest concentration is a threat to people, consequence managers would be prudent to remember that there is a whole other class of attack that may spread disease, or infect produce and destroy the economy of an agricultural region. Between 1977 and 1979, more than 40 percent of the Israeli European citrus market was curtailed by a Palestinian plot to inject Jaffa oranges with mercury. In 1989 a Chilean left-wing group that was part of an anti-Pinochet movement claimed that it had laced grapes bound for US markets with sodium cyanide, causing suspensions of Chilean fruit imports by the United States, Canada, Denmark, Germany, and Hong Kong. In the United States the USDA has eradicated diseases such as foot-and-mouth disease, a highly contagious disease affecting cloven hoofed animals.

If that were to be reintroduced accidentally or deliberately, the economic losses could be catastrophic. (In February 2001 there was an outbreak of foot-and-mouth disease in England, Scotland and Northern Ireland.)

A terrorist group is not a terrorist group until it has brought its commitment to fruition. The act of terror is meant to make tangible and visible all of its ideology. The act is choreographed for maximum effect on the audience. Steve Sloan calls this the "theater of the obscene." Therefore the target is the medium in which to accomplish the act of terrorist theater. Irony in the choice of target is a main factor as well as irony in the date chosen for the act. The most recent example of a significant date playing a deciding factor is the April 19, 1995, bombing of the Alfred P. Murrah Federal Building in Oklahoma City which may have been based on the April 19, 1993, death of Branch Davidian leader David Koresh.

To help identify potential targets, and then harden them, we use several methodologies which combine motivation and operational feasibility. One is "CARVER." Six simple factors are examined.

Criticality: How will the attack on the target impact the terrorists intended audience and the public on the whole?

Accessibility: Is the target accessible enough to complete the attack? Terrorists are success oriented and will tend to choose targets that will guarantee them success without being caught or the attempt thwarted.

Recoverability: The willingness to take the time and risk must also be based on the long-term effect on the target. It is not enough to sabotage a facility if the damage may be repaired without disruption to operations.

Vulnerability: What will it take to successfully accomplish the task of destroying the target and where are the points of vulnerability to allow for maximum damage. The bombing at the military housing in Dhahran, Saudi Arabia was obviously assessed for the target's vulnerability. Even to the point in which the terrorists made a dry run by running a vehicle into the security gate to test the reaction of the security force.

Effect: As a result of the attack, what will be the effect on the group? Will it receive favorable reaction from its supporters or, due to the lethality of the attacks, will they repel their desired audience. Will the local authorities frightened by the possibility of more attacks, desist their operations against the terrorists, or will the act be so horrendous that the international community will collaborate in their apprehension? This was the case in the Pan Am 103 bombing, the World Trade Center bombing and the Achille Lauro hijacking.

Risk: With the exception of suicide bombers whose fate is decided, the terrorist must also assess the risk of capture when analyzing a target. What are all the potential escape routes from the target and is a delayed attack or detection possible?

Possible targets abound, and it is only by analyzing the threat, and maintaining good intelligence they can be narrowed down to the most probable for any given locality.

To quote William Cohen, former US Secretary of Defense, "As the new millennium approaches, the United States faces a heightened prospect that regional aggressors, third rate armies, terrorist cells, and even religious cults will wield disproportionate power by using -- or even threatening to use -- nuclear, biological or chemical weapons against our troops in the field and our people at home."

ENDNOTES

1   Brent L. Smith, "Terrorism in America," 1994
2   Matt Bai *Newsweek*, September 29, 1997
3   1998 Strategic Assessment "Engaging Power for Peace, National Defense University, Chapter eleven.
4   Counterproliferation Program Review Committee's Report on Activities and Programs for Countering Proliferation and NBC Terrorism, May 1997.
5   Thomas J. Török et al., "A Large Community Outbreak of Salmonellosis Caused by Intentional Contamination of Restaurant Salad Bars," *JAMA (Journal of the American Medical Association)*, vol. 278, no. 5, 6 August 1997, pp. 389-395.
6   First Annual Report to The President and The Congress of the Advisory Panel To Assess Domestic Response Capabilities For Terrorism Involving Weapons Of Mass Destruction I. Assessing The Threat, December 15, 1999.
     "Terrorism in the United States," 1997. FBI annual report.
7   Report of the Accountability Review Boards on the Embassy Bombings in Nairobi and Dar es Salaam on August 7, 1998.

8   United States Army Medical Research Institute Of Chemical Defense Medical Management Of Chemical Casualties Handbook.

9   Dr. Sivo and Dr. Lobuono of the University of Bari: data from their studies on the continuing exposure of fisherman to mustard gas.

10   Ken Ward Jr., staff writer, *The Charleston Gazette.*

11   United States Army Institute for Infectious Diseases -- *Textbook of Military Medicine.*

12   Jenkins, Brian.

13   Maximillian Robespierre, "Republic of Virtue"

14   The Avalon Project at the Yale Law School. "The Barbary Treaties: Algeria, September 5, 1795," Hunter Miller's Notes.

15   "Terrorism in America," Brent L. Smith, 1994

16   Louis J. Freeh, Director, Federal Bureau of Investigation before the United States Senate Committee on Appropriations Subcommittee for the Departments of Commerce, Justice, and State, the Judiciary, and Related Agencies, February 4, 1999

Chapter 14

The Challenge of Cyberterrorism*
By Robert T. Thetford, J.D.

The first known cyberattack occurred in 1998, and was a limited attempt by Tamil guerrillas to swamp Sri Lankan embassies with e-mail, according to US officials. This attack may have been crude and ineffective but it set the stage for more serious cyber attacks in the future.

*Excerpted from "A survey of Terrorism," By Robert T. Thetford, Copyright 2000, Institute for Criminal Justice Education, Inc., P.O. Box 293, Montgomery, AL 36101. (www.ICJE.org). Used with permission.

While the use of "hacking" or more appropriately named "cracking" techniques have been used by unscrupulous individuals (mostly teenagers) for over ten years in the United States to gain unauthorized access to computer systems, the use of these techniques by states or organized groups to deliberately disable or destroy the computer systems of their enemies is a relatively recent phenomenon.

In 1999 an Associated Press report detailed an apparent coordinated electronic attack by the Chinese on Internet web sites operated by the Falun Gong meditation group. The report stated that at least one "hacking" attempt appeared to have been traced back to a Chinese national police bureau in Beijing.

ATTACK METHODS

The vast majority of electronic attacks involve amateurs who have copied programs from the Internet or from their friends. Armed with these programs, the attackers, most of whom are still in school or are school age, can and have caused damages running in the millions. Other hackers attack computer systems merely for the thrill of the attack itself, and leave "calling cards" as to their visits or simply do it in order to brag to their friends.

Often a hacker will gain access and open a "back door," a separate entry point to the computer system, which allows the hacker to enter the system undetected at will and provides a sense of ownership over the system. Knowing that the system is his for the taking provides a feeling of absolute power which is frequently necessary for the hacker's self-esteem.

A further measure of control involves inserting a "Trojan Horse" into the system files. This is a program which a system accepts, usually because it is not detected or because it is recognized as a benign file. Trojan Horses often contain malicious code in the form of "Logic Bombs," which are programs which reside in the system without interfering with the system operation until activated through the passage of a certain amount of time or the occurrence of a certain event. Upon activation, the Logic Bomb may do anything its designer has programmed it to do, including destroying the system files or spreading viruses.

A virus is by definition a program which reproduces itself. It may destroy or alter data or use system memory, or it may simply reproduce itself, but it generally stays within the computer system.

Worms are similar to viruses in that they copy themselves over and over, generally degrading system resources, but they are designed to reproduce across computers systems (for example, through e-mail) and are, therefore, potentially much more dangerous. Even the most innocuous of these are vicious, however, and cause serious problems for computer systems. Although the total number of viruses (and worms) is unknown, one leading manufacturer of anti-virus software advertises that its program protects against over 47,000 viruses.

Just how much damage do they cause? The latest estimates of the worldwide virus, the "Love Bug," which originated in the Philippines and quickly spread to both Europe and the United States, indicate that the damage to computer systems may run as high as $10 billion. This virus was allegedly created by college students as a prank. Imagine what a terrorist group could accomplish with determination and a fundamental understanding of computer technology.

A growing form of cyberterrorism common in Europe (but not unknown in the United States) is cyberextortion. The typical scenario in this criminal activity occurs when an individual or group threatens to destroy data files of a company if a certain fee is not paid or an action by the company is not undertaken.

Often the extortionists will have gained entry into the system files and left a "calling card" in order to prove the validity of the threat. Companies frequently accede to the demands rather than report the threat to the police because they understand the damage that can be done and also because they are afraid of the effect on their customer or client base if a security breach of client data becomes publicly known.

Perhaps the most devastating computer attacks occurring in 1999 and 2000 have been "Denial-of-Service" (DOS) attacks, often caused by "Mail Bombs." In this type of attack, third-party computer systems are in essence hijacked and used to flood the target system with requests for information or e-mails, thereby totally overwhelming the target system and shutting it down for commercial traffic. DOS attacks cost private industry only $77,000.00 in 1998, but cost an estimated $8 million in damages during the first two months of the year 2000 alone. In the United States, Mail Bombs have been used by eco-terrorists to tie up their adversaries, with over 50,000 e-mails being sent in 1998 to a Swedish facility that does research using monkeys.

The DOS attacks have caused considerable damage to major US corporations, yet they appear to have been directed by teenagers, not organized terrorist groups. The magnitude of damage which could be caused by a well organized and orchestrated attack carried out simultaneously from numerous locations is staggering to computer security professionals.

THE TARGETS

Most experts feel that military installations, power plants, air traffic control centers, banks and telecommunication networks themselves are the most likely targets for a cyberterrorist attack. Other targets include police, medical, fire and rescue systems, which could easily be damaged, along with Wall Street brokerage firms and water/sewage systems.

During the Gulf War in 1990, a group of Dutch hackers calling themselves "High Tech for Peace" approached diplomats in the Iraqi Embassy in Paris.

The hackers offered to disrupt the electronic network handling logistics messages between bases in the US and US military units in Saudi Arabia if the Iraqi Government paid a fee of $1 million. The Iraqis refused, but in reality they probably should have accepted the offer. A study later showed that 25 percent of the electronic messages coming into Saudi Arabia were uncoded and were totally vulnerable to interception and disruption. Had this offer been excepted the US military supply lines would have been severely affected.

In a briefing before the US Congress, George Tenet, Director of the US Central Intelligence Agency, said at least a dozen countries are developing programs to attack other nations' information and computer systems. China, Libya, Russia, Iraq, and Iran are among those developing such systems. Additionally, a new classified National Intelligence Estimate reports at least one instance to date of active cybertargeting of the United States by a foreign nation.

In 1996 a Swedish hacker, moving through cyberspace from London to Atlanta to Florida, rerouted and tied up telephone lines to 11 counties, put 911 emergency service systems out of commission, and impeded the emergency responses of police, fire, and ambulance services.

While many of the foreign cyberattacks grab the headlines, domestic cyberattacks are increasing at an alarming rate with the number of pending FBI cases involving cyberattacks increased from 128 in 1996, to 1,154 in 1999.

Nor are the cyberattacks limited to business and educational establishments. In 1998 the FBI executed search warrants on the homes of two California high school students after determining that they had gained entry to a number of government computer sites. Their hacker assaults on the Pentagon, NASA, and a US nuclear-weapons research lab were described by a deputy defense secretary as "the most organized and systematic attack" on US computers ever discovered. To make the Pentagon attack hard to trace, the hackers routed it through the United Arab Emirates. They were directed in this attack by a teenage hacker in Israel. While all of those involved were arrested, in a typical case little punishment is imposed on teen hackers due to their age.

The situation is even more complicated with the discovery of a teenage hacker in another country. In most recent situations, the United States has left the prosecution of teenagers to the discretion of their home country, even if extradition treaties would allow prosecution here.

The vulnerability of technologically advanced countries such as the United States to cyberattacks became acutely apparent through government studies of the Y2K problem in 1999. It was discovered that the "triad" of electric power, banking and telecommunications was especially susceptible to cyberattacks because of the heavy use of computers in these industries and the mandated use of telecommunications to link the computers. The interdependence of these industries makes protection against electronic intrusion vital to the continuation of an advanced society. When it is understood that without telecommunications, both banking and electric power will fail; that without electric power, both telecommunications and banking will fail; and that without banking, the economic infrastructure of a country will fail, then the magnitude of the problem can be seen.

James D. Kallstrom, former chief of engineering at the FBI laboratory in Quantico, Virginia, in discussing the possibility of computer network based cyberattacks, advised:

"We are using the efficiencies of technology and the Information Age to control everyday things like traffic lights, 911 systems, the environment of buildings, the communications network, and the power grid. We even control the water supply with computers. We are doing more and more things like that. In the old days ... Fort Knox was the symbol of how we protected things of great value: we put them in buildings with thick walls and concrete. We put armed guards at the doors, with sophisticated multiple locks and locking bars. We could even build a moat and fill it with alligators.

"Today [with] things of that same value, you wonder if some teenager is going to go in on the phone lines and steal it all. We are not equipped to deal with those issues both in the government and private industry."

Brian Jenkins, an analyst at the Rand Corporation, a US think tank, expressed a similar view:

"In the past, when terrorists wanted to conspire, they usually had to get together and meet in person. Nowadays, they can take to the Internet and find like-minded believers, even if they don't know them already.

"We have not even begun to comprehend the consequences of the Internet to create an army. Their ability to communicate with one another, to find reinforcement -- even justification -- for crazy views is of extraordinary importance."

THE FUTURE

It was estimated that by the end of the year 2000, 90 percent of all criminals would be computer literate. This percentage would indicate a dramatic increase in the number of computer crimes overall, including the use of computers for terrorist acts. As the computer literacy of terrorists increases, so should the number of cyberattacks by terrorist groups show a corresponding increase.

There has never been a greater need for joint government and private industry cooperation to meet what will likely be the next great threat to the security of our nation's infrastructure. Reaction on the part of cyberattack victims (in both government and private industry sectors) continues to vary widely to both published and unpublished attacks. Some companies have taken an extremely aggressive stance, even to the point of reversing DOS attacks and actually counterattacking the DOS originators. On the opposite end of the spectrum, many companies merely attempt to close the door to the attack and quietly look for ways to defeat attacks in the future, giving as little publicity as possible to the attack and hoping the attacker will seek another victim in the future. Still other companies have opted for litigation and criminal action to stop the attacks, understanding that only by pursuing actions which inflict legal pain will attacks be stopped.

Recent technology has enabled government agencies to electronically search an attacking computer for evidence of the attack, and the potential is not limited to purely defensive methods.

According to the *New York Times*, the US Department of Defense has set up a Cyberwarfare Center which provides offensive cyberwarfare capabilities, including strategies designed to "infect enemy software, upset enemy logistics, and disable enemy air defense systems." One immediate usage for the Center's programmers during the war in Kosovo was to conduct "attacks on Serbian computer systems in an effort to change banking records and deplete Serbian assets."

A review of published data indicates no unified approach in the defense of cyberattacks, whether they be from teenage computer hackers or from dedicated terrorist groups bent on destroying the United States. While recent changes in state and national criminal laws have closed some of the more obvious loopholes, the basic fact is that, as a nation, we have failed to recognize the enormous nature of the threat to our society. Law enforcement attempts to plug gaping holes in electronic fences have been repeatedly and effectively thwarted by those who consistently place privacy above security.

Until the threat is recognized as not random and isolated, not the pranks of a few talented but misguided individuals, but is rather the opening salvo of a massive and deadly serious assault against the very fabric of our technological culture, no effective steps will be taken to prevent and neutralize the threat. It may just be that, until we experience an "Electronic Pearl Harbor," we will continue to approach the problem in a piecemeal and ineffective manner, always playing catch-up with the other side and always at least one step behind in the on-going war against computer literate criminals and cyberterrorists.

EDITOR'S NOTE:

The FBI worked jointly with the National Security Council, the Department of Defense, and others to set up a plan to increase cybersecurity. The plan outlines who should meet in times of a cyberattack and puts the multi-agency National Infrastructure Protection Center on top.

The FBI's National Infrastructure Protection Center (NIPC) is where the FBI and other federal agencies investigate cybercrimes, including those by hackers. NIPC recommends that computers be updated with the latest anti-virus systems. To assist in this effort, the NIPC makes available detection tools. The NIPC was established in 1998 to serve as the US government's central organization to assess cyberthreats, issue warnings and coordinate responses. The Secret Service has also taken a major role in the war against computer attacks. A Secret Service spokesperson said, "This will be the crime of the future. The reason why we're expanding the number of people we have and dedicating more manpower and training is because we see the future."

The NIPC, located at FBI headquarters, is charged by the President with leading the US government's efforts to detect, warn of, investigate, and respond to significant, malicious cyberevents against the Nation's critical infrastructures. NIPC Director Michael Vatis said, "We believe that having these procedures in place will help ensure prompt and meaningful coordination among federal agencies whenever we are faced with cyberattacks that could have a significant impact on our national security, national economy, public safety or military operations."

Top US military and corporate security experts met in June 2000 to discuss strategies to protect vital technology from cyberattacks originating in foreign countries. The move was an indication of growing concern about the threat to national security from new methods of "information warfare." The National Defense Industrial Association's symposium on critical infrastructure addressed conventional threats to infrastructure such as telecommunications, banking and power supply, but also unveiled new products to defend these vital services from hacker attacks originating in foreign countries.

Terrorists are embracing the opportunities offered by recent leaps in information technology. To a greater and greater degree, terrorist groups, including Hizballah, HAMAS, the Abu Nidal organization, and bin Laden's al-Qa'ida organization are using computerized files, e-mail, and encryption to support their operations.

The US has had its share of successes, but really has only succeeded in buying time against an increasingly dangerous threat. The difficulty in destroying this threat lies in the fact that our efforts will not be enough to overcome the fundamental causes of the phenomenon -- poverty, alienation, disaffection, and ethnic hatreds deeply rooted in history. In the meantime, constant vigilance and timely intelligence are our best weapons.

While a number of excellent studies -- both classified and unclassified -- have been produced on the information warfare threat, popular journalism has also produced a great deal of hyperbole on this subject. That the National Information Infrastructure is vulnerable to an Information Warfare attack is unarguable. A recent National Intelligence Estimate verified this threat. The challenge comes in providing context and a proper appreciation of the nature of the vulnerabilities and the extent of the threat.

Traditionally, the information warfare threat has been associated with the telecommunications infrastructure and the ability to communicate. This remains a primary area of concern. But the US Government is also growing more and more dependent upon the commercial power, transportation, energy, and finance communities, and these communities are also vulnerable to attack.

All of these major national infrastructures share a common dependency on computer-driven, management-and-control systems. With the passage of time, technical and economic imperatives have driven these infrastructures to more and more dependence on networked computer-driven systems. Indeed, the complexity of the software involved in the "system-of-systems" that drive some of the major infrastructures is a significant concern.

By virtue of this increasing dependence on networked computer-driven systems, all of these infrastructures possess some degree of vulnerability to infowar attack. The question is how vulnerable?

Some of the critical infrastructures (e.g., the Public Switched Telephone Network (PSTN) have been the subject of hacker attacks for years. A number of the major companies operating networks that comprise the PSTN have very robust programs to defeat toll fraud and ensure network continuity. Others have placed less emphasis on this problem and, while a structure exists to facilitate cooperation among the various companies, the level and quality of the cooperation is mixed.

The continued globalization of the economy, information, and technology will provide significant new opportunities for those seeking to terrorize or intimidate. This is because the interdependencies created by such networking provide a broader base for greater destruction, especially in the areas of infowar. Concurrently, these very trends may also provide new and better means of tracking, capturing, preventing or deterring these same criminal elements. However, our own growing dependency on computer-driven systems in government, within industry, and throughout the Nation's infrastructures of oil and gas, finance, communications, power, and transportation undoubtedly increases our vulnerability.

The President's Commission on Infrastructure Protection has vigorously studied the vulnerabilities of our infrastructure, however, it remains to be seen if our society can effectively organize itself to protect these key assets of our nation. (The denial-of-service attacks launched against several major Internet sites in February 2000 graphically demonstrates this growing threat to our national security and well being.)

Whatever tools terrorists select, the fact of increasing cooperation between crime, narcotics and terrorist groups will provide terrorists with new, more creative ways to raise money and a marketplace to shop for weaponry and high tech equipment. Weapons of mass destruction are not the only highly destructive tools that terrorists may use. As the government becomes more and more dependent upon commercial off-the-shelf information technologies, products, and networks, it will become more vulnerable to the infowar threat.

This vulnerability will not be limited to potential infowar attack on the operation of support infrastructures, but also will include potential "time bomb" attack via pre-programmed imbedded software in operating systems, much of which software is written abroad.

In addition to foreign nations placing more emphasis on developing infowar capabilities, there is growing evidence that drug cartels and other transnational groups -- to include some terrorist groups -- have recognized the potential for infowar and are developing capabilities. In fact, some groups, like the FARC, ELN, Provisional IRA, and the Sendero Luminoso, already target information infrastructures today for the purposes of collecting intelligence, targeting data, and monitoring of law enforcement and other government activities. In time, with the increasing availability of infowar attack information on the Internet and in other public media, transnational groups will establish some modicum of capability in this arena.

It is the American character to believe we can solve all problems with our ingenuity and hard work. But even if the United States intelligence and law enforcement communities were given the means to correct these gaps, there still would remain a significant portion of terrorist planning, preparation, operations and attacks that will be unpredictable. Just as better defenses have turned some terrorists away from harder targets, the amorphous nature of the "new" terrorism, combined with the uncertainty inherent in predictive analysis of chaotic behaviors, means that some events will remain unforeseen.

We, as a nation, may not be able to prevent all acts of terrorism given the nature of our democratic society. However, the new vehemence of terrorist groups and their access to both high technology and weapons of mass destruction make it imperative that we do our utmost to prevent terrorist acts and prepare for the dire consequences if we fail.

A study conducted in December 2000, reflected that more than 100 million people now use the Internet and this number will increase exponentially in the years ahead. This increases the nation's vulnerabilities to cyberattack.

In late October 2000, hackers broke into Microsoft's computer network and gained access to blueprints for software under development. If Microsoft cannot protect itself from hackers, it illustrates how vulnerable every computer user really is. The intrusion reportedly was traced to a source in Russia.

A study by Kroll Associates, a business investigative firm, shows that executives of Internet companies are four times more likely to have an unsavory past than their counterparts at other companies. Nearly 40 percent of senior Internet managers have criminal convictions or connections to questionable organizations compared to 10 per cent at non-Internet companies. Out of 70 background checks conducted by Kroll Associates, 27 Internet executives were linked to white collar crimes or with ties to the Russian Mafia.

A September 2000 survey of corporate computer-security specialists reported that hackers had stolen proprietary information, sabotaged systems and vandalized web sites. Computer hacking or fraud cost three companies more than $5 million.

The FBI is sponsoring chapters of a networking group called Infra Gard in various cities to afford computer specialists an opportunity to meet and discuss security problems.

Larry Dalci, head of security at Kansas City Power and Light Company, reported that workers formerly manually opened and closed switches that control the power grid, but now those switches are controlled by computer. He said hackers at 5,000 different Internet sites use automated scans to try to break into the utility's computers. Dolce said, "It's just constant, 24 hours per day."

Early in 2000 a nationwide survey by the Computer Security Institute and the FBI found that 643 companies reported losing $265 million to computer hackers in 1999. The number goes up every year.

Of the tens of thousands of known computer viruses, the "Love Bug" which circulated in May 2000, was by far the fastest spreading. This virus sent copies from one computer to hundreds of other Internet users, overwhelming computer networks and destroying files.

The general defense against viruses is arming computers with anti-virus software and warning users not to open e-mail attachments that look suspicious.

In the case of the "Love Bug," the virus proliferated before the software could be updated and the creator of the virus lured in recipients with the heading, "I LOVE YOU" and listed sender addresses known to the recipient. Even after updates to defensive software were available, new versions of the virus appeared, some of which were even disguised as warnings about viruses.

In another case -- one of many -- a 20-year-old hacker penetrated sensitive National Aeronautics and Space Administration computers at the Jet Propulsion Laboratory in Pasadena, California, and Stanford University. He then used them to hack into other government and university systems. He admitted that he had hacked into "hundreds, maybe thousands of computers" over a two-year period.

In May 2000 the Department of Justice and the FBI launched a web site (http//www.ifccfbi.gov) on which consumers and businesses can report suspected Internet fraud. Complaints will be sent to the appropriate federal, state, local or foreign law enforcement agency.

Increased tension in the Middle East spawned cyberthreats targeting the computers of government and private companies. The FBI recommended that government agencies and private companies take certain security measures. Security officials should be prepared to take appropriate steps to prevent e-mail flooding attacks against computers, block source e-mail addresses in the event of flooding and make sure that appropriate patches are installed in operating systems to limit vulnerability to other types of denial-of-service attacks.

Some terrorists have set up web sites to disseminate their propaganda. The Colombian group ELN, which is noted for blowing up oil rigs and kidnapping foreign executives, is trying to extend its influence through its websites.

The Defense Intelligence Agency has a list of 70 terrorist websites. Under the US Constitution's First Amendment, these groups have a right to use their websites for propaganda as long as they do not engage in criminal acts.

Germany's Red Army Faction has supposedly disbanded after a 28-year reign of terror, but co-founder Horst Mahler still has a website (www.horst-mahler.de).

Terrorists use encrypted e-mail as a fast, reliable method for planning terrorist attacks. They also use the Internet for training and exchanging information. They often cooperate with each other in training and in operations. They also use the Internet for fundraising.

In the February 6, 2001, issue of <u>USA Today</u> reporter Jack Kelley wrote about a fascinating use of computer technology by terrorists. He reported that US officials say that Osama bin Laden and his associates, as well as other terrorist groups, are concealing messages to his operatives throughout the world in other people's images and web sites. They are hiding maps and photographs of terrorist targets and giving instructions for terrorist activities on Internet sites.

Hiding messages in pictures is called steganography. Images -- pictures or maps -- are created by a series of dots. There is a string of letters and numbers inside the dots which computers read to create the image. A coded message or another image can be hidden in those letters and numbers. The programs scramble the messages or pictures into existing images. The images can only be unlocked by using a private key or code.

Former FBI Director Louis Freeh told a US Senate committee in March 2000, "Uncrackable encryption is allowing terrorists to communicate without fear of outside intrusion. They're thwarting the efforts of law enforcement."

Bin Laden and his cohorts have used this technique to facilitate at least three operations.

Reuven Paz, academic director of the Institute for Counterterrorism in Israel, was quoted by Kelley as saying, "All the Islamists and terrorist groups are now using the Internet to spread their messages. The Internet has become another battleground."

Ben Venske, director of special intelligence projects for iDefense of Fairfax, Virginia, was quoted as saying, "There is a tendency out there to envision a stereotypical Muslim fighter standing with an AK-47 in Afghanistan, but HAMAS, Hezballah and bin Laden's groups have very sophisticated, well-educated people. Their technical equipment is good, and they have the bright, young minds to operate them."

He added that you could have sitting on your computer a photograph or other image which includes the time and information of a planned terrorist attack and you would never know it. It will look no different than a photograph exchanged between two friends.

US officials admit that it is very difficult to find encrypted messages and images and, even if you find them, it is impossible to read the hidden message without cracking the code, a very time-consuming process.

Although these terrorist groups began using this technique about five years ago, their use accelerated when they learned that US officials are tapping bin Laden's telephone calls from his base in Afghanistan. Encryption programs can also scramble telephone conversations. Law enforcement officers could be listening to a tapped telephone call in which a bombing attack is planned but be unable to get the hidden message to prevent the attack.

Ahmed Jabril, spokesperson for the Hezballah organization, said, "Encryption is brilliant. Now it's possible to send a verse from the Koran, an appeal for charity and even a call for jihad and know it will not be seen by anyone hostile like the Americans."

The State University of New York at Binghamton barred from its computer network, the guerrilla group Revolutionary Armed Forces of Columbia (FARC) which promptly moved to an Internet server at the University of California at San Diego (burn.ucsd.edu/~farc.ep).

Monitoring these sites seems to be an excellent way to keep track of them and have an early warning for an attack, but the FBI is prohibited from keeping files on these groups. It is absurd that the FBI is expected to keep tabs on these groups but is prohibited from keeping files on them unless it is connected to a criminal investigation. In a far wiser approach to the problem, Sri Lanka has outlawed the separatist group, the Liberation Tigers of Tamil Eelam, and officials continue to monitor its London-based web site (www.eelam.com).

Through its web page, Peru's vicious Sendero Luminoso (Shining Path) (www.blythe.org/peru/pcp) sets forth its four forms of struggle: propaganda, sabotage, combat and selective annihilation.

In May 2000 Russian ultranationalist Vladimir Zhirinovsky urged that the computer virus could be used to advance Russian foreign policy. He said, "The era of detective stories and James Bond has long been over. Now there is a different era -- the era of computers and the Internet. And we can bring the entire West to its knees with our Russian computer specialists. Let us put viruses into their secret programs like we did recently, and they will not be able to do anything." He continued, "It is time to put an end to the news focusing on Chechnya. It must be closed down as a combat spot, and we must track computer viruses more. Thanks to us, the West will soon suffer enormous losses." Obviously, Zhirinovsky only speaks for a minority in Russia, but it only takes a minority to do serious harm to our computer systems.

As mentioned above, the FBI is very concerned that a terrorist group will launch an electronic attack on US computers, raising havoc with the government and every aspect of our economy and national life. If such an attack were successful, it could shut down airports, power plants and communications systems.

A virus can take many forms and is intended by design to surreptitiously infiltrate, spread and damage computers. Computers which offer standard services are not capable of detecting or identifying these viruses, but many companies sell software to identify and block viruses on a case-by-case basis. Hacktivists (who merge hacking and activism) often launch hacking attacks as part of a protest against some event. As a defensive strategy, governments and companies should monitor their systems and networks for possible intrusion during major events and re-evaluate computer security procedures. Such procedures include up-to-date, appropriate virus detecting software, blocking or limiting unnecessary inbound traffic, regular checking of inactive user accounts, and making login and password changes.

ENDNOTES

1   "US: First Cyberattack by Terrorists," Reuters Report, May 5, 1998,
        <http://news.cnet.com/news/0-1005-200-
        328992.html?st.ne.fd.mdh > (April 25, 2000).

2   Claims Sites Under Attack," Associated Press, July 31, 1999,
        <http://www.jsonline.com/bym/tech/ap/jul99/ap-sect-
        hacking073199.asp> (April 25, 2000).

3   David Noack, "Love Bug" Damage Worldwide: $10 Billion," _ABP News_, May 8, 2000,
        Http://www.apbnews.com/newscenter/internetcrime/2000/05/08/lo
        vebug_impac t0508_01.html?s=syn.emil_lovebug_impact0508>
        (May 9, 2000).

4   Andrew Quinn, "Risky Business; Computer Security a Top Issue,"
        ABC News, March 22, 2000,
        <http://www.abcnews.go.com/sections/tech/DailyNews/survey000
        322.html > (March 25, 2000).

5   Miguel Llanos, "Eco-extremists Using e-mail Bombs," MSNBC,
        October 24, 1998,
        <http://www.freerepublic.com/forum/a363216430d16.htm>
        (November 2, 1998).

6   John J. Fialka, "War by Other Means," (New York: W.W. Norton,
        1997), pp. 104-105.

7   Douglas Pasternak and Bruce B. Auster, "Terrorism at the Touch
         of a Keyboard," *US News & World Report,* July 13, 1998, p.37,
         <http://www.usnews.com/usnews/issue/980713/13cybe.htm>
         (April 27, 2000).
8   Ibid.
9   Sue Pleming, "Freeh: Cyber Attacks Doubled in '99," Reuters,
         March 28, 2000< http://biz.yahoo.com/rf/000328/8y.html> (April
         1, 2000).
10   Douglas Pasternak and Bruce B. Auster, "Terrorism at the Touch
         of a Keyboard," *US News & World Report*, July 13, 1998, p.37.
         <http://www.usnews.com/usnews/issue/980713/13cybe.htm>
         (4/27/00).
11   Simson Garfinkel, "Database Nation," (Sebastopol, California: --
         Reilly & Associates, 2000), p. 224.
12   Jim Krane, "Terror's 'Dark Undercurrent' Rises in America," APB
         News, April 19, 2000,
         <http://www.apbnews.com/newscenter/breakingnews/2000/04/19/t
         error0419_01 .html> (April 20, 2000).
13   Richard S. Groover, "Overcoming Obstacles: Preparing For
         Computer-related Crime," *FBI Law Enforcement Bulletin*, August
         1996 <http://www.fbi.gov/library/leb/1996/aug962.txt> (April 26,
         2000).
14   "Can You Hack Back?" CNN News, June 1, 2000,
         <http://www.cnn.com/2000/TECH/computing/06/01/hack.back.idg
         /index.html> (June 3, 2000).
15   Patrick Riley, "Feds Use Convicted Pedophile To Create Internet
         Spy Software," Fox News, August 16, 2000,
         <http://www.foxnews.com/national/081500/pedophile_riley.sml>
         (August 17, 2000).
16   Elizabeth Becker, "Pentagon Sets Up New Center for Waging
         Cyberwarfare," *New York Times*, October 8, 1999, p. A16.
17   "US: First Cyberattack by Terrorists," Reuters Report, May 5,
         1998,<http://news.cnet.com/news/0-1005-200-
         328992.html?st.ne.fd.mdh > (April 25, 2000).
18   "China Sect Claims Sites Under Attack," Associated Press, July 31,
         1999, <http://www.jsonline.com/bym/tech/ap/jul99/ap-sect-
         hacking073199.asp> (April 25, 2000).
19   David Noack, "Love Bug -- Damage Worldwide: $10 Billion,"
         ABP News, May 8, 2000,

Http://www.apbnews.com/newscenter/internetcrime/2000/05/08/lo
vebug_impac t0508_01.html?s=syn.emil_lovebug_impact0508>
(May 9,2000).

20   Andrew Quinn, "Risky Business; Computer Security a Top Issue,"
ABC News, March 22, 2000,
<http://www.abcnews.go.com/sections/tech/DailyNews/survey000
322.html > (March 25, 2000).

21   Miguel Llanos, "Eco-extremists Using e-mail Bombs," MSNBC,
October 24, 1998,
<http://www.freerepublic.com/forum/a363216430d16.htm>
(November 2, 1998).

22   John J. Fialka, "War by Other Means," (New York: W.W. Norton,
1997), pp. 104-105.

23   Douglas Pasternak and Bruce B. Auster, "Terrorism at the Touch
of a Keyboard," *US News & World Report*, July 13, 1998, p.37,
<http://www.usnews.com/usnews/issue/980713/13cybe.htm>
(April 27, 2000).

24   Ibid.

25   Sue Pleming, "Freeh: Cyber Attacks Doubled in '99," Reuters,
March 3, 2000< http://biz.yahoo.com/rf/000328/8y.html> (April 1,
2000).

26   Douglas Pasternak and Bruce B. Auster, "Terrorism at the Touch
of a Keyboard," *US News & World Report*, July 13, 1998, p.37.
<http://www.usnews.com/usnews/issue/980713/13cybe.htm>
(April 27, 2000).

27   Simson Garfinkel, Database Nation, (Sebastopol, California:
O'Reilly & Associates, 2000), p. 224.

28   Jim Krane, "Terror's 'Dark Undercurrent' Rises in America," APB
News, April 4, 2000,
http://www.apbnews.com/newscenter/breakingnews/2000/04/19/te
rror0419_01. html> (April 4, 2000).

29   Richard S. Groover, "Overcoming Obstacles: Preparing For
Computer-related Crime," *FBI Law Enforcement Bulletin*, August
1996, <http://www.fbi.gov/library/leb/1996/aug962.txt> (April 26,
2000).

30   "Can You Hack Back?" CNN News, June 1, 2000,
<http://www.cnn.com/2000/TECH/computing/06/01/hack.back.idg
/index.html> (6/3/00).

31   Patrick Riley, "Feds Use Convicted Pedophile To Create Internet
        Spy Software," Fox News, August 16, 2000,
        <http://www.foxnews.com/national/081500/pedophile_riley.sml>
        (8/17/00).
32   Elizabeth Becker, "Pentagon Sets Up New Center for Waging
        Cyberwarfare," _New York Times_, October 08, 1999, p. A16.

Chapter 15

Terrorism Case Studies: New York World Trade Center, Tokyo Subway Attack, and Oklahoma City Federal Building Bombing

By Timothy R. S. Campbell

Terrorism has been with us since the United States Government was founded over 200 years ago. From the Whiskey rebellion through the International Workers of the World (IWW), also known as the "Wobblies," Americans have protested government actions, often in violent fashion. From the actions of Tory Loyalists during the American Revolution through the USS Cole, groups with some form of state sponsorship have attacked the United States and its symbols.

Until recently, these activities have been in the form of armed attack by gunmen, such as the Puerto Rican nationalist attack on Congress in the 1950s, or kidnappings such as those of the Beirut 7. Only today, do we see the use of weapons designed to create large numbers of casualties. These weapons, referred to as Weapons of Mass Destruction or WMD, have introduced a new aspect to the issues of civilian and government preparedness. Even organizations that stated that they were at war with the United States, such as extreme protest groups during the Vietnam War, may have used explosives and the like but never directed their attacks against civilians. The introduction of these weapons, generally of a chemical, biological or nuclear nature, though large explosive devices may also be referred to as WMD, creates issues that must be analyzed and incorporated into preparedness activities.

From a preparedness point of view, this sort of event would be the equivalent of the "Super Bowl." It would be a major disaster striking at the community. There may or may not be a warning. In that sense, there are some parallels with earthquakes or tornadoes. However, the community needs a well-defined, trained response system backed up by an equally competent disaster management system.

Case studies play a vital part in such preparedness. Every community experiences crimes and fires so that lessons are learned from these events, but due to the limited number of WMD events, communities do not have the history to guide them. Thus, they must learn from the events of others.

To do so, training officials must identify what areas of the community preparedness require strengthening. This can be accomplished through drills or other analysis. Then, this information should be matched with existing case studies. Parallels should be drawn between the case study community environment and the community working on preparedness.

Three case studies form the basis for any WMD terrorism preparedness: the World Trade Center explosion of February 1993 in New York City, New York, the Sarin vapor nerve agent attack on the commuter riders and facilities of the Tokyo Subway System in Tokyo, Japan, in March 1995 and the explosive attack on the persons in the Murrah Federal

Building in Oklahoma City, Oklahoma, in April 1995. These cases contain all the issues that may impact responders to terrorist attacks.

CASE STUDY I: WORLD TRADE CENTER, NEW YORK CITY, FEBRUARY 26, 1993

A light mid-day snow was falling on the New York City metropolitan area. The noon temperature was in the mid twenties at street level amid the high rises of New York's commercial districts. Workers in the financial district and throughout the city were heading for lunch. Suddenly, there was a large explosion from the direction of Wall Street.

A 1,200-pound bomb made of nitro-urea, supplemented by hydrogen cylinders, and mounted in a rented Ryder truck, exploded on the B-2 level of the underground parking area of the World Trade Center. It tore an L-shaped crater 130 by 150 feet at the maximum point. There was damage to six floors below grade as well as at ground level.

The explosion impacted the entire World Trade Center complex. Built as one interconnected complex, the Center consists of seven major buildings. Two are the famous Twin Towers 110 stories tall. There are also two 9-story office buildings and one 47-story office building. Finally, there is an 8-story customs house and a 22-story hotel. There is over 8 million interconnected square feet, including an underground commuter transit station. It is the heart of the financial district and is often seen as the heart of capitalistic America.

The explosion was centered under one corner of the hotel. The plan seems to have been to topple one of the twin towers into the other. This would then have collapsed the second into the neighborhood. Counting the 25,000 individuals in each tower and those in the surrounding area, the planned potential causalities were over 125,000. While there is some debate and question as to whether this is possible from an engineering standpoint, it is clear that the attackers planned carefully and researched the information required to create a tremendous amount of damage.

The attackers had reportedly trained for a period of time on a farm in Perry County, Pennsylvania, a rural county located between Harrisburg and State College. They had built and tested model devices there. After traveling to Jersey City, New Jersey, they built the final bomb and mounted it in the rented Ryder truck. Their research on the target reportedly included analyzing plans of the complex which were obtained from procurement authorities who were planning to make renovations to the buildings. These plans were available to any interested party for a fee.

The challenges faced by agencies responding to the explosion were many. Injuries were extensive and numerous. A large complex had to be searched for those missing and injured. Several agencies had to mount major responses. Impacts were felt across state lines.

Miraculously, there were only six deaths caused by the explosion. Four victims died in a work area adjacent to the explosion center and one was found on an access ramp to the garage. The sixth was found by police 17 days later under rubble during their investigation. There were 1,042 confirmed injuries from the incident though this number remains in question due to people leaving the area and seeking treatment elsewhere. Patients were reported as far away as Philadelphia, Pennsylvania, to the South and to Hartford and New Haven, Connecticut, to the north. Emergency Medical Service units transported only 642 patients.

Of the injuries, 124 were police, fire and EMS personnel injured during the rescue effort. Thirty were pregnant females who had to be checked by both trauma and obstetrical surgeons. Fifteen were major trauma cases and twenty were cardiac problems. These all had to be transported during the snow and traffic for medical care. All major medical facilities in New York City received patients.

Search and rescue efforts had to be carried out all over the complex. Sixteen people were found trapped in a collapsed locker room near the epicenter of the explosion. People were rescued from a room that was precariously teetering over the crater ripped through the floors of the underground area. There were 111 elevators that had to be checked for persons trapped in them. Ten people were found unconscious in one single elevator.

In another, 72 young children on a tour of the World Trade Center were trapped. Many people were trapped in one of the Twin Towers and the hotel by smoke infiltrating past fire-and-smoke barriers compromised by the explosion. In total, 50,000 people evacuated the complex on their own by walking down fire towers as firefighters carrying equipment climbed up them. Firefighters had to carry some victims down 60 stories or more after having climbed up those stairs to rescue them. It took some 11 hours for the fire department to search and evacuate the towers.

In the midst of what would turn out to be the largest single incident in the history of the New York City Fire department, reports were received of a missing firefighter. Search-and-rescue efforts to retrieve him caused the diversion of two chief officers and seven response units from the main incident. He had fallen into the crater while trying to reach persons trapped by the explosion. His injuries were severe and required major surgery.

The rescue of the missing firefighter compounded the problem of on-scene communications. There was only one portable radio channel available for all 187 responding fire department units and chief officers. Two command channels and a tactical channel supplemented it. Runners were used to transmit many messages. This was compounded by the size of the complex and the fact that units were operating over a 1,200-foot vertical distance.

Thousands of calls flooded the New York City 911 system about the event. Many were from people in the immediate area and in the complex seeking information and help. Over 1,000 911 calls were screened by telecommunicators and passed to the on-scene Fire Department command post for follow up. Cellular telephone channels were swamped in the area by the demand placed by evacuees calling out and friends and relatives trying to call for information, and persons, including emergency officials, could not get access.

Many of these calls were made to media outlets when emergency lines were overloaded and people could not get through. This produced the situation where media on-the-air personalities were giving out advice to persons trapped in the buildings and live on-the-scene reports. Sometimes the advice given compounded the problems such as telling people to throw fax machines through windows to get fresh air. Flying debris, including fax machines and broken glass, endangered responders and citizens on the streets below.

Additionally, as the event continued, media outlets contacted their own experts in high rise buildings and fires. These people, without knowledge of the damage and tactical situation, spread a vast amount of misinformation about the event. Yet, the people trapped in the various buildings for an extended period were listening to these broadcasts.

The cause for the calls was the scope of the damage suffered by the complex. The fire alarm and public address systems were damaged and out-of-service. The Port Authority command station was out-of-service. The complex firewater standpipes were only partially available due to damage. The sprinkler system was out of service in the area of the explosion and the resultant fire. Power to many parts of the complex failed.

The emergency generators shut down after 20 minutes due to loss of cooling water. A ceiling collapsed into the PATH train station. The B-2 level was a scene of total devastation with cars strewn everywhere. Masonry walls and steel reinforced concrete flooring were blown apart. Smoke barriers in the complex were damaged.

The impact was not just in the immediate area of the complex. Several broadcast outlets and governmental and private radios systems were dependent on the twin towers as antenna locations. Wireless communications were disrupted over the entire metropolitan area for everything from television to paging services. The failure of the emergency generators affected the Telephone Company switching center located in the World Trade Center. This unit supplied service to the regional air traffic control center for the three major and all minor airports in the New York metropolitan area. Battery backup existed, but preventing the shut down of this facility was a crucial priority.

"Defend in place," a concept that depends on building systems, was not possible due to the vast damage and the critical systems which were disrupted. So, evacuation and firefighting became the priority. The firefighting, as the most effective methods of smoke control, became the operational priority after rescue in the below-grade area where cars and building components burned.

This was the largest response in the history of the New York City Fire Department. 45 percent of the on-duty strength covering the five boroughs were involved. 34 engine companies, 60 ladder and tower companies, 5 heavy rescue units, 26 support companies and 37 chief officers were on the scene. Fire Department personnel would be on the scene for over a month. While fire units from surrounding communities responded, there was no fire mutual aid officially activated.

Support, including on-scene care and transportation following triage, was provided by the New York City EMS agency (now part of the Fire Department but then independent). Patients were transported to all medical facilities in the area. Ambulances from New Jersey responded since many NYC units were far away from the scene while New Jersey was just across the river. Reportedly, the two tunnels connecting New York and New Jersey were established as one way in and one way out for the incident. (Editor's Note: *The terrorists also planned to blow up these two vitally important tunnels.)*   New Jersey units transported patients back to their base hospitals per state protocols.

The New York City Police Department, along with 18 other agencies, responded to the scene. New York City has a police force that ranks as large as some of the world's largest standing armies. The Department maintains daily reserve allocations of officers to respond for crowd control and other special circumstances. These officers, along with the Port Authority police, provided on-scene security and crime scene preservation while preparing for a major investigation.

Some problems resulted from the dispersion of patients all over the area. The New York Police Department had to interview witnesses to the event to try to establish what happened and who was responsible. Even with eyewitnesses spread over at least four and possibly more states, quick investigative work identified the vehicle used and where it had been rented. Police were able to establish surveillance on the office and arrested someone who turned up to claim the deposit on a supposedly stolen truck.

CASE STUDY II: SUBWAY SARIN ATTACK
IN TOKYO, JAPAN, MARCH 1995

The next major event established that today's terrorists can use chemical agents as well as explosives. In March of 1995, a cult in Japan carried out a second attack with the nerve agent Sarin. This is one of the family of nerve agents that was developed in the mid 20th Century as a weapon of war. The cult was protesting cultural issues as well as actions taken or planned against their organization by authorities.

During the height of Tokyo's morning rush hour, eleven bags containing a solution of Sarin liquid were placed on five separate commuter subway trains and in some stations. Cult members punctured them and left the scene immediately.

Transit authorities and other passengers became aware of the event as choking passengers began to leave trains and stations. Within minutes, people were stricken and Tokyo authorities began a major mass casualty incident response. Over the next few hours, over 5,000 people flooded nearby hospitals, requiring evaluation and sometimes treatment.

Despite the evidence of choking fumes and large numbers of injuries, the incident was not identified as a nerve agent incident for approximately three hours after the attack. It is said that an emergency room physician, who had treated victims of an earlier attack the previous year in Matsumoto City, saw a television report that described the symptoms and he recognized them as Sarin. He advised authorities in Tokyo.

During that previous attack, cult members drove through a residential neighborhood spraying Sarin into the air. Seven people died in an attack aimed at judicial officials who lived in that community.

Only 688 patients were transported by the EMS system. The rest went on their own or were taken to hospitals by bystanders. Some even took buses. The nearest emergency room saw over 500 patients the first hour.

Approximately 1,000 patients suffered exposures. The remaining 4,500 appear to have heard the symptoms and then thought they had been exposed, including persons that had not even been on the subway that day.

There were 1,000 doses of atropine, an antidote, available in the hospital system that day, apparently because of Japan's proximity to North Korea with its stockpile of weapons. This allowed rapid treatment.

Decontamination was not performed on all the victims and riders. 135 emergency responders were affected by exposure to clothing of victims. Approximately 20 percent of the hospital staffs suffered from exposures. Many of these individuals then required treatment at a time that hospitals were activating disaster plans. Many persons who left the area returned to hospitals later.

The Tokyo Fire Department is regarded as the world's largest. The Department dispatched 1,364 personnel and 340 response vehicles to the incident. Support was received from police and the Army Chemical Corps.

Tokyo depends on the subway as a major transportation system. Supported by the Army Chemical Corps, the Transit Authority re-established service on two of the three affected lines the same day and on the other on the next day. Ridership dropped by 30 percent within the first week after the attack and took several years to return to pre-attack levels. As of five years later, 10 percent of the victims had either quit school or left their jobs.

Over 50 percent of the victims report some lingering effects from the attack five years later. This includes fear of crowded places or subway rides. Thirty-seven percent requested financial assistance of some sort from the government. $484,000 was awarded to 18 families for loss of loved ones or injuries suffered. $2,600,000 was spent on medical expenses related to the incident. Forty-two sued the cult, but cannot sue the government reportedly due to Japanese laws on liability.

The personal belongings of injured and evacuated persons were placed in plastic bags. They were returned to the appropriate individuals with instructions to take them home and burn them. Reports indicate some mild re-exposures as people attempted to retrieve valuables before disposing of them.

CASE STUDY III: ALFRED P. MURRAH FEDERAL BUILDING IN OKLAHOMA CITY, APRIL 1995

On the second anniversary of the Waco incident, just blocks from the courthouse where the Branch Davidian trials were held, a large explosion occurred. Initial reports flowed into Oklahoma City 911 from all over the city. Police and fire units responded on their own, reporting the explosion to be in their sectors. After a couple of minutes, units were directed to the Water Board building across from the Murrah Federal Office Building.

Soon it became apparent that the bomb had exploded at the Federal Building. A truckload of 4,000 pounds of ammonium nitrate fuel oil mix had been detonated in a Ryder truck parked alongside the street in front of the building. The building was occupied by some six hundred people, including children in a day care center on the second floor.

The challenges of this event were enormous. There was an extended crime scene stretching over 200 city blocks. It had to be stabilized, secured, searched and processed for evidence. More than 500 injured persons had to be transported to hospitals for treatment.

As in Tokyo and New York City, many arrived at the hospitals by non-EMS system transportation. 167 people died in the explosion. Many, living and dead, were trapped inside the building. The explosion had been felt for miles. It registered as 3.5 on the Richter scale in Denver, Colorado. The sound was heard and recorded 50 miles away. Over 1,800 calls to 911 were received during the first hour and the system was jammed to overcapacity with nonstop calls for over 5 days. Two-thirds of all 911 calls received busy signals.

The Murrah Federal Building was a nine-story reinforced concrete office building with over 100,000 square feet of office space. It would be worth about \$35 million in 2,000 prices. It housed 19 federal agencies. The south side of the building was entirely glass.

The explosion created a crater 12 feet deep and 30 feet wide in the road by the building. The debris pile was three stories high and 80 percent of the building's face was destroyed. The crankshaft of the Ryder truck was discovered two blocks away and a wheel from an adjacent car was found on the roof of the Hyatt Hotel more than two blocks away. Over 343 buildings in downtown Oklahoma City were damaged. Fifty needed to be demolished. 23 more were placarded as unsafe for occupancy. Windows were shattered up to two miles away. Many cars in the area caught on fire.

A major emergency response occurred with the Fire Department committing every unit and every staff member over the next several weeks. Fifty-one companies and 37 ambulances, supported by 29 mutual aid ambulances, were used on the incident. Over 1,000 firefighters were involved in the local response. Before it was over 17 days later, more than 3,000 persons would have responded.

Initially, rescue efforts included anyone in the area. Citizens and responders worked frantically until there was a report of a second device. This led to the evacuations of the building by rescuers even though people were still trapped inside alive. Though the device turned out to be some form of training device from one of the offices in the building, it was a good interruption since it allowed rescue to resume in a much more organized fashion.

This improved on-site safety though not before a nurse, who had responded as a citizen responder, died from a head injury, raising the death toll to 168. Teams were now made up and analysis of structural safety began.

There were over 130 different agencies at the scene. These included everything from K-9 dog search teams to medical response teams to investigative and logistics agencies. Eleven Urban Search and Rescue Teams were activated and sent over the next days with as many as four of these self-contained Federal Emergency Management Agency-supported teams in service at one time. 44 local, state and federal police agencies assisted with security and investigation. This included 37 sheriffs' agencies and two Indian tribal police departments.

All of the major damaged buildings had to be searched for survivors. Since this was a crime scene, access and egress had to be controlled and almost 20,000 entry passes had to be issued. 50,000 people had to be evacuated from their homes for varying periods of time. Parts of the National Medical Disaster System were activated to provide medical and mortuary support. The Federal Aviation Administration closed the air space to all traffic.

Public safety radio systems were overwhelmed. Cellular telephone systems were overwhelmed. There were no common frequencies available early on although some operational systems were set up later. Often messages had to be sent by runners. Liaison officers were used extensively. Food, water, clothing, shelter, staging and work space was needed for over 130 agencies, 3,000 responders for 17 days. Tools needed to be replaced and repaired. A parking garage near the site was taken over as a supply house. Equipment was laid out and handed out as needed. Logistics personnel were brought in from the forest-firefighting agencies and the military.

While the national media focused on the Murrah Building, officials had to deal with many problems. All electrical and telephone service in the central business district was out. Businesses not involved needed to relocate to resume operations. People needed access to their property. Several businesses were mission-critical operations in the downtown.

Information Management was critical. Oklahoma City held daily 4 PM press briefings. A small media pool group was allowed site access and had to report to the rest of the press. There was some problem with individual agency public information officers providing conflicting information very early on due to only having part of the picture. This was resolved by the use of joint briefings.

Investigative agencies had to deploy and set up in areas within the damaged portion of the city. Support such as secure telephone lines and offices had to be secured. Over 120 truckloads of debris were taken to a controlled landfill for second inspection and review.

After the event was stabilized and the investigation was moving into the prosecution phase, officials had to deal with the need for long-term revitalization of the downtown area. Between $150 and $200 million was used for building and infrastructure repair. $50 million was spent on business revitalization. Only 53 percent of businesses returned to operation.

Legal and liability issues were raised as several local personnel who had volunteered for evidence searching were psychologically traumatized by some of the material they came across. Mental health costs for Oklahoma City were over $4.1 million the first year. Recovery of all the deceased took two weeks. This was covered constantly by the media keeping it in the public's eye.

Community businesses and individuals stepped forward to help. The Oklahoma City Convention Center hosted the Oklahoma Restaurant Association Food Fair. This resulted in serving 25,000 meals in nine days and housing for all Urban Search-and-Rescue teams and volunteers provided them clean uniforms and bed linens every day. The local chapter of the American Red Cross spent $7.25 million dollars through 1999 on explosion-related matters.

Donated goods overwhelmed Oklahoma City and the agencies in the area. There was no prior plan for staging, refrigeration and allocation of all the goods and materials that arrived. This was cited in the After-Action Report as the single biggest problem.

Clear command and control was essential to an effective response. Initial command was assumed by the Oklahoma City Fire Department as it was reported as a natural gas explosion early on in the event. As a result of the withdrawal of forces from the building and the fact that it now appeared as a bomb explosion, a loose unified command was set up between the fire and police departments and the FBI within hours. A formal Unified Incident Command System was in place by the next morning when the first operational planning period began. The Fire Department maintained command until the bodies had been recovered and then transferred it to law enforcement.

Key points to remember from these three case studies:
- ♦ Because information sources will be scattered initially, beware of conflicts.
- ♦ Situation assessment takes time.
- ♦ The media will want information that may not exist.
- ♦ Competition will cause media organizations to break the "story" and stay with it.
- ♦ Media may not have access to correct technical information.
- ♦ Media "experts" may create problems. Beware of reacting to these media "experts."
- ♦ The community will be scared.

Terrorism Case Studies: New York World Trade Center,
Tokyo Subway Attack, and Oklahoma City Federal Building Bombing

271

♦ Emergency decontamination procedures will be problematic.
♦ Sheltering in place may be necessary for extended periods.
♦ The incident may involve widespread contamination.
♦ The public's expectations for effective government leadership and action will be high.
♦ The incident will be an international event within minutes.
♦ Provide a credible source of information.
♦ Establish the public's perception of the threat.
♦ Instill confidence that the government is in control.
♦ Liability for safety of responders, the public and volunteers will be an issue.
♦ "Mandatory" decontamination will be problematical.
♦ Long-term medical/psychological care will be needed.
♦ Temporary housing will be needed for evacuees.
♦ Business loss will be both short and long term.
♦ There should be a plan in place for management of donated goods.

OKLAHOMA CITY BOMBING
Chronology of Key Integrated Response Events on April 19-20

09:02	Explosion occurs
09:19	Incident Command System and Command Post established by the Oklahoma City Fire Department
09:20	Mutual aid requested and triage centers established
09:25	State Emergency Operation Center (EOC) operational
09:30	FEMA Regional EOC activated
09:45	Governor declares State of Emergency
10:00	Secondary device suspected; area evacuated. Mayor meets with Police and Fire Chief and FBI Special Agent in Charge
11:23	Agencies meet in Command Post -- Establish Unified Command
14:00	Disaster Mitigation Assessment Team (DMAT) arrives from Tulsa
16:00	President signs Federal Disaster Declaration and joint press briefings begin
17:00	All city departments and local military units integrated into response

19:00	DMORT arrives along with other federal assets
01:00	First US&R Task Forces and IST arrive on scene
06:00	First joint agency operational period begins
08:00	Disaster Field Office established by FEMA

EDITOR'S NOTE:

   Timothy McVeigh, convicted perpetrator of the Oklahoma City bombing, was executed on June 16, 2001. Another defendant, Terry Nichols, received a life sentence. On March 16, 2001, the 10th US Circuit Court of Appeals in Denver upheld Michael Fortier's 12-year prison sentence in the case, rejecting arguments that the judge was vindictive and improperly exceeded the sentencing guidelines. The Appeals court said that the judge could impose a longer sentence than the guidelines called for because of the enormity of the crime. Fortier, an Army buddy of Timothy McVeigh, pleaded guilty to failing to warn authorities about the plot to bomb the Federal Building in Oklahoma City which killed 168. He admitted that he helped McVeigh move and sell stolen weapons and that he lied to FBI Agents when they interviewed him following the bombing.

Chapter 16

PERSONAL PROTECTION*
By Lawrence J. Hogan, A.B., M.A., J.D.

The US State Department has warned citizens that they are targets of terrorists funded by Osama bin Laden who is offering bounties for anyone who kills an American. The FBI (which has bin Laden on its "Ten Most Wanted List") has issued a similar warning to businessmen who are urged to keep a low profile, vary their travel routes and treat people with suspicion.

Some of this material has been extracted from information provided by the US Department of State

In addition, the CIA Director has warned, "There is not the slightest doubt that Osama bin Laden, his worldwide allies and his sympathizers are planning further attacks against us." In a recruitment video circulated among Muslim militants, bin Laden's Afghanistan-based terrorist group boasted that they had bombed the USS Cole in Yemen's Aden harbor on October 12, 2000, killing 17 US sailors and wounding 39.

The former US Secretary of Defense said, "A biological attack on US soil is not a remote possibility but a real probability in the present." The commander of the US Army Research Institute of Infectious Diseases (USAMRIID) believes "a mass casualty-producing event could happen in 5 to 10 years." It behooves us all to learn as much as we possibly can about the threats facing us.

A SAFE TRIP ABROAD

Millions of US citizens travel abroad each year and use their US passports. When you travel abroad, the odds are in your favor that you will have a safe and incident-free trip. However, crime and violence, as well as unexpected difficulties, do befall US citizens in all parts of the world. No one is better able to tell you this than US consular officers who work in the more than 250 US embassies and consulates around the globe. Every day US embassies and consulates receive calls from American citizens in distress.

Fortunately, most problems can be solved over the telephone or through a visit by the US citizen to the Consular Section of the nearest US embassy or consulate. But there are occasions when US consular officers are called on to meet US citizens at foreign police stations, hospitals, prisons and even morgues. In these cases, the assistance that consular officers can offer is specific but limited.

BEFORE YOU GO

Safety begins when you pack. To avoid being a target, dress conservatively because a flashy wardrobe or one that is too casual can mark you as a tourist. Also, as much as possible, avoid the appearance of affluence. Always try to travel light so you can move quickly and be more likely to have a free hand. If your luggage is light you will be less likely to set your luggage down to rest, leaving it unattended.

Carry the minimum amount of valuables necessary for your trip and plan a place or places where you can conceal them. Your passport, cash and credit cards are most secure when locked in a hotel safe. When you must carry them with you, you may wish to conceal them in several places rather than putting them all in one wallet or pouch. Avoid hand bags, fanny packs and outside pockets which are easy targets for thieves. Inside pockets and a sturdy shoulder bag with the strap worn across your chest are somewhat safer. One of the safest places to carry valuables is in a pouch or money belt worn under your clothing.

If you wear glasses, pack an extra pair. Bring them and any medicines you might need in your carry-on luggage.

To avoid problems when passing through customs, keep medicines in their original, labeled containers. Bring a copy of your prescriptions and the generic names for the drugs. If a medication is unusual or contains narcotics, carry a letter from your doctor attesting to your need to take the drug. If you have any doubt about the legality of carrying a certain drug into a country, consult the embassy or consulate of that country first.

Bring travelers checks and one or two major credit cards instead of cash. Pack an extra set of passport photos along with a photocopy of your passport information page to make replacement of your passport easier in the event it is lost or stolen.

Put your name, address and telephone numbers inside and outside of each piece of luggage. Use covered luggage tags to avoid casual observation of your identity or nationality and, if possible, lock your luggage.

Consider getting a telephone calling card. It is a convenient way of keeping in touch. If you have one, verify that you can use it from your overseas location(s). Access numbers to US operators are published in many international newspapers. Find out your access number before you go.

Don't bring anything you would hate to lose. Leave at home: valuable or expensive-looking jewelry or watches, irreplaceable family objects, all unnecessary credit cards.

Leave a copy of your itinerary with family or friends at home in case they need to contact you in an emergency.

Make two photocopies of your passport identification page, airline tickets, driver's license and the credit cards that you plan to bring with you. Leave one photocopy of this data with family or friends at home; pack the other in a place separate from where you carry your valuables.

Leave a copy of the serial numbers of your travelers' checks with a friend or relative at home. Carry your copy with you in a separate place and, as you cash the checks, cross them off the list.

WHAT TO LEARN BEFORE YOU GO

Security. The Department of State's Consular Information Sheets are available for every country of the world. They describe unusual entry, currency regulations or unusual health conditions, the crime and security situation, political disturbances, areas of instability, special information about driving, road conditions and drug penalties.

They also provide addresses and emergency telephone numbers for US embassies and consulates. In general, the sheets do not give advice. Instead, they describe conditions so travelers can make their own informed decisions about their trips.

In some dangerous situations, however, the Department of State recommends that Americans defer travel to a particular country. In such a case, a Travel Warning is issued for the country in addition to its Consular Information Sheet.

Public Announcements are a means of disseminating information about terrorist threats and other relatively short-term and/or transnational conditions posing significant risks to the security of American travelers. They are issued when there is a perceived threat, usually involving Americans as a particular target group. In the past, Public Announcements have been issued to deal with short-term coups, pre-election disturbances, violence by terrorists and anniversary dates of specific terrorist events.

Consular Information Sheets, Travel Warnings and Public Announcements are available at the 13 regional passport agencies; at US embassies and consulates abroad; or by sending a self-addressed, stamped envelope to: Overseas Citizens Services, Room 4811, Department of State, Washington, D.C. 20520-4818. They are also available through airline computer reservation systems when you or your travel agent make your international air reservations.

In addition, you can access Consular Information Sheets, Travel Warnings and Public Announcements 24 hours a day in several ways.

Telephone: To listen to them, call (202) 647-5225 from a touch-tone phone.

Fax: From your fax machine, dial (202) 647-3000, using the hand set as you would a regular telephone. The system prompts you on how to proceed.

Internet: Information about travel and consular services is available on the Bureau of Consular Affairs' World Wide Web home page. The address is http://travel.state.gov. It includes Consular Information Sheets, Travel Warnings and Public Announcements, passport and visa information, travel publications, background on international adoption, international child abduction services, and international legal assistance. It also links to the State Department's main Internet site at http://www.state.gov which contains current foreign affairs information.

CONSULAR AFFAIRS BULLETIN BOARD

If you have a personal computer, modem and communication software, you can access the Consular Affairs Bulletin Board (CABB). To view or download the documents from a computer and modem, dial the CABB on (301) 946-4400. The login is travel; the password is info. There is no charge to use these systems other than normal long distance charges.

LOCAL LAWS AND CUSTOMS

When you leave the United States, you are subject to the laws of the country where you are located. Therefore, before you go, learn as much as you can about the local laws and customs of the places you plan to visit. Good resources are your library, your travel agent, and the embassies, consulates or tourist bureaus of the countries you will visit. In addition, keep track of what is being reported in the media about recent developments in those countries.

THINGS TO ARRANGE BEFORE YOU GO

Your Itinerary. As much as possible, plan to stay in larger hotels that have more elaborate security. Safety experts recommend booking a room from the second to seventh floors above ground level to deter easy entrance from outside, but low enough for fire equipment to reach.

Book Nonstop Flights. Because take-off and landing are the most dangerous times of a flight, book nonstop flights whenever possible. When there is a choice of airport or airline, ask your travel agent about comparative safety records.

Legal Documents. Have your affairs at home in order. If you leave a current will, insurance documents, and power of attorney with your family or a friend, you can feel secure about traveling and will be prepared for any emergency that may arise while you are away. If you have minor children, consider making guardianship arrangements for them. Prepare medical power of attorney for your minor children empowering a trusted adult.

Credit. Make a note of the credit limit on each credit card that you bring. Make certain not to charge over that amount on your trip. In some countries, Americans have been arrested for innocently exceeding their credit limit. Ask your credit card company how to report the loss of your card from abroad. 800 numbers do not work from abroad, but your company should have a number that you can call while you are overseas.

Insurance. Find out if your personal property insurance covers you for loss or theft abroad. More importantly, check if your health insurance covers you abroad. Medicare and Medicaid do not provide payment for medical care outside the US. Even if your health insurance will reimburse you for medical care that you pay for abroad, normal health insurance does not pay for medical evacuation from a remote area or from a country where medical facilities are inadequate. Consider purchasing one of the short-term health and emergency assistance policies designed for travelers. Also, make sure that the plan you purchase includes medical evacuation in the event of an accident or serious illness.

PRECAUTIONS TO TAKE WHILE TRAVELING
Some Tips for Personal Safety

Wherever possible, try to blend in with local citizens. Dress as local citizens do. Do not ostentatiously display manifestations of wealth such as Rolex watches, expensive jewelry or clothes.

Avoid large crowds and keep a low profile. Vary your routes and times of travel. Always let someone know where you are going and when you will return. If possible, don't travel alone. Don't go anywhere with strangers.

SAFETY ON THE STREET

Use the same common sense traveling overseas that you would use at home. Be especially cautious in, or avoid, areas where you are likely to be victimized. These include crowded subways, train stations, elevators, tourist sites, market places, festivals and "marginal" areas of cities.

Don't take short cuts or travel through narrow alleys or poorly lit streets. Try not to travel alone, especially at night.

Avoid public demonstrations and other civil disturbances. Keep a low profile and avoid loud conversations or arguments. Do not discuss travel plans or other personal matters with strangers. Avoid scam artists.

Beware of strangers who approach you, offering bargains or to be your guide.

Beware of pickpockets. They often have an accomplice who will: jostle you, ask you for directions or for the time of day, point to something spilled on your clothing, or otherwise distract you by creating a disturbance. A child or a woman carrying a baby can be a pickpocket. Beware of groups of vagrant children who create a distraction while picking your pocket. Wear the shoulder strap of your bag across your chest and walk with the bag away from the curb to avoid drive-by purse snatchers.

Try to seem purposeful when you move about. Even if you are lost, act as if you know where you are going. When possible, ask directions only from individuals in authority.

Know how to use a pay telephone and have the proper change or token on hand.

Learn a few phrases in the local language so you can signal your need for help, the police, or a doctor. Make a note of emergency telephone numbers you may need: police, fire, your hotel and the nearest US embassy or consulate. Have a business card or at least a handwritten name of your hotel in the local language so you can show it to a taxicab driver if you do not know the local language.

If you are confronted, don't fight back. Give up your valuables. Your money and passport can be replaced, but you cannot.

SAFETY IN YOUR HOTEL

Keep your hotel door locked with the safety chain on at all times. Meet visitors in the lobby, not in your room. Never invite strangers to your room. Never leave money and other valuables in your hotel room while you are out. Use the hotel's safe deposit boxes or room safe.

Arrange your briefcase so that you can tell if it has been rummaged through. Use devices to see if your room has been searched such as matches in the door jamb, hairs or toothpicks in dresser drawer openings etc. Remember, some cameras are less than 1/32 of an inch and electronic devices can be placed on a pinhead. In certain countries, assume that your hotel room is bugged and your phone is tapped. To determine if you have a two-way mirror in your room, conduct this simple test: Place the tip of your fingernail against the reflective surface and, if there is a gap between your fingernail and the image of the nail, then it is a genuine mirror. However, if your fingernail directly touches the image of your nail, then it is a two-way mirror.

Let someone (the hotel desk clerks if no one else) know where you are going and when you expect to return, especially if you are out late at night.

If you are alone, do not get on an elevator if there is a suspicious-looking person inside.

Read the fire safety instructions in your hotel room. Know how to report a fire. Be sure you know the location of the nearest fire exit and alternate exits. Count the doors between your room and the nearest exit. This could be a life-saver if you have to crawl through a zero-visibility, smoke-filled corridor.

SAFETY ON PUBLIC TRANSPORTATION

If a country has a pattern of tourists being targeted by criminals on public means of transport, that information will be mentioned in the Consular Information Sheets under the "Crime Information" section.

Taxis. Only take taxis clearly identified with official markings, preferably those called by your hotel's doorman. Beware of unmarked cabs, especially at airports.

Trains. Well organized, systematic robbery of passengers on trains along popular tourist routes is a serious problem. It is more common at night, especially on overnight trains. If you are in a sleeping compartment, keep the door locked and do not admit strangers. If it cannot be locked securely, take turns sleeping in shifts with your traveling companions. If that is not possible, stay awake. If you must sleep unprotected, tie down your luggage, strap your valuables to you and sleep on top of them as much as possible.

If you see your way being blocked by a stranger and another person is very close behind you, move away. This can happen in the corridor of the train or on the platform or station.

Do not accept food or drink from strangers. Criminals have been known to drug food or drink offered to passengers. Criminals may also spray sleeping gas into train compartments.

Do not be afraid to alert authorities if you feel threatened in any way. Extra police are often assigned to ride trains on routes where crime is a serious problem.

Buses. The same type of criminal activity found on trains can be found on public buses on popular tourist routes. For example, tourists have been drugged and robbed while sleeping on buses or in bus stations. In some countries whole bus loads of passengers have been held up and robbed by gangs of bandits.

SAFETY WHEN YOU DRIVE

When you rent a car, don't go for the expensive, exotic car. Choose a type commonly available locally. Where possible, ask that markings that identify it as a rental car be removed. Make certain it is in good repair. If available, choose a car with universal door locks and power windows, features that give the driver better control of access to the car. Make sure the car doors are locked at all times, when you are in the car and when it is unattended. An air conditioner, when available, is also a safety feature, allowing you to drive with the windows closed. Thieves can and do snatch purses through open windows of moving cars. They also open unlocked doors and snatch purses while the car is stopped at a traffic light.

Wear seat belts. As much as possible, avoid driving at night. Don't leave valuables in the car. If you must carry things with you, keep them out of sight locked in the trunk.

Don't park your car on the street overnight. If the hotel or municipality does not have a parking garage or other secure area, select a well-lit area.

Never pick up hitchhikers.

Don't get out of the car if there are suspicious-looking individuals nearby. Drive away.

PATTERNS OF CRIME AGAINST MOTORISTS

In many places frequented by tourists, including areas of southern Europe, victimization of motorists has been refined to an art. Where it is a problem, US embassies are aware of it and consular officers try to work with local authorities to warn the public about the dangers. In some locations, these efforts at public awareness have paid off, reducing the frequency of incidents. You may also wish to ask your rental car agency for advice on avoiding robbery while visiting tourist destinations.

Carjackers and thieves operate at gas stations, parking lots, in city traffic and along the highway. Be suspicious of anyone who hails you or tries to get your attention when you are in or near your car. Always check the back seat of your car before entering it. Carjackers might be hiding there.

Criminals use ingenious ploys. They may masquerade as good Samaritans, offering help for tires that they claim are flat or that they have made flat. Or they may flag down a motorist, ask for assistance, and then steal the rescuer's luggage or car. Usually they work in groups, one person carrying on the pretense while the others rob you.

Other criminals get your attention with abuse, either trying to drive you off the road, or causing an "accident" by rear-ending you or creating a "fender bender." When you leave your car to investigate, they rob you.

In some urban areas, thieves don't waste time on ploys, they simply smash car windows at traffic lights, grab your valuables or your car and get away. In cities around the world, "defensive driving" has come to mean more than avoiding auto accidents; it means keeping an eye out for potential criminal pedestrians, cyclists and scooter riders.

HOW TO HANDLE MONEY SAFELY

To avoid carrying large amounts of cash, change your travelers checks only as you need currency. Countersign travelers checks only in front of the person who will cash them.

Do not flash large amounts of money when paying a bill. Make sure your credit card is returned to you after each transaction.

Do not change money on the black market. In addition to being illegal, you are likely to get swindled in the process. A criminal might offer to exchange currency for you at attractive rates. He or she will then do a quick switch, cheating you in the exchange. Your unfamiliarity with the exchange rate might make you an easy victim. By the time you discover that you have been cheated, the criminal has disappeared. Deal only with authorized agents when you exchange money, buy airline tickets or purchase souvenirs.

If your possessions are lost or stolen, report the loss immediately to the local police. Keep a copy of the police report for insurance claims and as an explanation of your plight. After reporting missing items to the police, report the loss or theft of travelers checks to the nearest agent of the issuing company, credit cards to the issuing company, airline tickets to the airline or travel agent, passport to the nearest US embassy or consulate. Don't leave valuables such as these in your room while you are away.

Hotels in some countries want to keep your passport when you check in. Refuse. Suggest they make a photocopy of it instead.

HOW TO AVOID LEGAL DIFFICULTIES

When you are in a foreign country, you are subject to its laws and are under its jurisdiction, NOT the protection of the US Constitution and laws. You can be arrested overseas for actions that may be either legal or considered minor infractions in the United States. Be aware of what is considered criminal in the country where you are. Consular Information Sheets include information on unusual patterns of arrests in various countries when appropriate.

Some of the offenses for which US citizens have been arrested abroad are:

Drug Violations. More than 1/3 of US citizens incarcerated abroad are held on drug charges. Some countries do not distinguish between possession and trafficking. Many countries have mandatory sentences -- even for possession of a small amount of marijuana or cocaine. A number of Americans have been arrested for possessing prescription drugs, particularly tranquilizers and amphetamines, that they purchased legally in certain Asian countries and then brought to some countries in the Middle East where they are illegal. Other US citizens have been arrested for purchasing prescription drugs abroad in quantities that local authorities suspected were for commercial use. If in doubt about foreign drug laws, ask local authorities or the nearest US embassy or consulate.

Liquor. Some Muslim countries very strictly enforce their laws prohibiting possession of alcohol. Some American travelers have been arrested for possession of liquor miniatures furnished to them on an earlier connecting airline.

Possession of Firearms. The places where US citizens most often come into difficulties for illegal possession of firearms are nearby -- Mexico, Canada and the Caribbean. Sentences for possession of firearms in Mexico can be up to 30 years. In general, firearms, even those legally registered in the US, cannot be brought into a country unless a permit is first obtained from the embassy or a consulate of that country and the firearm is registered with foreign authorities on arrival.

(Note: If you take firearms or ammunition to another country, you cannot bring them back into the US unless you register them with US Customs before you leave the US.)

Photography. In many countries you can be harassed or detained for photographing such things as police and military installations, government buildings, border areas and transportation facilities. If you are in doubt, ask permission before taking photographs.

Purchasing Antiques. Americans have been arrested for purchasing souvenirs that were, or looked like, antiques and which local customs authorities believed were national treasures. This is especially true in Turkey, Egypt and Mexico. In countries where antiques are important, document your purchases as reproductions if that is the case, or if they are authentic, secure the necessary export permit (usually from the national museum). Similar problems can arise from purchasing animals or the skins, hides, horns, shells etc. of animals which are considered endangered by the country.

PROTECTION AGAINST TERRORISM

Terrorist acts occur at random and unpredictably, making it impossible to protect oneself absolutely. The first and best protection is to avoid travel to unsafe areas where there has been a persistent record of terrorist attacks or kidnapping. (See Appendix I. Page 349 for a list of countries where terrorism is supported by the government.) The vast majority of foreign states have good records of maintaining public order and protecting residents and visitors within their borders from terrorism.

Most terrorist attacks are the result of long and careful planning. Just as a car thief will first be attracted to an unlocked car with the key in the ignition, terrorists are looking for defenseless, easily accessible targets who follow predictable patterns. The chances that a tourist, traveling with an unpublished program or itinerary, would be the victim of terrorism are slight. In addition, many terrorist groups, seeking publicity for political causes within their own country or region, may not be looking for American targets. Other groups kidnap Americans for ransom to finance their activities.

Nevertheless, the following pointers may help you avoid becoming a target of opportunity. They should be considered as adjuncts to the tips listed in the previous sections on how to protect yourself against being a victim of crime. These precautions may provide some degree of protection, and can serve as practical and psychological deterrents to would-be terrorists.

- Schedule direct flights if possible and avoid stops in high-risk airports or areas. Consider other options for travel, such as trains.
- Be aware of what you discuss with strangers or what may be overheard by others.

♦ Try to minimize the time spent in the public area of an airport, which is a less protected area. Move quickly from the check-in counter to the secured areas. On arrival, leave the airport as soon as possible.

♦ As much as possible, avoid luggage tags, dress and behavior which may identify you as an American.

♦ Keep an eye out for suspicious abandoned packages or briefcases. Report them to airport security or other authorities and leave the area promptly.

♦ Avoid obvious terrorist targets such as places where Americans and Westerners are known to congregate.

TRAVEL TO HIGH-RISK AREAS

If you must travel in an area where there has been a history of terrorist attacks or kidnapping, make it a habit to:

♦ Discuss with your family what they would do in the event of an emergency.

♦ Make sure your affairs are in order before leaving home.

♦ Register with the US embassy or consulate upon arrival. Remain friendly but be cautious about discussing personal matters, your itinerary or program. Leave no personal or business papers in your hotel room.

♦ Watch for people following you or "loiterers" observing your comings and goings.

♦ Keep a mental note of safe havens, such as police stations, hotels, hospitals.

♦ Let someone else know what your travel plans are. Keep them informed if you change your plans.

♦ Avoid predictable times and routes of travel and report any suspicious activity to local police, and the nearest US embassy or consulate. When possible, travel with someone.

♦ Select your own taxicabs at random or those hailed by a doorman. Don't take a vehicle that is not clearly identified as a taxi. Compare the face of the driver with the one posted on his or her license. As stated above, never invite strangers to your room. If you do plan to meet a business contact or friend in your hotel room, be sure of the identity of such visitors before opening the door. Don't meet strangers at unknown or remote locations.

- Refuse unexpected packages.
- Formulate a plan of action for what you will do if a bomb explodes or there is gunfire nearby.
- Check for loose wires or other suspicious activity around your car.
- Be sure your vehicle is in good operating condition in case you need to resort to high-speed or evasive driving.
- Drive with car windows closed in crowded streets. Bombs can be thrown through open windows.
- If you are ever in a situation where somebody starts shooting, drop to the floor or get down as low as possible. Don't move until you are sure the danger has passed. Do not attempt to help rescuers and do not pick up a weapon. If possible, shield yourself behind or under a solid object. If you must move, crawl on your stomach.

HIJACKING/HOSTAGE SITUATIONS

While every hostage situation is different and the chance of becoming a hostage is remote, some considerations are important.

The US government's policy is to not negotiate with terrorists. When Americans are abducted overseas, the US Government looks to the host government to exercise its responsibility under international law to protect all persons within its territories and to bring about the safe release of hostages. US authorities work closely with these governments from the outset of a hostage-taking incident to ensure that US citizens and other innocent victims are released as quickly and safely as possible.

Normally, the most dangerous phases of a hijacking or hostage situation are the beginning and, if there is a rescue attempt, the end. At the outset, the terrorists typically are tense, high-strung and may behave irrationally. It is extremely important that you remain calm and alert and manage your own behavior.

- Avoid resistance and sudden or threatening movements. Do not struggle or try to escape unless you are certain of being successful.
- Make a concerted effort to relax. Breathe deeply and prepare yourself mentally, physically and emotionally for the possibility of a long ordeal.
- Try to remain inconspicuous, avoid direct eye contact and the appearance of observing your captors' actions.
- Avoid alcoholic beverages. Consume little food and drink.

♦ Consciously put yourself in a mode of passive cooperation. Talk normally. Do not complain, avoid belligerency, and comply with all orders and instructions.

♦ If questioned, keep your answers short. Don't volunteer information or make unnecessary overtures.

♦ Don't try to be a hero, endangering yourself and others.

♦ Maintain your sense of personal dignity and gradually increase your requests for personal comforts. Make these requests in a reasonable, low-key manner.

♦ If you are involved in a lengthier, drawn-out situation, try to establish a rapport with your captors, avoiding political discussions or other confrontational subjects.

♦ Establish a daily program of mental and physical activity. Don't be afraid to ask for anything you need or want -- medicines, books, pencils, papers.

♦ Eat what they give you, even if it does not look or taste appetizing. A loss of appetite and weight is normal.

♦ Think positively. Avoid a sense of despair. Rely on your inner resources. Remember that you are a valuable commodity to your captors. It is important to them to keep you alive and well.

ASSISTANCE ABROAD

If you plan to stay more than two weeks in one place, if you are in an area experiencing civil unrest or a natural disaster, or if you are planning travel to a remote area, it is advisable to register at the Consular Section of the nearest US embassy or consulate. This will make it easier if someone at home needs to locate you urgently or in the unlikely event that you need to be evacuated in an emergency. It will also facilitate the issuance of a new passport should yours be lost or stolen.

Another reason to contact the Consular Section is to obtain updated information on the security situation in a country.

If you are ill or injured, contact the nearest US embassy or consulate for a list of local physicians and medical facilities. If the illness is serious, consular officers can help you find medical assistance from this list and, at your request, will inform your family or friends. If necessary, a consul can assist in the transfer of funds from family or friends in the United States. Payment of hospital and other medical expenses is your responsibility.

If you run out of money overseas and have no other options, consular officers can help you get in touch with your family, friends, bank or employer and inform them how to wire funds to you.

Should you find yourself in legal difficulty, contact a consular officer immediately. Consular officers cannot serve as attorneys, give legal advice, or get you out of jail. What they can do is provide a list of local attorneys who speak English and who may have had experience in representing US citizens. If you are arrested, consular officials will visit you, advise you of your rights under local laws and ensure that you are held under humane conditions and are treated fairly under local law. A consular officer will also contact your family or friends if you desire. When necessary, consuls can transfer money from home for you and will try to get relief for you, including food and clothing in countries where this is a problem. If you are detained, remember that under international agreements and practice, you have the right to talk to the US consul. If you are denied this right, be persistent. Try to have someone get in touch for you.

TRAVEL WARNINGS AND CONSULAR INFORMATION SHEETS

The Department of State reminds American citizens worldwide of the need to remain vigilant with regard to their personal security. If the Department receives information concerning a specific and credible threat, that information will be shared with everyone who could be potentially affected by it.

From time to time the State Department receives unconfirmed reports which give rise to concern about the safety and security of US Government employees and private American citizens abroad. In addition, the possibility remains that terrorists and other groups or individuals may take actions against Americans and American interests. In the past these groups and individuals have not distinguished between US Government and civilian targets.

Periods on or about significant dates such as the August 7 anniversary of the bombings of the US Embassies in Nairobi, Kenya; and Dar es Salaam, Tanzania; may be chosen as opportunities for further terrorist acts. As a result, security continues to be a prime concern at US facilities worldwide. US citizens traveling or residing abroad are urged to review their own personal security practices, to be attentive to their surroundings and to exercise caution.

American citizens traveling or residing abroad should regularly monitor the US State Department's Consular Information Program Internet web site at http://travel.state.gov to review the Department's Consular Information Sheets, Public Announcements, Travel Warnings and regional brochures for up-to-date information on security conditions overseas.

Travel Warnings are issued when the State Department decides, based on all relevant information, to recommend that Americans avoid travel to a certain country. Countries where avoidance of travel is recommended will have Travel Warnings as well as Consular Information Sheets.

Consular Information Sheets are available for every country of the world. They include such information as location of the US Embassy or consulates in the subject country, unusual immigration practices, health conditions, political disturbances, unusual currency and entry regulations, crime conditions, security problems, drug penalties etc. If an unstable condition exists in a country that is not severe enough to warrant a Travel Warning, a description of the condition(s) may be included under an optional section entitled "Safety/Security".

On limited occasions, The State Department also restates in this section any US Embassy advice given to official employees. Consular Information Sheets generally do not include advice, but provide information in a factual manner so the traveler can make his or her own decisions concerning travel to a particular country. For information about a particular country, go to http://travel.state.gov/travel_warnings.html.

BE ALERT FOR POSSIBLE KIDNAPPERS

While kidnapping could take place anywhere, Colombia leads the world in kidnapping and Mexico is number two. In Colombia in 1998 there were officially more than 2,400 reported kidnappings, 2,757 in 1999 and 3,029 reported in the first eleven months of 2000. No one really knows the true numbers because many are not reported. Guerrillas are responsible for most of them and paramilitary units are also involved. Many hostages are taken at roadblocks along the highways. (This technique is called "pesca milagrosa" or "miraculous fishing.") There were more than 20,000 kidnappings for ransom in 2000.

The National Liberation Army (ELN) hijacked a commercial airliner in April 1999, flew it to a landing strip in drug country, and took the passengers into the forest as hostages. On another occasion, the ELN took 143 persons hostage from a Catholic Church in Cali, Colombia. The message here is that you might not even be safe in church!

EDITOR'S NOTE:

The US Army has developed a specialized "James Bond type" vehicle which would be useful against terrorists. The SmarTruck, a modified Ford F350 pickup truck is just a prototype but it illustrates the types of protective devices which can be adopted. On both sides of the truck there are pepper-spray dispensers capable of propelling pepper spray up to 12 feet. All the windows are tinted, bulletproof glass and all over the outside of the vehicle there is a layer of lightweight Kevlar armor capable to withstanding .44 magnum bullets. Super bright lights in the front and back can temporarily blind adversaries who are pursuing the truck or approaching it from the front. The door handles are electrified to stun intruders and thieves.

Pipes in the rear of the truck dispense an oil slick, blinding smoke and tacks which are designed to hit the ground face up to puncture tires. The truck's various devices can only be controlled from touch-screen panels which read the operator's fingerprints to activate them.

Appendix A
Introduction

Released by the Office of the Coordinator for Counterterrorism
April 2001

The year 2000 showed that terrorism continues to pose a clear and present danger to the international community. From the millennium-related threats at the beginning of the year to the USS Cole bombing and the rash of hostage takings at the end, the year 2000 highlighted the need for continued vigilance by our government and our allies throughout the world. The tragic death of 19 US citizens at the hands of terrorists is the most sober reminder.

While the threat continues, 2000 saw the international community's commitment to counterterrorism cooperation and ability to mobilize its resources grow stronger than ever. As a result, state-sponsored terrorism has continued to decline, international isolation of terrorist groups and countries has increased, and terrorists are being brought to justice. Indeed, the vigilance of all members of the international community is critical to limiting the mobility and capability of terrorists throughout the world, and both we and the terrorists know it.

We base our cooperation with our international partners on four basic policy tenets:

First, make no concession to terrorists and strike no deals.

Second, bring terrorists to justice for their crimes.

Third, isolate and apply pressure on states that sponsor terrorism to force them to change their behavior.

Fourth, bolster the counterterrorist capabilities of those countries that work with the United States and require assistance.

These points have been the basis for international cooperation and the foundation for important progress.

UN Security Council Resolution 1333, which levied additional sanctions on the Taliban for harboring Osama bin Laden and failing to close down terrorist training camps in Afghanistan, was a major victory for international cooperation against terrorism. This resolution, passed a year after its predecessor resolution 1267, showed the extent to which the international community is prepared to go to isolate those states that refuse to adhere to international norms.

The UN's action also reflected the understanding that Taliban-controlled Afghanistan remains a primary hub for terrorists and a home or transit point for the loosely organized network of "Afghan alumni," a web of informally linked individuals and groups that were trained and fought in the Afghan war. Afghan alumni have been involved in most major terrorist plots or attacks against the United States in the past 15 years and now engage in international militant and terrorist acts throughout the world. The leaders of some of the most dangerous terrorist groups to emerge in the past decade have headquarters or major offices in Afghanistan, and their associates threaten stability in many real and potential trouble spots around the globe -- from the Philippines to the Balkans, Central Asia to the Persian Gulf, Western China to Somalia, and Western Europe to South Asia. This is why the Taliban's continued support for these groups is now recognized by the international community as a growing threat to all countries.

International cooperation against agents linked to this network extended far beyond the collaboration on UNSCR 1333. Numerous countries have sent the message to the Taliban and its supporters that the international community -- as a whole and as individual member countries -- will not stand for such blatant disregard for international law. Good intelligence and law enforcement work -- exemplified by the Jordanian

Government -- enabled partner countries to thwart millennium attacks in early 2000. It has also led to invaluable coordination in the investigation of the October bombing of the USS Cole in Yemen's port of Aden. (It is worth noting that several suspects in the attack on the USS Cole fled back to, not surprisingly, Afghanistan.) We remain fervently committed to ensuring that those who committed and supported the attack on the USS Cole -- and killed 17 US service persons -- are brought to justice. We will continue to work closely with our allies to ensure that this terrorist incident and others like it do not go unpunished.

The opening in New York of the trial against those accused of perpetrating the bombings of the US embassies in Nairobi and Dar es Salaam in 1998 marked another major victory. Strong international cooperation with our allies -- Kenya, Germany, and South Africa, for example -- led to the apprehension of several suspects in those crimes. Their trial underlines the importance of cooperative diplomatic, law enforcement, and judicial efforts to combat terrorism. It sends the same strong message that is the cornerstone of US counterterrorism policy: we will be unrelenting in our efforts to bring to justice every individual who chooses terrorism against the United States to advance his or her agenda.

Afghanistan is not the only threat, nor the only rallying point for international cooperation. The conviction of Abdel Basset Ali Mohammed al-Megrahi to life imprisonment for his role in the downing of Pan Am flight 103 over Lockerbie, Scotland, in 1988 also sent a strong message about the international community's determination to bring to justice those responsible for terrorist acts, regardless of how much time has passed. The US Government remains dedicated to maintaining pressure on the Libyan Government until it complies fully with the stipulations required by the UN Security Council to lift sanctions.

Central Asian states have stepped up their fight against terrorist elements in their region, particularly those operating from Afghanistan. At a US Government-hosted conference in June 2000, representatives from five Central Asian states discussed the challenges in their region and committed themselves to developing mechanisms for cooperating to deny sanctuary and financial support to terrorists. We look forward to a follow-up conference and continued constructive engagement with the countries of the region.

While our cooperation with states such as Jordan and Egypt is strong, the terrorism picture in the Middle East remains grim, particularly given the recent escalation of violence in the region. Despite domestic political changes that suggest evolution towards a more moderate policy,

Iran remained the primary state sponsor of terrorism, due to its continued support for groups that violently oppose peace between Israel and its Arab neighbors. We expect those states in the region that are committed to peace to distance themselves from all forms of terrorism and to ensure that their countries do not become safe havens or launching points for terrorist acts.

During the past year, increased bilateral and multilateral cooperation with friendly nations has brought unified pressure and action against terrorism. We have expanded our bilateral dialogues with Russia, India, the United Kingdom, Israel, and Canada, and have extended cooperation in intelligence sharing, law enforcement, and antiterrorism training. In addition, we have worked closely with the member states of the G-8, which continued to condemn terrorism emanating from Afghanistan and Iran, and made strides in cutting off terrorist financing.

Like our G-8 counterparts, the United States places a high priority on denying terrorists their sources of financing and blocking their ability to use the funds they already control. In January 2000 we signed the new International Convention for the Suppression of Terrorist Financing. The Convention creates an international legal framework for investigating, apprehending, and prosecuting those involved in terrorist financing and describes preventive measures to identify and choke off sources of income for terrorists and to restrict the movements of such funds across international borders. We look to all members of the international community to join the 35 signatories and to ratify and implement the convention.

In addition, we are strengthening our efforts to fight the spate of hostage taking seen in 2000. Southeast Asia, Central Asia, and South America are just a few of the areas that have been plagued by hostage taking, often linked to terrorist elements. We maintain our policy that we will not concede to terrorist demands or pay ransom. Doing so only rewards the terrorist-criminals and encourages continued criminality. We do remain committed to negotiations with hostage takers for the safety of US citizens and other nationals. (*EDITOR'S NOTE: During 2000 there were 20,000 kidnappings for ransom.*)

The foundation of our efforts is diplomacy. Our diplomats and representatives maintain relations with countries that are the front-line of defense for US citizens at home and abroad. Our diplomatic efforts build crucial cooperation necessary for joint counterterrorism efforts and raise international political will to fight terrorism. We will continue to reach out to our allies while isolating those who are sympathetic to terrorism. We will continue to use all US tools and cooperation with these allies to disrupt terrorist activity and build a world that is intolerant of terrorists. And we will never rest until we have brought to justice each terrorist that has targeted the United States and its citizens.

Edmund J. Hull
Acting Coordinator for Counterterrorism

Note: Adverse mention in this report of individual members of any political, social, ethnic, religious, or national group is not meant to imply that all members of that group are terrorists. Indeed, terrorists represent a small minority of dedicated, often fanatical, individuals in most such groups. It is those small groups -- and their actions -- that are the subject of this report.

Furthermore, terrorist acts are part of a larger phenomenon of politically inspired violence, and at times the line between the two can become difficult to draw. To relate terrorist events to the larger context, and to give a feel for the conflicts that spawn violence, this report will discuss terrorist acts as well as other violent incidents that are not necessarily international terrorism.

LEGISLATIVE REQUIREMENTS

This report is submitted in compliance with Title 22 of the United States Code, Section 2656f(a), which requires the Department of State to provide Congress a full and complete annual report on terrorism for those countries and groups meeting the criteria of Section (a)(1) and (2) of the Act. As required by legislation, the report includes detailed assessments of foreign countries where significant terrorist acts occurred and countries about which Congress was notified during the preceding five years pursuant to Section 6(j) of the Export Administration Act of 1979 (the so-called terrorist-list countries that have repeatedly provided state support for international terrorism). In addition, the report includes all relevant information about the previous year's activities of individuals, terrorist organizations, or umbrella groups known to be responsible for the kidnapping or death of any US citizen during the preceding five years and groups known to be financed by state sponsors of terrorism.

In 1996, Congress amended the reporting requirements contained in the above-referenced law. The amended law requires the Department of State to report on the extent to which other countries cooperate with the United States in apprehending, convicting, and punishing terrorists responsible for attacking US citizens or interests. The law also requires that this report describe the extent to which foreign governments are cooperating, or have cooperated during the previous five years, in preventing future acts of terrorism. As permitted in the amended legislation, the Department is submitting such information to Congress in a classified annex to this unclassified report.

DEFINITIONS

No one definition of terrorism has gained universal acceptance. For the purposes of this report, however, we have chosen the definition of terrorism contained in Title 22 of the United States Code, Section 2656f(d). That statute contains the following definitions:

The term "terrorism" means premeditated, politically motivated violence perpetrated against noncombatant targets by subnational groups or clandestine agents, usually intended to influence an audience.

The term "international terrorism" means terrorism involving citizens or the territory of more than one country.

The term "terrorist group" means any group practicing, or that has significant subgroups that practice, international terrorism. The US Government has employed this definition of terrorism for statistical and analytical purposes since 1983.

Domestic terrorism is probably a more widespread phenomenon than international terrorism. Because international terrorism has a direct impact on US interests, it is the primary focus of this report. However, the report also describes, but does not provide statistics on, significant developments in domestic terrorism.

For purposes of this definition, the term "noncombatant" is interpreted to include, in addition to civilians, military personnel who at the time of the incident are unarmed or not on duty. For example, in past reports we have listed as terrorist incidents the murders of the following US military personnel: Col. James Rowe, killed in Manila in April 1989; Capt. William Nordeen, US defense attaché killed in Athens in June 1988; the two servicemen killed in the Labelle discotheque bombing in West Berlin in April 1986; and the four off-duty US Embassy Marine guards killed in a cafe in El Salvador in June 1985. We also consider as acts of terrorism attacks on military installations or on armed military personnel when a state of military hostilities does not exist at the site, such as bombings against US bases in Europe, the Philippines, or elsewhere.

APPENDIX B

US Government's Commitment to Anti-Terrorism

INTRODUCTION

US counterterrorist policies are tailored to combat what we believe to be the shifting trends in terrorism. One trend is the shift from well-organized, localized groups supported by state sponsors to loosely organized, international networks of terrorists. Such a network supported the failed attempt to smuggle explosives material and detonating devices into Seattle, Washington, in the United States in December 1999. With the decrease of state funding, these loosely networked individuals and groups have turned increasingly to other sources of funding, including private sponsorship, narcotrafficking, crime, and illegal trade.

This shift parallels a change from primarily politically motivated terrorism to terrorism that is more religiously or ideologically motivated. Another trend is the shift eastward of the locus of terrorism from the Middle East to South Asia, specifically Afghanistan. As most Middle Eastern governments have strengthened their counterterrorist response, terrorists and their organizations have sought safe haven in areas where they can operate with impunity.

US POLICY TENETS

Our policy has four main elements:

- First, make no concessions to terrorists and strike no deals.
- Second, bring terrorists to justice for their crimes.
- Third, isolate and apply pressure on states that sponsor terrorism to force them to change their behavior.
- Fourth, bolster the counterterrorist capabilities of those countries that work with the United States and require assistance.

The US Government uses two primary legislative tools -- the designations of state sponsors and of Foreign Terrorist Organizations (FTOs) -- as well as bilateral and multilateral efforts to implement these tenets.

STATE SPONSORS

After extensive research and intelligence analysis, the Department of State designates certain states as sponsors of terrorism in order to enlist a series of sanctions against them for providing support for international terrorism. Through these sanctions, the United States seeks to isolate states from the international community, which condemns and rejects the use of terror as a legitimate political tool. This year the Department of State has redesignated the same seven states that have been on the list since 1993: Cuba, Iran, Iraq, Libya, North Korea, Sudan, and Syria.

The designation of state sponsors is not permanent, however. In fact, a primary focus of US counterterrorist policy is to move state sponsors off the list by delineating clearly what steps these countries must take to end their support for terrorism and by urging them to take these steps.

As direct state sponsorship has declined, terrorists increasingly have sought refuge wherever they can. Some countries on the list have reduced dramatically their direct support of terrorism over the past years -- and this is an encouraging sign. They still are on the list, however, usually for activity in two categories: harboring of past terrorists (some for more than 20 years) and continuing their linkages to designated Foreign Terrorist Organizations. Cuba is one of the state sponsors that falls in this category.

The harboring of past terrorists, although not an active measure, is still significant in terms of US policy. International terrorists must know unequivocally that they cannot seek haven in states and "wait out" the period until international pressure diminishes. The US Government encourages all state sponsors to terminate all links to terrorism -- including harboring old "Cold War terrorists" -- and join the international community in observing zero tolerance for terrorism. Of course, if a state sponsor meets the criteria for being dropped from the terrorism list, it will be removed -- notwithstanding other differences we may have with a country's other policies and actions.

There have been encouraging signs recently suggesting that some countries are considering taking steps to distance themselves from terrorism. North Korea has made some positive statements condemning terrorism in all its forms. We have outlined clearly to the Government of North Korea the steps it must take to be removed from the list, all of which are consistent with its stated policies. A Middle East peace agreement necessarily would address terrorist issues and would lead to Syria being considered for removal from the list of state sponsors.

In addition to working to move states away from sponsorship, the Department of State constantly monitors other states whose policies and actions increase the threat to US citizens living and working abroad.

AREAS OF CONCERN

The primary terrorist threats to the United States emanate from two regions, South Asia and the Middle East. Supported by state sponsors, terrorists live in and operate out of areas in these regions with impunity. They find refuge and support in countries that are sympathetic to their use of violence for political gain, derive mutual benefit from harboring terrorists, or simply are weakly governed.

The United States will continue to use the designations of state sponsors Foreign Terrorist Organizations, political and economic pressure, and other means as necessary to compel those states that allow terrorists to live, move, and operate with impunity those which provide financial, and political patronage for terrorists, to end their direct or indirect support for terrorism.

In South Asia the major terrorist threat comes from Afghanistan which continues to be the primary safe haven for terrorists. While not directly hostile to the United States, the Taliban, which controls the majority of Afghan territory, continues to harbor Osama bin Laden and a host of other terrorists loosely linked to bin Laden, who directly threaten the United States and others in the international community. The Taliban is unwilling to take actions against terrorists trained in Afghanistan, many of whom have been linked to numerous international terrorist plots, including the foiled plots in Jordan and Washington State in December 1999. Pakistan continues to send mixed messages on terrorism. Despite significant and material cooperation in some areas -- particularly arrests and -- the Pakistani Government also has tolerated terrorists living and moving freely within its territory. Pakistan's government has supported groups that engage in violence in Kashmir, and it has provided indirect support for terrorists in Afghanistan.

In the Middle East, two state sponsors -- Iran and Syria -- have continued to support regional terrorist groups that seek to destroy the Middle East peace process. The Iranian Ministry of Intelligence and Security (MOIS) and the Islamic Revolutionary Guard Corps (IRGC) continue to provide training, financial, and political support directly to Lebanese Hizballah, HAMAS, and Palestinian Islamic Jihad operatives who seek to disrupt the peace process. These terrorist organizations, along with others, are based in Damascus, a situation that the Syrian Government made little effort to change in 1999.

The Syrian Government -- through harboring terrorists, allowing their free movement, and providing resources -- continued to be a crucial link in the terrorist threat emanating from this region during the past year. Lebanon also was a key -- although different -- link in the terrorist equation. The Lebanese Government does not exercise control over many parts of its territory where terrorist groups operate with impunity, often under Syrian protection, thus leaving Lebanon as another key safe haven for Hizballah, HAMAS, and several other groups the United States has designated as Foreign Terrorist Organizations.

FOREIGN TERRORIST ORGANIZATIONS (FTOS)

Former Secretary of State Albright in October 1999 designated 28 Foreign Terrorist Organizations, dropping three from the previous list (issued in 1997) and adding one. The removal or addition of groups shows our effort to maintain a current list that accurately reflects those groups that are foreign, engage in terrorist activity, and threaten the security of

US citizens or the national security of the United States. The designations make members and representatives of those groups ineligible for US visas and subject to exclusion from the United States. US financial institutions are required to block the funds of those groups and of their agents and to report the blocking action to the US Department of the Treasury. Additionally, it is a criminal offense for US persons or persons within US jurisdiction knowingly to provide material support or resources to such groups.

As in the case of state sponsorship, the goal of US policy is to eliminate the use of terrorism as a policy instrument by those organizations it designates as FTOs. Organizations that cease to engage in terrorist-related activities will be dropped from the list.

(A complete list of the designated Foreign Terrorist Organizations appears in Appendix K).

US DIPLOMATIC EFFORTS

In addition to continuing our cooperation with close allies and friends, such as the United Kingdom, Canada, Israel, and Japan, we made significant progress on our primary policy objectives with other key governments and organizations. In 2000 we began a bilateral counterterrorist working group with India, and we look forward to increasing US-Indian counterterrorist cooperation in the years ahead.

We worked closely with the Group of Eight (G-8) states and reached a common agreement about the threat that Iran's support for terrorist groups poses to the Middle East peace process. In the meeting in November 1999 of counterterrorist experts the G-8 representatives agreed that the Iranian Government had increased its activities and support for HAMAS, the Palestinian Islamic Jihad, and Hizballah with the aim of undermining the Middle East peace process. We explored with G-8 partners ways to exert influence on the Iranian Government to end its sponsorship of those groups.

In 1999 we also expanded our discussions with Russia and initiated dialogues with key Central Asian states, the Palestinian Authority, and other states eager to cooperate with the United States and strengthen their ability to counter terrorist threats.

The United States worked closely with the Government of Argentina and other hemispheric partners to bring about the creation of CICTE, the Organization of American States' (OAS) Inter-American Commission on Counterterrorism. As the first chair of CICTE, the United

States worked with other OAS members to develop new means to diminish the terrorist threat in this hemisphere.

The United States also hosted an important multilateral conference that brought together senior counterterrorist officials from more than 20 countries, primarily from the Middle East, Central Asia, and Asia. The conference promoted international cooperation against terrorism, the sharing of information on terrorist groups and countermeasures, and the discussion of policy choices.

After President Clinton issued an Executive Order levying sanctions against the Taliban for harboring terrorist suspect Osama bin Laden, the United Nations overwhelmingly passed Security Council Resolution 1267, which imposed a similar set of sanctions against the Taliban.

On 8 December 1999 the UN General Assembly also adopted the International Convention for the Suppression of the Financing of Terrorism, which grew out of the G-8's initiative to combat terrorist financing and was drafted and introduced by France. The convention fills an important gap in international law by expanding the legal framework for international cooperation in the investigation, prosecution, and extradition of persons who engage in terrorist financing.

The United States conducts a successful program to train foreign law enforcement personnel in such areas as airport security, bomb detection, maritime security, VIP protection, hostage rescue, and crisis management. To date, we have trained more than 20,000 representatives from over 100 countries. We also conduct an active research and development program to adapt modern technology for use in defeating terrorists.

WEAPONS OF MASS DESTRUCTION
(WMD) TERRORISM

In 1999 the possibility of another terrorist weapons of mass destruction (WMD) event -- a chemical, biological, radiological, nuclear (CBRN), or large explosive weapon -- continued to increase.

Although most terrorists continued to favor proven and conventional tactics, such as bombing, shooting, and kidnapping, some terrorist groups were attempting to obtain CBRN capabilities. For example, Osama bin Laden spoke publicly about acquiring such a capability and likened his pursuit of those weapons to a religious duty.

Some terrorist groups have demonstrated CBRN use and are actively pursuing CBRN capabilities for several reasons:

Increased publicity highlighted the vulnerability of civilian targets to CBRN attacks. Such attacks could cause lasting disruption and generate significant psychological impact on a population and its infrastructure. As of yearend, the largest attack involving chemical weapons against civilians was Aum Shinrikyo's Sarin nerve agent attack on the Tokyo subway system in March 1995.

Some groups, especially those motivated by distorted religious and cultural ideologies, had demonstrated a willingness to inflict greater numbers of indiscriminate casualties. Other less predictable, but potentially dangerous groups, also had emerged. Those groups may not adhere to traditional targeting constraints.

CBRN materials, information, and technology became more widely available, especially from the Internet and the former Soviet Union.

Sudan also continued to assist several Islamic and non-Islamic rebel groups based in East Africa. Nonetheless, Sudan's relations with its neighbors appeared to improve in 1999. Ethiopia renewed previously terminated air links, while Eritrea considered reestablishing diplomatic ties. Moreover, in early December, Sudan signed a peace accord with Uganda under which both nations agreed to halt all support for any rebel groups operating on each other's soil.

SUMMARY

The United States continues to make progress in fighting terrorism. The policy and programs of the past 20 years have reduced dramatically the role of state sponsors in directly supporting terrorism. The threat is shifting, and we are responding accordingly. It is our clear policy goal to get all seven countries and 28 Foreign Terrorist Organizations out of the terrorist business completely. We seek to have all state sponsors rejoin the community of nations committed to ending the threat. We must redouble our efforts, however, to "drain the swamp" in other countries -- whether hostile to the United States or not -- where terrorists seek to find safe haven for their planning and operations.

Terrorism will be with us for the foreseeable future. Some terrorists will continue using the most popular form of terrorism -- the truck or car bomb -- while others will seek alternative means to deliver their deadly message, including weapons of mass destruction (WMD) or cyberattacks. We must remain vigilant to these new threats, and we are preparing ourselves for them.

All terrorists -- even a "cyberterrorist" -- must occupy physical space to carry out attacks. The strong political will of states to counter the threat of terrorism remains the crucial variable of our success.

NOTE:

Adverse mention of individual members of any political, social, ethnic, religious, or national group is not meant to imply that all members of that group are terrorists. Indeed, terrorists represent a small minority of dedicated, often fanatical, individuals in most such groups. It is those small groups -- and their actions -- that are the subject of this report.

Furthermore, terrorist acts are part of a larger phenomenon of politically inspired violence, and at times the line between the two can become difficult to draw. To relate terrorist events to the larger context and to give a feel for the conflicts that spawn violence, this report will discuss terrorist acts as well as other violent incidents that are not necessarily international terrorism.

The Coordinator for Counterterrorism is required by law to give Congress complete report every year on terrorism for certain countries and groups. The report must include detailed assessments of foreign countries where significant terrorist acts occurred and countries about which Congress was notified during the preceding five years about the so-called terrorist list countries that repeatedly have provided state support for international terrorism.

In addition, the report includes all relevant information about the previous year's activities of individuals, terrorist organizations, or umbrella groups known to be responsible for the kidnapping or death of any US citizen during the preceding five years, and groups known to be financed by state sponsors of terrorism.

The Department of State is also required to report on the extent to which other countries cooperate with the United States in apprehending, convicting, and punishing terrorists responsible for attacking US citizens or interests and the extent to which foreign governments are cooperating, or have cooperated during the previous five years, in preventing future acts of terrorism. (As permitted in the legislation, the Department submitted such information to Congress in a classified annex to this unclassified report.)

LAW ENFORCEMENT EFFORTS

The United States brought the rule of law to bear against international terrorists in several ongoing cases throughout 1999:

On 19 May the US District Court in the Southern District of New York unsealed an indictment against Ali Mohammed, charging him with conspiracy to kill US nationals overseas. Ali, suspected of being a member of Osama bin Laden's al-Qa'ida terrorist organization, had been arrested in the United States in September 1998 after testifying before a grand jury concerning the US Embassy bombings in East Africa.

Authorities apprehended Khalfan Khamis Mohamed in South Africa on 5 October, after a joint investigation by the Department of State's Diplomatic Security Bureau, the Federal Bureau of Investigation (FBI), and South African law enforcement authorities. US officials brought him to New York to face charges in connection with the bombing of the US Embassy in Dar es Salaam, Tanzania, on 7 August 1998.

Three additional suspects in the Tanzanian and Kenyan US Embassy bombings currently are in custody in the United Kingdom, pending extradition to the United States: Khalid Al-Fawwaz, Adel Mohammed Abdul Almagid Bary, and Ibrahim Hussein Abdelhadi Eidarous. Eight other suspects, including Osama bin Laden, remain at large. The FBI added bin Laden to its Ten Most Wanted Fugitives list in June. The Department of State's Rewards for Justice program pays up to $5 million for information that leads to the arrest or conviction of these and other terrorist suspects.

On 15 October, Siddig Ibrahim Siddig Ali was sentenced to 11 years in prison for his role in a plot to bomb New York City landmarks and to assassinate Egyptian President Hosni Mubarak in 1993. Siddig Ali was arrested in June 1993 on conspiracy charges and pleaded guilty in February 1995 to all charges against him. His cooperation with authorities helped prosecutors convict Shaykh Umar Abd al-Rahman and nine others for their roles in the bombing conspiracy.

In September the US Justice Department informed Hani al-Sayegh, a Saudi Arabian citizen, that he would be removed from the United States and sent to Saudi Arabia. Authorities expelled him from the United States to Saudi Arabia on 11 October, where he remains in custody. He faces charges there in connection with the attack in June 1996 on US forces in Khubar, Saudi Arabia, that killed 19 US citizens and wounded more than 500 others. Al-Sayegh was paroled into the United States from Canada in June 1997. After he failed to abide by an initial plea agreement with the Justice Department concerning a separate case, the State Department terminated his parole in October 1997 and placed him in removal proceedings.

EDITOR's NOTE: *On June 21, 2001, Thirteen Saudis and one Lebanese were indicted in the 1996 bombing that killed 19 American servicemen and wounded nearly 400 in Saudi Arabia. A 46-count indictment by a federal grand jury in Alexandria, Virginia, charged that the defendants, under the direction of unnamed Iranian officials, conspired to kill U.S. citizens. The indictment charges that as early as 1993 members of Saudi Hezballah began extensive surveillance in search of a U.S. target, settling two years later on the American military housing high-rise near Dhahran. Most of the Saudis indicted are young male members of the Shiite branch of Islam who lived in the eastern province of Saudi Arabia near the Persian Gulf. The indictment said they were trained in Lebanon in Hezballah-controlled areas and also in Iran.*

The United States claims that certain Iranian figures "inspired, supported and supervised" the activities of the terrorists. Iran denied the allegation.

U.S. Attorney General John Ashcroft commented, "This indictment serves to underscore the commitment of the Bush administration and the Justice Department to bringing terrorists to account. Americans are a high-priority target for terrorists and our nation will vigorously fight to preserve justice for our citizens both here at home as well as abroad."

Appendix C
Africa Overview

Africa in 2000 witnessed an increase in the number of terrorist attacks against foreigners or foreign interests -- part of a growing trend in which the number of international terrorist incidents on the continent has risen steadily each year since 1995. Most attacks stemmed from internal civil unrest and spillover from regional wars as African rebel movements and opposition groups employed terrorism to further their political, social, or economic objectives. International terrorist organizations, including al-Qaida, Lebanese Hizballah, and Egyptian terrorist groups, continued to operate in Africa during 2000 and to pose a threat to US interests there.

Angola

Angola continued to be plagued by the protracted civil war between the National Union for the Total Independence of Angola (UNITA) and the Angolan Government. Several international terrorist attacks originating in this conflict occurred in 2000, while throughout the year members of the separatist group the Front for the Liberation of the Enclave of Cabinda (FLEC) took hostage several foreigners in Cabinda Province.

Unidentified militants, suspected of being UNITA rebels, ambushed a vehicle near Soyo on 25 January and killed a Portuguese citizen. During May, UNITA rebels attacked two World Food Program convoys in northern Angola, killing one person and causing significant property damage. On 18 and 19 August, suspected UNITA fighters attacked two diamond mines in northeast Angola, killing nine South Africans and abducting seven Angolans.

The group's most significant incident for the year occurred on 24 May, when FLEC rebels kidnapped three Portuguese construction workers and one Angolan in Cabinda Province.

Guinea

Spillover from fighting in Sierra Leone resulted in several international terrorist acts in Guinea during 2000. Revolutionary United Front (RUF) rebels crossed the border into Guinea from Sierra Leone on 7 September and kidnapped two foreign Catholic priests who escaped their captors in early December. On 17 September suspected RUF rebels from Sierra Leone attacked and killed a Togolese United Nations High Commissioner for Refugees staff employee and kidnapped an Ivorian secretary.

Namibia

During 2000 violence from the Angolan civil war spilled over into Namibia after Angolan Government troops were invited into border areas where Angolan National Union for the Total Independence of Angola (UNITA) rebels had been active for 20 years. Clashes in the border area killed nine individuals, including several foreigners. Three French children were killed on 3 January in the Caprivi region of Namibia when their vehicle was attacked by uniformed armed men of unknown affiliation. The local police commissioner blamed UNITA rebels for the attack, but a UNITA spokesman denied any responsibility. In other attacks on vehicles, gunmen of unknown affiliation also wounded two French citizens, two Danish aid workers, and a Scottish citizen.

Niger

In January, a suspected threat from Algerian terrorists forced organizers to cancel the Niger stage of the Paris-Dakar Road Rally. Race officials bypassed Niger and airlifted competitors to Libya after receiving information that Islamic extremists based in Niger were planning a terrorist attack. No terrorist attacks occurred on the 11,000-kilometer race through Senegal, Burkina Faso, Mali, Libya, and Egypt.

Nigeria

In 2000, impoverished ethnic groups in the southern oil-producing region of Nigeria continued to kidnap local and foreign oil workers in an effort to acquire a greater share of Nigeria's oil wealth. (Abductions in the oil region are common, and hostages are rarely harmed.) Some 300 persons, including 54 foreigners, were abducted between April and July. The most serious kidnapping incident occurred on 31 July when armed youths attacked two oil drilling rigs and took 165 hostages, including seven US citizens and five Britons. All hostages were released unharmed on 4 August.

Sierra Leone

Sierra Leone's warring factions carried out more high-profile terrorist attacks against foreign interests in 2000 than in 1999, killing and kidnapping United Nations Assistance Mission in Sierra Leone (UNAMSIL) peacekeepers, foreign journalists, and humanitarian aid workers.

The most violent attacks occurred in May when Revolutionary United Front (RUF) rebels resorted to terrorism in an effort to force out UN peacekeepers who had arrived to replace a regional peacekeeping force. In those attacks, RUF militiamen killed five UN peacekeepers and kidnapped some 500 others -- most of whom were later released. The RUF also is believed responsible for shooting down a UN helicopter and killing two foreign journalists -- including one US citizen -- in May. Armed militants kidnapped two British aid workers on 9 May and released them a month later.

Sporadic terrorist attacks continued from June until August, resulting in the deaths of four more peacekeepers and the kidnapping of at least 30 additional UN troops. RUF fighters were responsible for most of the attacks.

Somalia

According to the US Embassy in Nairobi, Kenya, unidentified Somali gunmen on 30 March opened fire on a UN aircraft departing the port city of Kismaayo in southern Somalia. No group claimed responsibility for the attack, which resulted in no injuries and only minor damage to the aircraft. The UN responded by temporarily suspending humanitarian operations in Kismaayo.

South Africa

Cape Town continued to experience a series of bombings and other acts of urban terrorism in 2000. Nine bombings resulted in some 30 injuries. Five of the nine attacks were car-bombings that targeted South African authorities, public places, and restaurants and nightclubs with Western associations. According to US Embassy reporting, the spate of bombings in 2000 -- the latest of several urban terrorism episodes that Cape Town has experienced since 1998 -- was distinguished by larger bombs triggered by more sophisticated remote detonation devices. Damage from a car-bomb explosion in a suburban Cape Town shopping center parking lot in August.

Two persons, including a 10-year-old boy, were injured.

South African authorities suspect that People Against Gangsterism and Drugs (PAGAD) -- South Africa's most militant Muslim organization -- was responsible for most of the bombings. According to press reports, anonymous calls to news reporters demanding the release of PAGAD cadre preceded four of the bombings. One unidentified individual called a local radio station before a bombing on 29 August and gave precise details of the timing and location of the attack. In raids in November, police arrested several suspects affiliated with PAGAD and confiscated several pipe bombs. There were no bombings or incidents after the arrests.

Uganda

The Sudanese-backed Lord's Resistance Army (LRA) in northern Uganda and the Sudanese- and Congolese-supported Allied Democratic Forces (ADF) in Western Uganda continued their insurgent campaigns to undermine the Ugandan Government in 2000 -- resulting in several terrorist attacks against foreign nationals. Suspected LRA rebels kidnapped two Italian missionaries on 4 March and released them unharmed several hours later. In October, LRA militants shot and killed another Italian priest as he drove to his church.

Government counterterrorist efforts initiated in 1999 helped prevent any major bombings during 2000 in the capital, Kampala. Islamist militants associated with the ADF are believed responsible for a series of deadly bombings and other urban terrorist incidents that occurred from 1997 to 1999.

Appendix D
Asia Overview

South Asia

In 2000, South Asia remained a focal point for terrorism directed against the United States, further confirming the trend of terrorism shifting from the Middle East to South Asia. The Taliban continued to provide safe haven for international terrorists, particularly Osama bin Laden and his network, in the portions of Afghanistan it controlled.

Smart Sanctions

United Nations Security Council Resolution 1333, passed in December 2000, targets the Taliban regime in Afghanistan. The Taliban ignored its obligations under UN Security Council Resolution 1267 (passed in November 1999) and has continued to provide shelter to Osama bin Laden. In UN Security Council Resolution 1333, the Security Council: Demands the Taliban comply with Resolution 1267 and cease providing training and support to international terrorists; Insists the Taliban turn over indicted international terrorist Osama bin Laden so he can be brought to justice; Directs the Taliban to close all terrorist camps in Afghanistan within 30 days.

Until the Taliban fully complies with its obligations under this resolution and Resolution 1267, member states of the United Nations should: Freeze the financial assets of Osama bin Laden; Observe an arms embargo against the Taliban that includes a prohibition against providing military weapons, training, or advice; Close all Taliban offices overseas; Reduce the staff at the limited number of Taliban missions abroad; Restrict travel of senior Taliban officials except for the purposes of participation in peace negotiations, compliance with the resolution, or for humanitarian reasons, including religious obligations; Ban the export to Afghan territory of a precursor chemical, acetic anhydride, which is used to manufacture heroin; Close all offices of Ariana Afghan Airlines and ban all nonhumanitarian assistance flights into and out of Afghanistan. Broad exemptions are given to humanitarian flights operated by, or on behalf of, nongovernmental organizations and government relief agencies providing humanitarian assistance to Afghanistan.

The sanctions imposed by these two resolutions are targeted sanctions. They are not economic sanctions. These "smart sanctions" provide for broad humanitarian exemptions to avoid harming the Afghan people.

They permit private-sector trade and commerce, including food, medicine, and consumer products.

They permit, without impediment, the work of the humanitarian organizations providing assistance to the civilian population of Afghanistan.

They permit Afghans to travel by air for urgent humanitarian reasons and to fulfill their religious obligations, such as the hajj, including on the banned Ariana Afghan Airline. The UN Sanctions Committee already has approved about 200 flights for 13,000 Afghans in 2001 for this purpose. The Committee never has denied a request for a legitimate humanitarian waiver.

They permit Taliban officials to travel abroad to participate in a peace process and to discuss fulfilling the demands of the Resolutions.

The Government of Pakistan increased its support to the Taliban and continued its support to militant groups active in Indian-held Kashmir, such as the Harakat ul-Mujahidin (HUM), some of which engaged in terrorism. In Sri Lanka the government continued its 17-year conflict with the Liberation Tigers of Tamil Eelam (LTTE), which engaged in several terrorist acts against government and civilian targets during the year.

Afghanistan

Islamic extremists from around the world -- including North America, Europe, Africa, the Middle East, and Central, South, and Southeast Asia -- continued to use Afghanistan as a training ground and base of operations for their worldwide terrorist activities in 2000. The Taliban, which controlled most Afghan territory, permitted the operation of training and indoctrination facilities for non-Afghans and provided logistics support to members of various terrorist organizations and mujahidin, including those waging jihads (holy wars) in Central Asia, Chechnya, and Kashmir.

Throughout 2000 the Taliban continued to host Osama bin Laden despite UN sanctions and international pressure to hand him over to stand trial in the United States or a third country. In a serious and ongoing dialogue with the Taliban, the United States repeatedly made clear to the Taliban that it would be held responsible for any terrorist attacks undertaken by Bin Laden while he is in its territory.

In October, a terrorist bomb attack against the USS Cole in Aden Harbor, Yemen, killed 17 US sailors and injured scores of others. Although no definitive link has been made to Bin Laden's organization, Yemeni authorities have determined that some suspects in custody and at large are veterans of Afghan training camps.

In August, Bangladeshi authorities uncovered a bomb plot to assassinate Prime Minister Sheik Hasina at a public rally. Bangladeshi police maintained that Islamic terrorists trained in Afghanistan planted the bomb.

India

Security problems associated with various insurgencies, particularly in Kashmir, persisted through 2000 in India. Massacres of civilians in Kashmir during March and August were attributed to Lashkar-e-Tayyiba (LT) and other militant groups. India also faced continued violence associated with several separatist movements based in the northeast of the country.

The Indian Government continued cooperative efforts with the United States against terrorism. During the year, the US-India Joint Counterterrorism Working Group -- founded in November 1999 -- met twice and agreed to increased cooperation on mutual counterterrorism interests. New Delhi continued to cooperate with US officials to ascertain the fate of four Western hostages -- including one US citizen -- kidnapped in Indian-held Kashmir in 1995, although the hostages' whereabouts remained unknown.

Pakistan

Pakistan's military government, headed by Gen. Pervez Musharraf, continued previous Pakistani Government support of the Kashmir insurgency, and Kashmiri militant groups continued to operate in Pakistan, raising funds and recruiting new cadre. Several of these groups were responsible for attacks against civilians in Indian-held Kashmir, and the largest of the groups, the Lashkar-e-Tayyiba, claimed responsibility for a suicide car-bomb attack against an Indian garrison in Srinagar in April.

In addition, the Harakat ul-Mujahidin (HUM), a designated Foreign Terrorist Organization, continues to be active in Pakistan without discouragement by the Government of Pakistan. Members of the group were associated with the hijacking in December 1999 of an Air India flight that resulted in the release from an Indian jail of former HUM leader Maulana Masood Azhar. Azhar since has founded his own Kashmiri militant group, Jaish-e-Mohammed, and publicly has threatened the United States.

The United States remains concerned about reports of continued Pakistani support for the Taliban's military operations in Afghanistan. Credible reporting indicates that Pakistan is providing the Taliban with materiel, fuel, funding, technical assistance, and military advisers. Pakistan has not prevented large numbers of Pakistani nationals from moving into Afghanistan to fight for the Taliban. Islamabad also failed to take effective steps to curb the activities of certain madrassas, or religious schools, that serve as recruiting grounds for terrorism. Pakistan publicly and privately said it intends to comply fully with UNSCR 1333, which imposes an arms embargo on the Taliban.

The attack on the USS Cole in Yemen in October prompted fears of US retaliatory strikes against Bin Laden's organization and targets in Afghanistan if the investigation pointed in that direction. Pakistani religious party leaders and militant groups threatened US citizens and facilities if such an action were to occur, much as they did after the US attacks on training camps in Afghanistan in August 1998 and following the US diplomatic intervention in the Kargil conflict between Pakistan and

India in 1999. The Government of Pakistan generally has cooperated with US requests to enhance security for US facilities and personnel.

Sri Lanka

The separatist group the Liberation Tigers of Tamil Eelam (LTTE) -- redesignated as a Foreign Terrorist Organization in 1999 -- remained violent in 2000, engaging in several terrorist acts against government and civilian targets. LTTE attacks, including those involving suicide bombers, killed more than 100 persons, including Minister of Industrial Development Goonaratne, and wounded dozens. Two US citizens and a British national were apparent incidental victims of the group in October, when an LTTE suicide bomber cornered by the police detonated his bomb near the Town Hall in Colombo. The LTTE continued to strike civilian shipping in Sri Lanka, conducting a naval suicide bombing of a merchant vessel and hijacking a Russian ship.

The war in the north between the Tigers and the Sri Lankan Government continued, although by year's end the government had re-taken 70 percent of the Jaffna Peninsula. The Government of Norway initiated efforts to broker peace between the two parties and may have contributed to an LTTE decision to announce unilaterally a cease-fire in December.

Several terrorist acts have been attributed to other domestic Sri Lankan groups. Suspected Sinhalese extremists protesting Norway's peace efforts used small improvised explosive devices to attack the Norwegian-run charity Save the Children as well as the Norwegian Embassy. Sinhalese extremists also are suspected of assassinating pro-LTTE politician G. G. Kumar Ponnambalam, Jr., in January.

East Asia

Japan continued to make progress in its counterterrorist efforts. Legal restrictions instituted in 1999 began to take effect on the Aum. Four Aum Shinrikyo members who had personally placed the Sarin on the subway in 1995 were sentenced to death. Tokyo also made substantial progress in its efforts to return several Japanese Red Army (JRA) members to Japan. The Government of Japan indicted four JRA members who were forcibly returned after being deported from Lebanon. Tokyo also took two others into custody: Yoshimi Tanaka, a fugitive JRA member involved in hijacking a Japanese airliner in 1970, who was extradited from Thailand, and Fusako Shigenobu, a JRA founder and leader, who had been on the run for 30 years and was arrested in Japan in November.

Several nations in East Asia experienced terrorist violence in 2000. Burmese dissidents took over a provincial hospital in Thailand; authorities stormed the hospital, killed the hostage takers, and freed the hostages unharmed. In Indonesia, there was a sharp increase in international and domestic terrorism, including several bombings, two of which targeted official foreign interests. Pro-Jakarta militia units continued attacks on UN personnel in East Timor. In one incident in September, three aid workers, including one US citizen, were killed.

Small-scale violence in Cambodia, Laos, and Vietnam occurred in 2000, some connected to antigovernment groups, allegedly with support from foreign nationals. Several small-scale bombings occurred in the Laotian capital, some of which targeted tourist destinations and injured foreign nationals. An attack on 24 November in downtown Phnom Penh, Cambodia, resulted in deaths and injuries. The US Government released a statement on 19 December that "deplores and condemns" alleged US national or permanent resident support, encouragement, or participation in violent antigovernment activities in several foreign countries with which the United States is at peace, specifically Vietnam, Cambodia, and Laos.

In the Philippines, the Abu Sayyaf Group (ASG) abducted 21 persons, including 10 foreign tourists, from a Malaysian resort in April, the first time the group conducted operations outside the southern Philippines. ASG members later abducted several foreign journalists, three Malaysians, and one US citizen in the southern Philippines. (The US citizen and one Filipino remained captive at year's end.) After breaking off peace talks in Manila in April, the Moro Islamic Liberation Front (MILF) mounted several terrorist attacks in the southern Philippines against Philippine security and civilian targets. Philippine officials also suspect MILF operatives conducted bombings in Manila, including two at popular shopping malls in May. Other groups, including the Communist Party of the Philippines New People's Army, and the Alex Boncayao Brigade, mounted attacks in the archipelago.

Burma

In January, 10 armed Burmese dissidents -- linked to the takeover in 1999 of the Burmese Embassy in Bangkok -- took over the Ratchaburi provincial hospital in Thailand. Thai security forces stormed the hospital and freed the victims. All the hostage takers were killed, and no hostages were injured during the assault. Separately, Burma sentenced to death one terrorist involved in the 1999 Embassy seizure.

Indonesia

Indonesia experienced a sharp rise in international and domestic terrorism during the year, as weakening central government control and a difficult transition to democracy provided fertile ground for terrorist activities.

Several bombings occurred in 2000, two of which targeted official foreign interests. Unidentified assailants detonated a car bomb in front of the Philippine Ambassador's residence in central Jakarta as the Ambassador was entering the compound on 1 August. The explosion killed two Indonesians, seriously injured three other persons -- including the Ambassador -- and slightly injured 18 bystanders, including one Filipino and two Bulgarians. Unidentified perpetrators also conducted a grenade attack against the Malaysian Embassy on 27 August, but no injuries resulted.

Six other bombings from July to November targeted domestic interests in the capital. The most destructive occurred on 13 September when a car bomb in the Jakarta stock exchange's underground parking garage killed 10 Indonesians. Other targets included the Attorney General's office, the Jakarta Governor's residence, a Jakarta hotel, a local nongovernmental organization, as well as the Ministry of Agriculture, which was used as the courtroom venue for former President Soeharto's corruption trial. Multiple bombings also occurred in major cities in North Sumatra, Riau, and East Java.

Indonesian officials made little progress in apprehending and prosecuting those responsible for the bombings. The Indonesian National Police arrested 34 persons suspected of involvement in the Malaysian Embassy and the stock-exchange bombings, but a lack of evidence forced the release of all suspects in mid-October. The police claim the Free Aceh Movement (GAM) -- a group seeking an independent state in northern Sumatra -- conducted both attacks and planned another against the US Embassy to "create chaos" in Jakarta. The evidence made public as of December, however, does not support elements of this theory. Nevertheless, the GAM or Achenese separatists did conduct sporadic attacks on ExxonMobil oil facilities in Aceh early in the year. The group's primary target was Indonesian security elements, some of which continued to guard ExxonMobil facilities.

Indonesian nationalists and some radical Islamic groups occasionally carried out violent protests outside US diplomatic facilities in response to perceived US interference in domestic affairs and support for Israel. One demonstration culminated in a mob attack against the US Consulate in Surabaya on 15 September, and another involved the Islamic militant Front Pembela Islam (Islamic Defenders' Front) threatening US citizens in the country. Other Islamic extremists in October searched for US citizens in a central Javanese city, warning them to leave the country.

Indonesian students attacked US Consulate gates during a protest in Surabaya on 15 September. The students were protesting perceived western intervention in Indonesian domestic politics.

Militiamen attacked a UNHCR aid office in Atambua, West Timor, on 6 September, killing three aid workers, including one US citizen. Suspected militia members also killed two UN peacekeepers -- a New Zealander and a Nepalese national -- during the year.

Japan

Aum Shinrikyo, which conducted the Sarin nerve agent attack in the Tokyo subway system in 1995, remained under active government surveillance. The Aum now is required by law to report regularly on its membership, residences, and other holdings. The Tokyo district court in 1999 and 2000 sentenced to death four of the five senior cultists who actually placed the Sarin on the subway. (The fifth culprit, Ikuo Hayashi, showed a repentant and cooperative attitude and, in 1998, received a less severe life sentence.) The prosecution of cult leader Shoko Asahara continued, with four drug-related charges dropped in October in an effort to expedite a verdict.

Aum leadership took further steps to improve the cult's image following up its public apology and admission of responsibility for the subway attack with an agreement to pay $40 million damage to attack victims, rejection of cult founder Asahara as a religious prophet, a pledge to remove teachings advocating murder from the cult's religious doctrine, and a change of its name to Aleph.

Separately, four Japanese Red Army (JRA) members were returned to Japan in March after being deported from Lebanon. They later were indicted on charges of attempted murder and forgery of official documents. Japanese officials continued to seek the extradition of a fifth colleague, Kozo Okamoto, who was granted political asylum by Lebanon because he had participated in operations against Israel. In June, the Japanese Government successfully extradited Yoshimi Tanaka -- one of the fugitive members of the JRA involved in hijacking a Japanese Airlines plane to North Korea in 1970 -- from Thailand. During a preliminary hearing before the Tokyo district court in July, Tanaka publicly apologized and submitted a signed report admitting to hijacking and assault charges. His trial began on 16 December.

In November, Osaka police successfully tracked down and arrested Fusako Shigenobu, a founder and leader of the JRA, who had been on the run for 30 years. Prosecutors have charged her with suspicion of conspiracy related to JRA's seizure of the French Embassy in The Hague in 1974, as well as attempted murder, and passport fraud. Police later seized two supporters who allegedly helped her evade detection while in Japan. Only a handful of JRA members remain at large. Fusako Shigenobu, JRA founder and leader, was arrested in November.

Japan has yet to sign the International Convention for the Suppression of Terrorist Financing.

Laos

Several small-scale bombings of undetermined origin occurred in Vientiane during 2000, some of which targeted tourist destinations and injured foreign nationals. Unidentified assailants threw an explosive device at a restaurant on 30 March, injuring 10 tourists from Britain, Germany, and Denmark. Bombings also occurred at Vientiane's morning market in May -- injuring four Thai nationals -- and the central post office in July, where two foreign tourists narrowly escaped injury. Unidentified perpetrators also detonated explosives at the Vientiane bus station, the domestic airport terminal, and a national monument. Authorities discovered other bombs planted at the morning market, a foreign embassy, and in a hotel outside Vientiane and rendered them safe.

Press reporting during the year indicated that political dissidents conducted some of the attacks in the capital, although the suspected groups denied involvement.

Malaysia

Malaysia experienced two incidents of international terrorism in 2000, both perpetrated by the Philippine-based Abu Sayyaf Group (ASG). The ASG abducted 21 persons, including 10 foreign tourists, from the Sipadan diving resort in eastern Malaysia on 23 April. A suspected ASG faction also kidnapped three Malaysians from a resort on Pandanan Island in eastern Malaysia on 10 September. The group released most of the hostages from both incidents but continued to hold one Filipino abducted from Sipadan as of the end of the year.

A Malaysian Islamic sect known as Al-Ma'unah targeted domestic security forces for the first time in July. Members of the group raided two military armories in Perak state, about 175 miles north of Kuala Lumpur, and took four locals hostage. Sect members killed two of the hostages -- a Malaysian police officer and soldier -- before surrendering on 6 July. Malaysian authorities arrested and detained several dozen members following the incident and suspect that 29 of those held also launched attacks against a Hindu temple, a brewery, and an electrical power tower.

Philippines

Islamic separatist groups in the Philippines increased attacks against foreign and domestic targets in 2000. The Abu Sayyaf Group (ASG) -- designated one of 29 Foreign Terrorist Organizations by the US Government -- conducted operations outside the southern Philippines for the first time when it abducted 21 persons -- including 10 foreign tourists -- from a Malaysian resort in April. In a series of subsequent, separate incidents, ASG group members abducted several foreign journalists, three Malaysians, and one US citizen in the southern Philippines. Although obtaining ransom money was a primary goal, the hostage takers issued several disparate political demands ranging from releasing international terrorists jailed in the United States to establishing an independent Islamic state. The group released most of the hostages by October allegedly for ransoms totaling several million dollars, while Philippine Government assaults on ASG positions paved the way for some other hostages to escape. The ASG, however, continued to hold the US citizen and a Filipino captive at year's end.

Manila made some legal progress against ASG kidnapping activities in 2000 when a regional trial court sentenced three group members to life in prison for abducting Dr. Nilo Barandino and 10 members of his household in 1992. The Philippine Government also filed charges against ASG members involved in multiple kidnapping cases, although the suspects remained at large.

The Moro Islamic Liberation Front (MILF) -- the largest remaining Philippine Islamic separatist group -- broke off stalled peace talks with Manila in late April. After the military launched an offensive capturing several MILF strongholds and attacking rebel checkpoints near Camp Abubakar -- the MILF headquarters in the southern Philippines -- the MILF mounted several terrorist attacks in the southern Philippines against

Philippine security and civilian targets. In July, Philippine Armed Forces captured Camp Abubakar, and the MILF responded by declaring a "holy war" against Manila and continuing attacks against civilian and government targets in the southern Philippines. Philippine law enforcement officials also have accused MILF operatives of responsibility for several bombings in Manila, including two at popular shopping malls in May and five at different locations in Manila on 30 December. Police arrested 26 suspected MILF members in connection with the May bombings and still held them at year's end.

Communist rebels also remained active in 2000, occasionally targeting businesses and engaging in sporadic clashes with Philippine security forces. Press reporting indicates that early in the year the Communist Party of the Philippines New People's Army (CPP/NPA) attacked a South Korean construction company and in March issued an order to target foreign businesses "whose operations hurt the country's economy and environment."

The Alex Boncayao Brigade (ABB) -- a breakaway CPP/NPA faction -- strafed Shell Oil offices in the central Philippines in March. The group warned of more attacks against oil companies, including US-owned Caltex, to protest rising oil prices.

Distinguishing between political and criminal motivation for many of the terrorist-related activities in the Philippines continued to be difficult, most notably in the numerous cases of kidnapping for ransom in the southern Philippines. Both Islamic and Communist insurgents sought to extort funds from businesses in their operating areas, occasionally conducting reprisal operations if money was not paid.

Thailand

In January 2000, 10 armed Burmese dissidents -- linked to the takeover in 1999 of the Burmese Embassy in Bangkok -- took over the Ratchaburi provincial hospital. Thai security forces stormed the hospital and freed the victims. Although no hostages were injured during the assault, all the hostage takers were killed. Separately, Burma sentenced to death one terrorist involved in the 1999 Embassy takeover. Authorities responded with military force and legal action to separatist activity in the south. In February, security forces dealt a severe blow to the New Pattani United Liberation organization -- a Muslim separatist group -- when they killed its leader Saarli Taloh-Meyaw. Authorities claim that he was responsible for 90 percent of the terrorist activities in Narathiwat, a southern Thai province.

In April, police arrested the deputy leader of the outlawed Barisan Revolusi Nasional (BRN) -- a Southern separatist group -- in Pattani. The case was still pending before the court at year's end.

Authorities suspect Muslim separatists conducted several small-scale attacks on public schools, a government-run clinic, and a police station in the south.

In June, a Thai criminal court ordered extradited to Japan Yoshimi Tanaka -- a member of the radical Japanese Red Army Faction, wanted for the hijacking in 1970 of a Japan Airlines plane. His trial in Tokyo began in mid-December.

Thai officials again publicly pledged to halt the use of Thailand as a logistics base by the Sri Lankan group the Liberation Tigers of Tamil Eelam (LTTE). The pledges, which echoed reassurances made by Bangkok in previous years, followed the discovery in June of a partially completed submersible at a shipyard in Phuket, Thailand, owned by an LTTE-sympathizer, as well as an unclassified paper by Canadian intelligence published in December that outlined the Tigers' use of front companies to procure weapons via Thailand.

Appendix E
Eurasia Overview

No major terrorist attacks occurred in Eurasia in 2000, but counterterrorist efforts, often in conjunction with counterinsurgency efforts, continued in the states of the former Soviet Union. Russia, China, and the United States were all involved in regional efforts to combat terrorism. In 2000, members of the Commonwealth of Independent States (CIS) discussed establishing a CIS-wide counterterrorism center in Bishkek, although past efforts have been unsuccessful. The heads of the CIS states security services put forward Gen. Boris Mylnikov, former First Deputy Director of the Russian Federal Security Service (FSB) Department for Protecting the Constitutional Order and Combating Terrorism, to lead the potential CIS Counter-terrorism Center, and on 1 December the CIS heads of state agreed on funding for the organization, half of which will be provided by Russia. The center began operations in

December 2000 and reportedly has been tasked by the CIS to maintain a database of information on terrorism.

The Shanghai Forum--Kyrgyzstan, Kazakhstan, Tajikistan, Russia, and China--met in July and discussed cooperation among the five states as well as with Uzbekistan against terrorism, insurgency, and Islamic extremism. The Forum supported a proposal to establish a regional counterterrorism center in Bishkek, although no progress had been made in implementing this decision by year's end.

All five Central Asian states participated in the Central Asian counterterrorism Conference in June sponsored by the US Department of State. Other participants included representatives from Russia, Egypt, and Spain. The United Kingdom, Turkey, China, and the Organization for Security and Cooperation in Europe (OSCE) sent observers.

Several Central Asian states also concluded counterterrorism agreements in 2000. Uzbekistan in early May signed an agreement with India that included an extradition treaty and mutual assistance in criminal investigations with an eye toward counterterrorist operations. In June, Kazakhstan and Kyrgyzstan separately reached bilateral agreements with China to cooperate on counterterrorist matters. In October and November, Uzbekistan also signed agreements on counterterrorism cooperation with Turkey, China, and Italy.

Azerbaijan

Azerbaijan took strong steps to curb the international logistics networks that support the fighters in Chechnya, to include closing international Islamic relief organizations believed to assist militants in Chechnya, strengthening border controls with Russia, and arresting and extraditing suspected mujahidin supporters. There has been good cooperation on counterterrorism cases between the Government of Azerbaijan and US law enforcement. In mid-September, Azerbaijani police arrested seven Dagestani men under suspicion of working with the mujahidin and extradited them to Russia. The government has cooperated closely and effectively with the United States on antiterrorism issues, and a program of antiterrorism assistance has been initiated.

Azerbaijan intends to join the CIS Counterterrorism Center.

Azerbaijan and Russia signed a border agreement extension in early June to limit the flow of arms and militants across the borders.

In early October, the Supreme Court in Baku found 13 members of Jayshullah, an indigenous terrorist group who may have had plans to attack the US Embassy, guilty of committing terrorist actions. The court sentenced them to prison terms ranging from eight years to life.

Georgia

Georgia faced the potential for spillover violence from the Chechen conflict and contended with international mujahidin seeking to use Georgian territory as a conduit for financial and logistic support to the mujahidin in Chechnya. Russia continued to pressure Georgia for stronger border controls. With international assistance, Georgia has steadily increased its border control presence on its northern border and invited monitors from the Organization for Security and Cooperation in Europe (OSCE). The OSCE has not recorded any movement of mujahidin across the Georgian border with Chechnya, although some evidence suggests that, despite these efforts, neither Russian nor Georgian border guards have been able to seal the border entirely from individuals and small groups passing to and from Chechnya.

Russia alleged that there are mujahidin in the Pankisi Gorge in northern Georgia. Georgia moved more Interior Ministry units into the region. Hostage taking for ransom by criminal gangs continued to be a problem in some parts of Georgia. Five persons were kidnapped in the Abkhazia region, including two unarmed UN military observers and an international NGO employee, in early June, then released without payment of ransom. Two International Red Cross staff employees were taken hostage on 4 August in the Pankisi Gorge and released one week later under the condition that their kidnappers would not face criminal charges.

Kazakhstan

In Almaty in September, Kazakhstani police killed four suspected Uighur separatist militants who were sought in connection with the murders of two policemen and a leader of the Uighur community in Kyrgyzstan.

Kyrgyzstan

The only clear instances of international terrorism in Central Asia this year occurred in Kyrgyzstan as the Islamic Movement of Uzbekistan's (IMU) insurgent efforts continued. Four US citizen mountain climbers were taken hostage by IMU militants operating in southern Kyrgyzstan in early August and held captive for several days before they escaped unharmed. IMU militants also took six German, three Russian, one Ukrainian, and two Uzbek mountaineers hostage, but later freed them.

Russia

Russian authorities continued to search for suspects in the four deadly apartment bombings that took place in August and September 1999. The trial of the six Dagestani men accused of conducting the bombing in Buinaksk, which killed 62 persons, began in December. There still are no suspects in custody for the bombings of two buildings in Moscow or a building in Volgodonsk. In November, Polish authorities arrested two Russian organized crime members, whom they suspect are connected to the August bombing in Moscow's Pushkin Square, which killed eight persons.

Tajikistan

Several incidents of domestic terrorism occurred in Tajikistan in 2000. A small car bomb, planted on a vehicle belonging to the European Community Humanitarian Organization (ECHO), exploded on 16 July in Dushanbe and injured several children. In addition, in October an unoccupied car belonging to the Chairman of the Democratic Party, Mahmadruzi Iskandarov, was bombed. Bombings and other violence marred Tajikistani Parliamentary elections in February, which concluded the Tajikistani Peace Process ending a five-year civil war.

On 1 October and 31 December four churches were bombed. Several deaths and numerous casualties resulted from the bombing in October. There is no evidence that any of the attacks, either on the churches or during the elections, involved international interests. While the Tajikistani Government does not support the Islamic Movement of Uzbekistan (IMU), it has been unable to prevent it from transiting its territory.

Uzbekistan

The Islamic Movement of Uzbekistan (IMU) infiltrated fighters into mountainous areas of Surkhandar'inskaya Oblast southern Uzbekistan during the spring and summer of 2000. Uzbekistani military forces discovered the fighters and drove them back into Tajikistan. Tohir Yuldashev and Juma Khodjiev (a.k.a. Juma Namangani), the leaders of the IMU, were tried in absentia together with 10 other persons accused of terrorism or anticonstitutional activity. All defendants were convicted at a trial that failed to conform to international standards for the protection of the human rights of the defendants. The court sentenced Yuldashev and Khodjiev to death and the remaining defendants to prison terms. On 25

September, the United States designated the IMU a Foreign Terrorist Organization, citing both its armed incursions into Uzbekistan and neighboring Kyrgyzstan and its taking of foreign hostages, including US citizens.

Appendix F
Europe Overview

Western Europe had the largest decline in the number of international terrorist incidents of any region in 2000. Several European states moved to strengthen and codify anti-terrorism legislation, and many signed the International Convention for the Suppression of Terrorist Financing, which was opened for signature on 10 January 2000. There were notable examples of counterterrorism cooperation among several countries, such as the US-UK-Greek collaboration on the British Defense Attache's assassination in Athens, Spanish-French cooperation against the Basque terrorist group Basque Fatherland and Liberty (ETA), and Italy and Spain's agreement to create common judicial space. Greece undertook a series of more stringent counterterrorism measures in the wake of the murder of the UK Defense Attaché by the terrorist group 17 November, but Athens still has not made any arrests in connection with any of the group's 21 murders over the past quarter century.

France and Turkey both made impressive strides in combating terrorism through aggressively pursuing the perpetrators and their terrorist groups.

In Southeastern Europe, groups of ethnic Albanians have conducted armed attacks against government forces in southern Serbia and in Macedonia since 1999. One group in southern Serbia calls itself the Liberation Army of Presevo, Medvedja, and Bujanovac (PMBLA). One group in Macedonia calls itself the National Liberation Army (NLA). Both groups include members who fought with the Kosovo Liberation Army (KLA) in 1998-99 and have used their wartime connections to obtain funding and weapons from Kosovo and elsewhere. The PMBLA has, on occasion, harassed and detained civilians traveling through areas it controls. Both the PMBLA and the NLA have fired indiscriminately upon civilian centers. (In the same region, ethnic Albanian assailants carried out a terrorist attack against a bus in Kosovo on 16 February 2001, killing at least seven civilians and wounding 43 others.)

Austria

In keeping with Austria's constructive security relationship with the United States, the Interior Minister discussed closer cooperation in countering crime and terrorism during a visit to Washington in August. Vienna also enacted an expanded police-powers bill enabling authorities to collect and analyze information more effectively.

On 26 February, Austrian letter bomber Franz Fuchs committed suicide in his prison cell where he had been serving a life sentence for masterminding a series of letter-bomb campaigns in Austria and Germany between 1993 and 1997.

Authorities held Halimeh Nimr, a suspected member of the terrorist Abu Nidal organization (ANO), in custody from January to May. In September, she failed to appear in court to be tried on charges of attempting to withdraw some $8 million from a bank account controlled by the ANO, which subsequently threatened to target Austrian interests if the funds were not released to the group.

In 2000, citing the statute of limitations, France declined an Austrian Government request that Illich Ramirez Sanchez, also known as Carlos the Jackal, be extradited to face criminal charges for a terrorist attack on the Vienna headquarters of OPEC in 1975.

The Austrian Government continued to allow the political front of the Kurdistan Workers' Party (PKK) to maintain its offices in Vienna, which have been open since 1995. Authorities estimate some 400 PKK militants and 4,000 sympathizers reside in Austria.

Belgium

The Interior Ministers of Belgium and Spain met in Brussels in June to discuss Belgium's refusal to extradite Basque Fatherland and Liberty (ETA) members suspected of terrorist acts. The Belgian minister pledged that his government would no longer refuse Spanish extradition requests.

In 2000, Belgium did reject Turkey's request for the extradition of suspected Turkish terrorist Fehriye Erdal to prosecute her for her alleged role in the 1996 handgun murder of a prominent Turkish industrialist and two associates in Istanbul. Erdal, arrested in Belgium in 1999, is allegedly a member of the Turkish Revolutionary People's Liberation Party/Front (DHKP/C) terrorist group. Belgian authorities denied Turkey's request on the grounds she could receive the death penalty if tried in Turkey. Belgium also declined to prosecute her under the 1977 European Convention on the Suppression of Terrorism, noting that it covers only terrorist acts using bombs or automatic weapons. After Brussels denied Ms. Erdal's political asylum request, she went on a hunger strike and subsequently was released from prison and placed under house arrest. She may be tried later on charges arising from criminal activities in Belgium.

In February, authorities paroled two members of the "Cellules Communistes Combattantes" after they had served 14 years of their life sentences for involvement in a series of bomb attacks against US, NATO, and Belgian interests in 1984 and 1985. One attack resulted in the deaths of two firefighters in Brussels.

Belgium has yet to sign the International Convention for the Suppression of Terrorist Financing.

France

During 2000, France maintained its traditional tough stance against terrorism. On the legal front, Paris was the first to sign the International Convention for the Suppression of Terrorist Financing, which was a French initiative. The French Government's nationwide "Vigi-Pirate" plan--which uses military forces to reinforce police security in Paris and other major cities to prevent a repeat of the Paris metro attacks by Algerian terrorists--remained in effect. Vigi-Pirate increased security at metro and train stations, enhanced border controls, and expanded identity checks countrywide.

In January, the Basque Fatherland and Liberty (ETA) relaunched its assassination and bombing campaign in Spain, and French police responded aggressively by interdicting cross-border operations, arresting group members, and shutting down logistics and supply cells in France. At year's end, ETA had killed 23 persons and wounded scores more.

On the judicial front, French courts tried and convicted numerous ETA terrorists. In January, Javier Arizkuren Ruiz, alias Kantauri, a former ETA military operations chief, was sentenced to eight years' imprisonment. A Paris appeals court in September reportedly authorized Ruiz's extradition to Spain to stand trial for an attempt to kill King Juan Carlos in 1995. Twelve other ETA militants received lengthy jail sentences. The court sent Daniel Derguy, believed to be the ETA chief in France, to prison for 10 years. In October, 10 senior French and Spanish ETA members were convicted of criminal conspiracy in connection with a terrorist organization. Ignacio Gracia Arregui, alias Inaki de Renteria, reportedly a top ETA leader, was sentenced in December to five years in jail. Others convicted received prison sentences of five to 10 years. France often has extradited convicted ETA terrorists to Spain when they have completed their prison sentences.

In October, a French judge ruled in favor of a suit charging Libyan leader Muammar Qadhafi with "complicity to murder" in the bomb attack in 1989 against a UTA airliner over the Niger desert that killed 170 persons. In November, French courts also convicted seven Spanish citizens of membership in First of October Anti-Fascist Resistance Group (GRAPO), a Spanish leftist terrorist group. In raids during the year, police officials seized bomb-making paraphernalia, false identity documents, and large amounts of cash. French courts convicted a number of Algerian nationals on terrorist-related charges. Amar Bouakaze, an Algerian, was convicted in June for criminal conspiracy in connection with a terrorist organization. Evidence linked Bouakaze to Ahmed Ressam, a suspected terrorist being held in the United States. Another Algerian national was convicted of an attack that derailed a train in France in June, leaving two persons dead.

The Breton Resistance Army (ARB) claimed responsibility for a bomb attack in April that damaged a McDonald's restaurant at Pornic, but the group denied involvement in another attack the same month against a McDonald's restaurant near Dinan that killed a French employee. French police arrested four members of the Breton nationalist group Emgann (Combat) on charges of involvement in the Dinan bombing.

Six proindependence Corsican groups joined in proclaiming a cease-fire in late 1999, but bomb attacks against government offices on the island continued intermittently in 2000. One such Corsican group claimed responsibility for a failed attack in Paris in June. In October, Corsican separatists placed a car bomb in front of the police station in Marseilles. The device was not built to detonate but to serve as a warning for a possible future attack and to highlight the group's capabilities. Also in October, French courts sentenced 10 Corsican nationalists to four years' imprisonment for an attack that damaged an estate complex on Corsica in 1994.

France's counterterrorism efforts have been less robust on the diplomatic front where it has blocked concerted action by the G-8 aimed at Iranian-sponsored terrorism in the Middle East. Also, France's presidency of the EU yielded little practical US-EU counterterrorism cooperation.

Germany

Extreme right-wing violence against foreign nationals in Germany increased in 2000 and became a major political issue. Interior ministers from the German states met in November to address the problem and recommended the federal authorities adopt control measures, including establishing databases to track right-wing and left-wing extremists.

German officials detected no revival of organized extreme left-wing terrorist activity in 2000. Authorities sought several former members of the Red Army Faction (RAF), which was dissolved in 1998, and continued to prosecute former RAF members in court. Johannes Weinreich, a former RAF member and lieutenant to Carlos the Jackal, was convicted in January of committing murder and attempted murder during an attack in 1983 on a French cultural center in then-West Berlin. In November, RAF member Andrea Klump went on trial on charges of participation in a failed attack on the NATO base at Rota, Spain, in 1988. In December, Foreign Minister Joschka Fischer testified at the trial of former acquaintance Hans-Joachim Klein, who was charged with three murders in connection with the 1975 attack in Vienna on petroleum ministers from OPEC states by "Carlos"-led terrorists.

The courts convicted Metin Kaplan, leader of the violent Turkish Islamic group Kalifatstaat, and sentenced him to four years in prison for publicly calling for the death of a rival. The trial of five defendants accused of the 1986 Libyan-sponsored bombing against the Labelle Discotheque, which killed two US servicemen, continued to progress slowly. The 1993 ban on the Kurdistan Workers' Party (PKK) and its affiliates remained in effect.

The PKK ceased to conduct violent demonstrations in 2000, following the seizure of the group's leader Ocalan.

Germany continued to cooperate multilaterally and bilaterally-- notably with the United States--to combat terrorism. In 2000, German authorities arrested and extradited to the United States a suspect in the bombings in 1998 of the US embassies in East Africa.

Greece

The Greek Government undertook some meaningful steps to combat terrorism--especially in the wake of the Revolutionary Organization 17 November's (17 November) murder of UK Defense Attaché Saunders in Athens--including efforts to persuade a historically skeptical public of the damage inflicted by terrorism on Greece's interests and international reputation. The government strengthened the police counterterrorism unit, implemented a multimillion-dollar reward program, and began drafting legislation to provide a legal basis for more vigorous counterterrorism efforts. Greek, British, and US experts cooperated closely in the still ongoing investigation of the Saunders murder. Nonetheless, despite these and other promising initiatives, as well as closer Greek-US cooperation, Athens resolved no outstanding terrorist incident and arrested no terrorist suspects in 2000.

In June, two motorcyclists shot and killed British Defense Attaché Stephen Saunders in Athens' rush hour traffic.

Revolutionary Organization 17 November, a violent far-left nationalist group, claimed the murder as revenge against NATO's military action in 1999 against Serbia. The group simultaneously claimed responsibility for attacks it had mounted in 1999 on the German and Dutch ambassadors' residences, on three Western banks, and on offices of the governing PASOK party. In a follow-up communiqué released in December, 17 November defended itself against mounting public criticism by trying to appeal to populist, pro-Serb sentiments and also by urging Greeks not to cooperate with the government's counterterrorism efforts.

The Saunders murder and Greek preparations for the 2004 Olympics contributed to a political and public opinion climate more supportive of effective counterterrorism measures. The Prime Minister, his cabinet colleagues, and opposition leaders denounced the murder of Saunders and spoke out against terrorism in general. The Greek media provided extensive coverage of Heather Saunders' eloquent public statements in the aftermath of her husband's murder. The public widely observed a national moment of silence for all victims of terrorism, and Orthodox Archbishop Christodoulos held an unprecedented memorial service for all Greek and foreign victims of terrorism in Greece.

The police sought to involve the public in the Saunders investigation and encouraged witnesses to come forward. Minister of Public Order (MPO) Khrisokhoidhis led the government's efforts, which included increasing the reward for information on terrorist attacks to $2.5 million. The police also opened toll-free hot lines to enable informants to pass tips anonymously. Although failure to cordon off the Saunders crime scene initially hampered the investigation, the Greek police subsequently worked effectively with British investigators to pursue a small number of useful leads. At year's end, the British Defense Attache's murder remained unsolved.

In the spring, Revolutionary Nuclei, another far-left, nationalist terrorist group, bombed buildings belonging to two Greek construction companies linked to the Greek Government, military, and NATO. Police safely removed a bomb the group had left outside the Peiraiefs (Piraeus) office of a former PASOK minister. On 12 November, the group mounted three separate but nearly simultaneous attacks against a British bank, a US bank, and the studio and home of the Greek sculptor whose statue of Gen. George C. Marshall is displayed at the US Embassy.

Throughout the year, a host of anarchist groups claimed responsibility for an average of two arson or bomb attacks per week on offices, shops, and vehicles, almost always in Athens. Many of the targeted vehicles belonged to foreign diplomats, foreign companies, Greek officials, and Greek public-sector executives. The two most prolific groups, Black Star and Anarchist Faction, together carried out 31 attacks in 2000. No fatalities or arrests resulted from these attacks.

Suspected terrorist Avraam Lesperoglou, already imprisoned since December 1999 for passport fraud and draft dodging, was convicted in October of attempting to murder a policeman and sentenced to 17 years. Lesperoglou, who is suspected of being linked to Revolutionary People's Struggle (ELA) and possibly other groups, still awaits trial on several terrorism-related murder charges.

In late November, a Justice Ministry expert committee began drafting legislation on terrorism and organized crime for presentation to Parliament. The controversial legislation is expected to provide for greater admissibility of evidence from undercover police operations, use of DNA evidence, adjudication by all-judge panels of certain classes of terrorist cases, and protection of witnesses. The Greek Government has indicated the legislation will be consistent with EU standards and international norms.

In 2000, Greece and the United States ratified a mutual legal assistance treaty and signed a police cooperation memorandum to enhance bilateral cooperation on law enforcement, including terrorism. During the year, MPO Khrisokhoidhis met with cabinet-level officials in the United States and in the United Kingdom and signed a bilateral counterterrorism agreement in London. By year's end, Greece had signed all 12 and ratified all but two of the UN counterterrorism conventions.

Italy

Italy's counterterrorism efforts in 2000 focused primarily on the assassination in 1999 of Labor Ministry Adviser Massimo d'Antona by individuals who claimed to be from the extreme leftist Red Brigades-Combatant Communist Party (BR-PCC). Leaks from the investigation, however, complicated the arrest and interrogation of several suspects. One much-publicized suspect was released because of lack of evidence but remains under investigation. Later in the year, the Revolutionary Proletarian Nucleus, a leftist-anarchist group, issued a communiqué claiming responsibility for placing a bomb at the Milan office of the Italian Confederation of Free Trade Unions in July.

In February, Interior Minister Bianco warned of a possible resurgence of right-wing terrorism, and the Italian Government subsequently dissolved the neofascist organization Fronte Nazionale (National Front) and in October confiscated its assets. Bianco maintained, however, that left-wing and anarchist violence, exemplified by the BR-PCC and the Territorial Anti-Imperialist Nuclei (NTA), posed the greater threat. A spin-off group of the NTA--an anti-US, anti-NATO group -- was behind several low-level bombing and incendiary attacks on Aviano Airbase in 1999.

In October authorities in Naples issued arrest warrants for 11 members of Al-Takfir w'al Hijra, a North African Muslim extremist group. Seven were apprehended in Naples, France, and Algeria, but four eluded arrest.

Officials noted that members of the group, also active in Milan and other cities, engaged primarily in forging travel documents and raising funds from expatriate Muslims.

In January, the government expelled to his native country illegal immigrant and Algerian national Yamin Rachek, husband of Italian-

Canadian dual national Lucia Garofolo who was arrested in December for carrying explosives from Canada into the United States. In June, the government pardoned Turkish national Ali Agca for his attack on the Pope in 1981 and extradited him to his native Turkey.

In late 2000, Italy and Spain signed an agreement to create a common judicial space between them, eliminating extradition procedures in the case of serious felonies, including terrorist activities.

Spain

Spain was wracked by domestic terrorism in 2000. After abandoning its cease-fire in late 1999, the terrorist group Basque Fatherland and Liberty (ETA) began a countrywide bombing and assassination campaign, killing 23 and wounding scores more by year's end. ETA traditionally targets police, military personnel, and politicians, as well as journalists and businessmen. As 2000 progressed, however, the group appeared to become increasingly indiscriminate in its attacks, targeting, for example, intersections and shopping areas. The public responded with huge demonstrations in major cities, demanding an end to the violence. Also in 2000, the Spanish and French Basque youth groups united and continued their campaign of street violence and arson.

Spanish authorities diligently prosecuted ETA members on terrorism and criminal charges, and the Aznar government reiterated its determination to eliminate terrorism and not negotiate over independence for the constitutionally autonomous Basque provinces. After difficult discussions over the role of moderate Basques represented by the Basque Nationalist Party (PNV), the governing and opposition Socialist parties signed a common anti-ETA pact at year's end.

The First of October Anti-Fascist Resistance Group (GRAPO), quiescent in recent years, stepped up its activity in 2000. In November, the group murdered a Spanish policeman following the arrest of seven GRAPO leaders in Paris, killed two security guards during a botched armed robbery attempt of a security van in May, and carried out several bombings that damaged property but caused no injuries. In November, the Spanish Interior Minister stated that arrests of GRAPO operatives in France had effectively dismantled the leadership and operational command of the group.

In June, Spain's Interior Minister Jaime Mayor Oreja visited Washington in keeping with the active, high-level dialogue on terrorism between the United States and Spain. Spain also played an important role in the Central Asian Counterterrorism Conference sponsored by the US

Department of State held in Washington in June. A Spanish court convicted Ramon Aldasoro, whom the United States extradited to Spain in December 1999, for his participation in the bombing of a police barracks in 1988.

Spanish and French interior ministries cooperated closely in combating terrorism, including arresting numerous ETA members and raiding logistics and support cells. France regularly delivered detained ETA terrorists, including several senior leaders, into Spanish custody. Spain also secured a pledge from Mexico to deny safe haven to ETA members. Spain welcomed the condemnation of ETA in November by all Ibero-American presidents -- except Cuba's Castro, whose refusal harmed bilateral relations.

Spain has urged the European Union to adopt more vigorous measures against terrorism, including creating a common judicial space. Spain and Italy signed such an agreement.

Turkey

Combating terrorism remained a top Turkish domestic and foreign policy priority as ethnic, Islamic, leftist, and transnational terrorist groups continued to threaten Turkey. In 2000, previous Turkish successes in fighting these groups were consolidated, producing a dramatically lowered incidence of terrorist activity. The Turkish Government remained in the forefront of cooperative international counterterrorism efforts and worked closely with Washington on combating groups that target US personnel and facilities.

At the direction of its imprisoned leader, Abdullah Ocalan, the Kurdistan Workers' Party (PKK), which long had sought to achieve an independent Kurdish state through violence, asserted that it now seeks, through a political campaign, only guarantees of Kurdish political, economic, social, and cultural rights in a democratic Turkey. The government did not respond to the PKK's declared change in tactics and goals. Prime Minister Ecevit warned that his government would reconsider its decision not to press for the death sentence against Ocalan if the PKK renewed its violence while the European Court of Human Rights reviewed his trial. The Court took up Ocalan's appeal in November.

Meanwhile, the number of violent clashes between PKK and government forces in Turkey declined significantly with 45 confrontations in the first 11 months of 2000, according to the Turkish General Staff, compared with thousands in previous years. Turkish forces mounted vigorous operations against the few hundred PKK guerrillas in southeastern Turkey and the several thousand who had withdrawn to northern Iraq, enlisting the aid of Iraqi Kurdish groups that have fought sporadically with the PKK over the last several years. Turkish officials and newspapers noted that Syria observed its commitment made in 1998 to abjure support to the PKK.

In contrast, Iran allegedly continued to provide at least a safe haven to armed PKK militants.

Turkish security forces continued their effective campaign against the extreme-left terrorist group Revolutionary People's Liberation Party/Front (DHKP/C, formerly Dev Sol). The group was able to mount only a few attacks. In August, the police arrested seven suspected DHKP/C terrorists that allegedly planned to attack the airbase at Incirlik, from which a joint US-British-Turkish force maintains "Operation Northern Watch" over the no-fly zone in Iraq. Several European countries, including Belgium, have declined Turkish requests to extradite PKK, DHKP/C, and other terrorists, citing Turkey's retention of the death penalty and the political motivation of the suspects' crimes.

The DHKP/C, joined by small extreme leftist factions, staged repeated violent uprisings in prisons to protest the government's efforts to transfer prisoners from overcrowded older prisons--in which terrorist and criminal groups effectively controlled entire wards--to newer prisons with cells for two or three prisoners. In December, the outlawed terrorist group Turkish Communist Party/Marxist-Leninist showed its opposition to the transfer program by killing two policemen. "Operation Return to Life," undertaken in December by security forces to gain control of the prison wards, left about 30 prisoners dead, some by their own hand.

The police and the judiciary dealt heavy blows to domestic Islamic terrorist groups in 2000, including the Turkish Hizballah, a domestic terrorist group of mostly Kurdish Sunni Islamics with no known ties to Lebanese Hizballah. Turkish officials and media assert that Turkish Hizballah has received limited Iranian support. Turkish Hizballah's adherents are anti-Western but primarily target Kurds who are viewed as insufficiently Islamic or unwilling to meet the group's extortion demands. They have not targeted US citizens. Through October, 723 police operations, mostly in predominantly Kurdish southeastern Turkey, netted more than 2,700 Turkish Hizballah suspects, approximately 1,700 of whom were arrested. The trial of 15 Turkish Hizballah suspects accused of 156 murders began in July in Diyarbakir.

Turkish authorities arrested members of the Jerusalem Warriors, a small ethnic Turkish Sunni Islamic group with tenuous links to the

Turkish Hizballah. Turkish officials and media reported that they had received direction, training, and support from Iran. In August, 17 Warriors went on trial for involvement in 22 murders, including assassinations of several prominent Turkish secularist intellectuals. Four have been accused of killing USAF Sgt. Victor Marvick in a car-bombing in 1991.

United Kingdom

The United Kingdom enacted two far-reaching counterterrorism laws and continued its close cooperation with the United States and other nations in the fight against terrorism. As in previous years, UK authorities focused primarily on the threat posed by dissident Republican and Loyalist terrorist groups in Northern Ireland, while continuing their efforts to combat transnational Islamic terrorists settled in or transiting the United Kingdom.

The Terrorism Act, enacted in July and effective February 2001, replaces temporary and emergency laws that dealt with Northern Ireland-related terrorism. It broadens the definition of domestic and transnational terrorism throughout the United Kingdom to cover violent acts and threats against individuals and property--including electronic systems--intended to influence the government or promote political, religious, or ideological causes. The Act authorizes the government to ban groups involved in domestic or transnational terrorism and to use special arrest powers to prosecute their members or supporters. The Regulation of Investigatory Powers Act, effective July 2000, created a statutory basis for intercepting communications and for covert surveillance.

London continued to work vigorously to combat Northern Ireland-related terrorism, but British press reports indicated that terrorist killings in the north increased from seven in 1999 to 18 in 2000. The dissident Real Irish Republican Army (RIRA) is credited in press reports to have been responsible for attacks in Northern Ireland as well as in central London. The most spectacular incident involved a rocket attack in September that caused minor damage to the headquarters of Britain's foreign intelligence service, MI6, in central London. UK officials continued to prosecute dissidents suspected in previous attacks. Authorities repeatedly urged witnesses to come forward with evidence relating to RIRA's 1998 bombing in Omagh, which left 29 dead, and to the murder in 1999 of Republican defense lawyer Rosemary Nelson by Loyalist Red Hand Defenders.

Making the most of close US ties to the United Kingdom and Ireland, Washington continued its efforts to encourage normalization of political, law enforcement, and security arrangements in Northern Ireland as called for in the Good Friday Agreement. The US supports achieving lasting peace in the troubled region.

London and Washington worked together to bring to justice suspects in the bombing of two US embassies in East Africa in 1998 and in the Pan Am 103 bombing over Lockerbie, Scotland, in 1988. UK courts found Khaled al-Fawwaz, Ibrahim Hussein Abd al-Hadi Eidarous, and Abel Mohammed Abd al-Majid--indicted in the United States for involvement in the embassy attacks--extraditable to the United States. The three men are appealing the decision. In April, Manchester police, responding to a US request, searched two residences of associates of Osama bin Laden and his al-Qaida terrorist network. In May, a Scottish court sitting in the Netherlands commenced the trial of two Libyans accused of murder, conspiracy, and breach of the UK Aviation Security Act in perpetrating the Pan Am 103 bombing. All charges but murder were later dropped. (In January 2001, one of the Libyans was found guilty of murder in connection with that attack. The judges found that he acted "in furtherance of the purposes of Libyan Intelligence Services". Concerning the other defendant, Al-Amin Kalifa Fahima, the court concluded that the Crown failed to present sufficient evidence to satisfy the high standard of "proof beyond reasonable doubt" that is necessary in criminal cases.)

British authorities assisted Greek officials in investigating the assassination in June of Britain's Defense Attaché in Athens by the terrorist group 17 November. London continues to investigate the murder of British and US citizens in Yemen in 1998 and a bomb incident in its Embassy in Sanaa in 2000, the day after the bombing of the USS Cole.

Appendix G
Latin America Overview

Latin America witnessed an increase in terrorist attacks from the previous year, from 121 to 193. In Colombia, leftist guerrilla groups abducted hostages and attacked civil infrastructure, while right-wing paramilitary groups abducted congressional representatives, killed political candidates, and massacred civilians in an attempt to thwart the guerrillas. In Ecuador, organized criminal elements with possible links to terrorists and terrorist groups abducted 10 oil workers and also claimed responsibility for oil pipeline bombings that killed seven civilians.

Extremist religious groups continued to pose a terrorist concern in the triborder area of Argentina, Brazil, and Paraguay. Terrorist incidents continued a downward trend in Peru despite a deteriorating political situation and the abrupt resignation of hard-line President Fujimori.

Colombia

Despite ongoing peace talks, Colombia's two largest guerrilla groups, the Revolutionary Armed Forces of Colombia (FARC) and the National Liberation Army (ELN), continued to conduct international terrorist acts, including kidnapping private US and foreign citizens and extorting money from businesses and individuals in the Colombian countryside.

A significant development during the year involved a series of FARC attacks on interests of US coal firm Drummond, Inc., in Colombia, which publicly refused to pay the group millions of dollars annually in extortion under the terms of FARC Law 002, a tax on entities valued at more than $1 million. As a result of FARC actions, Drummond did not bid on a state-owned coal company, potentially costing Bogota tens of millions of dollars in lost privatization revenue. Colombia's second-largest crude oil pipeline, the Cano Limon, was attacked 152 times in 2000 -- a record -- which the army blames mostly on the ELN. The attacks forced Occidental Petroleum to halt exports through most of August and September.

In October, the Colombian police rescued a five-year-old US citizen who had been held six months by individuals connected with the FARC.

The FARC and the ELN continued to reach out to government and non-government groups throughout the world and especially in Europe and Latin America through international representatives and attendance at regional conferences and meetings, such as the Sao Paulo Forum. The FARC also continued to target security forces and other symbols of government authority to demonstrate its power and to strengthen its negotiating position. President Pastrana in December extended the FARC's demilitarized zone to 31 January 2001 and pledged to place government controls over the zone. The FARC -- which said it would not return to the table until Bogota reined in the right-wing paramilitaries -- unilaterally froze peace talks in November.

Meanwhile, right-wing paramilitary groups continued to grow and expanded their reach in 2000, most notably in southern Colombia's prime coca growing areas. The groups, in addition to massacring civilians in their attempts to erode FARC and ELN areas of influence, also abducted seven national congressional representatives in December, demanding negotiations with the government.

Ecuador

On 12 October, organized criminal elements with possible links to terrorists and terrorist groups abducted 10 aviation company employees and oil workers (five US citizens, two French, one Chilean, one Argentine, and one New Zealander) in the northern canton of Sucumbios. In December, the kidnappers also claimed responsibility for multiple bomb attacks on the Trans-Ecuadorian Oil pipeline, one of which killed seven Ecuadorian bystanders. At year's end, the terrorists were demanding $80 million in ransom for eight hostages (two escaped), and the situation had not been resolved. The exact identity of the terrorists remained uncertain. (The group executed one of their hostages, a US citizen, in January 2001. Following extended negotiations with representatives of the oil companies that employed the hostages, the remaining captives were released on 1 March 2001. The United States has pledged to bring those responsible to justice.)

Peru

There were no international acts of terrorism in Peru in 2000, but the Peruvian judicial system continued to prosecute vigorously individuals accused of committing domestic terrorist acts. Of the 314 persons Peruvian authorities arrested for involvement in significant acts of terrorism, 30 were sentenced to life imprisonment and 25 were sentenced to 20 to 30 years. Lima requested the extradition from Bolivia of suspected terrorist Justino Soto Vargas. La Paz granted the request, but at year's end Soto's asylum status remained unchanged, impeding his extradition.

In April, government authorities captured Shining Path (SL) commander Jose Arcela Chiroque (a.k.a. Ormeno) and as of late November 2000 continued large-scale efforts to apprehend SL leaders Macario Ala (also known as Artemio) and "Comrade Alipio." Government operations targeted pockets of terrorist activity in the Upper Huallaga River Valley and the Apurimac/Ene River Valley, where SL columns continued to conduct periodic attacks.

The Peruvian Government continued to oppose strongly support to terrorists, but investigations continued into allegations that a small group of Peruvian military officers sold a substantial quantity of small arms to the Revolutionary Armed Forces of Colombia. Lima remained receptive to US Government-sponsored antiterrorism training and cooperated fully to prevent terrorist attacks by providing valuable information, including access to law enforcement files, records, and databases concerning domestic terrorist groups.

Triborder (Argentina, Brazil, and Paraguay)

In 2000, the triborder region of South America -- where the borders of Argentina, Brazil, and Paraguay meet -- remained a focal point for Islamic extremism in Latin America, but no acts of international terrorism occurred in any of the three countries. The Governments of Argentina, Brazil, and Paraguay continued efforts to stem criminal activities of individuals linked to international Islamic terrorist groups, but limited resources, porous borders, and corruption remained obstacles.

Paraguayan authorities in February arrested Ali Khalil Mehri, a Lebanese businessman having financial links to Hizballah, for violating intellectual property rights laws and aiding a criminal enterprise involved in distributing CDs espousing Hizballah's extremist ideals. He fled the country in June after faulty judicial procedures allowed his release. In November, Paraguayan authorities arrested Salah Abdul Karim Yassine, a Palestinian who allegedly threatened to bomb the US and Israeli Embassies in Asuncion, and charged him with possession of false documents and entering the country illegally. Yassine remained in prison at year's end. Paraguayan counternarcotics police in October also arrested an individual believed to be representing the FARC for possible involvement in a guns-for-cocaine ring between Paraguay and the Colombian terrorist group. Despite these successes, an ineffective judicial system and pervasive corruption, which facilitate criminal activity supporting terrorist groups, hampered counterterrorism efforts in Paraguay.

Argentina continued investigations into the bombings of the Israeli Embassy in 1992 and the Argentine-Israeli Community Center (AMIA) in 1994, both in Buenos Aires. In early February, the magistrate in the AMIA case presented his conclusions, which included charges of complicity against numerous former police officials and local civilians and a determination that a car bomb loaded with 300 kilograms of explosives was used to execute the attack. In May, INTERPOL agents also arrested a Paraguayan businessman for suspected links to the AMIA bombing. Trials were set to begin in early 2001.

Appendix H
Middle East Overview

Middle Eastern terrorist groups and their state sponsors continued to plan, train for, and carry out acts of terrorism throughout 2000. The last few months of the year brought a significant increase in the overall level of political violence and terrorism in the region, especially in Israel and the occupied territories. Much of the late-year increase in violence was driven by a breakdown in negotiations and counterterrorism cooperation between Israel and the Palestinian Authority. The breakdown sparked a cycle of violence between Israelis and Palestinians that continued to spiral at the end of the year and which continued into 2001.

Israeli-Palestinian violence also prompted widespread anger at Israel, as well as the United States, throughout the Middle East, demonstrated in part by numerous, occasionally violent protests against US interests in several Middle Eastern countries. Palestinian terrorist groups, with the assistance of Iran and the Lebanese Hizballah, took advantage of Palestinian and regional anger to escalate their terrorist attacks against Israeli targets.

Other terrorists also keyed on Israeli-Palestinian difficulties to increase their rhetorical and operational activities against Israel and the United States. Osama bin Laden's al-Qaida organization, the Egyptian Islamic Jihad, and other terrorist groups that focus on US and Israeli targets escalated their efforts to conduct and promote terrorism in the Middle East. Several disrupted plans to attack US and Israeli targets in the Middle East purportedly were intended to demonstrate anger over Israel's sometimes disproportionate use of force to contain protests and perceptions that the United States "allowed" Israel to act.

Al-Qaida and its affiliates especially used their ability to provide money and training as leverage to establish ties to and build the terrorist capabilities of a variety of small Middle Eastern terrorist groups such as the Lebanese Asbat al-Ansar.

The most significant act of anti-US terrorism in the region in 2000 -- the bombing of the USS Cole in Yemen on 12 October -- was not driven by events in the Levant. Although the joint US-Yemeni investigation into the savage bombing -- which killed 17 US sailors and wounded 39 others -- continued through the end of 2000, initial indications suggested the attack may have originated in Taliban-controlled Afghanistan, where al-Qaida, the Egyptian Islamic Jihad, and other terrorist groups are based and some of the alleged USS Cole attackers received training. The Yemeni Government, as much a victim of the attack as the United States, was working closely with the US Government to bring to justice those responsible for the act.

Many other Middle Eastern governments also increased their efforts to counter the threat from regional and Afghanistan-based terrorists, including the provision of enhanced security for high-risk US Government targets.

The Government of Kuwait, for instance, cooperated with regional counterparts in November to disrupt a suspected international terrorist cell. Kuwait arrested 13 individuals and recovered a large quantity of explosives and weapons. The cell reportedly was planning to attack both Kuwaiti officials and US targets in Kuwait and the region.

Algeria

President Bouteflika's Law on Civil Concord in 2000 initially contributed to a decrease in violence against civilians inside Algeria. Nonetheless, two main armed groups continued to reject the government's amnesty program for terrorists, and it is estimated that domestic terrorism kills between 100 to 300 there persons each month.

Antar Zouabri's Armed Islamic Group (GIA) actively targeted civilians, although such tactics caused his group to lose popular support. In contrast, Hassan Hattab's splinter faction -- the Salalfi Group for Call and Combat (GSPC) -- stated it would limit attacks on civilians, enabling it to co-opt Zouabri's supporters and eclipse the GIA as the most effective terrorist group operating inside Algeria.

Although at year's end the GSPC had not staged an anti-Western terrorist attack, various security services in January suspected Algerian extremists associated with the GSPC of planning to disrupt the Paris-Dakar Road Rally, leading organizers to re-route the race.

No foreign nationals were killed in Algeria during 2000, although in May GSPC troops crossed into Tunisia and attacked an outpost, killing three border guards. The GSPC frequently used false roadblocks to rob passengers of money. In one incident on 3 May, 19 persons were killed and 26 injured when militants sprayed a bus with bullets after the driver refused to stop.

Egypt

No terrorist attacks in Egypt or by Egyptian groups were reported in 2000. The Egyptian Government continued to regard terrorism as its most serious threat. Cairo tried and convicted numerous terrorists in 2000, including 14 al-Gama'a al-Islamiyya members, in connection with attempts to reactivate al-Gama'a in Egypt. Two Egyptian Islamic Jihad members, who were convicted in 1999 for planning an attack against the US Embassy in August 1998, were executed in February. Security forces attacked a terrorist hideout in Aswan in late October, killing two al-Gama'a members, including the group's military leader in charge of armed operations in Qina, Suhaj, and Luxor.

International counterterrorism cooperation remained a key foreign policy priority for the Egyptian Government throughout the year. In September, at the UN General Assembly Millennium Summit, Egypt signed the International Convention for the Suppression of Terrorist Financing.

The Egyptian Government worked closely with the United States on a broad range of counterterrorism issues in 2000. It cooperated with US authorities after the bombing in October of the USS Cole in Yemen, conducting a security survey of the Suez Canal and recommending measures to protect ships from possible terrorist attacks while transiting the canal. Egypt also played an important role in sharing its expertise at the Central Asian Counterterrorism Conference sponsored by the US Department of State and held in Washington in June.

In 2000, Egyptian security forces and government agencies continued to place a high priority on protecting US citizens and facilities in Egypt from terrorist attacks. The Egyptian Government increased security for the US Embassy and other official facilities in light of disturbances in Israel and the Palestinian territories and related threats against US interests.

Israel, the West Bank, and the Gaza Strip Terrorism by Palestinian extremist groups opposed to the peace process increased in late 2000 against the backdrop of violent Palestinian-Israeli clashes. The Palestine Islamic Jihad (PIJ) and Islamic Resistance Movement (HAMAS) claimed responsibility for several attacks during the crisis, ending a period of more than two years without a large-scale successful terrorist operation. Both groups publicly threatened more anti-Israeli attacks to avenge Palestinian casualties.

In an operation almost certainly timed to mark the anniversary of the death of PIJ founder Fathi Shaqaqi in 1995, on 26 October a PIJ operative on a bicycle detonated an explosive device near a Jewish settlement in Gaza, killing himself and injuring an Israeli soldier. The PIJ also claimed responsibility for a car bomb that exploded near a Jerusalem market on 2 November, killing two Israeli civilians -- including the daughter of Israeli National Religious Party leader Yitzhak Levy -- and wounding nine. The bomb -- which was concealed in a parked car -- reportedly was remotely detonated; the perpetrators escaped. On 28 December, PIJ operatives detonated explosive charges near the Sufa crossing in Gaza, injuring four Israeli explosives-disposal experts, two of whom later died. The PIJ claimed the attack in honor of a PIJ member killed by Israeli forces earlier that month and promised further revenge attacks.

The PIJ stepped up its rhetoric condemning Israeli-Palestinian peace talks at Camp David and Israel for its role in clashes with the Palestinians and vowed to continue attacks against Israel. Before the crisis, PIJ leader Shallah had issued threats against US interests in response to speculation during the summer that Washington was considering moving the US Embassy from Tel Aviv to Jerusalem.

HAMAS also claimed responsibility for several attacks during the unrest, including the bombing of an Israeli bus on 22 November in downtown Hadera that killed two Israeli civilians and wounded more than

20. Resembling the car bombing on 2 November, the bomb apparently also was hidden in a parked car and detonated as the bus passed. At year's end no suspects had been arrested for the attack. The group also took responsibility for launching an explosives-laden craft against an Israeli naval patrol boat off the Gaza coast on 7 November. The operative died in the explosion, according to a HAMAS statement, but the Israeli boat suffered no damage. A suicide bomber killed himself and injured three Israeli soldiers at a cafe in Moshav Mehola on 22 December; HAMAS's military wing claimed responsibility four days later.

In addition, other groups or individuals may have carried out terrorist attacks during the year. Three little-known groups -- Palestinian Hizballah, Umar al-Mukhtar Forces, and the Martyrs of al-Aqsa -- claimed responsibility for the bombing of an Israeli settler school bus in Gaza on 20 November that killed two Israelis. The al-Aqsa group also claimed responsibility for killing prominent Jewish extremist Binyamin Kahane, himself the leader of a terrorist organization, and his wife on 31 December. Kahane's death prompted heightened concern among Israeli security services that Jewish extremists would extend their violent attacks against Palestinian civilians to include "spectacular" operations, including against the Haram al-harif/Temple Mount. A group calling itself Salah al-Din Battalions claimed responsibility for bombing a bus in Tel Aviv on 28 December, injuring 13 persons. Israeli authorities accused Palestinian Authority (PA) security officials of facilitating the attack. The Salah al-Din Battalions reportedly also carried out a shooting attack in mid-November that killed at least one Israeli soldier.

In late summer, Israeli authorities arrested Nabil Awkil, a militant they suspect has links to HAMAS and Osama bin Laden. Israeli officials claim that Awkil underwent terrorist training in bin Laden-affiliated camps in Afghanistan before returning to the West Bank and Gaza to establish terrorist cells.

Earlier in the year, PA and Israeli security forces disrupted HAMAS networks that were planning several large-scale anti-Israeli attacks. On 10 February a botched bombing plot in Nabulus led to the discovery of a HAMAS explosives lab, several caches, and a multicell network in the West Bank. The network was preparing major terrorist operations designed to inflict mass casualties, including the bombing of a high-rise building in Jerusalem. The Israelis linked those arrested to a series of pipe-bomb attacks in Hadera in 1999. In March, an Israeli raid on a HAMAS hideout in the predominantly Israeli-Arab town of Et Taiyiba uncovered an extensive HAMAS network with ties to Gaza that was planning multiple terrorist attacks in Israel. The cell planned to carry out four-to-five simultaneous suicide bombings against Israeli targets, including bus stops and hitchhiking stations inside Israel frequented by Israeli soldiers. The PA discovered additional explosives in a Gaza kindergarten and arrested a bodyguard of HAMAS leader Shaykh Yasin on suspicion of having links to the Et Taiyiba cell. Israeli authorities arrested a Jewish settler and indicted an Israeli Arab for allegedly assisting the cell.

Israeli and PA security officials took additional measures, often coordinated, to further disrupt HAMAS terrorist planning. PA police in mid-March, following up on the Et Taiyiba raid, uncovered a HAMAS explosives lab in Tulkarm. Separate Israeli and PA operations disrupted HAMAS cells in Janin later that month. The PA also disrupted in mid-July another HAMAS explosives lab in Nabulus and made at least a dozen arrests. The PA inflicted additional damage on HAMAS's military wing with the arrest of two key leaders in 2000. In May, PA security forces arrested Gaza military wing leader Mohammed al-Dayf. In November, Dayf escaped from PA custody. West Bank military wing leader Mahmud al-Shuli (a.k.a. Abu Hanud) surrendered to PA security officials in August after a firefight with IDF soldiers in his hometown of Asirah ash Shamaliyah near the West Bank town of Nabulus. Three IDF soldiers were killed by friendly fire in the incident. At year's end Abu Hanud remained in Palestinian custody, serving a 12-year sentence handed down by a PA security court.

During the unrest HAMAS issued numerous statements calling for Palestinians to fight the Israelis with all means available and threatened to continue attacks to avenge Palestinian casualties. The group also vowed revenge for the killing of several HAMAS operatives during the unrest at year's end, including Ibrahim `Awda, who was killed on 23 November in Nabulus. HAMAS issued public statements accusing the Israelis of assassinating Awda, who reportedly died when the headrest in the car he was driving exploded, although the Israelis claim he died transporting an explosive device. HAMAS vowed revenge for the killing of activist Abbas Othman Ewaywi, who was gunned down by Israeli security forces in front of a shop in Hebron on 13 December.

Despite demonstrated Palestinian efforts to uproot terrorist infrastructure earlier in the year, Israeli officials publicly expressed their dissatisfaction with PA counter-terrorism efforts during the crisis. The Israelis also accused PA security officials and Fatah members of facilitating and taking part in shooting and bombing attacks against Israeli targets, including the bus bombing in Tel Aviv on 28 December. The Israelis charged that the release of several prisoners during the crisis had facilitated terrorist planning by the groups and that Palestinian security officials had not been responsive to their calls for more decisive measures against the violence.

Israeli officials publicly expressed well-founded concern that Iran supported Palestinian rejectionist efforts to disrupt the Middle East peace process. The Israelis also stated Palestinian rejectionists increasingly were influenced by Lebanese Hizballah. Public statements by HAMAS, the PIJ, and other Palestinian rejectionist officials since the Israeli withdrawal from southern Lebanon in May lauded Hizballah's actions and called for emulating Hizballah's victory in the territories.

Jordan

Jordan remained vigilant against terrorism in 2000. On 18 September, the State Security Court convicted several Sunni extremists, some in absentia, for plotting terrorist attacks against US and Israeli targets during the millennium celebrations in late 1999. The accused allegedly acted on behalf of Osama bin Laden. The three-member military tribunal sentenced eight defendants to death but immediately commuted two of the sentences to life imprisonment at hard labor, citing family reasons. Six others, including a minor, were acquitted, while the remaining 14 received prison sentences ranging from seven-and-a-half to 15 years. Lawyers for 10 of the convicted men have appealed the verdicts.

On 9 December the State Security Court indicted Ra'id Hijazi, a US-Jordanian dual national who had been sentenced to death in absentia in January for having had a role in the millennial plot. He had been recently remanded by Syria. Khalil Deek, another US-Jordanian dual citizen, was brought to Jordan from Pakistan in December 1999 to face charges in the plot but at year's end had not yet been tried. Jordanian authorities were handling his case separately from the other suspects.

Two Israeli diplomats in Jordan were targets of shooting attacks in the latter part of the year. An unidentified gunman shot at Israeli Vice Consul Yoram Havivian outside his home in Amman on 19 November. On 5 December, an unidentified gunman wounded another Israeli diplomat, Shlomo Ratzabi, as he, his wife, and bodyguard left a grocery store in Amman. Both diplomats suffered minor injuries and returned to Israel soon after the attacks. By year's end, Jordanian authorities had detained several suspects and were continuing their investigation. Two previously unknown groups, the Movement for the Struggle of the Jordanian Islamic

Resistance and the Holy Warriors of Ahmad Daqamseh, claimed responsibility for the attacks, which coincided with rising public sympathy in Jordan for Palestinians in ongoing violence with Israel. (Ahmad Daqamseh is a Jordanian soldier currently serving a life sentence for killing six Israeli school girls in 1997.)

Jordan continued to ban all HAMAS activity, and the Supreme Court upheld the expulsion of four Political Bureau leaders. Jordan's Prime Minister reiterated the government's conditions for their return at a meeting with HAMAS leaders during the Organization of the Islamic Conference summit in Doha in November. The conditions reportedly included a renunciation of their HAMAS affiliation. In December, lawyers for the group announced their intention to appeal once again to Jordan's Supreme Court to contest the deportation. Jordan refused to permit HAMAS military-wing members to reside or operate in the country but allowed other lower-level HAMAS members to remain in Jordan provided they did not conduct activities on the group's behalf.

Several low-level incidents kept security forces focused on combating threats to Jordan. Police in the southern city of Ma'an in January detained 15 suspects in connection with two shooting attacks against a female dormitory at Al-Hussein University. Four women were injured slightly in one attack. Police sources reported that the suspects were affiliated with a group called the Islamic Renewal and Reform Organization. Before the attacks, leaflets denouncing coeducation and calling for women to wear veils were distributed on campus.

The Government of Jordan also regularly interdicted the smuggling across Jordan's borders of weapons and explosives, which, in many cases, may have been destined for Palestinian rejectionist groups in the West Bank and Gaza. The government prosecuted individuals suspected of such activity.

In March, the government expelled eight Libyans it suspected of having terrorist links, and in September it refused entry to the leader of Israel's Islamic Movement, Shaykh Ra'id Salah. The Israelis publicly claimed that followers of Shaykh Salah have links to HAMAS and were involved in plans to conduct terrorist operations against Israeli interests earlier in the year.

Jordanian security forces coordinated closely with the US Embassy on security matters and acted quickly to bolster security at US Government facilities in response to other threats, including one against the US Embassy in June 2000.

Kuwait

In November the Government of Kuwait disrupted a suspected international terrorist cell. Working with regional counterparts, Kuwaiti security services arrested 13 individuals and recovered a large quantity of explosives and weapons. The terrorist cell reportedly was planning to attack both Kuwaiti officials and US targets in Kuwait and the region.

Lebanon

Throughout the year, the Lebanese Government's continued lack of control in portions of the country -- including parts of the Bekaa Valley, Beirut's southern suburbs, Palestinian refugee camps, and the southern border area -- as well as easy access to arms and explosives, contributed to an environment with a high potential for acts of violence and terrorism.

A variety of terrorist groups -- including Hizballah, Osama bin Laden's (UBL) al-Qaida network, HAMAS, the PIJ, the PFLP-GC, `Asbat al-Ansar, and several local Sunni extremist organizations -- continued to operate with varying degrees of impunity, conducting training and other operational activities. Hizballah continued to pose the most potent threat to US interests in Lebanon. Although Hizballah has not attacked US targets in Lebanon since 1991, it continued to pose a significant terrorist threat to US interests globally from its base in Lebanon. Hizballah voiced its support for terrorist actions by Palestinian rejectionist groups in Israel and the occupied territories. While the Lebanese Government expressed support for "resistance" activities along its southern border, it has only limited influence over Hizballah and the Palestinian rejectionists.

UBL's al-Qaida network maintained a presence in Lebanon. Although the Lebanese Government actively monitored and arrested UBL-affiliated operatives, it did not control the Palestinian refugee camps where the operatives conducted terrorist training and anti-US indoctrination.

In the fall, Hizballah kidnapped an Israeli noncombatant whom it may have lured to Lebanon on a false pretense. Hizballah has been using hostages, including captured IDF soldiers, as bargaining chips to win the release of Lebanese prisoners in Israel.

In January, Lebanese security forces clashed in the north with a Sunni extremist movement that had ambushed and killed four Lebanese soldiers. The group had ties to UBL operatives. The same month, Asbat al-Ansar launched a grenade attack against the Russian Embassy. In October, the Sunni extremist group, Takfir wa Hijra, claimed responsibility for a grenade attack against a Christian Member of

Parliament's residence, though there are indications others may have been behind this attack.

The Lebanese Government continued to support some international counterterrorist initiatives and moved against UBL-affiliated operatives in 2000. In February, Lebanese authorities arrested members of a UBL cell in Lebanon. In March, the government fulfilled a Japanese Government request and deported four Japanese Red Army (JRA) members after it had refused to do so for years. It allowed one JRA member to remain in Lebanon.

It did not act, however, on repeated US requests to turn over Lebanese terrorists involved in the hijacking in 1985 of TWA flight 847 and in the abduction, torture, and -- in some cases -- murders of US hostages from 1984 to 1991.

Saudi Arabia

Several threats against US military and civilian personnel and facilities in Saudi Arabia were reported in 2000, but there were no confirmed terrorist incidents. At year's end Saudi authorities were investigating a shooting by a lone gunman who opened fire on British and US nationals near the town of Khamis Mushayt in early August 2000. The gunman fired more than 100 rounds on a Royal Saudi Air Force checkpoint, killing one Saudi and wounding two other Saudi guards. The gunman was wounded in the exchange of fire.

Terrorist Osama bin Laden, whose Saudi citizenship was revoked in 1994, continued to publicly threaten US interests in Saudi Arabia during the year. In a videotaped statement released in September, bin Laden once again publicly threatened US interests.

The Government of Saudi Arabia continued to investigate the bombing in June 1996 of the Khubar Towers housing facility near Dhahran that killed 19 US military personnel and wounded some 500 US and Saudi personnel. The Government of Saudi Arabia publicly stated that it still was looking for three Saudi suspects whom it wanted for questioning in connection with the bombing and whom authorities believed to be currently outside Saudi Arabia. The Saudis continued to hold in detention a number of Saudi citizens linked to the attack, including Hani al-Sayegh, whom the United States expelled to Saudi Arabia in 1999.

The Government of Saudi Arabia reaffirmed its commitment to combating terrorism. It required nongovernmental organizations and private voluntary agencies to obtain government authorization before soliciting contributions for domestic or international causes. It was not clear that these regulations were enforced consistently; however, allegations continued to surface that some international terrorist organization representatives solicited and collected funds from private citizens in Saudi Arabia.

Yemen

On 12 October a boat carrying explosives was detonated next to the USS Cole, killing 17 US sailors and injuring another 39. The US destroyer, en route to the Persian Gulf, was making a prearranged fuel stop in the Yemeni port of Aden when the attack occurred. At least three groups reportedly claimed responsibility for the attack, including the Islamic Army of Aden, Mohammed's Army, and a previously unknown group called the Islamic Deterrence Force.

The Yemeni Government strongly condemned the attack on the USS Cole and actively engaged in investigative efforts to find the perpetrators. On 29 November, Yemen and the United States signed a memorandum of agreement delineating guidelines for joint investigation to further facilitate cooperation between the two governments. The Yemeni Government's ability to conduct international terrorism investigations was enhanced by joint investigative efforts undertaken pursuant to these guidelines.

Several terrorist organizations maintained a presence in Yemen. HAMAS and the Palestinian Islamic Jihad continued to be recognized as legal organizations and maintained offices in Yemen but did not engage in terrorist activities there. Other international terrorist groups that have an illegal presence in Yemen included the Egyptian Islamic Jihad, al-Gama'a al-Islamiyya, Libyan opposition groups, the Algerian Armed Islamic Group, and al-Qaida. Press reports indicated indigenous groups such as the Islamic Army of Aden remained active in Yemen.

The Government of Yemen did not provide direct or indirect support to terrorists, but its inability to control fully its borders, territory, or its own travel documents did little to discourage the terrorist presence in Yemen.

Improved cooperation with Saudi Arabia as a result of the Yemeni-Saudi border treaty, concluded in June, promised to reduce illegal border crossings and trafficking in weapons and explosives, although border clashes continued after the agreement's ratification. The government attempted to resolve some of its passport problems in 2000 by requiring proof of nationality when submitting an application, although terrorists continued to have access to forged Yemeni identity documents.

Appendix I
Overview of State-Sponsored Terrorism

The designation of state sponsors of terrorism by the United States -- and the imposition of sanctions -- is a mechanism for isolating nations that use terrorism as a means of political expression. US policy seeks to pressure and isolate state sponsors so they will renounce the use of terrorism, end support to terrorists, and bring terrorists to justice for past crimes. The United States is committed to holding terrorists and those who harbor them accountable for past attacks, regardless of when the acts occurred. The US Government has a long memory and will not simply expunge a terrorist's record because time has passed. The states that choose to harbor terrorists are like accomplices who provide shelter for criminals. They will be held accountable for their "guests'" actions. International terrorists should know, before they contemplate a crime, that they cannot hunker down in safe haven for a period of time and be absolved of their crimes.

The United States is firmly committed to removing countries from the list once they have taken necessary steps to end their link to terrorism. In fact, the Department of State is engaged in ongoing discussions with North Korea and Sudan with the object of getting those governments completely out of the terrorism business and off the terrorism list.

Iran, Iraq, Syria, Libya, Cuba, North Korea, and Sudan continue to be the seven governments that the US Secretary of State has designated as state sponsors of international terrorism. Iran remained the most active state sponsor of terrorism in 2000. It provided increasing support to numerous terrorist groups, including the Lebanese Hizballah, HAMAS, and the Palestine Islamic Jihad (PIJ), which seek to undermine the Middle East peace negotiations through the use of terrorism. Iraq continued to provide safe haven and support to a variety of Palestinian rejectionist groups, as well as bases, weapons, and protection to the Mujahedin-e-Khalq (MEK), an Iranian terrorist group that opposes the current Iranian regime. Syria continued to provide safe haven and support to several terrorist groups, some of which oppose the Middle East peace negotiations. Libya at the end of 2000 was attempting to mend its international image following its surrender in 1999 of two Libyan suspects for trial in the Pan Am 103 bombing. (In early 2001, one of the suspects was convicted of murder. The judges in the case found that he acted "in furtherance of the purposes of ... Libyan Intelligence Services.") Cuba continued to provide safe haven to several terrorists and US fugitives and maintained ties to state sponsors and Latin American insurgents. North Korea harbored several hijackers of a Japanese Airlines flight to North Korea in the 1970s and maintained links to other terrorist groups. Finally, Sudan continued to serve as a safe haven for members of al-Qaida, the Lebanese Hizballah, al-Gama'a al-Islamiyya, Egyptian Islamic Jihad, the PIJ, and HAMAS, but it has been engaged in a counterterrorism dialogue with the United States since mid-2000.

State sponsorship has decreased over the past several decades. As it decreases, it becomes increasingly important for all countries to adopt a "zero tolerance" for terrorist activity within their borders. Terrorists will seek safe haven in those areas where they are able to avoid the rule of law and to travel, prepare, raise funds, and operate. The United States continued actively researching and gathering intelligence on other states that will be considered for designation as state sponsors. If the United States deems a country to "repeatedly provide support for acts of international terrorism," the US Government is required by law to add it to the list. In South Asia, the United States has been increasingly concerned about reports of Pakistani support to terrorist groups and elements active in Kashmir, as well as Pakistani support, especially military support, to the Taliban, which continues to harbor terrorist groups, including al-Qaida, the Egyptian Islamic Jihad, al-Gama'a al-Islamiyya, and the Islamic Movement of Uzbekistan. In the Middle East, the United States was concerned that a variety of terrorist groups operated and trained inside Lebanon, although Lebanon has acted against some of those groups. Lebanon also has been unresponsive to US requests to bring to justice terrorists who conducted attacks against US citizens and property in Lebanon in previous years.

Cuba

Cuba continued to provide safe haven to several terrorists and US fugitives in 2000. A number of Basque ETA terrorists who gained sanctuary in Cuba some years ago continued to live on the island, as did several US terrorist fugitives.

Havana also maintained ties to other state sponsors of terrorism and Latin American insurgents. Colombia's two largest terrorist organizations, the Revolutionary Armed Forces of Colombia and the National Liberation Army, both maintained a permanent presence on the island.

Iran

Despite the victory for moderates in Iran's Majles elections in February, aggressive countermeasures by hard-line conservatives have blocked most reform efforts. Iran remained the most active state sponsor of terrorism in 2000. Its Revolutionary Guard Corps (IRGC) and Ministry of Intelligence and Security (MOIS) continued to be involved in the planning and the execution of terrorist acts and continued to support a variety of groups that use terrorism to pursue their goals.

Iran's involvement in terrorist-related activities remained focused on support for groups opposed to Israel and peace between Israel and its neighbors. Statements by Iran's leaders demonstrated Iran's unrelenting hostility to Israel. Supreme Leader Khamenei continued to refer to Israel as a "cancerous tumor" that must be removed; President Khatami, labeling Israel an "illegal entity," called for sanctions against Israel during the intifadah; and Expediency Council Secretary Rezai said, "Iran will continue its campaign against Zionism until Israel is completely eradicated." Iran has long provided Lebanese Hizballah and the Palestinian rejectionist groups -- notably HAMAS, the Palestine Islamic

Jihad, and Ahmad Jibril's PFLP-GC -- with varying amounts of funding, safe haven, training, and weapons. This activity continued at its already high levels following the Israeli withdrawal from southern Lebanon in May and during the intifadah in the fall. Iran continued to encourage Hizballah and the Palestinian groups to coordinate their planning and to escalate their activities against Israel.

Iran also provided a lower level of support -- including funding, training, and logistics assistance -- to extremist groups in the Gulf, Africa, Turkey, and Central Asia.

Although the Iranian Government has taken no direct action to date to implement Ayatollah Khomeini's fatwa (death warrant) against Salman Rushdie, the decree has not been revoked, and the $2.8 million bounty for his assassination has not been withdrawn. Moreover, hard-line Iranians continued to stress that the decree is irrevocable. On the anniversary of the fatwa in February, the IRGC released a statement that the decree remains in force, and Ayatollah Yazdi, a member of the Council of Guardians, reiterated that "the decree is irrevocable and, God willing, will be carried out."

Iran also was a victim of Mujahedin-e-Khalq (MEK)-sponsored terrorism. The Islamic Republic presented a letter to the UN Secretary General in October citing seven acts of sabotage by the MEK against Iran between January and August 2000. The United States has designated the MEK as a Foreign Terrorist Organization.

Iraq

Iraq planned and sponsored international terrorism in 2000. Although Baghdad focused on antidissident activity overseas, the regime continued to support various terrorist groups. The regime has not attempted an anti-Western terrorist attack since its failed plot to assassinate former President Bush in 1993 in Kuwait.

Czech police continued to provide protection to the Prague office of the US Government-funded Radio Free Europe/Radio Liberty (RFE/RL), which produces Radio Free Iraq programs and employs expatriate journalists.

The police presence was augmented in 1999, following reports that the Iraqi Intelligence Service (IIS) might retaliate against RFE/RL for broadcasts critical of the Iraqi regime.

To intimidate or silence Iraqi opponents of the regime living overseas, the IIS reportedly opened several new stations in foreign capitals during 2000. Various opposition groups joined in warning Iraqi dissidents abroad against newly established "expatriates' associations," which, they asserted, are IIS front organizations. Opposition leaders in London contended that the IIS had dispatched women agents to infiltrate their ranks and was targeting dissidents for assassination. In Germany, an Iraqi opposition figure denounced the IIS for murdering his son, who had recently left Iraq to join him abroad. Dr. Ayad `Allawi, Secretary General of the Iraqi National Accord, an opposition group, stated that relatives of dissidents living abroad are often arrested and jailed to intimidate activists overseas.

In northern Iraq, Iraqi agents reportedly killed a locally well-known religious personality who declined to echo the regime line. The regional security director in As Sulaymaniyah stated that Iraqi operatives were responsible for the car-bomb explosion that injured a score of passersby. Officials of the Iraqi Communist Party asserted that an attack on a provincial party headquarters had been thwarted when party security officers shot and wounded a terrorist employed by the IIS.

Baghdad continued to denounce and delegitimize UN personnel working in Iraq, particularly UN de-mining teams, in the wake of the killing in 1999 of an expatriate UN de-mining worker in northern Iraq under circumstances suggesting regime involvement. An Iraqi who opened fire at the UN Food and Agriculture Organization (FAO) office in Baghdad, killing two persons and wounding six, was permitted to hold a heavily publicized press conference at which he contended that his action had been motivated by the harshness of UN sanctions, which the regime regularly excoriates.

The Iraqi regime rebuffed a request from Riyadh for the extradition of two Saudis who had hijacked a Saudi Arabian Airlines flight to Baghdad, but did return promptly the passengers and the aircraft. Disregarding its obligations under international law, the regime granted political asylum to the hijackers and gave them ample opportunity to ventilate in the Iraqi Government-controlled and international media their criticisms of alleged abuses by the Saudi Arabian Government, echoing an Iraqi propaganda theme.

While the origins of the FAO attack and the hijacking were unclear, the Iraqi regime readily exploited these terrorist acts to further its policy objectives.

Several expatriate terrorist groups continued to maintain offices in Baghdad, including the Arab Liberation Front, the inactive 15 May Organization, the Palestine Liberation Front (PLF), and the Abu Nidal organization (ANO). PLF leader Abu `Abbas appeared on state-controlled television in the fall to praise Iraq's leadership in rallying Arab opposition to Israeli violence against Palestinians. The ANO threatened to attack Austrian interests unless several million dollars in a frozen ANO account in a Vienna bank were turned over to the group.

The Iraq-supported Iranian terrorist group, Mujahedin-e Khalq (MEK), regularly claimed responsibility for armed incursions into Iran that targeted police and military outposts, as well as for mortar and bomb attacks on security organization headquarters in various Iranian cities. MEK publicists reported that in March group members killed an Iranian colonel having intelligence responsibilities. An MEK claim to have wounded a general was denied by the Iranian Government. The Iraqi regime deployed MEK forces against its domestic opponents.

Libya

In 2000, Libya continued efforts to mend its international image in the wake of its surrender in 1999 of two Libyans accused of the bombing of Pan Am flight 103 over Lockerbie, Scotland, in 1988. Trial proceedings for the two defendants began in the Netherlands in May and were ongoing at year's end. (The court issued its verdict on 31 January 2001. It found Abdel Basset al-Megrahi guilty of murder, concluding that he caused an explosive device to detonate on board the airplane resulting in the murder of the flight's 259 passengers and crew as well as 11 residents of Lockerbie, Scotland. The judges found that he acted "in furtherance of the purposes of ... Libyan Intelligence Services." Concerning the other defendant, Al-Amin Kalifa Fahima, the court concluded that the Crown failed to present sufficient evidence to satisfy the high standard of "proof beyond reasonable doubt" that is necessary in criminal cases.)

In 1999, Libya paid compensation for the death of a British policewoman, a move that preceded the reopening of the British Embassy. (In April 1984, the British policewoman had been killed and 11 demonstrators wounded when gunmen in the Libyan People's Bureau in London fired on a peaceful anti-Qadhafi demonstration outside their building.)

Libya also paid damages to the families of victims in the bombing of UTA flight 772. Six Libyans were convicted in absentia in that case, and the French judicial system is considering further indictments against other Libyan officials, including Libyan leader Muammar Qadhafi.

Libya played a high-profile role in negotiating the release of a group of foreign hostages seized in the Philippines by the Abu Sayyaf Group, reportedly in exchange for a ransom payment. The hostages included citizens of France, Germany, Malaysia, South Africa, Finland, the Philippines, and Lebanon. The payment of ransom to kidnappers only encourages additional hostage taking, and the Abu Sayyaf Group, emboldened by its success, did seize additional hostages -- including a US citizen -- later in the year. Libya's behavior and that of other parties involved in the alleged ransom arrangement served only to encourage further terrorism and to make that region far more dangerous for residents and travelers.

At year's end, Libya had yet to comply fully with the remaining UN Security Council requirements related to Pan Am 103: accepting responsibility, paying appropriate compensation, disclosing all it knows, and renouncing terrorism. The United States remains dedicated to maintaining pressure on the Libyan Government until it does so. Qadhafi stated publicly that his government had adopted an antiterrorism stance, but it remains unclear whether his claims of distancing Libya from its terrorist past signify a true change in policy.

Libya also remained the primary suspect in several other past terrorist operations, including the Labelle discotheque bombing in Berlin in 1986 that killed two US servicemen and one Turkish civilian and wounded more than 200 persons. The trial in Germany of five suspects in the bombing, which began in November 1997, continued in 2000. Although Libya expelled the Abu Nidal organization and distanced itself from the Palestinian rejectionists in 1999, it continued to have contact with groups that use violence to oppose the Middle East Peace Process, including the Palestine Islamic Jihad and the Popular Front for the Liberation of Palestine-General Command.

North Korea

In 2000 the Democratic People's Republic of Korea (DPRK) engaged in three rounds of terrorism talks that culminated in a joint DPRK-US statement wherein the DPRK reiterated its opposition to terrorism and agreed to support international actions against such activity. The DPRK, however, continued to provide safe haven to the Japanese Communist League-Red Army Faction members who participated in the hijacking of a Japanese Airlines flight to North Korea in 1970. Some evidence also suggests the DPRK may have sold weapons directly or indirectly to terrorist groups during the year. Philippine officials publicly declared that the Moro Islamic Liberation Front had purchased weapons from North Korea with funds provided by Middle East sources.

Sudan

The United States and Sudan in mid-2000 entered into a dialogue to discuss US counterterrorism concerns. The talks, which were ongoing at the end of the year, were constructive and obtained some positive results. By the end of the year Sudan had signed all 12 international conventions for combating terrorism and had taken several other positive counterterrorism steps, including closing down the Popular Arab and Islamic Conference, which served as a forum for terrorists.

Sudan, however, continued to be used as a safe haven by members of various groups, including associates of Osama bin Laden 's al-Qaida organization, Egyptian al-Gama'a al-Islamiyya, Egyptian Islamic Jihad, the Palestine Islamic Jihad, and HAMAS. Most groups used Sudan primarily as a secure base for assisting compatriots elsewhere.

Khartoum also still had not complied fully with UN Security Council Resolutions 1044, 1054, and 1070, passed in 1996 -- which demand that Sudan end all support to terrorists. They also require Khartoum to hand over three Egyptian Gama'a fugitives linked to the assassination attempt in 1995 against Egyptian President Hosni Mubarak in Ethiopia. Sudanese officials continued to deny that they had a role in the attack.

Syria

Syria continued to provide safe haven and support to several terrorist groups, some of which maintained training camps or other facilities on Syrian territory. Ahmad Jibril's Popular Front for the Liberation of Palestine-General Command (PFLP-GC), the Palestine Islamic Jihad (PIJ), Abu Musa's Fatah-the-Intifada, and George Habash's Popular Front for the Liberation of Palestine (PFLP) maintained their headquarters in Damascus. The Syrian Government allowed HAMAS to open a new main office in Damascus in March, although the arrangement may be temporary while HAMAS continues to seek permission to reestablish its headquarters in Jordan. In addition, Syria granted a variety of terrorist groups -- including HAMAS, the PFLP-GC, and the PIJ -- basing privileges or refuge in areas of Lebanon's Bekaa Valley under Syrian control. Damascus generally upheld its agreement with Ankara not to support the Kurdish PKK, however.

Although Syria claimed to be committed to the peace process, it did not act to stop Hizballah and Palestinian rejectionist groups from carrying out anti-Israeli attacks. Damascus also served as the primary transit point for terrorist operatives traveling to Lebanon and for the resupply of weapons to Hizballah. Damascus appeared to maintain its long-standing ban on attacks launched from Syrian territory or against Western targets.

Weapons-of-Mass-Destruction (WMD) Terrorism

At the dawn of a new millennium, the possibility of a terrorist attack involving weapons of mass destruction (WMD) -- chemical, biological, radiological, nuclear (CBRN), or large explosive weapons -- remained real. As of the end of 2000, however, the most notorious attack involving chemical weapons against a civilian target remained Aum Shinrikyo's Sarin nerve agent attack against the Tokyo subway in March 1995.

Most terrorists continued to rely on conventional tactics, such as bombing, shooting, and kidnapping, but some terrorists -- such as Osama bin Laden and his associates -- continued to seek CBRN capabilities.

Popular literature and the public dialog focused on the vulnerability of civilian targets to CBRN attacks. Such attacks could cause lasting disruption and generate significant psychological impact on a population and its infrastructure.

A few groups, notably those driven by distorted religious and cultural ideologies, showed signs they were willing to cause large numbers of casualties. Other potentially dangerous but less predictable groups had emerged, and those groups may not abide by traditional targeting constraints that would prohibit using indiscriminate violence or CBRN weapons.

Some CBRN materials, technology, and especially information continued to be widely available, particularly from commercial sources and the Internet.

Terrorist Use of Information Technology

Terrorists have seized upon the worldwide practice of using information technology (IT) in daily life. They embrace IT for several reasons: it improves communication and aids organization, allows members to coordinate quickly with large numbers of followers, and provides a platform for propaganda. The Internet also allows terrorists to reach a wide audience of potential donors and recruits who may be located over a large geographic area.

In addition, terrorists are taking note of the proliferation of hacking and the use of the computer as a weapon. Extremists routinely post messages to widely accessible Web sites that call for defacing Western

Internet sites and disrupting on-line service, for example. The widespread availability of hacking software and its anonymous and increasingly automated design make it likely that terrorists will more frequently incorporate these tools into their on-line activity. The appeal of such tools may increase as news media continue to sensationalize hacking.

Appendix J
Chronology of Significant Incidents, 2000

January

3 January

Namibia

Unidentified assailants attacked four vehicles in Rundu, killing three French children and wounding their parents. The gunmen also injured two humanitarian aid workers -- one Scottish citizen and one Namibian national. National Union for the Total Independence of Angola (UNITA) guerrillas are suspected, but UNITA leaders denied the group's involvement in the attack.

8 January

Sudan

Humanitarian Aid Commission officials reported Sudanese People's Liberation Army (SPLA) rebels attacked a CARE vehicle in Al Wahdah State, killing the CARE office director and his driver, and abducting two others. An SPLA spokesperson denied the group's involvement.

9 January

Namibia

Five suspected UNITA rebels entered a private residence in western Kavango and attacked the occupants, killing two Namibian nationals and injuring one other, according to police officials. No one claimed responsibility.

14 January

Namibia

Military officials reported UNITA gunmen attacked a privately owned vehicle near Divundu, killing four persons and injuring five others.

18 January

Yemen

Armed tribesmen kidnapped two French nationals and their two Yemeni guides, according to press reports. The Al-Shamian tribe claimed responsibility. The tribesmen released the hostages on 18 January but recaptured them the same day after authorities attempted to arrest the kidnappers. The hostages were released again unharmed on 19 January.

21 January

Namibia

UNITA gunmen entered a private residence near Mayara and opened fire, killing three persons and injuring six others, according to local press accounts.

25 January

Angola
Local press reported UNITA militants ambushed a vehicle near Soyo, killing one Portuguese national. No one claimed responsibility.

26 January

Yemen
Armed tribesmen in Ma'rib kidnapped a US citizen working for the Halliburton Company, according to press reports. On 10 February, the kidnappers released the hostage unharmed.

27 January

Spain
Police officials reported unidentified individuals set fire to a Citroen car dealership in Iturreta, causing extensive damage to the building and destroying 12 vehicles. The attack bore the hallmark of the Basque Fatherland and Liberty (ETA).

29 January

Colombia
According to press reports, suspected Revolutionary Armed Forces of Colombia (FARC) or National Liberation Army (ELN) rebels bombed a section of the Cano-Limon pipeline in Arauquita, causing major damage and suspending oil production for three days.

February

2 February

Yugoslavia
Government officials reported unidentified individuals fired an antitank missile at a refugee convoy escorted by KFOR soldiers in Mitrovica, killing two Serbians and injuring five others. No one claimed responsibility.

3 February

Colombia

In Putumayo, according to press reporting, suspected FARC or ELN rebels bombed a section of the Cano-Limon pipeline, causing major damage, including an oil spill, and halting production for three days.

8 February

Colombia

Government officials reported suspected ELN guerrillas bombed the ONCESA (Canadian-British-Colombian consortium) oil pipeline near Campo Hermoso, causing extensive damage to the pipeline, an oil spill, and a forest fire.

11 February

Spain

Four individuals set fire to and destroyed a Citroen car dealership in Amorebieta, according to press reports. The attack bore the hallmark of the ETA.

13 February

Yugoslavia

According to press accounts, unidentified individuals shot and wounded two French KFOR soldiers in Mitrovica. No one claimed responsibility.

27 February

India

A bomb exploded at a railroad station in New Delhi, injuring eight persons and causing major damage, according to military reporting. Indian authorities suspect Kashmiri Militants or Sikhs were responsible.

29 February

Yugoslavia

According to press accounts, an unidentified assailant shot and killed a Russian KFOR soldier while he was on patrol in Srbica. An ethnic Albanian youth was arrested. Near Pristina, an unidentified gunman shot a UN official, according to press reports. No one claimed responsibility.

March

2 March

Yemen

Armed tribesmen kidnapped the Polish Ambassador in Sanaa, according to press reports. The Khawlan tribe claimed responsibility. On 4 March, the Ambassador was released unharmed.

3 March

India

A bomb exploded on a bus in Sirhand, Punjab, killing eight persons and injuring seven others. The Indian Government suspects either Kashmiri militants or Sikhs were responsible.

4 March

Uganda

Armed militants kidnapped two Italian missionaries in Kampala, according to press reports. The hostages were released unharmed several hours later. The Lord's Resistance Army (LRA) probably was responsible.

10 March

El Salvador

US Embassy officials reported unidentified gunmen kidnapped a US citizen and his El Salvadoran nephew from their vehicle near San Antonio Pajonal. On 21 March, the hostages were released unharmed following a ransom payment of $34,000.

14 March

Nigeria

Press reported armed youths occupied Shell Oil Company buildings in Lagos and held hostage 30 Nigerian employees and four guards of the Anglo-Dutch-owned company. No group claimed responsibility. On 15 March the Nigerian army rescued the 34 hostages unharmed.

21 March

India

Armed militants killed 35 Sikhs in Chadisinghpoora Village, according to press reports. Police officers arrested Muslim militants, who confessed to helping two groups suspected in the massacre -- the Lashkar-e-Tayyiba and the Hizb ul-Mujahedin -- two of the principal Muslim groups in Kashmir.

27 March

India

Armed militants threw a grenade at a group of police officers, missing their target but killing three civilians and injuring 11 others in Srinagar, according to press reports. The Hizb ul-Mujahedin may be responsible.

April

4 April

Pakistan

Armed militants fired on an Afghan vehicle, killing the Governor of the Taliban-held northern Afghan province of Kondoz and his militia commander, and wounding his driver and another passenger, according to press reports. No one claimed responsibility.

7 April

Nigeria

Armed militants kidnapped 40 persons -- 15 British, 15 French, and 10 Korean citizens -- from residences belonging to the Elf Aquitaine Oil Company in Port Harcourt, according to press reports. The 40 hostages were released unharmed several hours later. Disgruntled landowners were suspected.

12 April

Colombia

Police officials reported ELN rebels kidnapped a Mexican citizen in Cali and demanded $5 million ransom. On 16 April, police arrested three of the kidnappers and freed the hostage unharmed.

India

Militants using a remote-controlled device detonated a car bomb near an army convoy in Srinagar, killing one bystander, according to press reports. No one claimed responsibility.

13 April

Colombia

Press reported a bomb exploded on the Cano-Limon oil pipeline near La Cadena, causing major damage and suspending oil production for several days. Police suspect either FARC or ELN rebels were responsible.

14 April

Nigeria

In Warri, armed militants kidnapped 19 employees of the Noble Drilling Oil Company, a firm contracted by the Anglo-Dutch-owned Shell Oil Company, according to press reports. Ijaw youths probably were responsible.

15 April

India

Armed militants killed 12 persons, wounded seven others, and torched several huts in Tripura, according to press reports. No one claimed responsibility.

19 April

France

Press reported a bomb exploded at a McDonald's restaurant in Quevert, killing one person and causing major damage. Although no group claimed responsibility, authorities suspect the Breton Liberation Army (ARB). Nine persons associated with ARB were arrested.

20 April

Pakistan

A bomb exploded near the Jamaat-E-Islami headquarters in Mansuren, injuring two persons in a nearby residence, according to press reports. No one claimed responsibility.

24 April

Malaysia

In Kampong Pulau Tiga, Abu Sayyaf Group (ASG) militants kidnapped 21 persons -- two French, three Germans, two South Africans, two Finns, two Filipinos, one Lebanese, and nine Malaysians -- according to press reports.

Tajikistan

According to government officials, a group of armed Afghans broke into a residence in Khatlon Oblast and opened fire, killing one person, injuring another, and kidnapping one other. No one claimed responsibility.

28 April

India

A bomb exploded at a police checkpoint in Srinagar, killing one civilian and wounding four police officers and one civilian, according to press reports. No one claimed responsibility.

In Srinagar, militants threw a grenade at a security patrol but hit a bus stop instead, injuring two civilians, according to press accounts. No one claimed responsibility.

May

1 May

Sierra Leone

On 1 May in Makeni, Revolutionary United Front (RUF) militants kidnapped at least 20 members of the United Nations Assistance Mission in Sierra Leone (UNAMSIL) and surrounded and opened fire on a UNAMSIL facility, according to press reports. The militants killed five UN soldiers in the attack.

In Kailahun, RUF militants kidnapped 27 members of the UNAMSIL. The hostages were released unharmed on 28 May.

2 May

Sierra Leone

Unidentified militants kidnapped five Kenyan soldiers from the UNAMSIL peacekeeping force in Magburaka, according to press reports. RUF militants were probably responsible. On 10 May, the hostages escaped.

3 May

Angola

Armed militants attacked a World Food Program humanitarian convoy in Luanda, killing one person, wounding one other, and setting the trucks on fire. The UNITA was probably responsible.

5 May

Sierra Leone

RUF militants kidnapped 300 UNAMSIL peacekeepers throughout the country, according to press reports. On 15 May in Foya, Liberia, the kidnappers released 139 hostages. On 28 May, on the Liberia and Sierra Leone border, armed militants released unharmed the last of the UN peacekeepers.

8 May

Sierra Leone

In Freetown, armed militants shot down a United Nations helicopter, causing major damage to the helicopter but no injuries, according to press reports. The RUF was probably responsible.

9 May

Sierra Leone

In Freetown, armed militants kidnapped two British citizens working for a humanitarian organization, according to press reports. The RUF was probably responsible. On 19 June one of the hostages was released unharmed.

10 May

India

In Kupwara, armed militants kidnapped a civilian from his residence and then killed him, according to press reports. No one claimed responsibility.

11 May

India

In Bihar, according to press reports, armed militants killed 11 persons and injured four others. No one claimed responsibility.

14 May

Colombia

Press reported unidentified individuals kidnapped an Australian missionary and three Colombians in Canito. Several hours later, the Colombian hostages were released unharmed. No group claimed responsibility.

Iran

A bomb exploded in the cultural/sports center in Kermanshah, injuring two civilians, according to press reports. The Mujahedin-e Khalq claimed responsibility.

15 May

India

A land mine exploded in Chabran, killing Kashmir's power minister and four other government employees and destroying their vehicle, according to press reports. No one claimed responsibility.

19 May

India

In Amludesa, armed militants killed six persons -- one magistrate, four police officers, and one civilian -- according to press reports. No one claimed responsibility.

A rocket hit a private residence in Srinagar, injuring six persons, according to press reports. No one claimed responsibility.

20 May

India

Armed militants threw several bombs at a government vehicle near a bus stop in Srinagar, injuring four police officers and three civilians, according to press reports. No one claimed responsibility.

23 May

India

Militants fired six grenades at the Civil Secretariat building in Kashmir, killing one civilian and injuring three others, according to press reports. No one claimed responsibility.

24 May

Angola

Press reported suspected Front for the Liberation of the Cabinda Enclave rebels kidnapped three Portuguese construction company workers in Cabinda. No one claimed responsibility.

25 May

Sierra Leone

In Freetown, according to press reports, armed militants ambushed two military vehicles carrying four journalists. A Spaniard and one US citizen were killed, and one Greek and one South African were injured in the attack. The RUF was probably responsible.

27 May

Indonesia

According to press reporting, armed militants, who claimed to be members of the Free Aceh Movement, occupied a Mobil Oil production plant. The rebels ordered the workers and all Indonesian nationals to shut down production and held six hostages for several hours before releasing them unharmed and allowing production to resume. The militants demanded $500,000 ransom to restore operations.

June

1 June

Georgia

In Kodori Gorge, police officials reported unidentified gunmen kidnapped two Danish UN military observers, a British Government employee, and two Abkhaz citizens, demanding a $500,000 ransom. On 3

June, one Abkhaz hostage was released. On 5 June, the remaining hostages were released unharmed.

2 June

Namibia

In Mut'jiku, press reported suspected UNITA militants kidnapped a woman from her residence. No one claimed responsibility. In Rundu, according to press accounts, suspected UNITA militants kidnapped a man.

India

Police officials reported a bomb exploded at a religious meeting in Srinagar, killing 12 persons and injuring seven others, including a senior legislator. The Hizb ul-Mujahedin claimed responsibility.

6 June

Sierra Leone

Suspected RUF rebels kidnapped 21 Indian UN peacekeepers in Freetown, according to press accounts. No one claimed responsibility.

8 June

Greece

In Athens, press reported two unidentified gunmen killed British Defense Attaché Stephen Saunders in an ambush. The Revolutionary Organization 17 November claimed responsibility.

India

Press reported unidentified individuals threw a hand grenade into a crowded marketplace in Sopur, injuring 30 civilians and causing major damage. No one claimed responsibility.

11 June

Yemen

Four unidentified gunmen kidnapped a Norwegian diplomat and his son, according to press reports. Later the same day, Yemeni police opened fire on the kidnappers, killing the diplomat and one gunman. The son escaped unharmed. The three remaining assailants escaped. No one claimed responsibility.

16 June

Yemen

In the Ma'rib region, according to press reports, armed tribesmen kidnapped an Italian archaeologist. On 20 July, the kidnappers released the hostage unharmed. Yemeni tribesmen claimed responsibility.

17 June

India

Armed militants shot and injured four civilians in Jammu and Kashmir, according to press reports.

18 June

Nigeria

In the Niger Delta region, press reported armed militants kidnapped 22 Nigerian citizens and two unidentified foreign nationals working for Chevron, a US-owned oil company. The militants later released the two foreign nationals and four Nigerians. No one claimed responsibility.

26 June

Yugoslavia

In Prizren, press reported a bomb exploded outside a shop located below a UN police officer's residence, slightly injuring the officer and destroying the shop. No one claimed responsibility.

27 June

Colombia

In Bogota, according to press reporting, ELN militants kidnapped a five-year-old US citizen and his Colombian mother, demanding an undisclosed ransom.

30 June

India

A land mine exploded in Srinagar, killing one person, injuring three military personnel and five civilians, damaging several vehicles, and shattering the windows in several nearby hotels, according to press reports. No one claimed responsibility.

July

2 July

Philippines

Unidentified militants kidnapped a German journalist working for Der Spiegel magazine, according to police authorities. The Abu Sayyaf Group (ASG) claimed responsibility. On 27 July, the journalist was released unharmed.

4 July

India

In Jammu and Kashmir, armed militants killed one person and injured one other, according to press reports. No one claimed responsibility.

9 July

Democratic Republic of the Congo

Near the Rwandan border, Rwandan Interahamwe militiamen attacked a refugee camp, killing 30 persons and kidnapping four others, according to press accounts.

10 July

Afghanistan

Press reported a bomb exploded at the Pakistani Embassy, causing major damage but no injuries. No one claimed responsibility.

13 July

India

In Leh, Kashmir, armed militants killed three Buddhist monks, according to press reports. No one claimed responsibility.

14 July

India

In the Himalaya Mountains, press reported armed militants attacked two German hikers, killing one and injuring the other. No one claimed responsibility.

15 July

India

In Doda, Kashmir, armed militants killed the Doda National Conference district president and his bodyguard, according to press reports. No one claimed responsibility.

Sierra Leone

Press reported suspected RUF militants attacked UNAMSIL troops, near Kailahun, killing one Indian soldier and wounding one other Indian soldier. No one claimed responsibility.

India

In Srinagar, Kashmir, militants fired nine rifle grenades toward the Civil Secretariat building, according to press reports. The Chief Minister was in his office at the time but was unharmed in the attack, which injured four civilians and damaged two vehicles nearby. The Jaish-e-Mohammed claimed responsibility.

India

In Tangmarg, Kashmir, armed militants killed one Indian soldier and one civilian, according to press reports. No one claimed responsibility.

16 July

Sierra Leone
Unidentified militants killed a Nigerian UNAMSIL soldier in Rogberi, press reported. No one claimed responsibility.

Germany
In Ludwigshafen, the US Consulate reported unidentified individuals firebombed a refugee shelter housing Albanian Kosovars, injuring three children and causing minor damage. No one claimed responsibility.

18 July

Angola
Press reported UNITA troops kidnapped 14 clergy members from the Dunge Catholic Mission in Benguela. According to press accounts, two persons were killed and several escaped during the kidnapping. On 26 July all remaining hostages were released unharmed.

20 July

Angola
Unidentified militants kidnapped four Namibian citizens from their residence in Kavango, according to press accounts. The militants shot and killed two of the hostages. A third hostage was injured but escaped with a child. UNITA is suspected.

24 July

India
A bomb exploded on a private bus in Ballen, killing six persons and injuring 10 others, according to press reports. Kashmiri militants or Sikhs may have been responsible.

27 July

Colombia
In Bogota, suspected Guevarist Revolutionary Army (ARG) militants kidnapped a French aid worker affiliated with Doctors Without

Borders, according to press reports. The ARG is a suspected faction of the ELN.

29 July

Namibia
In Nginga, suspected UNITA rebels crossed into Namibia and kidnapped five Namibian men, according to press reports. No one claimed responsibility.

30 July

India
Militants threw a grenade into a crowded marketplace in Gulmarg, killing one person and injuring five others, according to press reports. No one claimed responsibility.

Sierra Leone
In Masiaka, suspected RUF militants fired on Jordanian UNAMSIL troops, killing one soldier and wounding three others, according to press accounts. No one claimed responsibility.

31 July

India
A remote-controlled land mine exploded in Gulmarg, killing one person, injuring five others, and destroying their vehicle, according to press reports. No one claimed responsibility.

Nigeria
Press reported armed youth stormed two oil drilling rigs, taking 165 persons hostage. The hostages included 145 Nigerians, seven US citizens, five Britons, eight Australian and Lebanese nationals. All were employed by service contractors of Shell Oil Company. No one claimed responsibility, but the gunmen were believed to be ethnic Ijaw. On 4 August all hostages were released unharmed.

Sierra Leone
Press reported RUF militants ambushed a UNAMSIL patrol in Freetown, killing one Nigerian soldier. No one else was injured.

August

2 August

India

In Rajwas, armed militants killed 30 persons and injured 47 others when they threw a grenade and then opened fire on a community kitchen, according to press reports. The Lashkar-e-Tayyiba claimed responsibility.

4 August

Georgia

Ethnic Kists kidnapped two Red Cross workers and their driver in Pankisi. No injuries were reported, and all hostages were released on 13 August.

Namibia

Press reported suspected UNITA rebels shot and killed one Namibian rebel inside her residence in Mwitjiku. No one claimed responsibility.

8 August

Angola

Suspected UNITA rebels attacked a diamond mine in Lunda Norte Province, killing eight South African security personnel, according to press accounts. No one claimed responsibility.

9 August

Angola

Press reported suspected UNITA rebels shot and killed one South African national and abducted seven Angolan workers during a raid on a diamond mine in northeast Angola. No one claimed responsibility.

10 August

India

A remote-controlled car bomb exploded in Srinagar, killing nine persons, injuring 25 others, and damaging four cars, according to press reports. Eight police officers were among those killed, and five journalists were among the wounded. No one claimed responsibility.

11 August

Colombia

Police authorities reported suspected ELN militants kidnapped a group of 27 tourists in Antioquia. A US professor and a German student were among the hostages. On 12 August the rebels released all hostages unharmed.

In Tolima, according to press reports, the FARC kidnapped then killed two persons -- one Colombian and one Irish citizen.

12 August

India

A grenade exploded near an historic mosque in Srinagar, injuring four persons -- two Hungarians and two Indians -- according to press accounts. No one claimed responsibility.

Kyrgyzstan

In the Kara-Su Valley, according to press accounts, Islamic Movement of Uzbekistan rebels took four US citizens and one Kyrgyzstani soldier hostage. The rebels killed the soldier, but the four US citizens escaped on 18 August.

14 August

India

Armed militants kidnapped three persons from their residences in Kot Dhara and later killed them, according to press reports. No one claimed responsibility.

Militants threw a grenade at a bus in Pulwama, injuring 14 passengers. No one claimed responsibility.

16 August

Greece

Militants in Athens set fire to a car belonging to an Italian Embassy official, according to press accounts. No one was injured. The Mavro Asteri (Black Star) called a local newspaper and claimed responsibility.

September

6 September

Indonesia

A militia-led mob attacked a UNHCR aid office in Atambua, West Timor, killing three aid workers -- one US citizen, one Ethiopian, and a Croatian -- and destroying the compound.

7 September

Guinea

Suspected RUF rebels kidnapped three Catholic missionaries -- one US citizen and two Italian priests -- in Pamlap, according to press accounts. In early December, the two Italian priests escaped.

13 September

Colombia

According to press reports, ELN militants set up a fake roadblock in Antioquia and kidnapped two Russian civil engineers. On 21 September the hostages were freed.

15 September

Colombia

According to police officials, a group of armed militants kidnapped three Italians in Medellin. No one claimed responsibility.

17 September

Guinea

Unidentified rebels attacked and killed a Togolese United Nations refugee agency employee in Macenta, according to press accounts. The rebels also kidnapped an Ivorian secretary. No one claimed responsibility.

30 September

India

Armed militants killed five persons in their private residence in Jammu, according to press reports. No one claimed responsibility.

October

1 October

Tajikistan

Unidentified militants detonated two bombs in a Christian church in Dushanbe, killing seven persons and injuring 70 others, according to press reports. The church was founded by a Korean-born US citizen, and most of those killed and wounded were Korean. No one claimed responsibility.

2 October

Uganda

Press reported LRA rebels shot and killed an Italian priest as he drove to church in Kitgum. No one else was injured.

12 October

Ecuador

In Napo, according to press reports, possible FARC members hijacked an Ecuadorian-owned helicopter and took hostage 10 aviation company employees and oil workers -- five US citizens, two French nationals, one Argentine, one Chilean, and one Ecuadorian. On 16 October the two French citizens escaped. (On 31 January, the US Embassy in Quito confirmed the death of one US hostage.)

Yemen

In Aden, a small dingy carrying explosives rammed the US destroyer, USS Cole, killing 17 sailors and injuring 39 others. Supporters of Osama bin Laden are suspected.

13 October

Bosnia

In Sarajevo, four German NATO-led Stabilization Force (SFOR) soldiers were injured when they attempted to arrest a Bosnian, according to press accounts. The suspect detonated a hand grenade, killing himself and wounding the soldiers and one civilian.

Indonesia

A powerful bomb exploded in Lombok, damaging the offices of the PT Newmont Nusa Tenggara Mining Company, which is jointly owned by the United States, Japan, and Indonesia, according to press reports. No one claimed responsibility.

Yemen

A small bomb detonated on the compound of the British Embassy in Sanaa, but there were no injuries.

14 October

South Africa

Demonstrators, possibly supported by PAGAD members, vandalized and threw rocks at a McDonald's restaurant in Cape Town, according to press reports. No one was injured, but significant damage was done to the restaurant and customers' vehicles.

19 October

Sri Lanka

In Colombo, a suicide bomber detonated the explosives he was wearing near the town hall, killing four persons and wounding 23 others, including two US citizens, according to press reports. The Liberation Tigers of Tamil Eelam (LTTE) were probably responsible.

November

14 November

Yemen

In Sanaa, an armed group from the Gahm Tribe kidnapped a Swedish employee of a local power station. On 30 November the hostage was released.

19 November

Namibia

Armed militants in Mahane Village kidnapped seven men and their cattle and moved them to Angola. Three men escaped. UNITA rebels were probably responsible.

Jordan

In Amman, armed militants attempted to assassinate the Israeli Vice Consul, according to press reports. The Movement for the Struggle of the Jordanian Islamic Resistance Movement and Ahmad al-Daqamisah Group both claimed responsibility.

24 November

India

In Akhala, armed militants kidnapped six persons from a bus stop and killed five of them, according to press reports. The fate of the sixth individual was unknown. The Lashkar-e-Tayyiba was probably responsible.

27 November

Chile

In Santiago, a bomb planted in front of the Colombian Embassy exploded, causing some property damage. No one was injured. No one claimed responsibility.

December

1 December

India

A grenade thrown at a passing security vehicle missed its target and exploded in a crowded street in Pattan, injuring 12 persons, according to press reports. No one claimed responsibility.

Press reported armed militants barged into the private residence of a village defense committee member in Udhampur, killing four children and injuring two others. No one claimed responsibility.

Militants threw a grenade at a military vehicle in Srinagar, missing their target but injuring three civilians. No one claimed responsibility.

5 December

Burundi

Small-arms fire struck a Sabena airliner as it was landing in Bujumbura, injuring two persons, a Belgian flight attendant, and a Tunisian passenger, according to press reports. The airliner was on a routine flight from Brussels. No one claimed responsibility.

Jordan

In Amman, an unidentified assailant shot and wounded an Israeli diplomat as he, his wife, and his bodyguard were leaving a grocery store. The Movement for the Struggle of the Jordanian Islamic Resistance claimed responsibility.

6 December

India

A bomb destroyed a vendor's cart, injuring four persons and damaging roadside shops in Muzaffarabad, according to press reporting. No one claimed responsibility.

7 December

India

Armed militants threw a grenade at a bus stop in Kupwara, injuring 24 persons, including one special police officer, according to press reports. No one claimed responsibility.

A bomb exploded near a mosque in Shopian, injuring 31 persons, including three police officers, according to press reports. No one claimed responsibility.

A bomb exploded in Gohlan, killing a father and injuring his son, according to press reports. No one claimed responsibility.

9 December

India

A bomb exploded in Neelum Valley, killing three persons, including a young boy, according to press accounts. No one claimed responsibility.

12 December

India

A grenade thrown at an outdoor marketplace in Chadoura injured 12 civilians and four police officers, according to press reports. The Jaish-e-Mohammed was probably responsible.

In Qamarwari, a police vehicle activated a remote-controlled bomb, killing five police officers and injuring five civilians. The Jaish-e-Mohammed claimed responsibility.

13 December

Nambia

A land mine placed near a private residence in Shighuru exploded, injuring the owner, according to press reports. UNITA was probably responsible.

25 December

India

A car bomb exploded at the main gate of a military base in Srinagar, killing nine persons -- six military personnel and three civilians -- and injuring 23 civilians, according to press reports. The Jaish-e-Mohammed and Jamiat-ul-Mujahedin claimed responsibility.

Greece

A bomb placed at a Citibank ATM in Athens exploded, causing major damage to the exterior ATM and to the bank interior, according to press reports. The Anarchists Attack Team claimed responsibility for the attack to show support for the dead prisoners in Turkey.

30 December

Philippines

A bomb exploded in a plaza across the street from the US Embassy in Manila, injuring nine persons, according to press reports. The Moro Islamic Liberation Front was possibly responsible.

31 December

Thailand

Armed militants attacked a grocery store in Suan Phung during New Year celebrations, killing six persons, according to press reports. The Burmese group, God's Army, was probably responsible.

Spain

A vehicle carrying explosives exploded in Seville, but no injuries resulted. The vehicle had been stolen from Toulouse, France. No one claimed responsibility.

Appendix K:
Background Information on Terrorist Groups

The following descriptive list of terrorist groups is presented in two sections. The first section lists the 29 groups that currently are designated by the Secretary of State as Foreign Terrorist Organizations (FTOs), pursuant to section 219 of the Immigration and Nationality Act, as amended by the Antiterrorism and Effective Death Penalty Act of 1996. The designations carry legal consequences:

- *It is unlawful to provide funds or other material support to a designated FTO.*
- *Representatives and certain members of a designated FTO can be denied visas or excluded from the United States.*

- *US financial institutions must block funds of designated FTOs and their agents and must report the blockage to the US Department of the Treasury.*

The second section includes other terrorist groups that were active during 2000. Terrorist groups whose activities were limited in scope in 2000 are not included.

I.   Designated Foreign Terrorist Organizations

Abu Nidal Organization (ANO)
a.k.a. Fatah Revolutionary Council, Arab Revolutionary Brigades, Black September, and Revolutionary Organization of Socialist Muslims

Description
    International terrorist organization led by Sabri al-Banna. Split from PLO in 1974. Made up of various functional committees, including political, military, and financial.

Activities
    Has carried out terrorist attacks in 20 countries, killing or injuring almost 900 persons. Targets include the United States, the United Kingdom, France, Israel, moderate Palestinians, the PLO, and various Arab countries. Major attacks included the Rome and Vienna airports in December 1985, the Neve Shalom synagogue in Istanbul and the Pan Am flight 73 hijacking in Karachi in September 1986, and the City of Poros day-excursion ship attack in Greece in July 1988.
    Suspected of assassinating PLO deputy chief Abu Iyad and PLO security chief Abu Hul in Tunis in January 1991. ANO assassinated a Jordanian diplomat in Lebanon in January 1994 and has been linked to the killing of the PLO representative there. Has not attacked Western targets since the late 1980s.

Strength
    A few hundred plus limited overseas support structure.

Location/Area of Operation

Al-Banna relocated to Iraq in December 1998, where the group maintains a presence. Has an operational presence in Lebanon, including in several Palestinian refugee camps. Financial problems and internal disorganization have reduced the group's activities and capabilities. Authorities shut down the ANO's operations in Libya and Egypt in 1999. Has demonstrated ability to operate over wide area, including the Middle East, Asia, and Europe.

External Aid

Has received considerable support, including safe haven, training, logistic assistance, and financial aid from Iraq, Libya, and Syria (until 1987), in addition to close support for selected operations.

Abu Sayyaf Group (ASG)

Description

The ASG is the smallest and most radical of the Islamic separatist groups operating in the southern Philippines. Some ASG members have studied or worked in the Middle East and developed ties to mjuahidin while fighting and training in Afghanistan. The group split from the Moro National Liberation Front in 1991 under the leadership of Abdurajik Abubakar Janjalani, who was killed in a clash with Philippine police on 18 December 1998. Press reports place his younger brother, Khadafi Janjalani, as the nominal leader of the group, which is composed of several factions.

Activities

Engages in bombings, assassinations, kidnappings, and extortion to promote an independent Islamic state in western Mindanao and the Sulu Archipelago, areas in the southern Philippines heavily populated by Muslims. Raided the town of Ipil in Mindanao in April 1995 -- the group's first large-scale action -- and kidnapped more than 30 foreigners, including a US citizen, in 2000.

Strength

Believed to have about 200 core fighters, but more than 2,000 individuals, motivated by the prospect of receiving ransom payments for foreign hostages, allegedly joined the group in August.

Location/Area of Operation

The ASG primarily operates in the southern Philippines with members occasionally traveling to Manila, but the group expanded its operations to Malaysia this year when it abducted foreigners from two different resorts.

External Aid

Probably receives support from Islamic extremists in the Middle East and South Asia.

Armed Islamic Group (GIA)

Description

An Islamic extremist group, the GIA aims to overthrow the secular Algerian regime and replace it with an Islamic state. The GIA began its violent activities in 1992 after Algiers voided the victory of the Islamic Salvation Front (FIS) -- the largest Islamic opposition party -- in the first round of legislative elections in December 1991.

Activities

Frequent attacks against civilians and government workers. Between 1992 and 1998 the GIA conducted a terrorist campaign of civilian massacres, sometimes wiping out entire villages in its area of operation. Since announcing its campaign against foreigners living in Algeria in 1993, the GIA has killed more than 100 expatriate men and women -- mostly Europeans -- in the country.

The group uses assassinations and bombings, including car bombs, and it is known to favor kidnapping victims and slitting their throats. The GIA hijacked an Air France flight to Algiers in December 1994. In late 1999 several GIA members were convicted by a French court for conducting a series of bombings in France in 1995.

The Salafi Group for Call and Combat (GSPC) splinter faction appears to have eclipsed the GIA since approximately 1998 and is currently assessed to be the most effective remaining armed group inside Algeria. Both the GIA and GSPC leadership continue to proclaim their rejection of President Bouteflika's amnesty, but in contrast to the GIA, the GSPC has stated that it limits attacks on civilians. The GSPC's planned attack against the Paris-Dakar Road Rally in January 2000 demonstrates, however, that the group has not entirely renounced attacks against high-profile civilian targets.

Strength
> Unknown; probably several hundred to several thousand.

Location/Area of Operation
> Algeria.

External Aid
> Algerian expatriates and GSPC members abroad, many of whom reside in Western Europe, provide financial and logistic support. In addition, the Algerian Government has accused Iran and Sudan of supporting Algerian extremists.

Aum Supreme Truth (Aum)
a.k.a. Aum Shinrikyo, Aleph

Description
> A cult established in 1987 by Shoko Asahara, the Aum aimed to take over Japan, then the world. Approved as a religious entity in 1989 under Japanese law, the group ran candidates in a Japanese parliamentary election in 1990. Over time the cult began to emphasize the imminence of the end of the world and stated that the United States would initiate Armageddon by starting World War III with Japan. The Japanese Government revoked its recognition of the Aum as a religious organization in October 1995, but in 1997 a government panel decided not to invoke the Anti-Subversive Law against the group, which would have outlawed the cult. In 2000, Fumihiro Joyu took control of the Aum following his three-year jail sentence for perjury. Joyu was previously the group's spokesman and Russia Branch leader. Under Joyu's leadership the Aum changed its name to Aleph and claims to have rejected the violent and apocalyptic teachings of its founder.

Activities
> On 20 March 1995, Aum members simultaneously released the chemical nerve agent Sarin on several Tokyo subway trains, killing 12 persons and injuring up to 6,000. (Recent studies put the number of persons who suffered actual physical injuries closer to 1,300, with the rest

suffering from some form of psychological trauma.) The group was responsible for other mysterious chemical accidents in Japan in 1994. Its efforts to conduct attacks using biological agents have been unsuccessful. Japanese police arrested Asahara in May 1995, and he remained on trial, facing 17 counts of murder at the end of 2000. Since 1997 the cult continued to recruit new members, engage in commercial enterprise, and acquire property, although the cult scaled back these activities significantly in 2000 in response to public outcry. The cult maintains an Internet home page.

Strength
        The Aum's current membership is estimated at 1,500 to 2,000 persons. At the time of the Tokyo subway attack, the group claimed to have 9,000 members in Japan and up to 40,000 worldwide.

Location/Area of Operation
        The Aum's principal membership is located only in Japan, but a residual branch comprising an unknown number of followers has surfaced in Russia.

External Aid
        None.

Basque Fatherland and Liberty (ETA)
a.k.a. Euzkadi Ta Askatasuna

Description
        Founded in 1959 with the aim of establishing an independent homeland based on Marxist principles in the northern Spanish provinces of Vizcaya, Guipuzcoa, Alava, and Navarra and the southwestern French departments of Labourd, Basse-Navarra, and Soule.

Activities
        Primarily bombings and assassinations of Spanish Government officials, especially security and military forces, politicians, and judicial figures. ETA finances its activities through kidnappings, robberies, and extortion. The group has killed more than 800 persons since it began lethal attacks in the early 1960s. In November 1999, ETA broke its "unilateral and indefinite" cease-fire and began an assassination and bombing

campaign that killed 23 individuals and wounded scores more by the end of 2000.

Strength
    Unknown; may have hundreds of members, plus supporters.

Location/Area of Operation
    Operates primarily in the Basque autonomous regions of northern Spain and southwestern France, but also has bombed Spanish and French interests elsewhere.

External Aid
    Has received training at various times in the past in Libya, Lebanon, and Nicaragua. Some ETA members allegedly have received sanctuary in Cuba while others reside in South America. Also appears to have ties to the Irish Republican Army through the two groups' legal political wings.

Al-Gama'a al-Islamiyya
(Islamic Group, IG)

Description
    Egypt's largest militant group, active since the late 1970s; appears to be loosely organized. Has an external wing with a worldwide presence. The group issued a cease-fire in March 1999, but its spiritual leader, Shaykh Umar Abd al-Rahman, incarcerated in the United States, rescinded his support for the cease-fire in June 2000. The Gama'a has not conducted an attack inside Egypt since August 1998. Rifa'i Taha Musa -- a hard-line former senior member of the group -- signed Osama bin Laden's February 1998 fatwa calling for attacks against US civilians.
    The IG since has publicly denied that it supports bin Laden and frequently differs with public statements made by Taha Musa. Taha Musa has in the last year sought to push the group toward a return to armed operations, but the group, which still is led by Mustafa Hamza, has yet to break the unilaterally declared cease-fire. In late 2000, Taha Musa appeared in an undated video with bin Laden and Ayman al-Zawahiri threatening retaliation against the United States for Abd al-Rahman's continued incarceration. The IG's primary goal is to overthrow the

Egyptian Government and replace it with an Islamic state, but Taha Musa also may be interested in attacking US and Israeli interests.

Activities

Group specialized in armed attacks against Egyptian security and other government officials, Coptic Christians, and Egyptian opponents of Islamic extremism before the cease-fire. From 1993 until the cease-fire, al-Gama'a launched attacks on tourists in Egypt, most notably the attack in November 1997 at Luxor that killed 58 foreign tourists. Also claimed responsibility for the attempt in June 1995 to assassinate Egyptian President Hosni Mubarak in Addis Ababa, Ethiopia. The Gama'a has never specifically attacked a US citizen or facility but has threatened US interests.

Strength

Unknown. At its peak the IG probably commanded several thousand hard-core members and a like number of sympathizers. The 1998 cease-fire and security crackdowns following the attack in Luxor in 1997 probably have resulted in a substantial decrease in the group's numbers.

Location/Area of Operation

Operates mainly in the Al-Minya, Asyu't, Qina, and Sohaj Governorates of southern Egypt. Also appears to have support in Cairo, Alexandria, and other urban locations, particularly among unemployed graduates and students. Has a worldwide presence, including Sudan, the United Kingdom, Afghanistan, Austria, and Yemen.

External Aid

Unknown. The Egyptian Government believes that Iran, bin Laden, and Afghan militant groups support the organization. Also may obtain some funding through various Islamic nongovernmental organizations.

HAMAS (Islamic Resistance Movement)

Description

Formed in late 1987 as an outgrowth of the Palestinian branch of the Muslim Brotherhood.

Various HAMAS elements have used both political and violent means, including terrorism, to pursue the goal of establishing an Islamic Palestinian state in place of Israel. Loosely structured, with some elements working clandestinely and others working openly through mosques and social service institutions to recruit members, raise money, organize activities, and distribute propaganda. HAMAS's strength is concentrated in the Gaza Strip and a few areas of the West Bank. Also has engaged in peaceful political activity, such as running candidates in West Bank Chamber of Commerce elections.

Activities
HAMAS activists, especially those in the Izz el-Din al-Qassam Brigades, have conducted many attacks -- including large-scale suicide bombings -- against Israeli civilian and military targets. In the early 1990s, they also targeted suspected Palestinian collaborators and Fatah rivals.
Claimed several attacks during the unrest in late 2000.

Strength
Unknown number of hard-core members; tens of thousands of supporters and sympathizers.

Location/Area of Operation
Primarily the occupied territories, Israel. In August 1999, Jordanian authorities closed the group's Political Bureau offices in Amman, arrested its leaders, and prohibited the group from operating on Jordanian territory.

External Aid
Receives funding from Palestinian expatriates, Iran, and private benefactors in Saudi Arabia and other moderate Arab states. Some fundraising and propaganda activities take place in Western Europe and North America.

Harakat ul-Mujahidin (HUM)

Description
Formerly known as the Harakat al-Ansar, the HUM is an Islamic militant group based in Pakistan that operates primarily in Kashmir. Long-time leader of the group, Fazlur Rehman Khalil, in mid-February stepped

down as HUM emir, turning the reins over to the popular Kashmiri commander and his second-in-command, Farooq Kashmiri. Khalil, who has been linked to bin Laden and signed his fatwa in February 1998 calling for attacks on US and Western interests, assumed the position of HUM Secretary General. Continued to operate terrorist training camps in eastern Afghanistan.

Activities

Has conducted a number of operations against Indian troops and civilian targets in Kashmir.

Linked to the Kashmiri militant group al-Faran that kidnapped five Western tourists in Kashmir in July 1995; one was killed in August 1995 and the other four reportedly were killed in December of the same year. The new millennium brought significant developments for Pakistani militant groups, particularly the HUM. Most of these sprang from the hijacking of an Indian airliner on 24 December by militants believed to be associated with the HUM. The hijackers negotiated the release of Masood Azhar, an important leader in the former Harakat ul-Ansar imprisoned by the Indians in 1994. Azhar did not, however, return to the HUM, choosing instead to form the Jaish-e-Mohammed (JEM), a rival militant group expressing a more radical line than the HUM.

Strength

Has several thousand armed supporters located in Azad Kashmir, Pakistan, and India's southern Kashmir and Doda regions. Supporters are mostly Pakistanis and Kashmiris and also include Afghans and Arab veterans of the Afghan war. Uses light and heavy machine guns, assault rifles, mortars, explosives, and rockets. HUM lost some of its membership in defections to the JEM.

Location/Area of Operation

Based in Muzaffarabad, Rawalpindi, and several other towns in Pakistan and Afghanistan, but members conduct insurgent and terrorist activities primarily in Kashmir. The HUM trains its militants in Afghanistan and Pakistan.

External Aid

Collects donations from Saudi Arabia and other Gulf and Islamic states and from Pakistanis and Kashmiris. The sources and amount of HUM's military funding are unknown.

Hizballah (Party of God)
a.k.a. Islamic Jihad, Revolutionary Justice Organization, Organization of the Oppressed on Earth, and Islamic Jihad for the Liberation of Palestine

Description
Radical Shia group formed in Lebanon; dedicated to increasing its political power in Lebanon and opposing Israel and the Middle East peace negotiations. Strongly anti-West and anti-Israel.

Closely allied with, and often directed by, Iran but may have conducted operations that were not approved by Tehran.

Activities
Known or suspected to have been involved in numerous anti-US terrorist attacks, including the suicide truck bombing of the US Embassy and US Marine barracks in Beirut in October 1983 and the US Embassy annex in Beirut in September 1984. Elements of the group were responsible for the kidnapping and detention of US and other Western hostages in Lebanon. The group also attacked the Israeli Embassy in Argentina in 1992 and is a suspect in the 1994 bombing of the Israeli cultural center in Buenos Aires. In fall 2000, it captured three Israeli soldiers in the Shabaa Farms and kidnapped an Israeli noncombatant whom it may have lured to Lebanon under false pretenses.

Strength
Several thousand supporters and a few hundred terrorist operatives.

Location/Area of Operation
Operates in the Bekaa Valley, the southern suburbs of Beirut, and southern Lebanon. Has established cells in Europe, Africa, South America, North America, and Asia.

External Aid
Receives substantial amounts of financial, training, weapons, explosives, political, diplomatic, and organizational aid from Iran and Syria.

Islamic Movement of Uzbekistan (IMU)

Description
    Coalition of Islamic militants from Uzbekistan and other Central Asian states opposed to Uzbekistani President Islom Karimov's secular regime. Goal is the establishment of an Islamic state in Uzbekistan. The group's propaganda also includes anti-Western and anti-Israeli rhetoric.

Activities
    Believed to be responsible for five car bombs in Tashkent in February 1999. Took hostages on several occasions in 1999 and 2000, including four US citizens who were mountain climbing in August 2000, and four Japanese geologists and eight Kyrgyzstani soldiers in August 1999.

Strength
    Militants probably number in the thousands.

Location/Area of Operation
    Militants are based in Afghanistan and Tajikistan. Area of operations includes Uzbekistan, Tajikistan, Kyrgyzstan, and Afghanistan.

External Aid
    Support from other Islamic extremist groups in Central and South Asia. IMU leadership broadcasts statements over Iranian radio.

Japanese Red Army (JRA)
a.k.a. Anti-Imperialist International Brigade (AIIB)

Description
    An international terrorist group formed around 1970 after breaking away from Japanese Communist League-Red Army Faction. The JRA was led by Fusako Shigenobu until her arrest in Japan in November 2000. The JRA's historical goal has been to overthrow the Japanese Government and monarchy and to help foment world revolution. After her arrest Shigenobu announced she intended to pursue her goals using a legitimate political party rather than revolutionary violence. May control or at least have ties to Anti-Imperialist International Brigade (AIIB); also may have links to Antiwar Democratic Front -- an overt leftist political organization -- inside

Japan. Details released following Shigenobu's arrest indicate that the JRA was organizing cells in Asian cities, such as Manila and Singapore. Has history of close relations with Palestinian terrorist groups -- based and operating outside Japan -- since its inception, primarily through Shigenobu. The current status of these connections is unknown.

Activities

During the 1970s, the JRA carried out a series of attacks around the world, including the massacre in 1972 at Lod Airport in Israel, two Japanese airliner hijackings, and an attempted takeover of the US Embassy in Kuala Lumpur. In April 1988, JRA operative Yu Kikumura was arrested with explosives on the New Jersey Turnpike, apparently planning an attack to coincide with the bombing of a USO club in Naples, a suspected JRA operation that killed five, including a US service woman. He was convicted of the charges and is serving a lengthy prison sentence in the United States. Tsutomu Shirosaki, captured in 1996, is also jailed in the United States. In 2000, Lebanon deported to Japan four members it arrested in 1997, but granted a fifth operative, Kozo Okamoto, political asylum. Longtime leader Shigenobu was arrested in November 2000 and faces charges of terrorism and passport fraud.

Strength

About six hard-core members; undetermined number of sympathizers.

Location/Area of Operations

Location unknown, but possibly traveling in Asia or Syrian-controlled areas of Lebanon.

External Aid

Unknown.

Al-Jihad
a.k.a. Egyptian Islamic Jihad, Jihad Group, Islamic Jihad

Description

Egyptian Islamic extremist group active since the late 1970s. Close partner of bin Laden's al-Qaida organization. Suffered setbacks as a result of numerous arrests of operatives worldwide, most recently in Lebanon and Yemen. Primary goals are to overthrow the Egyptian Government and replace it with an Islamic state and attack US and Israeli interests in Egypt and abroad.

Activities

Specializes in armed attacks against high-level Egyptian Government personnel, including cabinet ministers, and car-bombings against official US and Egyptian facilities. The original Jihad was responsible for the assassination in 1981 of Egyptian President Anwar Sadat. Claimed responsibility for the attempted assassinations of Interior Minister Hassan al-Alfi in August 1993 and Prime Minister Atef Sedky in November 1993. Has not conducted an attack inside Egypt since 1993 and has never targeted foreign tourists there. Responsible for Egyptian Embassy bombing in Islamabad in 1995; in 1998, planned attack against US Embassy in Albania was thwarted.

Strength

Not known but probably has several hundred hard-core members.

Location/Area of Operation

Operates in the Cairo area. Has a network outside Egypt, including Yemen, Afghanistan, Pakistan, Sudan, Lebanon, and the United Kingdom.

External Aid

Not known. The Egyptian Government claims that both Iran and bin Laden support the Jihad. Also may obtain some funding through various Islamic nongovernmental organizations, cover businesses, and by committing criminal acts.

Kach and Kahane Chai

Description

Stated goal is to restore the biblical state of Israel. Kach (founded by radical Israeli-American rabbi Meir Kahane) and its offshoot Kahane Chai, which means "Kahane Lives" (founded by Meir Kahane's son Binyamin following his father's assassination in the United States), were declared to be terrorist organizations in March 1994 by the Israeli Cabinet under the 1948 Terrorism Law.

This followed the groups' statements in support of Dr. Baruch Goldstein's attack in February 1994 on the al-Ibrahimi Mosque -- Goldstein was affiliated with Kach -- and their verbal attacks on the Israeli Government. Palestinian gunmen killed Binyamin Kahane and his wife in a drive-by shooting on 31 December in the West Bank.

Activities

Organize protests against the Israeli Government. Harass and threaten Palestinians in Hebron and the West Bank. Have threatened to attack Arabs, Palestinians, and Israeli Government officials. Have vowed revenge for the death of Binyamin Kahane and his wife.

Strength

Unknown.

Location/Area of Operation

Israel and West Bank settlements, particularly Qiryat Arba' in Hebron.

External Aid

Receives support from sympathizers in the United States and Europe.

Editor's Note: On December 31, 2000, Binyamin Kahane and his wife Talia were killed in an ambush when gunmen opened fire on their car. Five of their six children were also injured, one seriously, when their bullet-ridden car went off the road into a ditch.

On January 4, 2000, FBI Agents pursuant to a search warrant, raided the Hatikva Jewish Identity Center in Brooklyn, New York which is alleged to be headquarters for Kach and Kahane Chai. This group has fomented hatred against Arabs and advocates expelling all Arabs from Israel. In 1994 its members murdered 29 Muslims in a Hebron mosque and have reportedly attacked Palestinians repeatedly. The FBI Agents reportedly seized 84 boxes of material, a filing cabinet and six computers.

Kurdistan Workers' Party (PKK)

Description
Founded in 1974 as a Marxist-Leninist insurgent group primarily composed of Turkish Kurds. The group's goal has been to establish an independent Kurdish state in southeastern Turkey, where the population is predominantly Kurdish. In the early 1990s, the PKK moved beyond rural-based insurgent activities to include urban terrorism. Turkish authorities captured Chairman Abdullah Ocalan in Kenya in early 1999; the Turkish State Security Court subsequently sentenced him to death. In August 1999, Ocalan announced a "peace initiative," ordering members to refrain from violence and withdraw from Turkey and requesting dialogue with Ankara on Kurdish issues. At a PKK Congress in January 2000, members supported Ocalan's initiative and claimed the group now would use only political means to achieve its new goal, improved rights for Kurds in Turkey.

Activities
Primary targets have been Turkish Government security forces in Turkey. Conducted attacks on Turkish diplomatic and commercial facilities in dozens of West European cities in 1993 and again in spring 1995. In an attempt to damage Turkey's tourist industry, the PKK bombed tourist sites and hotels and kidnapped foreign tourists in the early-to-mid-1990s.

Strength
Approximately 4,000 to 5,000, most of whom currently are located in northern Iraq. Has thousands of sympathizers in Turkey and Europe.

Location/Area of Operation
Operates in Turkey, Europe, and the Middle East.

External Aid
Has received safe haven and modest aid from Syria, Iraq, and Iran. The Syrian Government expelled PKK leader Ocalan and known elements of the group from its territory in October 1998.

Liberation Tigers of Tamil Eelam (LTTE)
Other known front organizations: World Tamil Association (WTA), World Tamil Movement (WTM), the Federation of Associations of Canadian Tamils (FACT), the Ellalan Force, the Sangilian Force.

Description

Founded in 1976, the LTTE is the most powerful Tamil group in Sri Lanka and uses overt and illegal methods to raise funds, acquire weapons, and publicize its cause of establishing an independent Tamil state. The LTTE began its armed conflict with the Sri Lankan Government in 1983 and relies on a guerrilla strategy that includes the use of terrorist tactics.

Activities

The Tigers have integrated a battlefield insurgent strategy with a terrorist program that targets not only key personnel in the countryside but also senior Sri Lankan political and military leaders in Colombo and other urban centers. The Tigers are most notorious for their cadre of suicide bombers, the Black Tigers. Political assassinations and bombings are commonplace. The LTTE has refrained from targeting foreign diplomatic and commercial establishments.

Strength

Exact strength is unknown, but the LTTE is estimated to have 8,000 to 10,000 armed combatants in Sri Lanka, with a core of trained fighters of approximately 3,000 to 6,000. The LTTE also has a significant overseas support structure for fundraising, weapons procurement, and propaganda activities.

Location/Area of Operations

The Tigers control most of the northern and eastern coastal areas of Sri Lanka but have conducted operations throughout the island. Headquartered in northern Sri Lanka, LTTE leader Velupillai Prabhakaran has established an extensive network of checkpoints and informants to keep track of any outsiders who enter the group's area of control.

External Aid
        The LTTE's overt organizations support Tamil separatism by lobbying foreign governments and the United Nations. The LTTE also uses its international contacts to procure weapons, communications, and any other equipment and supplies it needs. The LTTE exploits large Tamil communities in North America, Europe, and Asia to obtain funds and supplies for its fighters in Sri Lanka. Information obtained since the mid-1980s indicates that some Tamil communities in Europe are also involved in narcotics smuggling. Tamils historically have served as drug couriers moving narcotics into Europe.

Mujahedin-e Khalq Organization (MEK or MKO)
a.k.a. The National Liberation Army of Iran (NLA, the militant wing of the MEK), the People's Mujahidin of Iran (PMOI), National Council of Resistance (NCR), Muslim Iranian Student's Society (front organization used to garner financial support)

Description
        Formed in the 1960s by the college-educated children of Iranian merchants, the MEK sought to counter what it perceived as excessive Western influence in the Shah's regime. Following a philosophy that mixes Marxism and Islam, has developed into the largest and most active armed Iranian dissident group. Its history is studded with anti-Western activity, and, most recently, attacks on the interests of the clerical regime in Iran and abroad.

Activities
        Worldwide campaign against the Iranian Government stresses propaganda and occasionally uses terrorist violence. During the 1970s the MEK staged terrorist attacks inside Iran and killed several US military personnel and civilians working on defense projects in Tehran. Supported the takeover in 1979 of the US Embassy in Tehran. In April 1992 conducted attacks on Iranian embassies in 13 different countries, demonstrating the group's ability to mount large-scale operations overseas. The normal pace of anti-Iranian operations increased during the "Operation Great Bahman" in February 2000, when the group claimed it launched a dozen attacks against Iran. During the remainder of the year,

the MEK regularly claimed that its members were involved in mortar attacks and hit-and-run raids on Iranian military, law enforcement units, and government buildings near the Iran-Iraq border. The MEK also claimed six mortar attacks on civilian government and military buildings in Tehran.

Strength

Several thousand fighters based in Iraq with an extensive overseas support structure. Most of the fighters are organized in the MEK's National Liberation Army (NLA).

Location/Area of Operation

In the 1980s the MEK's leaders were forced by Iranian security forces to flee to France. Most resettled in Iraq by 1987. In the mid-1980s the group did not mount terrorist operations in Iran at a level similar to its activities in the 1970s. In the 1990s, however, the MEK claimed credit for an increasing number of operations in Iran.

External Aid

Beyond support from Iraq, the MEK uses front organizations to solicit contributions from expatriate Iranian communities.

National Liberation Army (ELN) -- Colombia

Description

Marxist insurgent group formed in 1965 by urban intellectuals inspired by Fidel Castro and Che Guevara. Began a dialogue with Colombian officials in 1999 following a campaign of mass kidnappings -- each involving at least one US citizen -- to demonstrate its strength and continuing viability and to force the Pastrana administration to negotiate. Bogota and the ELN spent most of 2000 discussing where to establish an ELN safe haven in which to hold peace talks. A proposed location in north central Colombia faces stiff local and paramilitary opposition.

Activities

Kidnapping, hijacking, bombing, extortion, and guerrilla warfare. Modest conventional military capability. Annually conducts hundreds of kidnappings for ransom, often targeting foreign employees of large corporations, especially in the petroleum industry. Frequently assaults energy infrastructure and has inflicted major damage on pipelines and the electric distribution network.

Strength
Approximately 3,000 to 6,000 armed combatants and an unknown number of active supporters.

Location/Area of Operation
Mostly in rural and mountainous areas of north, northeast, and southwest Colombia and Venezuela border regions.

External Aid
Cuba provides some medical care and political consultation.

The Palestine Islamic Jihad (PIJ)

Description
Originated among militant Palestinians in the Gaza Strip during the 1970s. Committed to the creation of an Islamic Palestinian state and the destruction of Israel through holy war. Because of its strong support for Israel, the United States has been identified as an enemy of the PIJ, but the group has not specifically conducted attacks against US interests in the past. In July 2000, however, publicly threatened to attack US interests if the US Embassy is moved from Tel Aviv to Jerusalem. Also opposes moderate Arab governments that it believes have been tainted by Western secularism.

Activities
Conducted at least three attacks against Israeli interests in late 2000, including one to commemorate the anniversary of former PIJ leader Fathi Shaqaqi's murder in Malta on 26 October 1995. Conducted suicide bombings against Israeli targets in the West Bank, Gaza Strip, and Israel.

Strength
Unknown.

Location/Area of Operation
Primarily Israel and the occupied territories and other parts of the Middle East, including Jordan and Lebanon. Headquartered in Syria.

External Aid
Receives financial assistance from Iran and limited logistic assistance from Syria.

Palestine Liberation Front (PLF)

Description
Broke away from the PFLP-GC in mid-1970s. Later split again into pro-PLO, pro-Syrian, and pro-Libyan factions. Pro-PLO faction led by Mohammed Abbas (Abu Abbas), who became member of PLO Executive Committee in 1984 but left it in 1991.

Activities
The Abu Abbas-led faction is known for aerial attacks against Israel. Abbas's group also was responsible for the attack in 1985 on the cruise ship Achille Lauro and the murder of US citizen Leon Klinghoffer. A warrant for Abu Abbas's arrest is outstanding in Italy.

Strength
Unknown.

Location/Area of Operation
PLO faction based in Tunisia until Achille Lauro attack. Now based in Iraq.

External Aid
Receives support mainly from Iraq. Has received support from Libya in the past.

Popular Front for the Liberation of Palestine (PFLP)

Description
Marxist-Leninist group founded in 1967 by George Habash as a member of the PLO. Joined the Alliance of Palestinian Forces (APF) to oppose the Declaration of Principles signed in 1993 and suspended participation in the PLO. Broke away from the APF, along with the DFLP, in 1996 over ideological differences. Took part in meetings with Arafat's Fatah party and PLO representatives in 1999 to discuss national unity and

the reinvigoration of the PLO but continues to oppose current negotiations with Israel.

Activities
Committed numerous international terrorist attacks during the 1970s. Since 1978 has conducted attacks against Israeli or moderate Arab targets, including killing a settler and her son in December 1996.

Strength
Some 800.

Location/Area of Operation
Syria, Lebanon, Israel, and the occupied territories.

External Aid
Receives safe haven and some logistic assistance from Syria.

Popular Front for the Liberation of Palestine-General Command (PFLP-GC)

Description
Split from the PFLP in 1968, claiming it wanted to focus more on fighting and less on politics. Violently opposed to Arafat's PLO. Led by Ahmad Jabril, a former captain in the Syrian Army. Closely tied to both Syria and Iran.

Activities
Carried out dozens of attacks in Europe and the Middle East during 1970s-80s. Known for cross-border terrorist attacks into Israel using unusual means, such as hot-air balloons and motorized hang gliders. Primary focus now on guerrilla operations in southern Lebanon, small-scale attacks in Israel, West Bank, and Gaza Strip.

Strength
Several hundred.

Location/Area of Operation
Headquartered in Damascus with bases in Lebanon.

External Aid
        Receives logistic and military support from Syria and financial
support from Iran.

al-Qaida

Description
        Established by Osama bin Laden in the late 1980s to bring together
Arabs who fought in Afghanistan against the Soviet invasion. Helped
finance, recruit, transport, and train Sunni Islamic extremists for the
Afghan resistance. Current goal is to establish a pan-Islamic Caliphate
throughout the world by working with allied Islamic extremist groups to
overthrow regimes it deems "non-Islamic" and expelling Westerners and
non-Muslims from Muslim countries. Issued statement under banner of
"the World Islamic Front for Jihad Against the Jews and Crusaders" in
February 1998, saying it was the duty of all Muslims to kill US citizens --
civilian or military -- and their allies everywhere.

Activities
        Plotted to carry out terrorist operations against US and Israeli
tourists visiting Jordan for millennial celebrations. (Jordanian authorities
thwarted the planned attacks and put 28 suspects on trial.) Conducted the
bombings in August 1998 of the US Embassies in Nairobi, Kenya, and
Dar es Salaam, Tanzania, that killed at least 301 persons and injured more
than 5,000 others.
        Claims to have shot down US helicopters and killed US
servicemen in Somalia in 1993 and to have conducted three bombings that
targeted US troops in Aden, Yemen, in December 1992. Linked to the
following plans that were not carried out: to assassinate Pope John Paul II
during his visit to Manila in late 1994, simultaneous bombings of the US
and Israeli Embassies in Manila and other Asian capitals in late 1994, the
midair bombing of a dozen US trans-Pacific flights in 1995, and to kill
President Clinton during a visit to the Philippines in early 1995. Continues
to train, finance, and provide logistic support to terrorist groups in support
of these goals.

Strength
        May have several hundred to several thousand members. Also
serves as a focal point or umbrella organization for a worldwide network

that includes many Sunni Islamic extremist groups such as Egyptian Islamic Jihad, some members of al-Gama'at al-Islamiyya, the Islamic Movement of Uzbekistan, and the Harakat ul-Mujahidin.

Location/Area of Operation
Al-Qaida has a worldwide reach, has cells in a number of countries, and is reinforced by its ties to Sunni extremist networks. Bin Laden and his key lieutenants reside in Afghanistan, and the group maintains terrorist training camps there.

External Aid
Bin Laden, son of a billionaire Saudi family, is said to have inherited approximately $300 million that he uses to finance the group. Al-Qaida also maintains money-making front organizations, solicits donations from like-minded supporters, and illicitly siphons funds from donations to Muslim charitable organizations.

Revolutionary Armed Forces of Colombia (FARC)

Description
Established in 1964 as the military wing of the Colombian Communist Party, the FARC is Colombia's oldest, largest, most capable, and best-equipped Marxist insurgency. The FARC is governed by a secretariat, led by septuagenarian Manuel Marulanda, a.k.a. "Tirofijo," and six others, including senior military commander Jorge Briceno, a.k.a. "Mono Jojoy." Organized along military lines and includes several urban fronts. In 2000, the group continued a slow-moving peace negotiation process with the Pastrana Administration, which has gained the group several concessions, including a demilitarized zone used as a venue for negotiations.

Activities
Bombings, murder, kidnapping, extortion, hijacking, as well as guerrilla and conventional military action against Colombian political, military, and economic targets. In March 1999 the FARC executed three US Indian rights activists on Venezuelan territory after it kidnapped them in Colombia. Foreign citizens often are targets of FARC kidnapping for ransom. Has well-documented ties to narcotics traffickers, principally through the provision of armed protection.

Strength
Approximately 9,000 to 12,000 armed combatants and an unknown number of supporters, mostly in rural areas.

Location/Area of Operation
Colombia with some activities -- extortion, kidnapping, logistics, and R&R -- in Venezuela, Panama, and Ecuador.

External Aid
Cuba provides some medical care and political consultation.

Revolutionary Organization 17 November (17 November)

Description
Radical leftist group established in 1975 and named for the student uprising in Greece in November 1973 that protested the military regime. Anti-Greek establishment, anti-US, anti-Turkey, anti-NATO, and committed to the ouster of US bases, removal of Turkish military presence from Cyprus, and severing of Greece's ties to NATO and the European Union (EU).

Activities
Initial attacks were assassinations of senior US officials and Greek public figures. Added bombings in 1980s. Since 1990 has expanded targets to include EU facilities and foreign firms investing in Greece and has added improvised rocket attacks to its methods. Most recent attack claimed was the murder in June 2000 of British Defense Attaché Stephen Saunders.

Strength
Unknown, but presumed to be small.

Location/Area of Operation
Athens, Greece.

Revolutionary People's Liberation Party/Front (DHKP/C) a.k.a. Devrimci Sol (Revolutionary Left), Dev Sol

Description
       Originally formed in 1978 as Devrimci Sol, or Dev Sol, a splinter faction of the Turkish People's Liberation Party/Front. Renamed in 1994 after fractional infighting, it espouses a Marxist ideology and is virulently anti-US and anti-NATO. Finances its activities chiefly through armed robberies and extortion.

Activities
       Since the late 1980s has concentrated attacks against current and retired Turkish security and military officials. Began a new campaign against foreign interests in 1990. Assassinated two US military contractors and wounded a US Air Force officer to protest the Gulf war. Launched rockets at US Consulate in Istanbul in 1992. Assassinated prominent Turkish businessman and two others in early 1996, its first significant terrorist act as DHKP/C. Turkish authorities thwarted DHKP/C attempt in June 1999 to fire light antitank weapon at US Consulate in Istanbul. Series of safe house raids, arrests by Turkish police over last two years has weakened group significantly. Turkish security forces stormed prison wards controlled by the DHKP/C in December 2000, transferring militants to cell-type penitentiaries and further undermining DHKP/C cohesion.

Strength
       Unknown.

Location/Area of Operation
       Conducts attacks in Turkey, primarily in Istanbul, Ankara, Izmir, and Adana. Raises funds in Western Europe.

External Aid
       Unknown.

Revolutionary People's Struggle (ELA)

Description
       Extreme leftist group that developed from opposition to the military junta that ruled Greece from 1967 to 1974. Formed in 1971, ELA

is a self-described revolutionary, anti-capitalist, and anti-imperialist group that has declared its opposition to "imperialist domination, exploitation, and oppression." Strongly anti-US and seeks the removal of US military forces from Greece.

Activities

Since 1974 has conducted bombings against Greek Government and economic targets as well as US military and business facilities. In 1986 stepped up attacks on Greek Government and commercial interests. Raid on a safe house in 1990 revealed a weapons cache and direct contacts with other Greek terrorist groups, including 1 May and Revolutionary Solidarity. In 1991, ELA and 1 May claimed joint responsibility for more than 20 bombings. Greek police believe they have established links between ELA and Revolutionary Organization 17 November. Although ELA has not claimed an attack since January 1995, other groups have emerged with similar modus operandi. Of these, Revolutionary Nuclei (a.k.a. Revolutionary Cells) appears most likely to be the successor group to ELA.

Strength

Unknown.

Location/Area of Operation

Greece.

External Aid

Received weapons and other assistance from international terrorist Carlos during 1980s. Currently no known foreign sponsors.

Sendero Luminoso (Shining Path, or SL)

Description

Former university professor Abimael Guzman formed Sendero Luminoso in the late 1960s, and his teachings created the foundation of SL's militant Maoist doctrine. In the 1980s, SL became one of the most ruthless terrorist groups in the Western Hemisphere. Approximately 30,000 persons have died since Shining Path took up arms in 1980. Its stated goal is to destroy existing Peruvian institutions and replace them with a communist peasant revolutionary regime. It also opposes any influence by foreign governments, as well as by other Latin American guerrilla groups, especially the Tupac Amaru Revolutionary Movement (MRTA). In 2000, government authorities continued to arrest and prosecute active SL members, including, in April, commander Jose Arcela Chiroque, a.k.a. Ormeno. Counterterrorist operations targeted pockets of terrorist activity in the Upper Huallaga River Valley and the Apurimac/Ene River Valley, where SL columns continued to conduct periodic attacks.

Activities
Conducted indiscriminate bombing campaigns and selective assassinations. Detonated explosives at diplomatic missions of several countries in Peru in 1990, including an attempt to car-bomb the US Embassy in December. SL continued in 2000 to clash with Peruvian authorities and military units in the countryside and conducted periodic raids on villages. Despite numerous threats, the remaining active SL guerrillas were unable to cause any significant disruption to the Peruvian national elections held on 9 April.

Strength
Membership is unknown but estimated to be 100 to 200 armed militants. SL's strength has been vastly diminished by arrests and desertions.

Location/Area of Operation
Peru, with most activity in rural areas.

External Aid
None.

Tupac Amaru Revolutionary Movement (MRTA)

Description
Traditional Marxist-Leninist revolutionary movement formed in 1983 from remnants of the Movement of the Revolutionary Left, a Peruvian insurgent group active in the 1960s. Aims to establish a Marxist regime and to rid Peru of all imperialist elements (primarily US and Japanese influence). Peru's counterterrorist program has diminished the group's ability to carry out terrorist attacks, and the MRTA has suffered

from infighting, the imprisonment or deaths of senior leaders, and loss of leftist support. Several MRTA members also remain imprisoned in Bolivia.

Activities

Previously conducted bombings, kidnappings, ambushes, and assassinations, but recent activity has fallen drastically. In December 1996, 14 MRTA members occupied the Japanese Ambassador's residence in Lima and held 72 hostages for more than four months. Peruvian forces stormed the residence in April 1997, rescuing all but one of the remaining hostages and killing all 14 group members, including the remaining leaders. The group has not conducted a significant terrorist operation since and appears more focused on obtaining the release of imprisoned MRTA members.

Strength

Believed to be no more than 100 members, consisting largely of young fighters who lack leadership skills and experience.

Location/Area of Operation

Peru with supporters throughout Latin America and Western Europe. Controls no territory.

External Aid

None.

II.   Other Terrorist Groups

Alex Boncayao Brigade (ABB)

Description

The ABB, the breakaway urban hit squad of the Communist Party of the Philippines New People's Army, was formed in the mid-1980s.

Activities

Responsible for more than 100 murders and believed to have been involved in the murder in 1989 of US Army Col. James Rowe in the Philippines. In March 1997 the group announced it had formed an alliance with another armed group, the Revolutionary Proletarian Army. In March

2000, the group claimed credit for a rifle grenade attack against the Department of Energy building in Manila and strafed Shell Oil offices in the central Philippines to protest rising oil prices.

Strength
Approximately 500.

Location/Area of Operation
Operates in Manila and central Philippines.

External Aid
Unknown.

Army for the Liberation of Rwanda (ALIR)
a.k.a. Interahamwe, Former Armed Forces (ex-FAR)

Description
The FAR was the army of the Rwandan Hutu regime that carried out the genocide of 500,000 or more Tutsis and regime opponents in 1994. The Interahamwe was the civilian militia force that carried out much of the killing. The groups merged after they were forced from Rwanda into the Democratic Republic of the Congo (then Zaire) in 1994. They are now often known as the Army for the Liberation of Rwanda (ALIR), which is the armed branch of the PALIR or Party for the Liberation of Rwanda.

Activities
The group seeks to topple Rwanda's Tutsi-dominated government, reinstitute Hutu control, and, possibly, complete the genocide. In 1996, a message -- allegedly from the ALIR -- threatened to kill the US Ambassador to Rwanda and other US citizens. In 1999, ALIR guerrillas critical of alleged US-UK support for the Rwandan regime kidnapped and killed eight foreign tourists, including two US citizens, in a game park on the Congo-Uganda border. In the current Congolese war, the ALIR is allied with Kinshasa against the Rwandan invaders.

Strength
Several thousand ALIR regular forces operate alongside the Congolese Army on the front lines of the Congo civil war, while a like

number of ALIR guerrillas operate behind Rwanda lines in eastern Congo closer to the Rwandan border and sometimes within Rwanda.

Location/Area of Operation
Mostly Democratic Republic of the Congo and Rwanda, but a few may operate in Burundi.

External Support
From the Rwandan invasion of 1998 until his death in early 2001, the Laurent Kabila regime in the Democratic Republic of the Congo provided the ALIR with training, arms, and supplies.

Continuity Irish Republican Army (CIRA) a.k.a. Continuity Army Council

Description
Radical terrorist splinter group formed in 1994 as the clandestine armed wing of Republican Sinn Fein (RSF), a political organization dedicated to the reunification of Ireland and to forcing British troops from Northern Ireland. RSF formed after the Irish Republican Army announced a cease-fire in September 1994.

Activities
Bombings, assassinations, extortion, and robberies. Targets include British military and Northern Ireland security targets and Northern Ireland Loyalist paramilitary groups. Also has launched bomb attacks against civilian targets in Northern Ireland. Does not have an established presence or capability to launch attacks on the UK mainland.

Strength
Fewer than 50 hard-core activists.

Location/Area of Operation
Northern Ireland, Irish Republic.

External Aid
Suspected of receiving funds and arms from sympathizers in the United States. May have acquired arms and materiel from the Balkans in cooperation with the Real IRA.

First of October Antifascist Resistance Group (GRAPO)
Grupo de Resistencia Anti-Fascista Premero de Octubre

Description
 Formed in 1975 as the armed wing of the illegal Communist Party of Spain of the Franco era. Advocating the overthrow of the Spanish Government and replacement with a Marxist-Leninist regime, GRAPO is vehemently anti-US, calls for the removal of all US military forces from Spanish territory, and has conducted and attempted several attacks against US targets since 1977.

Activities
 GRAPO has killed more than 80 persons and injured more than 200. The group's operations customarily have been designed to cause material damage and gain publicity rather than inflict casualties, but the terrorists have conducted lethal bombings and close-range assassinations. In November 2000, GRAPO operatives shot to death a Spanish policeman in reprisal for the arrest that month in France of several group leaders, while in May, GRAPO operatives murdered two guards during a botched robbery against an armored security van.

Strength
 Unknown but likely fewer than a dozen hard-core activists. Numerous GRAPO members also currently are in Spanish prisons.

Location/Area of Operation
 Spain.

External Aid
 None.

Irish Republican Army (IRA)
a.k.a. Provisional Irish Republican Army (PIRA), the Provos

Description
 Terrorist group formed in 1969 as clandestine armed wing of Sinn Fein, a legal political movement dedicated to removing British forces from

Northern Ireland and unifying Ireland. Has a Marxist orientation. Organized into small, tightly knit cells under the leadership of the Army Council.

Activities
Bombings, assassinations, kidnappings, punishment beatings, extortion, smuggling, and robberies. Targets have included senior British Government officials, British military and police in Northern Ireland, and Northern Ireland Loyalist paramilitary groups. Bombing campaigns have been conducted against train and subway stations and shopping areas on mainland Britain, as well as against British and Royal Ulster Constabulary targets in Northern Ireland, and a British military facility on the European Continent. The IRA has been observing a cease-fire since July 1997 and previously observed a cease-fire from 1 September 1994 to February 1996.

Strength
Largely unchanged -- several hundred members, plus several thousand sympathizers -- despite the defection of some members to the dissident splinter groups.

Local/Area of Operation
Northern Ireland, Irish Republic, Great Britain, Europe.

External Aid
Has in the past received aid from a variety of groups and countries and considerable training and arms from Libya and the PLO. Is suspected of receiving funds, arms, and other terrorist-related materiel from sympathizers in the United States. Similarities in operations suggest links to the ETA.

Jaish-e-Mohammed (JEM) (Army of Mohammed)

Description
The Jaish-e-Mohammed (JEM) is an Islamic group based in Pakistan that has rapidly expanded in size and capability since Maulana Masood Azhar, a former ultrafundamentalist Harakat ul-Ansar (HUA) leader, announced its formation in February. The group's aim is to unite

Kashmir with Pakistan. It is politically aligned with the radical, pro-Taliban, political party, Jamiat-i lema-i Islam (JUI-F).

Activities

The JEM's leader, Masood Azhar, was released from Indian imprisonment in December 1999 in exchange for 155 hijacked Indian Airlines hostages in Afghanistan. The 1994 HUA kidnappings of US and British nationals in New Delhi and the July 1995 HUA/Al Faran kidnappings of Westerners in Kashmir were two of several previous HUA efforts to free Azhar. Azhar organized large rallies and recruitment drives across Pakistan throughout 2000. In July, a JEM rocket-grenade attack failed to injure the Chief Minister at his office in Srinagar, India, but wounded four other persons. In December, JEM militants launched grenade attacks at a bus stop in Kupwara, India, injuring 24 persons, and at a marketplace in Chadoura, India, injuring 16 persons. JEM militants also planted two bombs that killed 21 persons in Qamarwari and Srinagar.

Strength

Has several hundred armed supporters located in Azad Kashmir, Pakistan, and in India's southern Kashmir and Doda regions. Following Maulana Masood Azhar's release from detention in India, a reported three quarters of Harakat ul-Mujahedin (HUM) members defected to the new organization, which has managed to attract a large number of urban Kashmiri youth.

Supporters are mostly Pakistanis and Kashmiris and also include Afghans and Arab veterans of the Afghan war. Uses light and heavy machine guns, assault rifles, mortars, improvised explosive devices, and rocket grenades.

Location/Area of Operation

Based in Peshawar and Muzaffarabad, but members conduct terrorist activities primarily in Kashmir. The JEM maintains training camps in Afghanistan.

External Aid

Most of the JEM's cadre and material resources have been drawn from the militant groups Harakat ul-Jihad al-Islami (HUJI) and the Harakat ul-Mujahedin (HUM). The JEM has close ties to Afghan Arabs and the Taliban. Osama bin Laden is suspected of giving funding to the JEM.

Lashkar-e-Tayyiba (LT) (Army of the Righteous)

Description
The LT is the armed wing of the Pakistan-based religious organization, Markaz-ud-Dawa-wal-Irshad (MDI) -- a Sunni anti-US missionary organization formed in 1989. One of the three largest and best-trained groups fighting in Kashmir against India, it is not connected to a political party. The LT leader is MDI chief, Professor Hafiz Mohammed Saeed.

Activities
Has conducted a number of operations against Indian troops and civilian targets in Kashmir since 1993. The LT is suspected of eight separate attacks in August that killed nearly 100, mostly Hindu Indians. LT militants are suspected of kidnapping six persons in Akhala, India, in November 2000 and killing five of them. The group also operates a chain of religious schools in the Punjab.

Strength
Has several hundred members in Azad Kashmir, Pakistan, and in India's southern Kashmir and Doda regions. Almost all LT cadres are foreigners -- mostly Pakistanis from seminaries across the country and Afghan veterans of the Afghan wars. Uses assault rifles, light and heavy machine guns, mortars, explosives, and rocket propelled grenades.

Location/Area of Operation
Based in Muridke (near Lahore) and Muzaffarabad. The LT trains its militants in mobile training camps across Pakistan-administered Kashmir and Afghanistan.

External Aid
Collects donations from the Pakistani community in the Persian Gulf and United Kingdom, Islamic NGOs, and Pakistani and Kashmiri businessmen. The amount of LT funding is unknown. The LT maintains ties to religious/military groups around the world, ranging from the Philippines to the Middle East and Chechnya through the MDI fraternal network.

Loyalist Volunteer Force (LVF)

Description
      Terrorist group formed in 1996 as a faction of the mainstream loyalist Ulster Volunteer Force (UVF) but did not emerge publicly until February 1997. Composed largely of UVF hard-liners who have sought to prevent a political settlement with Irish nationalists in Northern Ireland by attacking Catholic politicians, civilians, and Protestant politicians who endorse the Northern Ireland peace process. Has been observing a cease-fire since 15 May 1998. The LVF decommissioned a small but significant amount of weapons in December 1998, but it has not repeated this gesture and in fact threatened in 2000 to resume killing Catholics.

Activities
      Bombings, kidnappings, and close-quarter shooting attacks. LVF bombs often have contained Powergel commercial explosives, typical of many loyalist groups. LVF attacks have been particularly vicious: the group has murdered numerous Catholic civilians with no political or terrorist affiliations, including an 18-year-old Catholic girl in July 1997 because she had a Protestant boyfriend. The terrorists also have conducted successful attacks against Irish targets in Irish border towns. In 2000, the LVF also engaged in a brief but violent feud with other loyalists in which several individuals were killed.

Strength
      Approximately 150 activists.

Location/Area of Operation
      Northern Ireland, Ireland.

External Aid
      None.

New People's Army (NPA)

Description
      The military wing of the Communist Party of the Philippines (CPP), the NPA is a Maoist group formed in March 1969 with the aim of overthrowing the government through protracted guerrilla warfare.

Although primarily a rural-based guerrilla group, the NPA has an active urban infrastructure to conduct terrorism and uses city-based assassination squads called sparrow units. Derives most of its funding from contributions of supporters and so-called revolutionary taxes extorted from local businesses.

Activities

The NPA primarily targets Philippine security forces, corrupt politicians, and drug traffickers. Opposes any US military presence in the Philippines and attacked US military interests before the US base closures in 1992. Press reports in 1999 indicated that the NPA would target US troops participating in joint military exercises under the Visiting Forces Agreement and US Embassy personnel.

Strength

Estimated between 6,000 and 8,000.

Location/Area of Operations

Operates in rural Luzon, Visayas, and parts of Mindanao. Has cells in Manila and other metropolitan centers.

External Aid

Unknown.

Orange Volunteers (OV)

Description

Terrorist group comprised largely of disgruntled loyalist hard-liners who split from groups observing the cease-fire. OV seeks to prevent a political settlement with Irish nationalists by attacking Catholic civilian interests in Northern Ireland.

Activities

The OV declared a cease-fire in September 2000, but the group maintains ability to conduct bombings, arson, beatings, and possibly robberies.

Strength
      Up to 20 hard-core members, some of whom are experienced in
terrorist tactics and bomb making.

Location/Area of Operations
      Northern Ireland.

External Aid
      None.

People Against Gangsterism and Drugs (PAGAD)

Description
      PAGAD was formed in 1996 as a community anti-crime group
fighting drugs and violence in the Cape Flats section of Cape Town but by
early 1998 had also become anti-government and anti-Western. PAGAD
and its Islamic ally Qibla view the South African Government as a threat
to Islamic values and consequently promote greater political voice for
South African Muslims.
      The group is led by Abdus Salaam Ebrahim. PAGAD's G-Force
(Gun Force) operates in small cells and is believed responsible for
carrying out acts of terrorism. PAGAD uses several front names, including
Muslims Against Global Oppression (MAGO) and Muslims Against
Illegitimate Leaders (MAIL), when launching anti-Western protests and
campaigns.

Activities
      PAGAD is suspected of conducting recurring bouts of urban
terrorism -- particularly bomb sprees -- in Cape Town since 1998,
including nine bombings in 2000. Bombing targets have included South
African authorities, moderate Muslims, synagogues, gay nightclubs,
tourist attractions, and Western-associated restaurants. PAGAD is
believed to have masterminded the bombing on 25 August 1998 of the
Cape Town Planet Hollywood.

Strength
      Estimated at several hundred members. PAGAD's G-Force
probably contains fewer than 50 members.

Location/Area of Operation
Operates mainly in the Cape Town area, South Africa's foremost tourist venue.

External Aid
Probably has ties to Islamic extremists in the Middle East.

Real IRA (RIRA)
a.k.a. True IRA

Description
Formed in February-March 1998 as clandestine armed wing of the 32-County Sovereignty Movement, a "political pressure group" dedicated to removing British forces from Northern Ireland and unifying Ireland. The 32-County Sovereignty Movement opposed Sinn Fein's adoption in September 1997 of the Mitchell principles of democracy and nonviolence and opposed the December 1999 amendment of Articles 2 and 3 of the Irish Constitution, which lay claim to Northern Ireland. Former IRA "quartermaster general" Mickey McKevitt leads the group; Bernadette Sands-McKevitt, his common-law wife, is the vice-chair of the 32-County Sovereignty Movement.

Activities
Bombings, assassinations, smuggling, extortion, and robberies. Many Real IRA members are former IRA who opposed the IRA's cease-fire and bring to RIRA a wealth of experience in terrorist tactics and bomb making. Targets include British military and police in Northern Ireland and Northern Ireland civilian targets. Has attempted several unsuccessful bomb attacks on the UK mainland. Claimed responsibility for the car bomb attack in Omagh, Northern Ireland, on 15 August 1998 that killed 29 and injured 220 persons. The group declared a cease-fire following Omagh but in early 2000 resumed attacks in Northern Ireland and on the UK mainland. These include a bombing of Hammersmith Bridge and a rocket attack against MI-6 headquarters in London.

Strength
150 to 200 activists plus possible limited support from IRA hard-liners dissatisfied with the IRA cease-fire and other republican sympathizers.

Location/Area of Operation
    Northern Ireland, Irish Republic, Great Britain.

External Aid
    Suspected of receiving funds from sympathizers in the United States. RIRA also is thought to have purchased sophisticated weapons from the Balkans, according to press reports.

Red Hand Defenders (RHD)

Description
    Extremist terrorist group composed largely of Protestant hard-liners from loyalist groups observing a cease-fire. RHD seeks to prevent a political settlement with Irish nationalists by attacking Catholic civilian interests in Northern Ireland.

Activities
    RHD was quiet in 2000, following a damaging security crackdown in late 1999. In recent years, however, the group has carried out numerous pipe bombings and arson attacks against "soft" civilian targets, such as homes, churches, and private businesses, to cause outrage in the Republican community and to provoke IRA retaliation. RHD claimed responsibility for the car-bombing murder on 15 March 1999 of Rosemary Nelson, a prominent Catholic nationalist lawyer and human rights campaigner in Northern Ireland.

Strength
    Up to 20 members, some of whom have considerable experience in terrorist tactics and bomb making.

Location/Area of Operation
    Northern Ireland.

External Aid
    None.

Revolutionary United Front (RUF)

Description
The RUF is a loosely organized group -- but an effective guerrilla force because of its flexibility and brutal discipline -- seeking to topple the current government of Sierra Leone and to retain control of the lucrative diamond-producing regions of the country. The group funds itself largely through the extraction and sale of diamonds obtained in areas of Sierra Leone that it controls.

Activities
The RUF uses guerrilla, criminal, and terror tactics, such as murder, torture, and mutilation, to fight the government, intimidate civilians, and keep UN peacekeeping units in check. In 2000 they held hundreds of UN peacekeepers hostage until their release was negotiated, in part, by the RUF's chief sponsor Liberian President Charles Taylor. The group also has been accused of attacks in Guinea at the behest of President Taylor.

Strength
Estimated at several thousand fighters and possibly a similar number of supporters and sympathizers.

Location/Area of Operation
Sierra Leone, Liberia, Guinea.

External Aid
A UN experts panel report on Sierra Leone said President Charles Taylor of Liberia provides support and leadership to the RUF. The UN has identified Libya, Gambia, and Burkina Faso as conduits for weapons and other materiel for the RUF.

United Self-Defense Forces/Group of Colombia (AUC-Autodefensas Unidas de Colombia)

Description
The AUC -- commonly referred to as autodefensas or paramilitaries -- is an umbrella organization formed in April 1997 to consolidate most local and regional paramilitary groups each with the

mission to protect economic interests and combat insurgents locally. The AUC -- supported by economic elites, drug traffickers, and local communities lacking effective government security -- claims its primary objective is to protect its sponsors from insurgents. The AUC now asserts itself as a regional and national counterinsurgent force. It is adequately equipped and armed and reportedly pays its members a monthly salary. AUC leader Carlos Castaño in 2000 claimed 70 percent of the AUC's operational costs were financed with drug-related earnings, the rest from "donations" from its sponsors.

Activities
        AUC operations vary from assassinating suspected insurgent supporters to engaging guerrilla combat units. Colombian National Police reported the AUC conducted 804 assassinations, 203 kidnappings, and 75 massacres with 507 victims during the first 10 months of 2000. The AUC claims the victims were guerrillas or sympathizers. Combat tactics consist of conventional and guerrilla operations against main force insurgent units. AUC clashes with military and police units are increasing, although the group has traditionally avoided government security forces. The paramilitaries have not taken action against US personnel.

Strength
        In early 2001, the government estimated there were 8,000 paramilitary fighters, including former military and insurgent personnel.

Location/Areas of Operation
        AUC forces are strongest in the north and northwest: Antioquia, Cordoba, Sucre, Bolivar, Atlantico, and Magdalena Departments. Since 1999, the group demonstrated a growing presence in other northeastern and southwestern departments and a limited presence in the Amazon plains. Clashes between the AUC and the FARC insurgents in Putumayo in 2000 demonstrated the range of the AUC to contest insurgents throughout Colombia.

External Aid
        None.

APPENDIX L
US Counterterrorism Efforts

The United States Government is engaged in a long-term struggle against international terrorism. We use a wide variety of foreign policy tools, from military force when necessary, to vigorous diplomacy, law enforcement, improvements in US security, and the development of new technology. In cooperation with other governments, we go after terrorist finances, shut down illegal activities, restrict travel, disrupt training, break up support cells, and bring suspects to justice.

Our determination to bring terrorists to justice was rewarded in April 1999 when the two Libyan suspects in the Pan Am 103 bombing were turned over for trial. This was the result of a sustained, eight-year-long international effort to put pressure on Libya to comply with UN Security Council requirements in this case.

Since 1993, a dozen suspected international terrorist fugitives have been apprehended overseas and turned over to the United States to stand trial for various terrorist crimes.

Two Presidential Directives were issued in 1998 to coordinate efforts to prevent and respond to unconventional attacks, and to shield our information and transportation facilities.

The President signed an Executive Order imposing financial and other commercial sanctions on the Afghan Taliban for its support of Osama bin Laden and his terrorist network.

In addition, as stated above, the Secretary of State has formally designated 30 foreign terrorist organizations, making it illegal for US citizens and institutions to provide funds or other forms of material support to such groups.

The United States is engaged in a vigorous campaign to promote the universal adoption and ratification of all eleven existing international terrorist conventions. Every nation has the responsibility to arrest or expel terrorists, shut down their finances, and deny them safe haven. Our goal is to strengthen the rule of law against terrorism globally.

In June 1999 the State Department hosted an important counterterrorism conference that included representatives from 22 nations in the Middle East, South Asia, Central Asia, Europe, and Canada. The conference promoted international cooperation against terrorism and the sharing of information on terrorist groups and countermeasures.

The United States conducts the successful Anti-terrorism Training Assistance program, which trains foreign law enforcement personnel in such areas as airport security, bomb detection, maritime security, VIP protection, hostage rescue, and crisis management. To date, we have trained more than 20,000 representatives from more than 100 countries.

We also conduct an active research and development program to adapt modern technology for use in defeating terrorists.

APPENDIX M
National Commission on Terrorism Recommendations

The full Report, which was issued on June 5, 2000, is available at:
http://www.fas.org/irp/threat/commission.html

EXECUTIVE SUMMARY

International terrorism poses an increasingly dangerous and difficult threat to America. This was underscored by the December 1999 arrests in Jordan and at the US/Canadian border of foreign nationals who were allegedly planning to attack crowded millennium celebrations.

Today's terrorists seek to inflict mass casualties, and they are attempting to do so both overseas and on American soil. They are less dependent on state sponsorship and are, instead, forming loose, transnational affiliations based on religious or ideological affinity and a common hatred of the United States. This makes terrorist attacks more difficult to detect and prevent.

Countering the growing danger of the terrorist threat requires significantly stepping up US efforts. The government must immediately take steps to reinvigorate the collection of intelligence about terrorists' plans, use of all available legal avenues to disrupt and prosecute terrorist activities and private sources of support, convince other nations to cease all support for terrorists, and ensure that federal, state, and local officials are prepared for attacks that may result in mass casualties. The Commission has made a number of recommendations to accomplish these objectives:

- ◆ CIA (Central Intelligence Agency) guidelines adopted in 1995 restricting recruitment of unsavory sources should not apply when recruiting counterterrorism sources.
- ◆ The Attorney General should ensure that the FBI (Federal Bureau of Investigation) is exercising fully its authority for investigating

suspected terrorist groups or individuals, including authority for electronic surveillance.

♦ Funding for counterterrorism efforts by the CIA, NSA (National Security Agency), and FBI must be given higher priority to ensure continuation of important operational activity and to close the technology gap that threatens their ability to collect and exploit terrorist communications.

♦ The FBI should establish a cadre of reports officers to distill and disseminate terrorism-related information once it is collected. US policies must firmly target all states that support terrorists.

♦ Iran and Syria should be kept on the list of state sponsors until they stop supporting terrorists.

♦ Afghanistan should be designated a sponsor of terrorism and subjected to all the sanctions applicable to state sponsors.

♦ The President should impose sanctions on countries that, while not direct sponsors of terrorism, are nevertheless not cooperating fully on counterterrorism. Candidates for consideration include Pakistan and Greece.

♦ Private sources of financial and logistical support for terrorists must be subjected to the full force and sweep of the US and international laws.

♦ All relevant agencies should use every available means, including the full array of criminal, civil, and administrative sanctions to block or disrupt non-governmental sources of support for international terrorism.

♦ Congress should promptly ratify and implement the International Convention for the Suppression of the Financing of Terrorism to enhance international cooperative efforts.

♦ Where criminal prosecution is not possible, the Attorney General should vigorously pursue the expulsion of terrorists from the United States through proceedings which protect both the national security interest in safeguarding classified evidence and the right of the accused to challenge that evidence.

♦ A terrorist attack involving a biological agent, deadly chemicals, or nuclear or radiological material, even if it succeeds only partially, could profoundly affect the entire nation. The government must do more to prepare for such an event.

◆ The President should direct the preparation of a manual to guide the implementation of existing legal authority in the event of a catastrophic terrorist threat or attack. The President and Congress should determine whether additional legal authority is needed to deal with catastrophic terrorism.

◆ The Department of Defense (DOD) must have detailed plans for its role in the event of a catastrophic terrorist attack, including criteria for decisions on transfer of command authority to DOD in extraordinary circumstances.

◆ Senior officials of all government agencies involved in responding to a catastrophic terrorism threat or crisis should be required to participate in national exercises every year to test capabilities and coordination.

◆ Congress should make it illegal for anyone not properly certified to possess certain critical pathogens and should enact laws to control the transfer of equipment critical to the development or use of biological agents.

◆ The President should establish a comprehensive and coordinated long-term research and development program for catastrophic terrorism.

◆ The Secretary of State should press for an international convention to improve multilateral cooperation on preventing or responding to cyberattacks by terrorists.

◆ The President and Congress should reform the system for reviewing and funding departmental counterterrorism programs to ensure that the activities and programs of various agencies are part of a comprehensive plan.

◆ The executive branch official responsible for coordinating counterterrorism efforts across the government should be given a stronger hand in the budget process.

◆ Congress should develop a mechanism for a comprehensive review of the President's counterterrorism policy and budget.

POSTSCRIPT: TERRORISTS ATTACK AMERICA

September 11, 2001, will go down in American history as another *"Day of Infamy."*

Two passenger planes were hijacked from Boston, Massachusetts, and were intentionally crashed by the terrorists into both of the 110-story twin towers of the World Trade Center in New York City. Both buildings soon collapsed. An ancillary building collapsed later.

A passenger plane hijacked from Washington's Dulles Airport crashed into the Department of Defense's Pentagon office building in Virginia outside Washington, D.C. A fourth plane, hijacked from Newark International in Newark, New Jersey, whose intended mission is unknown, crashed in a rural area of Pennsylvania.

Thousands were killed in the various incidents, including passengers, emergency responders and building occupants. The complete United States air transport system was closed down.

President George W. Bush and other government leaders of both political parties pledged to find those responsible and appropriately punish them. Suspects were taken into custody by the FBI the day following the events.

The vulnerabilities of US airports, which were described in the Editor's Notes following Chapter 6, contributed to the terrorists' ability to carry out these vicious attacks. Chapter 15 covered the February 1993 attack on the World Trade center.

This postscript is being written the day following these attacks, so information on numbers of victims and the results of on-going investigations is fragmentary. It is clear, however, that this attack on the World Trade Center incorporated lessons which the terrorists learned from the failure of the 1993 terrorist attack to topple the towers.

First responders and other emergency personnel throughout the United States must also learn lessons from these events as well as from the preceding information in this book.

Everything
You Need to
Know About

Measles and Rubella

Measles and rubella have plagued people around the world for thousands of years. This Japanese woodcut shows people trampling the measles demon.

Everything You Need to Know About

Measles and Rubella

Trisha Hawkins

The Rosen Publishing Group, Inc.
New York

For Elizabeth Duffy Hawkins

Published in 2001 by The Rosen Publishing Group, Inc.
29 East 21st Street, New York, NY 10010

Library of Congress Cataloging-in-Publication Data

Hawkins, Trisha.
    Everything you need to know about measles and rubella / by Trisha Hawkins. — 1st ed.
        p. cm. — (The need to know library)
Includes bibliographical references (p.) and index.
        ISBN 0-8239-3322-9 (library binding)
    1. Measles—Juvenile literature. 2. Rubella—Juvenile literature. [1. Measles. 2. Rubella. 3. Diseases.] I. Title. II. Series.
    RC168 .M4 H39 2000
    616.9'15—dc21

                                                        00-009721

Manufactured in the United States of America

Contents

	Introduction	6
Chapter One	**Understanding Measles**	**10**
Chapter Two	**Understanding Rubella**	**23**
Chapter Three	**Why Does Vaccination Work?**	**29**
Chapter Four	**Getting Your MMR Shots**	**39**
Chapter Five	**Measles, Rubella, and the People of the World**	**46**
	Glossary	**56**
	Where to Go for Help	**58**
	For Further Reading	**61**
	Index	**63**

Introduction

Measles and rubella are infectious diseases. Conditions such as heart disease and diabetes can be lifelong, chronic problems, but they cannot be passed from one person to another. You cannot "catch" heart disease or diabetes. But you can catch measles very easily if you haven't had your measles shots. It's one of the most highly contagious diseases in the world. Contagious, or infectious, means it can spread from person to person. Highly contagious means it can spread like wildfire. As recently as 1999, a million kids died of measles in countries around the world.

Measles and rubella are ancient. They have been making people sick every year in human history since around 2500 BC. Before that date, the homes of human beings were scattered over the countryside; after that date, people started living in towns and cities. They came into closer contact with each other. Closer contact brought more trade, more culture, more communication, and more services. But it also brought more infectious disease.

Sometimes a disease struck a whole community, and became an epidemic. When there's an epidemic, there is a chain of infection. The more people get it, the more chances the disease has to spread. If one person in a family gets it, then everyone in that family is at risk. If many families get sick, soon the whole town or country is infected. Throughout human history, there have been epidemics of infectious diseases, including measles, rubella, smallpox, polio, and, in our own day, AIDS.

Kids and young adults are the people who are most often infected by measles and rubella. A doctor who lived in Baghdad around AD 800 thought measles was a natural process kids went through, like losing baby teeth. He was wrong. Measles is not a natural process, it is a serious infectious disease. Measles can make you deaf; it can infect your brain; it can kill. Rubella is dangerous, too; it can infect a child in its mother's womb and cause it to be born with birth defects like mental retardation or blindness.

How does an infectious disease jump from one person to another? For many centuries, no one knew. Over the centuries, millions of children have been infected by disease and died before they had a chance to grow up. Today we know that many infectious diseases are caused by tiny germs called viruses. The viruses that cause measles and rubella are not the most dangerous germs that human beings can be exposed to, but they have been persistent, returning year after year to infect and sometimes to kill.

If you catch measles or rubella, there are no pills you can take or high-tech treatments that you can undergo. There are no cures for these diseases. But luckily there is a very effective way of preventing them. Prevention means that you do something, and because you did it, you won't get sick and you won't make other people sick. How can you prevent measles and rubella? Get vaccinated.

When a doctor or nurse vaccinates you, he or she gives you a shot, injecting vaccine into your body. Vaccination, immunization, getting your shots—they all mean the same thing. Given a choice, most people would say no thanks. Nobody likes to get a needle stuck in his or her arm or thigh. But vaccination works.

If you're reading this book in North America and were born after 1957, chances are you've never had measles. You've probably never had rubella either. You live in a time and place where most people get vaccinated against these two diseases as very young children, and today many people also get the now-required second measles shot. There is even a shot that vaccinates you against both diseases at once. It's called the MMR shot. MMR stands for measles, mumps (which is another infectious disease), and rubella.

Thanks to vaccination, measles and rubella are now quite rare in many countries. It's easy to forget how dangerous they can be. It's easy to take our good health for granted. But if kids stop getting vaccinated, the epidemics of measles and rubella will return. The measles and rubella viruses are not dead. They're just laying low.

Chapter One

Understanding Measles

If you're in good health and you get measles, you will probably be able to make a full recovery. But if your body is not strong enough to fight the disease and win, measles can be dangerous and even deadly. Before doctors and scientists discovered how to vaccinate kids against measles, everyone had to take their chances. You hoped you were strong enough to recover, but you could never be sure.

Measles Time Travel—If You Were You in 1962

Picture this: You're a kid living right there in your town, but it's 1962, and there's no such thing as a measles shot. Every two or three years, in your neighborhood, there's an outbreak of measles. It

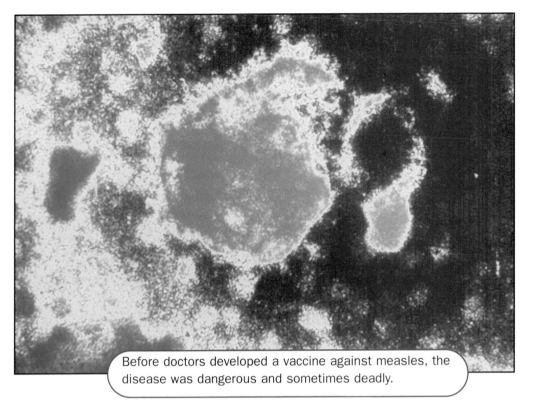

Before doctors developed a vaccine against measles, the disease was dangerous and sometimes deadly.

spreads from one person to another. Teenagers, younger kids, and babies become infected, and some adults, too.

Imagine you're the age you are right now. Some years, so many people get sick, they don't call it an outbreak, they call it an epidemic. It's 1962, and it's one of those years.

The cough might come first, or your eyes might get swollen and red. When you go outside, the light seems too bright. It hurts your eyes. The next day, you're sneezing, and when you blow your nose, you wind up wiping your eyes, too.

Your uncle calls and says that your cousin Gary is sick with measles. He thinks you may get it, too.

But the last time you saw Gary was a week ago. He was fine then, so he couldn't have infected you . . . could he?

The next morning you feel a little warm. You try to act normal but then you start to cough. Your mom feels your forehead and your dad puts a thermometer in your mouth. You've got a fever, it turns out. You tell your parents what your uncle said about Gary being sick, and your mom says there's no mystery anymore about what's wrong with you: You've caught measles from Gary.

Your dad takes you to your room and puts you to bed. He pulls down the shade on the window to protect you from the bright winter sun. "It's measles, all right," he says.

A day later you happen to notice a funny looking spot on the inside of your cheek. When you look closely, you realize that the inside of your mouth is covered with them. Another day goes by, and then the rash starts. First the red spots show up on your forehead and behind your ears. Then they start to spread down over your neck and shoulders. Your fever hits 105 degrees. The family doctor pays you a visit. There's no cure for measles, he tells you, you'll just have to wait it out.

You're in quarantine, isolated from the world. You're not allowed to see your friends because you're contagious, but it could be that you have

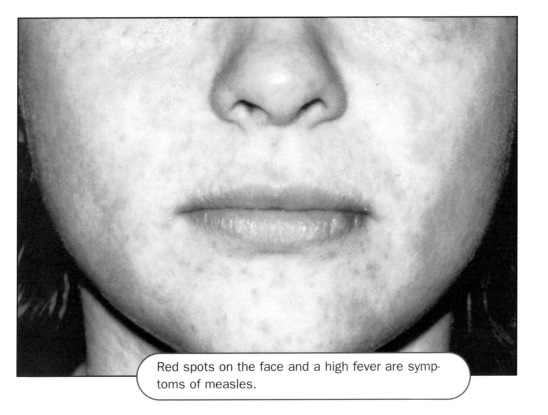

Red spots on the face and a high fever are symptoms of measles.

given it to them already. After all, Gary gave it to you and at the time he seemed perfectly healthy.

Your mom and dad take care of you, bringing you food and liquids and trying to keep your fever down. They've both already had measles, so they are immune—they can't get sick with measles a second time. But they forbid you to have any contact with your baby brother. They're still hoping that he won't catch it. They're hoping that you didn't infect him days ago, before you even knew you were sick.

The spots inside your mouth disappear. The fever finally goes away. You feel stronger. The red rash on your face and body gets dry and peels off.

You look out the window and you want to be out there more than anything, getting on with your life. But it's not time yet. The doctor says that you could still be contagious. You have to wait.

Finally it's over. Your body has won. You're fine. Good as new. You can't infect anyone now, you're not contagious anymore. You go downstairs and walk into the kitchen. Your dad is drinking a cup of coffee. He looks like he has been crying. You ask him what the matter is. Finally he tells you. Your mother is at the hospital; she has been there all night. They've been so afraid for your baby brother. They haven't wanted to worry you. The truth is, your brother is in the hospital, too. He's sick with measles and he is dying.

Viruses

In ancient Rome, a man named Varro had a hunch that diseases were caused by tiny creatures that flew from one person to another. The other people who lived in Rome at that time thought his theory was ridiculous. It wasn't until much later that scientists discovered the truth in Varro's hunch.

We live surrounded by countless tiny microorganisms. Luckily, most of these tiny germs are harmless to us, or even beneficial. But some of them cause infection and disease.

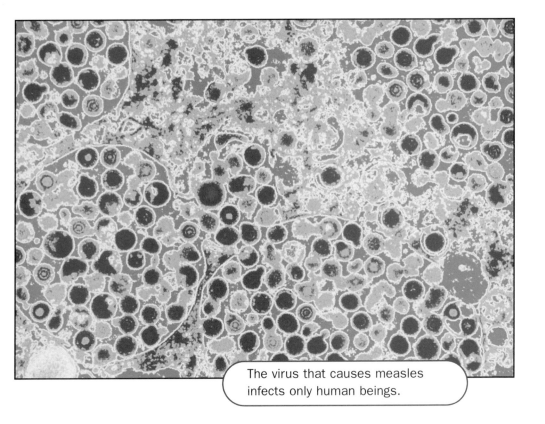

The virus that causes measles infects only human beings.

A Kind of Parasite

All germs are parasites—they live off other living things. They enter and infect a host. The host can be a plant, an animal, or a human being. Germs come in two varieties: (1) bacteria, which are living, single-celled animals and may cause disease, and (2) viruses.

Unlike bacteria, viruses are not animals. They're not plants either. They're in a class by themselves. They are not really alive at all until they enter a living thing, but once they get inside they can take over a host's body like pirates taking over a ship and run it to benefit themselves. Diseases that are caused by different kinds of viruses include measles, rubella, mumps, chicken pox, influenza (the flu), polio, and AIDS. Since we do not have drugs that can cure diseases that are caused by viruses, we must try to use vaccination to prevent them from happening in the first place.

Like every other creature on Earth, viruses want to survive and reproduce. Some viruses first infect animals like rats, ticks, and mosquitoes and then move from there to infect humans. But the measles virus infects only human bodies, usually young bodies. No one knows where and when the chain of infection began, but measles has been living and reproducing inside human beings for thousands of years. No other home will do.

Actually, this is lucky. We can vaccinate all the kids in the world and hope to eventually destroy the measles and rubella viruses by depriving them of their only homes—it would be pretty hard to vaccinate all the ticks and mosquitoes!

Measles: An Acute Infection

Another lucky thing about measles is that you can get it only once. The common cold, which is also caused by a virus, can attack and make you sick over and over again. But measles is an acute infection. You catch it, it incubates in your body, it infects you, and then, if there are no complications, you recover.

These three stages usually take no longer than three weeks. And if you recover, then you can never get measles again: you will be immune. To survive, the virus that causes measles needs a good-sized human population—about 200,000 people—living in close contact with each other. That way it can move from one person to another more easily and always find fresh bodies to infect, year after year.

First You Have to Catch It

Before the virus can infect you, it has to get inside your body. When someone who has measles sneezes or coughs, little drops of moisture spray into the air, sprinkling the measles virus all around. If you happen to breathe in that air or come into contact with the droplets with your mouth or eyes, the virus gets a free ride into your body. Then you "catch" measles. When the measles virus moves into a community, it infects everyone it can. You can even catch the measles virus by walking into an empty room that someone with measles has just spent time in, if you come into contact with the saliva or other respiratory secretions that are still in the air.

Incubation

The symptoms, or outward signs, of measles don't show up until about nine or ten days after the measles virus first enters your body. This waiting period is called the incubation period.

During the incubation period, you may not even know you're sick, but the virus is attaching itself to cells in your respiratory tract and starting to invade

17

A person with measles can spread the virus by coughing or sneezing near other people .

them. Every part of your body is made of different types of cells. A virus can invade only cells that it can fit itself into, like a key into a lock. Unfortunately, many different kinds of human cells have receptors that the measles virus can fit into. That's why measles is so infectious.

Infection—the Battle Begins

When the virus gets inside a human cell, it uses its genetic makeup to take over the cell. The cell is forced to start helping the virus to make copies of itself. Soon there is an army of viruses. This army starts moving through the bloodstream, invading more and more human cells.

Meanwhile, the body starts to fight back. Special cells sound the alarm. They are part of the immune system. Different types of immune system cells fight the virus in different ways. Some of them start making cells called antibodies that are specifically matched up with the invading virus. For instance, in response to the measles virus, the immune system will start making measles antibodies. These specifically created antibodies will help the body fight the measles virus.

Symptoms—Now You Know You're Sick

Early symptoms are tiredness, a runny nose, red eyes, coughing, and a low fever. Then bluish white specks surrounded by bright red areas start to appear inside the mouth.

Two or three days later, you break out in a rash and the fever goes up to around 105 degrees Fahrenheit (40.6 degrees Celsius). The rash starts behind the ears and spreads downward. It is made up of flat red or brown blotches and raised bumps. It lasts for four to seven days. There may be diarrhea, vomiting, and stomach pain. The coughing and sneezing continue. This is the time when the infection can spread most easily to others.

While you're sick, one of the only things a doctor can do for you is to recommend a nonaspirin pain reliever to keep your fever down. (Aspirin is not recommended for an infection caused by a virus.)

Recovery—Now You Are Immune

The rash fades. The fever goes down. And after you have gotten well, some of the measles antibodies that your immune system has made remain in your bloodstream. They will stay there for many years, ready to protect you if the measles virus tries to attack again. Also, special "memory" cells in your immune system will remember this war with the measles virus and what exactly your immune system did to allow you to win it. The measles virus may try to make you sick again, but your body will be too smart. It will fight off the virus so easily that you won't even know it's happening. You will be immune to measles.

Complications—Sometimes It's Not So Easy

But remember, measles is an infectious, highly contagious disease. If you get sick, you may spread the disease to those around you, and there is no cure for measles. The people you infect may be weak; their immune systems may not be as strong as yours. You are now immune—you are lucky. But they may be the unlucky ones for whom getting sick with measles means serious complications, lifelong problems, or even death.

Complications happen when the immune system is too busy fighting off the measles virus to notice that another disease is also attacking the body. With nothing to stop them, these other, secondary infections can be dangerous.

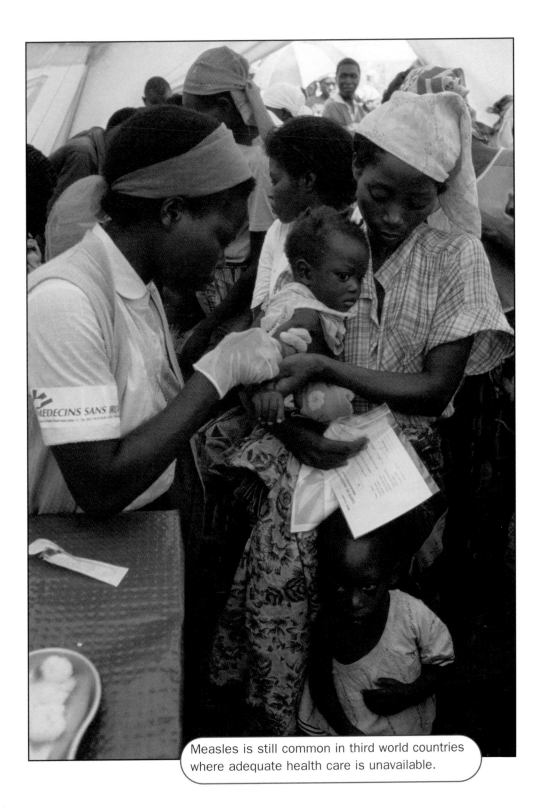

Measles is still common in third world countries where adequate health care is unavailable.

One of the most common complications of measles is pneumonia, an infection of the lungs. Sixty percent of the deaths that result from measles are from pneumonia.

Severe cough, diarrhea, and ear infections are other complications. Inflammation of the brain (encephalitis) occurs in less than 1 in 1,000 people, but 25 percent of those who do get it are left with brain damage.

SSPE (subacute sclerosing panencephalomyelitis) is yet another possible complication. It occurs years after a person is first infected by the virus. SSPE is a brain infection that starts with mental retardation and eventually leads to death. Mercifully, it is extremely rare.

Another danger is that if a woman who is pregnant catches measles, she may lose the baby or the baby may be born prematurely.

Death

One in 3,000 cases of measles ends in death, but in third world countries in Africa and elsewhere, measles is more common and the death rate is much higher. Kids in poorer countries have less money for vaccinations, health care, food, and shelter; and diseases like measles can infect them more easily and more dangerously.

Serious complications and death are most likely in children under the age of twelve months, children with weakened immune systems, and children who are starving or have a poor diet.

Chapter Two

Understanding Rubella

Rubella is sometimes called German measles. During the nineteenth century, a group of German doctors were the first to research the disease. But rubella is not measles. It is caused by the rubella virus. It is a separate disease and is dangerous for different reasons.

A healthy person usually recovers from rubella very quickly and may not even realize they are sick. But if a woman is infected with the rubella virus while she is in the first months of a pregnancy, the virus can infect the baby in her womb. Because of vaccination, rubella, like measles, is quite rare today. But outbreaks do occur.

Gina's Story

I live in Greece. In 1993, I married a boy who lived just down the street. I had known him all my life.

When we were seventeen we realized we loved each other. We got married and pretty soon I got pregnant. Everything went well until partway into the second month, when I got a little sick. I had a cold and a small rash on my face that lasted only a day. I didn't worry about it too much. But when I told the doctor at the clinic about it, he gave me a blood test right away, to check for rubella. He asked me if I had ever been vaccinated against rubella. I said no.

The test came back positive. What I had thought was a cold was the disease of rubella. The doctor told me that many people in Greece had become infected with rubella that year. And he gave me some news that frightened me. I had caught rubella in the second month of my pregnancy, and the doctor said there was a seven out of ten chance that my baby had been infected in my womb and would suffer from congenital rubella syndrome (CRS). A congenital disease is one that you are born with. If my daughter was born with CRS, she might be born blind, with cataracts covering her eyes; she might be born deaf; or she might develop bone disease or mental retardation. The doctor was very sad, but he suggested that I have an abortion. It was the best choice, under the circumstances, he said.

My husband and I stayed up fifty hours straight, making our decision. Finally we decided

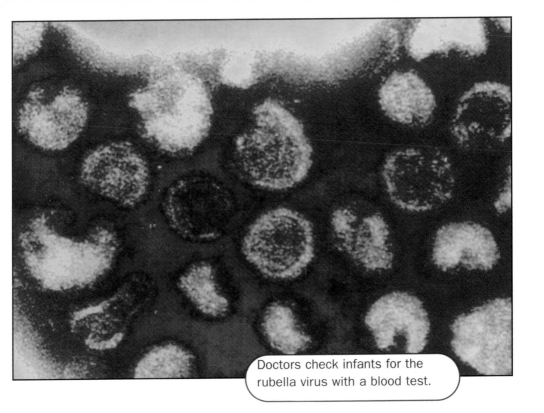

Doctors check infants for the rubella virus with a blood test.

I would go ahead with the pregnancy. During the next six months we prayed every night.

When I gave birth to our daughter, we felt blessed. The doctor examined her and tested her blood for the virus. He found no trace of rubella in her body. That's the only time I've ever seen my husband cry—he was crying with joy! We named our daughter Sofia. She has developed normally and is a smart, beautiful girl. And, of course, we have made sure that she has her vaccinations against rubella.

Greece learned its lesson from that epidemic of rubella. Now doctors in my country and all over the world know that all teenagers, especially young girls at the beginning of their childbearing years, must be immunized against rubella. Many people get the rubella shot when they are a baby, but it is so important that young girls make sure they have been vaccinated. I tell everyone in my town, the best protection is to get the second rubella shot, too. If you've been vaccinated twice, you are sure to be immune. I was lucky in 1993, but other girls who were pregnant that year had babies with congenital rubella syndrome. Others had abortions. Whatever country you live in, learn from what happened to me!

Rubella—Infection and Symptoms

You catch rubella the same way that you catch measles. Tiny droplets, which are released whenever someone who has the disease coughs or sneezes, carry the rubella virus from one human being to another. The rubella virus invades your body the same way the measles virus does. But rubella is not as contagious as measles, and living through it does not make you quite as miserable.

The first symptoms of rubella are like having a cold. There is a low fever. If and when the rash develops, it may last for one to five days. This rash is fine and pink, and spreads from the forehead and face downward. Some of the lymph nodes may become enlarged, especially

Rubella is especially dangerous to pregnant women and their unborn children.

behind the ears and on the back of the head. Teenage girls and adult women sometimes develop pain and swelling in the large joints of their bodies.

Rubella: A Danger to Pregnant Women

Rubella is a very serious threat if you are a pregnant woman. If a woman is infected with rubella while she is in the first trimester (first four months) of her pregnancy, she may miscarry, or the baby may be stillborn or born prematurely.

If the baby is born, it may have been infected with rubella while it was in its mother's womb. This is the most heartbreaking outcome of rubella: congenital rubella syndrome (CRS).

Congenital Rubella Syndrome

One out of every four babies whose mothers are infected with rubella during the first trimester of pregnancy is born with CRS. The earlier a woman is infected, the greater the risk to her child. A baby with this disease may suffer from many different kinds of birth defects, including mental retardation, cataracts, deafness, heart problems, or bone lesions. A child can die of CRS.

In 1941 an Australian doctor named Norman Gregg discovered that rubella causes congenital rubella syndrome. But it wasn't until 1969 that the rubella vaccine was licensed and made available in the United States. Today it is included in the MMR (measles, mumps, and rubella) shot. Protection against rubella is one more reason to make sure you have had your first and second MMR vaccinations, especially if you are female and in or approaching your childbearing years. If you're a girl age eleven or twelve or older, be especially sure you have had two doses of rubella vaccine. With high immunization levels—if enough people get vaccinated—the rubella virus will be stuck without enough human bodies to keep itself alive.

Chapter Three | Why Does Vaccination Work?

When you are vaccinated against a disease like measles, rubella, polio, or the flu, you become immune to that disease. Vaccination prevents you from getting sick. Vaccination saves lives around the world. Why is vaccination so effective? How does it work?

A Vaccine Stimulates Your Immune System

The substance that a doctor or nurse puts into the syringe and injects into your arm or thigh is called a vaccine. When the doctor presses on the plunger part of the syringe, it pushes the vaccine through the needle and into your body. The measles vaccine is made from the measles virus itself. The rubella vaccine is made from the rubella virus. Amazingly, the prevention for these diseases comes from the very viruses that cause the diseases in the first place!

The virus that infects you and makes you sick with measles or rubella is called a wild virus. It travels the world, and it is dangerous. But the virus that is used to make the measles or rubella vaccine is a weakened, or attenuated, form of the virus, and it is not wild; it is grown in a laboratory. Scientists have discovered how to grow a virus, weaken it, and turn it into a vaccine that is very safe and very effective.

When you receive your vaccination, this weakened form of the disease is injected into your body. The weakened virus in the measles vaccine will not make you sick, and it won't infect anyone around you. But it is strong enough to be recognized as a foreign substance by the cells of your immune system. The vaccine infects the body just enough to get the immune system to fight it. But because the virus in the vaccine is so weakened by its time in the laboratory, the immune system has a very easy time defeating it. After that you will have antibodies in your blood, and the "memory" cells of your immune system will know how to fight the virus if it ever attacks you again. Without having to go through the disease, you have become immune. If there is ever an outbreak of measles or rubella, your body will stop the chain of infection.

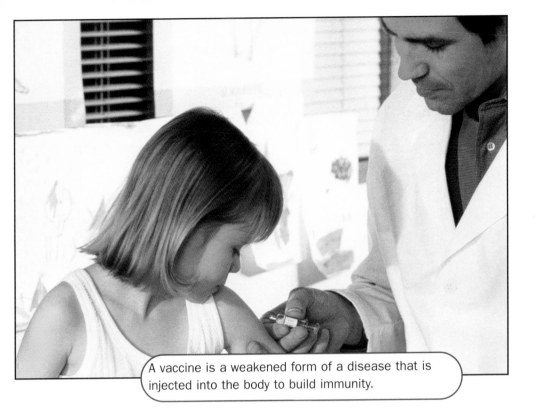

A vaccine is a weakened form of a disease that is injected into the body to build immunity.

Two Vaccinations Work Best

After one MMR vaccination, 95 out of 100 people will be immune to measles and rubella for the rest of their lives. After a second measles shot, 99 out of 100 people will become immune. Doing the math, that's a 4 percent improvement. Four percent may not seem like much of a difference, but if 4 people out of 100 are unprotected, then 4 out of 100 people can get measles or rubella and spread it to other people who are not yet immune. The MMR vaccination is good but not perfect. Once in a while it doesn't "take." Four infected people out of 100 can cause an outbreak of disease—that's why everyone should get two MMR shots.

Vaccination—Links to the Past

The idea of vaccination—injecting a weakened form of the virus that causes a disease into a person's body in order to make the person immune—is an unusual one. Today we know why vaccination works (see the previous pages), but early forms of vaccination existed long before modern science knew how to weaken viruses in a laboratory.

Smallpox

Throughout its history, measles has been linked to a viral disease that doesn't exist today—smallpox. The early symptoms sometimes made it difficult to tell whether you had been attacked by the smallpox virus or the measles virus. Both diseases were spread by armies, migrations of people, and traders.

But smallpox was far deadlier than measles. Even if you survived smallpox, you were left with pockmarks on your skin—you were scarred for life.

Variolation

In China in the first century AD, doctors were already trying to prevent smallpox. The method they used was called variolation: They took some of the scabs or pus from the skin of a person who was infected with smallpox and put it into the body of a healthy person who wanted to become immune and avoid getting the disease. Sometimes smallpox scabs were dried, made into a powder, and

Lady Mary Wortley Montagu, an Englishwoman who lived in Turkey during the eighteenth century, had her young son protected from smallpox through variolation.

Edward Jenner's vaccinations were safer than variolation because the cowpox virus was much weaker than the smallpox virus.

inhaled through the nose. Sometimes the method was to remove the liquid from one person's smallpox sore and rub it into a cut or needle scratch on the arm of another. Variolation was practiced in India, Persia, and Turkey.

In 1718, Lady Mary Wortley Montagu, an Englishwoman who was living in Turkey, observed the variolation procedure. She had been infected with smallpox at twenty-six, and her face had been permanently scarred. She wanted to protect her six-year-old son from the disease. She had him variolated by Dr. Maitland, an Englishman who had learned how to do the procedure. Her chaplain was against it and told her it was un-Christian, but she went ahead with it anyway, and her son remained free of smallpox.

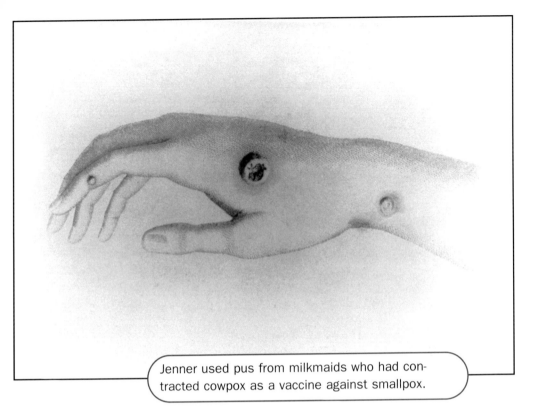

Jenner used pus from milkmaids who had contracted cowpox as a vaccine against smallpox.

Edward Jenner and Milkmaids

Variolation often worked, but it was risky. It involved cutting open the skin and putting a little bit of smallpox virus right into the bloodstream. It immunized many people, but other people got very sick and died. In 1798, Edward Jenner discovered a safer way. Jenner observed the smooth cheeks of milkmaids. He wondered why none of them seemed to have smallpox scars and pockmarks. He realized it was because they had been exposed to cowpox, a much less serious disease. The young women had caught cowpox from the cows they milked. When they recovered from cowpox, they became immune, and that immunity turned out to protect them against the dread disease of smallpox as well.

Jenner started using the pus from people who had cowpox to protect people against smallpox. The scientific name for cowpox virus is vaccinia. That's where we get the word "vaccination." Jenner's vaccinations were much safer than variolation, because the virus he used—cowpox—was much weaker than the smallpox virus.

Since Jenner's time, because of efforts all over the world to vaccinate people against it, smallpox has disappeared. There is no smallpox virus in the world today, except in a test tube, and hopefully even that bit of weakened virus will soon be thrown away. Smallpox is the only infectious disease that mankind has totally destroyed.

In 1977, the smallpox virus infected its last victim—there weren't any people left who were not immune. Because there is no longer any smallpox virus roaming earth, it is no longer necessary for people to be vaccinated against it.

Vaccination: For and Against

In 1798, many people were revolted by Jenner's vaccination method, even though it worked. They formed the Antivaccination Society. They argued that it was disgusting to infect a healthy person with material taken from a cow. They scoffed that soon all the vaccinated people would start turning into cows. Some were against vaccination because they said that it was not in the Bible.

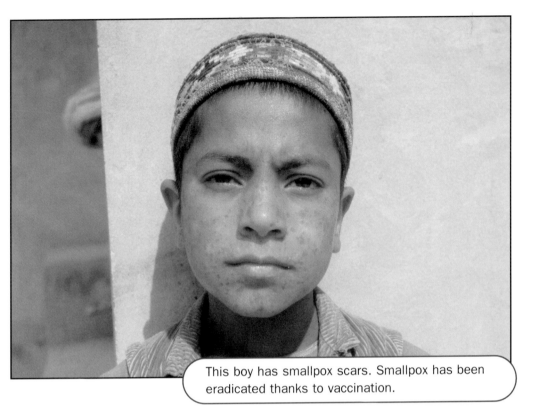

This boy has smallpox scars. Smallpox has been eradicated thanks to vaccination.

Even today, some people don't like the idea of vaccination—perhaps because they don't understand how it works together with the human immune system to protect people against infectious disease.

Measles and Rubella Vaccines Are Developed and Used

Even though Jenner had found a safe way to vaccinate people against smallpox, finding a safe vaccine against measles took time. In 1958, J. F. Enders developed a vaccine that used a dead measles virus. It was a first step, but the dead virus vaccine was not very effective and had some dangerous results. It is no longer used. In 1963, Enders found a way to make a vaccine that

J. F. Enders developed the measles vaccine.

used a live measles virus that had been attenuated, or weakened, in a laboratory. This vaccine was very safe and effective. In 1965, the United States started a mass immunization program, trying to vaccinate all kids and young adults. In 1969, a vaccine for rubella was developed, and vaccination programs against rubella began. As a result of vaccination programs, there were only 100 cases of measles in the United States in 1997.

Chapter Four

Getting Your MMR Shots

Even though 95 percent of American children are now properly vaccinated against measles and rubella by the time they enter kindergarten, 5 percent, or one million preschool children, are not. And even though most eleven- and twelve-year-olds have already received the recommended two MMR shots, many have not. Visit your doctor or health clinic for a preventive check-up. Make sure you are fully vaccinated against measles and rubella.

Vaccine for Free

Because of lack of adequate health insurance, some families may not have a family doctor or regular health care provider and may skip their vaccinations because of cost considerations. As president of the United States from 1993 to the year 2001, Bill Clinton wanted to make sure that all the children in the country were able to receive the proper vaccinations, including their MMR shots. One program that was set up is the Vaccines for Children program, which provides free vaccines to doctors and clinics for their patients who need them.

Connecting with a Doctor or Health Care Provider

If you need to be connected to a doctor or health clinic so you can be given your vaccinations for free, there are toll-free information hotlines that can refer you to clinics in your local area. For information in English, call 1-800-232-2522. For information in Spanish, call 1-800-232-0233.

Recommended Vaccination Schedule

- **First MMR Shot.** Kids should get their first MMR shot between the ages of twelve and fifteen months. Getting it earlier than that won't work, because for the first year or so of life, babies inherit passive immunity from their mothers. As long as the baby is passively immune, the vaccine won't be able to stimulate the baby's immune system to produce its own antibodies. After the inherited passive immunity fades, then the first MMR shot should be given. Check with your doctor about the best time to vaccinate a young baby.

- **Second MMR Shot.** Kids usually get their second MMR shot when they are between four and six years old or when they turn eleven or twelve. But these shots can be given at any age, as long as there is a period of time between the first and second.

◆ **Visiting Your Doctor and Keeping a Vaccination Record.** Your doctor or clinic can keep track of your medical history, including your vaccination records. Very young kids need to get a number of different shots in addition to the MMR vaccinations. Keeping a record is important, especially if you move or change health care providers. You will also need a record of your two MMR vaccinations because schools and some colleges will want to make sure that you have received your shots. Kids and young adults work and play in close contact with each other in schools and day-care centers, so diseases can spread easily. Most schools have a "no shots, no school" policy.

◆ **If You Are Unprotected.** If you have not been properly vaccinated and think that you have been exposed to someone who has measles or rubella, contact your doctor or your local health department immediately. It's possible that if you get vaccinated within a day or two, you will be able to protect yourself from the disease.

Sometimes doctors give shots of immunoglobulin to unvaccinated people who have been exposed to the measles or rubella virus. This is a shot that injects the antibodies directly into your body, but it is only a partial, short-term protection. It does not stimulate your immune system and teach your body how to protect itself and produce its own antibodies. Immunoglobulin gives you passive immunity to measles or rubella. But what you really need is the active immunity that the MMR vaccinations can provide.

Reportable Diseases

Measles and rubella are "reportable" diseases. A person who becomes infected by measles or rubella should report the illness to his or her doctor or health clinic, and doctors are required to report every case of measles or rubella they diagnose to the local health department. That way, all the doctors and health workers can be on the alert for other people who may be infected. To keep the disease from spreading, the local health department may decide to vaccinate certain groups of children and adults who live or work in the area.

Vaccination programs are a very important part of the work of public health agencies like the Centers for Disease Control and Prevention.

If the disease has already spread, infected people of all ages can get prompt and correct diagnosis and medical supervision.

Public Health

There are governmental departments and agencies that work to improve people's health in your community, the country, and the world. Vaccination programs are a very important part of what they do. Every county, state, and province has a health department. There are also national public health agencies like the Centers for Disease Control and Prevention (CDC) in the United States, Health Canada in Canada, and international agencies like the World

Health Organization (WHO), which is sponsored by the United Nations.

For a Few Kids, Measles and Rubella Vaccinations Are Not Recommended

+ **Postponing.** If you are fighting off another serious type of infection, you should put off getting your MMR shot until you have recovered. You don't want to overload your immune system. If you are pregnant, your doctor may tell you to wait. You can reschedule your vaccination for a later date.

+ **Who Shouldn't Have the Shots at All?** For a very small number of kids, getting vaccinated against measles and rubella is not recommended. Some kids are born with very weak immune systems. They might not be able to fight off even the weakened forms of the viruses that are used in the vaccines. Those with the symptoms of AIDS should generally not get the shots (but those with HIV but no symptoms should be vaccinated). Kids who are undergoing some types of treatment for cancer and kids undergoing treatment with steroids or other drugs that can suppress the immune system should not get the MMR shots. These people must depend on the rest of us to get our shots and thus prevent the measles and rubella viruses from ever reaching them. This protection of the few by the many is called herd immunity.

Herd Immunity

When most people have been vaccinated, a society or country is said to have achieved herd immunity. Today in some countries the vaccination rate is so high that even if a few kids aren't healthy enough to get the shots, the measles virus probably won't infect them because it doesn't have a chain of people that it can use to get to them. Society is like a herd of animals, and the few who can't be vaccinated are unlikely to get sick because they are living in the midst of a herd of people who are immune. Of course, herd immunity isn't 100 percent effective. With people traveling all around the globe, you can't be sure that you won't meet up with someone who is infected with measles or with rubella. Don't use the idea of herd immunity as an excuse not to get your shots! You can't afford to be that selfish. If you are healthy enough to be vaccinated—just do it!

Chapter Five

Measles, Rubella, and the People of the World

The most interesting—and tragic—stories about measles and rubella recount how these diseases have attacked whole communities. When a large group of people is infected, it's called an epidemic. When the diseases flare up in small groups of people, it's called an outbreak.

The measles and rubella viruses depend on being able to spread from person to person, forming a chain of infection. By the time one person recovers, someone else is coming down with the disease. The virus is on the move, entering body after body. Today, every vaccinated and fully immunized person breaks that chain of infection. But without vaccination, epidemics can strike.

Examples of Measles Epidemics

Mexico

Almost 500 years ago, measles and other infections crossed the Atlantic Ocean for the first time and came to the Americas inside the bodies of the Spanish soldiers who invaded Mexico.

The native peoples who lived in Mexico had never had measles before, and if a group of people has never been exposed to a certain virus, it hits them much harder. Within fifty years, out of a population of 30 million, only 3 million of the Mexican people were left alive. The Spanish soldiers were cruel, but their measles killed far more people than their weapons did.

Fiji

In 1875, the chief of the Fiji Islands made a sea voyage to Australia to sign a treaty. When the chief and his followers sailed for home aboard an Australian ship, one of the chief's sons got sick with measles—though unknown in Fiji, measles was common in Australia. The Australian sailors knew how contagious measles could be, so the sick son was isolated from everyone else, or quarantined. The Australians built a little hut for him on the deck, and those among them who had already had measles and were immune brought him food and water. No one else was allowed near him. The quarantine seemed successful. It seemed as though none of the other people from Fiji who were on board became sick.

When the chief and his followers got home to Fiji, they prepared a great celebration in honor of the signing of the treaty. Suddenly, another of the chief's sons who had also been on the ship got very sick. Because they were so involved in preparing the celebration, they did not quarantine him. Soon other people were sick. And then more. Some died from the complications of measles, some starved to death—so many people were sick, there weren't enough healthy people to gather food, cook, and keep the society going. One out of four people—30,000 in all—died from the complications of measles.

Outbreaks in the United States, 1989–1991

Let's jump ahead to our own time. In the 1980s, the United States had a measles vaccination program and was aiming to completely eliminate measles from the country by the year 1990. But because more and more people were getting vaccinated and fewer and fewer people were getting sick, it seemed as though measles was no longer any real threat. People forgot. Doctors, parents, and public health workers began to take young people's health for granted.

The nation was shocked when measles made a comeback, infecting 55,000 young people, mostly in inner city neighborhoods and at colleges. Thousands were hospitalized, and 132 people, mostly kids, died.

In some of the areas where the measles outbreaks occurred, only 50 percent of two-year-olds had gotten their first measles shot. Most of the college students had been vaccinated as young children, but some of them still came down with measles—doctors learned the hard way that the first measles shot is effective only 95 percent of the time. And a 5 percent failure rate—which leaves 5 out of every 100 kids unprotected—is enough to give the measles virus enough unprotected bodies to attack and infect. At Siena College in Albany, New York, the basketball team wound up playing their championship game in an empty gym. Unlike the people of Fiji, Siena College officials realized that in a large crowd, the measles virus would be able to infect large numbers of people. The game went on, but no crowd was allowed in the gym.

Today—Who Is Getting Vaccinated?

Today, vaccination rates in the United States, Canada, and most of the other countries in the world are higher than ever before. The United State learned from the outbreaks of 1989–1991. Today the policy is: No shots, no school. We can still do better, but we are on the right track.

Today—Who Is Not Getting Vaccinated?

◆ **War and Famine.** In countries where there is war or famine, it is difficult for people to receive preventive health care, including vaccinations. Sometimes the measles vaccine is just not available. In countries like Iraq, which have been put under economic sanctions by other countries, many children do not get the vaccinations they need.

◆ **Religious Objections.** Some parents in the United States and other countries do not get their kids vaccinated because it goes against their religious beliefs. In the Netherlands, 1,750 cases of measles were reported from April 1999 to January 2000. Forty children were admitted to hospitals with serious complications including encephalitis, pneumonia, and ear and eye infections. Three children died. Ninety-nine percent of the sick kids had never been vaccinated against measles because their parents felt it was against their religion.

◆ **The Current MMR Vaccine Controversy.** In the United States and England, some parents whose children have become autistic believe that the condition may have been triggered by the MMR shot. Autism is a disorder that starts in infancy and causes an inability to interact with others, repetitive behavior, and problems with language. But there is no medical evidence that autism can be caused by an MMR shot. Recent research shows that autism is caused by something in a child's genetic makeup. But some parents are still fearful. More studies will continue whenever fears about vaccination arise. It's important to make sure vaccinations are safe, and to make sure people know they are safe. If parents stop vaccinating their kids, measles and rubella will start up again.

Imported Measles

Most of the measles cases that have been reported in the United States in recent years have been "imported." Just as products made in other countries are imported into the United States to be sold to American customers, so the measles virus finds ways to enter the United States inside the bodies of travelers and visitors from foreign countries. For example, in 1994, a Rutgers University student caught measles while vacationing in Spain—after his return, the virus spread and infected twenty other students. The New Jersey Health Department declared a measles emergency. To keep the disease from spreading further, 22,000 Rutgers students, faculty, and staff were vaccinated at free immunization clinics. Today, almost every case of measles

Many immigrants to the United States were turned away at Ellis Island because they carried infectious diseases.

and rubella in the United States is traced to someone who has come from or visited a foreign country.

Can You Build a Wall Around a Country?

It's hard to protect a country from disease by keeping foreigners out, but in the past, it has been tried.

Back in the 1300s, members of the government of Venice, Italy, stopped ships from landing in their harbor if they thought that the people on board had an infectious disease. The people who governed and lived in Venice were frightened; they were trying to protect the people of their city from disease.

At Ellis Island, in the New York harbor, where many immigrants came in the nineteenth and early twentieth centuries as they tried to enter the United States, many people were turned back because they were sick with infectious diseases.

This strategy of keeping a country healthy by keeping out foreigners who have or may have diseases doesn't work anymore, if it ever did. Today, international travel is so fast, there isn't a way to screen people for disease—they may have no symptoms when they enter the country, but later they may become ill and infect others. Dr. Samuel Katz, a pediatrician at Duke University, says that since vaccine-preventable diseases such as measles still occur worldwide, they are "not further than a jet ride away."

The Future—Getting the Vaccines to the People

Health care issues are inseparable from politics and economics. One of the most difficult problems is delivery—getting medications and vaccines to kids and adults who need them. Bill Gates, head of the Microsoft Corporation, has pledged $750 million to a fund to buy and distribute vaccines to developing countries. The group that will carry out this effort is called Global Alliance for Vaccines and Immunization (GAVI). GAVI is funded by governments and private foundations. When GAVI announced its new vaccination campaign, The Children's Challenge, in 1999, the organization said that getting more kids vaccinated could save three million lives a year.

Carol Bellamy of Unicef is hoping that GAVI will achieve its goal of making vaccinations available worldwide, but she admits that: "This is a crazy world we live in and . . . one of the problems we have is how many countries are at war and how we can get immunizations to the children in those areas."

Can Measles and Rubella Be Eradicated?

Health organizations have wanted to eradicate measles and rubella for a long time. But the viruses hang on. Eradication would mean that there would no longer be any measles or rubella viruses left alive. So far, smallpox is the only infectious disease that has been eradicated by mankind. Vaccination and careful reporting of individual cases of the disease are what did it. Some people think that measles and rubella can be destroyed, too. Others say that worldwide measles eradication is an impossible dream, and we should just give up. Still others are working hard to make the dream a reality.

Today we must face the facts: If we want to be healthier, everyone on the planet has to get healthier, too. Our sense of compassion makes us want to improve people's health all over our country and the world. And in addition, our own self-interest demands that we make everyone's health our business. We're all in this together, and we all need to get our shots. More and more, our community includes everyone on Earth.

E-mail from the Year 2010

Hi. I'm speaking to you from the year 2010.

I know all about viruses. In the past few years, there have been a lot of diseases in my city. Our scientists are working on developing new vaccines, but some viruses are so new, they're still a mystery.

But at least we don't have to worry about measles and rubella anymore. A year ago, WHO, the World Health Organization, announced that measles had been eradicated. Eradicated means that it's dead and it's not coming back. Just yesterday, the news said that rubella, too, has been destroyed.

I want to thank all of you kids who were young at the beginning of the twenty-first century. You got your measles and rubella shots, and you helped all the other people who were kids back then to get their shots, too. I guess the measles virus got tired of looking for people to infect—it just gave up and died!

Now, in 2010, kids don't need to get measles and rubella shots anymore because there are no measles or rubella viruses left alive. Yeah! One less needle!

I just had to thank you.

Diego

Glossary

acute Having a sudden onset, sharp rise, and quick ending.

antibiotics Medicine used to treat some bacterial infections and diseases.

antibodies Proteins produced in the body as a reaction to an infectious disease. They help the body fight the disease and stay in the bloodstream for years afterward, ready to protect the body if the same disease should strike again.

attenuated Made weak.

bacteria Tiny creatures that cause infection and some diseases.

chronic Long-lasting, constantly weakening.

contagious Communicable, or spread, by contact.

epidemic Outbreak of a disease that affects a large number of people within a population or community.

eradicate   To do away with something; to destroy something completely.

immune   Having resistance to and protection from a disease.

immune system   The bodily system that protects the body from foreign substances and disease.

immunization   The process of giving someone protection against a disease, usually by vaccination.

infectious   Capable of spreading from person to person.

injection   A shot.

microorganisms   Tiny creatures such as viruses and bacteria.

quarantine   To isolate from other people in order to prevent disease from spreading.

vaccinate   To administer a vaccine, usually by injection.

vaccine   Preparation that is given to prevent a disease. Usually given by injection.

viruses   Tiny creatures, smaller than bacteria, that may cause disease.

Where to Go for Help

In the United States

Centers for Disease Control and Prevention (CDC)
1600 Clifton Road
Atlanta, GA 30333
(404) 639-3311
Web site: http://www.cdc.gov/

Immunization Action Coalition
1573 Selby Avenue, Suite 234
St. Paul, MN 55104
(651) 647-9009
Web site: http://www.immunize.org/

National Institutes of Health (NIH)
Bethesda, MD 20892
Web site: http://www.nih.gov/

National Library of Medicine
8600 Rockville Pike
Bethesda, MD 20894
Web site: http://www.nlm.nih.gov/

World Health Organization (WHO)
2 United Nations Plaza, DC-2 Building
New York, NY 10017
(212) 963-4388
Web site: http://www.who.int/

In Canada

Canadian Immunization Awareness Program
Canadian Public Health Association
400-1565 Carling Avenue
Ottawa, ON K1Z 8R1
(613) 725-3769
Web site: http://www.ciap.cpha.ca/

Health Canada
Bureau of Infectious Diseases
Division of Immunization, Health Protection Branch
Tunney's Pasture
Ottawa, ON K1A 0L2
Postal Locator: 0603E1
Web site:
http://www.hc-sc.gc.ca/hpb/lcdc/bid/di/index.html

Web Sites

American Academy of Pediatrics
http://www.aap.org/family/parents/vaccine.htm

Children's Vaccine Initiative
http://www.vaccines.ch/vaccines-diseases/safety

Growing Healthy Canadians
http://www.growinghealthykids.com

Infectious Disease Society of America
http://www.idsociety.org/

Institute for Vaccine Safety
http://www.vaccinesafety.edu/

National Vaccine Information Center
http://www.909shot.com

VaccinesbyNet
http://www.vaccinesbynet.com/

For Further Reading

Bazin, Hervé. *The Eradication of Smallpox: Edward Jenner and the First and Only Eradication of a Human Infectious Disease*. San Diego, CA: Academic Press, 1999.

Benenson, Abram S., ed. *Control of Communicable Diseases Manual*. 16th edition. Washington, DC: American Public Health Association, 1995.

Biddle, Wayne. *A Field Guide to Germs*. New York: Henry Holt and Company, Inc., 1995.

DeSalle, Rob, ed. *Epidemic! The World of Infectious Disease* New York: New Press, 1999.

Humiston, Sharon G., and Cynthia Good. *Vaccinating Your Child Questions and Answers for the Concerned Parent*. Atlanta, GA: Peachtree Publishers Ltd., 2000

McNeill, William H. *Plagues and Peoples*. Garden City, NY: Anchor Press/Doubleday, 1976.

Mitchell, Violaine S., Nalini M. Philipose, and Jay P. Sanford, eds. *The Children's Vaccine Initiative: Achieving the Vision.* Washington, DC: National Academy Press, 1993.

Offit, Paul A., and Louis M. Bell. *Vaccines: What Every Parent Should Know.* New York: IDG Books Worldwide, 1999.

Radetsky, Peter. *The Invisible Invaders: The Story of the Emerging Age of Viruses.* Boston: Little, Brown and Company, 1991.

Silverstein, Alvin, et al., *Measles and Rubella.* Springfield, NJ: Enslow, 1997.

Index

A
acute infection, 16
antibodies, 19, 20, 30, 40, 42
Antivaccination Society, 36

C
Centers for Disease Control and
    Prevention (CDC), 43
chain of infection, 7, 16, 30, 46
Children's Challenge, 54
complications from measles, 20–22
congenital disease, 24
congenital rubella syndrome (CRS),
    24, 26, 28
cowpox, 35–36

E
Enders, J. F., 37–38
epidemic, 7, 9, 11, 25, 46, 47
eradication, 54, 55

G
German measles, 23
Global Alliance for Vaccines and
    Immunization (GAVI), 53–54
Gregg, Norman, 28

H
Health Canada, 43
herd immunity, 45
host, 15

I
immunoglobulin, 42
immune system, 19, 20, 30, 37, 44
immunization, 8, 28, 54
incubation period, 17
infectious diseases, 7, 8, 36, 52
    AIDS, 7, 15, 44
    common cold, 15, 16, 29
    mumps, 9, 15
    smallpox, 7, 32, 35, 36, 37, 54

J
Jenner, Edward, 34, 35–36, 37

M
mass immunization program, 38
measles, mumps, and rubella vac-
    cine (MMR), 8–9, 28, 31, 39, 40,
    41, 42, 44, 50
    and autism, 50, 51

O
outbreaks, 23, 30, 31, 46, 48, 49

P
passive immunity, 40, 42
pregnant women
    and measles, 22
    and rubella, 23–26, 27–28
    and vaccination, 44
prevention, 8
public health agencies, 43

Q
quarantine, 47, 48

R
receptors, 18
recommended vaccine schedule, 40
reportable diseases, 42

S
secondary infections, 20
symptoms of measles, 19
symptoms of rubella, 26–27

V
vaccination for free, 40
vaccine, 8, 29, 30, 37, 38, 40, 50
Vaccines for Children program, 40
variolation, 32, 34, 35, 36
Varro, 14

W
wild virus, 30
World Health Organization (WHO), 43, 55

About the Author

Trisha Hawkins is a writer and copy editor who lives in Brooklyn, New York. She is a graduate of Harvard College.

Photo Credits

Cover photos and pp. 11, 13, 15, 25 © Custom Medical Stock Photo; pp. 2, 33, 34, 35 courtesy of the National Library of Medicine; p. 18 © Lester V. Bergman/Corbis; p. 21 © Howard Davies/Corbis; p. 27 © Corbis; p. 31 © FPG International; p. 37 © Paul Almasy/Corbis; pp. 38, 52 © Bettmann/Corbis; p. 43 © Photo Researchers.

Layout

Laura Murawski

ML   6/01